The Field of Social Work

The Field of

8th
edition

COAUTHORS

Paul Abels
Sonia Abels
George Hoshino
Peter J. Johnson
Alan Keith-Lucas
Dorothy J. Kiester
Norman A. Polansky
P. Nelson Reid
Lois R. Taber
Richard H. Taber

CONTRIBUTORS OF CASE MATERIAL

Allan A. Bloom
Lane Cooke
Philip W. Cooke
Roberta Kyle
Linda Reifsnyder
Janice Jacobson Ryan
Federico Souflee
Ann Sullivan
John B. Turner
Sibyl M. Wagner

WITHDRAWN

361.3
F459f8

Social Work

Arthur E. Fink
Jane H. Pfouts
Andrew W. Dobelstein

SAGE PUBLICATIONS
Beverly Hills   London   New Delhi

Copyright © 1985 by Sage Publications, Inc.

All rights reserved. No part of this book may be reproduced or utilized in any form or by any means, electronic or mechanical, including photocopying, recording, or by any information storage and retrieval system, without permission in writing from the publisher.

For information address:

SAGE Publications, Inc.
275 South Beverly Drive
Beverly Hills, California 90212

SAGE Publications India Pvt. Ltd.  SAGE Publications Ltd
M-32 Market   28 Banner Street
Greater Kailash I   London EC1Y 8QE
New Delhi 110 048 India   England

Printed in the United States of America

Library of Congress Cataloging in Publication Data

Main entry under title:

The field of social work.

    Includes bibliographies and index.
    1. Social service—Addresses, essays, lectures.
2. Social service—United States—Addresses, essays,
lectures. I. Fink, Arthur E. (Arthur Emil), 1903-
II. Pfouts, Jane H. (Jane Hoyer), 1921-1982.
III. Dobelstein, Andrew W.
HV40.F45   1984   361.3   84-18082
ISBN 0-8039-2268-X

FIRST PRINTING

Contents

Foreword   9

PART I   **Foundations of Social Work: Values, Skills, and Knowledge of the Profession**   **15**

    1. The Value Base for Social Work
      Dorothy J. Kiester
      Jane H. Pfouts   19

    2. The Helping Art of Social Work
      Alan Keith-Lucas   33

    3. The Knowledge Base of Social Work
      Norman A. Polansky   50

PART II   **Policies and Programs of Modern Social Work Practice**   **69**

    4. Development of Social Programs in the United States
      Jane H. Pfouts
      Arthur E. Fink   73

    5. Public Welfare Policy: A Background for Understanding Welfare Services in the United States
      Andrew W. Dobelstein   98

    6. Public Welfare Programs: Federal, State, and Local
      George Hoshino   128

PART III   **Social Work Methods of Practice**   **157**

    7. Social Casework
      Lois R. Taber
      Richard H. Taber   163

    8. Social Group Work
      Sonia Abels
      Paul Abels   188

CAT Mar 31 '86

3-14-86 mrs 19.48

ALLEGHENY COLLEGE LIBRARY

85-5912

9. Community Organization
   P. Nelson Reid   222

10. Social Work with Families
    Jane H. Pfouts   244

11. Case Management
    Peter J. Johnson   269

PART IV Social Work Practice in Varied Settings   **297**

Case 1. Profiles of Abuse and Neglect:
         Protective Services for Children in
         a Department of Social Services
         Lane Cooke
         Roberta Kyle
         Linda Reifsnyder   301

Case 2. Nickie's Story: Specialized Adoption
         Services in a Department of Social Services
         Ann Sullivan   313

Case 3. Family Crisis: Medical Social Work
         in a Teaching Hospital
         Janice Jacobson Ryan   322

Case 4. Women with Weight Problems: Group
         Treatment in Social Work Practice
         Sibyl M. Wagner   330

Case 5. Helping a Community Grow: Community
         Organization with a Minority Population
         Federico Souflée   346

Case 6. The Search for Self-Understanding:
         Long-Term Treatment in a
         Family Service Agency
         Allan A. Bloom   360

Case 7. Industrial Social Work: Direct and
         Indirect Services and Consultation
         Philip W. Cooke   377

Epilogue: Reflections on the Future of the
           Field of Social Work
           John B. Turner   386

Index   393

This book is
dedicated to Jane Hoyer Pfouts
1921-1982
Teacher, Scholar, and Friend

She was an inspiration and role model as a social worker and a person. She helped us know what to take seriously and what to laugh at. Jane was our loyal and enthusiastic fan, and we hers.

Connie Renz,
Social Worker and Former Student
November 11, 1982

Foreword

It has been said that the more things change, the more they stay the same. This astute observation concerning progress in human affairs (first made in 1849 by Alphonse Karr) seems particularly apt to me as I look back over the forty-year history of the field of social work. The United States has changed enormously over that span of time, and so have social work and the size of its professional membership, its organizational structure, and the sophistication of its practice methods. And yet, because human nature continues to be much as it always was, the same kinds of personal and social problems remain, always recognizable, although sometimes appearing under new labels or in new guises.

These all-too-familiar problems should challenge the present generation of social work students reading the eighth edition of this text, just as they challenged students reading the first edition in the early 1940s. The present edition, like the seven before it, aims to confront students with two basic themes central to the profession: How do we help people deal with personal misfortune? What can we do to help achieve a just society?

The original manuscript of *The Field of Social Work* was written during the years 1938-1941. When the first edition came out, World War II had just begun. When that war was over, students in unprecedented numbers went back to school, and among other course offerings there was an accelerating demand at the under-graduate level for instruction in the helping professions, including social work—hence, an updating in 1949. In that second edition, Kenneth Pray's presidential address before the 1949 National Conference on Social Work reminded students and the whole social work community about the important place of social work in American society:

> If American social work can stand true to its own faith, in its daily practice and in its broader relations with the whole society; if it can purge itself of the last lingering vestiges of benevolent paternalism and pretense of omniscience; . . . if it can then find the courage and wisdom to add its full strength to the concert of democratic forces now struggling toward a free, united, cooperative world of peace, and justice, and progress—it can reach in our time an achievement of incalculable value to mankind, by bravely and competently helping at least some part of this troubled world, caught in the turmoil of a social revolution, to discover and to fulfill their own permanent, positive values and their own truly creative purpose.

In a subsequent edition of *The Field of Social Work* a decade later, as the country prospered, it was an economist, William Haber, who observed:

> Affluence does not automatically wipe out social ills. . . . Social ills are by no means an affliction of the poor alone. Adequate family income is no protection against mental illness, unwanted pregnancies, alcoholism, drug addiction, crippling accidents, or personal failure. The social ills that are with us today were with us yesterday and will still be with us tomorrow . . . skilled counseling and guidance have never been more needed. . . . An attack on poverty is an inevitable consequence of our affluence. . . . I am persuaded, however, that even though costly, when the present expenditures on the poverty program become a matter of history, they will be recalled as an investment rather than an expenditure.

The decisions of the voters in the 1980 elections placed a new president in the White House and gave control of the U.S. Senate to that president's party. That president and Senate were determined to reduce federal commitments for welfare purposes, and the states and local communities have been unable to provide appropriate support for those in need. This is in marked contrast to the activities of the federal government fifty years earlier, which placed a political party in power that then was committed to the organization of programs on behalf of the disadvantaged, and to the use of federal funds for implementation. The words of Kenneth Pray and William Haber remain pertinent today, as *The Field of Social Work* appears in its eighth edition.

Many students will begin to read this book with some confusion about social work, some uncertainty about whether social work is a possible career for them, and a lot of anxiety about meeting a client face to face, in a social work situation. All of the contributors to this book have faced similar concerns throughout their social work careers. They join to welcome you to explore a career that has great potential for serving others and for bringing personal satisfaction. Through this book we hope to share with you some of the things we learned about social work, but not all of the things you will need to know in order to be a social worker.

Many students will not know who Jane Pfouts was. She was a social worker and a social work educator who worked and taught in North Carolina. She was interested in families—how they work and what could be done to help them stay strong enough to provide a nurturing environment. She was particularly interested in the children in families, and how the order in which children were born into a family affected the way these children developed into adults. Her work was sound, and many of her research reports were published in professional journals.

Jane Pfouts taught a course in undergraduate social work and she loved her interaction with the students. For her, beginning social work students held the future of social work in their hands. She was often impatient because there was so much to teach and not enough time to teach it. She was a very good teacher and the students were very fond of her. Jane saw in this well-known textbook, *The Field of Social Work,* the opportunity to communicate to her students, and many students like hers, the essential elements of social work practice. She devoted much of her time to revising *The Field of Social Work,* but before she could finish the task, she died suddenly. It is therefore fitting that this textbook be dedicated to Jane for the labor she spent but could not enjoy and for her commitment to social work education.

This textbook has been prepared for beginning social work students, to help them get started. There are four main parts to the book. The first part offers some different perspectives about social work and the kinds of things social workers do. The second part describes and discusses the major policies and programs that social workers use to help people. The third part presents the different social work helping methods. Social work methods can be thought of as the ways social workers connect people with social resources. The final part of the book contains a number of examples of the social work helping processes in action. These case studies provide the opportunity for students to see how the materials presented in the first three parts may be applied in actual situations. Although the case studies are at the end of the textbook, students may prefer to examine and discuss some of the case studies as they study other parts of the book.

Throughout its many years of usefulness the textbook has tried to present materials from a wide range of social work practitioners and educators. This eighth edition is no exception. We have selected authors for this edition who bring a balance of what is new about the field of social work and what has been tested and found desirable and basic to the profession. For example, Dorothy Kiester and Alan Keith-Lucas write from the perspective of many years of teaching and practicing social work. Both are now retired. Norman Polansky is an active teacher and researcher at the University of Georgia, and he brings a new perspective to the foundations of social work. George Hoshino is an active researcher and teacher at the University of Minnesota. Lois Taber is retired and brings the wisdom of many years of practice to understanding social casework.

Sonia Abels teaches undergraduate students and Paul Abels teaches graduate social work students. For a number of years both Sonia and Paul have been at the center of new developments in social group-work theory and practice. P. Nelson Reid, too, teaches undergraduate social work students. He brings a depth of practice experience and research to the discussion of community organization. Peter Johnson teaches graduate social work students and consults extensively with mental health agencies. His material represents an important new development in social work practice.

Lane Cooke, Roberta Kyle, and Linda R. Reifsnyder all work at a large public welfare agency, and they have extensive experience in child welfare. Ann Sullivan worked for many years in child welfare before beginning her current work of training child welfare practitioners. Federico Souflée headed the Chicano Training Center before he undertook his present teaching and research responsibilities. Janice Ryan is a practicing social worker well recognized for her work in a teaching hospital. Sibyl Wagner is a private practitioner with many years of social work training and experience. Allan Bloom is a social work therapist with a family counseling agency. Phil Cooke teaches graduate students and has consulted widely with private and public organizations. John Turner has had a lifelong concern and interest in social work students and social work education.

We think there is a good balance in our efforts to convey the scope and nature of the field of social work to beginning social work students. We welcome you as you begin to explore this exciting and stimulating profession, and we will look forward to meeting some of you in person, in the years to come, as you take your places beside the many fine people who have made social work their career.

—Arthur E. Fink
Andrew W. Dobelstein
Chapel Hill, North Carolina

PART I

FOUNDATIONS OF SOCIAL WORK
Values, Skills, and Knowledge of the Profession

Social work is a profession committed to helping people. Social work has a uniqueness about the way it helps people, and because social work is a special way of helping people to achieve many and varied personal and social goals, social work appears far-reaching in its professional commitments. The question that is frequently asked about social work is, "What pulls everything together so that social work can be defined as a profession?" Part I of this text answers this question. The values, the helping skills, and the knowledge base of social work provide the professional foundation for social work. Social work is a recognized profession because all social workers share common values, a common helping commitment, and a common base of knowledge.

In Chapter 1, Kiester and Pfouts describe the wide-ranging situations in which social workers carry out their professional helping activities. Lawyers and doctors, for example, may be defined by where they work and what tasks they perform, but social workers can

15

ALLEGHENY COLLEGE LIBRARY

not easily be understood by a discussion about where they are employed and by what they do. Kiester and Pfouts discuss the hazy boundaries of social work practice that have given rise to frequent questions as to social work's professional claims. Kiester and Pfouts assert that the social work code of ethics, a philosophical commitment to idealism, and core values of respect for the individual establish the professional definition of social work and social values.

There is more than ethics, values, and ideology to define the profession of social work. As a way of helping people, social work is also an art that requires the application of recognized skills. These helping skills are at the very core of the profession of social work, and because helping skills are so important to social work, the most frequently used skills are identified and discussed in great detail in Part III. In Chapter 2, however, Keith-Lucas provides an introduction to the social work art of helping, and he suggests some important distinctions and similarities among the various skills that social workers must use when practicing their art. Keith-Lucas cautions that all social work helping is a two-way street. Help may be given, but it also must be taken. Giving help so that it can be used by the taker is part of the social work *art* that acts to define the professional character of social work.

Finally, but no less important, social work is a definable profession because it has a base in knowledge that is both the same and different than the knowledge that supports other professional disciplines. In Chapter 3, Polansky identifies the various sources of knowledge that form the base of the profession of social work. Like Kiester and Pfouts, Polansky sketches the wide diversity of social work, and concludes that such a wide-ranging profession requires a wide-ranging knowledge base. Thus Polansky identifies a social work knowledge base in literature and the arts as well as in social research, which is commonly acknowledged as the base for social work knowledge.

Polansky draws particular attention to the importance of social theory as a foundation for social work knowledge. It is social theory that gives guidance to the art of helping. It is theory that helps social workers order what seems to be chaos in most practice situations. Social work theory is dynamic, both shaping practice and being shaped by it, but social work depends upon this theory to affirm its profession stature. Thus the beginning social work student must be prepared to explore and integrate the various sources of social work knowledge into the art of social work helping. Social work is not all doing. Social work is thinking as well.

The three chapters that follow offer each social work student the opportunity to understand what social work is all about. Once students have this foundation, they are ready to explore some of these foundation principles in greater depth as they progress through the text.

1

THE VALUE BASE FOR SOCIAL WORK

DOROTHY J. KIESTER
**Professor Emeritus, Institute of Government
University of North Carolina, Chapel Hill**

JANE H. PFOUTS
**Professor, School of Social Work
University of North Carolina, Chapel Hill**

A question frequently asked by students who are considering a social work career is, "What is it exactly that social workers do?" This is an eminently reasonable question, but one that is surprisingly difficult to answer, considering the fact that social workers have practiced whatever it is they do in our society for nearly a century. What do the many thousands of social workers—variously employed as therapists, grassroots organizers, group workers, policy analysts, welfare workers, administrators in human service agencies, and so on—have in common with one another? Almost all of them consider themselves social workers and are recognized as such by the social work community. Yet, the more we try to catch and hold for examination the commonalities which give social workers a strong sense of professional identity, the more elusive they seem. Social workers practice in such widely diverse settings, and use such a variety of techniques and methods, that it sometimes seems they have more in common with colleagues in related disciplines in the settings where they practice than they have with other social workers in different types of settings. Role overlap with other professionals (e.g., psychologists, marriage counselors, chaplains) has led to confusion about what it is that gives social work a claim to professional uniqueness. Explaining this wide-ranging profession is further complicated by the fact that the products of social work are intangible: human services to meet human needs. The most serious problem, however, is that social workers themselves lack consensus on these issues of identity, a situation that complicates their ability to give neat answers to the public and to the funding agencies that support them. Students should be forewarned, but not unduly discouraged, by this state of affairs; it is an accurate reflection of the vitality and complexity, as well as the confusion, of a many-faceted profession.

STRIVING FOR DEFINITIONAL CLARITY

Because many people believe that "social work has no exclusive domain" and "its uniqueness lies in its diversity,"[1] social work leaders are keenly aware of the necessity of finding a way to achieve a clearer professional definition. To facilitate this process, the publications committee of *Social Work,* the official journal of the National Association of Social Workers, convened a group of distinguished educators and practitioners in 1979 to develop a statement of social work's purpose and objective that would be applicable to all segments of the profession. The work of the committee was based on and extended the recommendations of a similar group that had met in 1974. The following working statement was drafted by the committee

1. William J. Reid, "Social Work for Social Problems," *Social Work* 22 (September 1977), p. 376.

and published in *Social Work* in January 1981, serving as the focus for an entire journal issue on conceptual frameworks.

The purpose of social work is to promote or restore a mutually beneficial interaction between individuals and society in order to improve the quality of life for everyone. Social workers hold the following beliefs:
1. The environment (social, physical, organizational) should provide the opportunity and resources for the maximum realization of the potential and aspirations of all individuals, and should provide for their common human needs and for the alleviation of distress and suffering.
2. Individuals should contribute as effectively as they can to their own well-being and to the social welfare of others in their immediate environment as well as to the collective society.
3. Transactions between individuals and others in their environment should enhance the dignity, individuality, and self-determination of everyone. People should be treated humanely and with justice.

Clients of social work may be an individual, a family, a group, a community or an organization.

Objectives

Social workers focus on person-and-environment in interaction. To carry out their purpose, they work with people to achieve the following objectives:
1. Help people enlarge their competence and increase their problem-solving and coping abilities.
2. Help people obtain resources.
3. Make organizations responsive to people.
4. Facilitate interaction between individuals and others in their environment.
5. Influence interactions between organizations and institutions.
6. Influence social and environmental policy.

To achieve these objectives, social workers work with other people. At different times, the target of change varies—it may be the client, others in the environment, or both.[2]

This valiant attempt to define the boundaries of social work's domain may not completely satisfy the need for a simple and specific

---

2. "Working Statement on the Purpose of Social Work," developed by the participants at the Second Meeting on Conceptual Frameworks; *Social Work* 26 (January 1981), p. 6.

answer to the question, What do social workers do? but it is the best the field can offer at this point in its development. Clearly defined or not, the reality is that social workers do recognize one another as colleagues in a common professional endeavor, and they are also more or less correctly recognized by agencies, clients, and the general public as a group of practitioners who are united by a common base of characteristics, values, and competencies.

THE QUESTION OF
WHO IS A SOCIAL WORKER

Traditionally, social work has been a profession with very permeable boundaries. Even today, practitioners holding Bachelor of Social Work (BSW) and Master of Social Work (MSW) degrees still constitute a minority among people engaged in social work. However, since 1955, when the National Association of Social Workers was formed through the merger of seven separate social work societies, NASW has taken leadership in setting higher and more uniform standards for membership in the profession. For example, in 1961 NASW established the Academy of Certified Social Workers (ACSW). To become a member of ACSW, a social worker must be a member of NASW, must have a minimum of two years of post-master's practice experience, and must pass a written examination.

By 1982, social workers in twenty-seven states had gained state certification that limits the use of the title of *social worker* to those who are able to meet specified educational and practice criteria. In a few states, social workers have become licensed, a procedure that further restricts who can practice and under what circumstances. Although there is a consensus in the field that some kind of quality control is necessary to protect the public and the profession, opinions differ sharply on the means of doing this. Some groups within the profession, who favor the goal of state certification or licensing based on credentials, are vigorously opposed by other groups who consider this approach to be elitist and self-serving. The latter groups also take the view that formal credentials do not necessarily ensure competence; they argue that until there is an agreed-upon, objective measure of practice competence, people without formal credentials should not be excluded. Whatever one's position in the debate, everyone agrees that somehow a way must be found for the profession to ensure practice competence. The problem has acquired additional urgency as more practitioners, with varying levels of expertise, who call themselves social workers have begun to move into unsupervised private practice in states with no restrictions on who can practice.

SOCIAL WORK'S CODE OF ETHICS

A written code of ethics is a crucial component of any profession. Such a code is not a set of hard-and-fast rules; rather, it serves as a guide for members in their daily professional lives by making explicit the standards of ethical behavior held by the profession. A code of ethics speaks to the common base of characteristics, values, and competencies binding all members.

In 1960, the Delegate Assembly of the NASW strengthened social work's professionalism by developing a Code of Ethics. It is fitting that NASW took the lead in this endeavor because, in organizational terms, NASW exemplifies the unity of all aspects of the profession. For over 25 years, the Code of Ethics (most recently revised in 1980) has been accepted, with occasional expansions and revisions, as a standard of requirements for ethical practice by all NASW members. The Code specifies the ethical responsibilities of all social workers regarding professional conduct and competence as well as relationships with clients, colleagues, employers, the profession, and the society.[3]

Social work's Code of Ethics is not easy to live by (no good code of ethics ever was), and, as the profession attempts to translate its stated beliefs into practice, it sometimes falls short of the mark. Its less-than-perfect record in relation to minority groups is a case in point. Social work has always strongly affirmed, and the Code of Ethics states, that individuals should be treated equally, regardless of color, gender, sexual orientation, age, religion, national origin, marital status, political beliefs, or mental or physical handicap. To a degree, this value has always been honored; yet, until one minority after another insisted on full rights as citizens, beginning in the 1960s, much remained undone. Social work schools and agencies were almost entirely populated by white, middle-class teachers, students, and practitioners; social work's understanding of and empathy with

3. National Association of Social Workers, *Code of Ethics of the National Association of Social Workers* (Washington, DC: NASW, 1980), p. 9.

the position of minority clients was incomplete; and an unconscious acceptance by practitioners of cultural myths that equated difference with inferiority was more pervasive than was realized. As the larger society has moved toward achieving greater equity for minorities, however, so has social work. The Council on Social Work Education, the profession's academic accrediting body, has taken a strong stand by withholding accreditation from undergraduate or graduate school programs not having a curriculum that adequately explores minority issues. At the same time, spurred on by NASW, by their own convictions, and by clients themselves, agency directors have begun to hire and promote minority employees and to pay greater attention to ensuring equity in services to all client groups. The social work profession still falls short of its ideals in this area, but it is making a conscientious effort to come to grips with its deficiencies and to live up more fully to the convictions stated in its Code of Ethics.

SOCIAL WORK'S COMMON BASE

Social work could not have developed a national association or a code of ethics in the absence of a common professional base of characteristics, values, and competencies. It is the common base that makes social work a profession and that provides the glue to hold together a highly diverse membership.

Perhaps the foremost characteristic shared by social workers is that of idealism. Most students who choose a social work career are motivated by a desire to make things better for people, and by the belief that things can be made better. The natural corollary of that conviction is that social work is a reformist profession, firmly committed to constructive change for people and systems. Given this idealistic stance, the saving grace for social workers as individuals and for the profession is that, by and large, social workers are reality-based and aware of their limits in knowledge and power. They are also very conscious of the complex interplay, in the helping professions, between the personal needs and the professional behaviors of workers. To protect themselves and their clients, therefore, social workers make self-awareness a cardinal virtue.

These three characteristics—idealism, desire for reform, and self-awareness—are intertwined with two primary values: belief in the dignity of the individual and belief in the right of self-determination. Upon this foundation of characteristics and values are built the competencies that are acquired through academic study and supervised practice. In essence, it is the common base of characteristics, values, and competencies that distinguishes social work as a profession.

Characteristics

Idealism

However discouraged the best motivated of social workers may become in working with clients, and however cynical after repeated, fruitless battles against entrenched injustice and inequity, most social workers continue to believe in the perfectability of human beings and society. In this optimistic view of human nature and social progress, social workers are philosophically closer to eighteenth-century beliefs of the Age of Enlightenment than to the pessimism and sense of limits that have marked the United States in the late twentieth century.

If it were not for their somewhat old-fashioned optimism, practitioners could not persevere in social work. On good days and bad, the goal remains constant: to alleviate human suffering and to improve the quality of life for clients. As individuals, social workers may lose sight of their ideals occasionally and succumb to self-interest; but even when they do—and try to rationalize their failure to live up to their own standards—they still know what they want to see for society as a whole, and especially for individuals in trouble. Idealism is never completely lost, even when the shine is dulled by too much daily exposure to human weakness (including one's own) and the painful recognition of the profession's very limited ability to bring about structural changes in the society.

This kind of idealism is not unique to social work; it is shared with many other altruistic groups. It is a reflection of a societal idealism which co-exists and does battle with the darker aspects of our culture. Social workers sometimes down-play their idealism because of the "bleeding heart" image that has been equated with quixotic ineffectiveness. Nonetheless, the commitment to social justice and to dependent and troubled people remains firm, even in the face of deliberate or uninformed misrepresentation of the profession's goals and motives. Most social workers, however, are flexible enough to acknowledge that honorable people may agree on ends while differing on the means of accomplishing their goals. At such times, a large measure of self-awareness is needed to prevent self-righteous proclamations about aims and programs. In order to be effective in translating ideals into programs, social workers must have a clear sense of the ambiguity and mixed outcomes that are inherent in all "solutions" to social problems. There are no sure answers, and there are undesirable side effects in even the best of our policies and programs. Effective idealists dream and work toward society as it could be, even while they act with a clear vision of society as it is.

Reform

A steadfast determination to do something about deplorable social conditions and destructive human problems marks social work as a reformist profession. It is in trying to bring about change for the individual or the community, however, that social workers are most likely to arouse antagonism. For those to whom change in the status quo represents a threat, social workers are unwelcome meddlers, or worse. When criticism becomes attack, it is difficult to retain one's professional objectivity. As a result, social workers sometimes succumb to the temptation to over-promise in an effort to gain support for controversial programs. Inevitably, when more is promised than can be delivered, both the clients and the public are disappointed, even though considerable gains may have been made. Partial successes are labeled as complete failures because the outcomes have fallen below unrealistic expectations. An excellent example of such over-promising and consequent disappointment is the much maligned War on Poverty in the 1960s.

Social workers also can be made to feel defensive by critics in the general public—that faceless, amorphous, tax-paying "general public"—who react to workers' efforts by blaming them for the very problems they are trying to solve. These critics, in the process of denying the reality of poverty and human misery, seek to remove themselves from any feeling of responsibility or any need for structural change by accusing those who are treating the problem of having created it. Any social worker who has ever worked in public welfare understands this phenomenon. Because no one wants to pay for someone else's failure, and because we are not supposed to fail, society has invented the convenient device of "blaming the victim,"[4]

4. William Ryan, *Blaming the Victim* (New York: Random House, 1971).

thus making those who work with the victim guilty by association. Public welfare and other programs to serve the poor have been traditional societal scapegoats,[5] a stigma that is likely to become even more onerous during the 1980s, when money and services for scapegoats appear to be decreasing and antagonism toward them is likely to increase.

Social work cannot completely control its own reform agenda. Its accomplishments are determined, in large part, by the national agenda of social problems that society chooses to address at any given time.[6] In the early 1960s, mental illness and mental retardation claimed center stage in the national reform theater; they were followed, in mid-decade, by the civil rights movement and the War on Poverty. The women's movement enjoyed the limelight in the 1970s; social work's attention was focused on rape victims and battered women. Drug abuse, gay rights, child abuse, and permanency planning for children in foster care also had a place on the national agenda of the 1970s. What society will choose to emphasize in the 1980s is still unclear; but certainly, some items will be dropped from the agenda and others will be added. Social causes go in and out of fashion rapidly, but the problems themselves remain for social workers to deal with, whether they are popular and well-funded or not.

Social workers would like to have a greater part in shaping public opinion in matters of social justice, but, to date, they have had little success in influencing public opinion or the politics of public policy. This is unfortunate, because it is a fact of political life that money is secured by those special interest groups who can successfully persuade appropriating bodies that their constituents want and will vote for a given program. To state the obvious, the special interests of social agencies—popular or not—are dependent upon such appropriations.

The current social and economic climate, conservative by some lights but radical in its reduction of support for human services, will inevitably put pressure on local communities to find ways of meeting human needs with less tax money. In this endeavor, social work will face its most demanding challenge since the 1930s. Even the "old guard" admit that many of the solutions of the past fifty years may no

5. Erving Goffman, *Stigma* (Englewood Cliffs, NJ: Prentice-Hall, 1963).

6. Jane Pfouts and Connie Renz, "The Future of Wife Abuse Programs," *Social Work* 26 (November 1981), pp. 451-455.

longer be applicable. It is time to devise new approaches and seek new solutions to the old problems. Perhaps the most difficult reform of all will involve social work's own willingness to modify or discard some of its cherished theories about how to correct social ills.

Self-Awareness

It is always easier to see the problems and weaknesses of others than to see our own; so, also, it is easier and more pleasant to analyze someone else's motivations and rationalizations. For this reason, one of the most important and often most painful parts of becoming a professional social worker is the process of achieving an understanding of oneself. In order to do good social work, it is necessary to be conscious of the impact of one's own attitudes and behaviors on interactions with clients. Without this awareness, social workers are in danger of imposing a set of values that, although important to themselves, may be wrong—even counterproductive—for clients. Hard questions for the social worker, regardless of professional setting or worker's status, are "Are my needs or the needs of my client concerning me most?" and "Am I willing to risk creating problems for myself to meet the needs of my client?"

In all types of interaction with clients, self-awareness and sensitivity to the impact of one's helping behavior are the best guarantees against imposition of the worker's solution on the client's problem. After all, "help" lies in the perception of the recipient, not in the intention of the helper. Without a reasonable degree of self-awareness, social workers find it almost impossible to know whether they are giving more than mere lip service to such fundamental values as respect for the dignity of the individual and respect for the right of self-determination.

Primary Values

Dignity of the Individual

The expression "dignity of the individual" is so familiar and has been incorporated into the jargon of so many disciplines that it requires a bit of thought to work through its overlay of superficiality and get a sense of what the words actually mean in the practice of social work. Dignity is, in itself, a concept with broad implications. Can a person who lives in harshest poverty, with none of the advantages of cleanliness, social grace, physical health, education—even good will—be said to have dignity? Is it something that can be imparted by courteous treatment? Does a person have dignity by virtue of personal humanity, without regard to external judgments?

Two of the statements in *A Social Worker's Creed*, enunciated many years ago by Linton B. Swift, speak to both the inherent nature of human dignity and the importance of external validation of its existence:

> I believe in the dignity of the individual human personality as the basis for all social relationships.

And

> I shall always base my opinion of another person on a genuine attempt to understand him—to understand not merely his words, but the man himself and his whole situation and what it means to him.[7]

A genuine attempt to understand begins with some kind of communication that conveys a courteous interest in the client as a person, not just as a "case." If the relationship is to progress, the client must begin to trust the worker's genuine desire to understand; and the worker must, indeed, have such a genuine desire. A relationship based on mutual acceptance can begin to develop only as stereotypical preconceptions held by both worker and client are laid aside.

Because social workers, like everyone else, are products of their own life experiences and are affected by social and cultural conditioning, there are elements of professional competence that require disciplined behavior and personal change. Social workers have an obligation to understand themselves well enough to be able to recognize their own prejudices. To respect the dignity of someone who is "different," it is essential to control personal biases and modify them. In practice, a genuine effort to understand the other person makes prejudices less salient. As the worker begins to understand the client, the client becomes not a stereotype but a fellow human being who has a problem. At the same time, as the client becomes engaged in the helping process, the worker is seen in a different, less stereotyped way.

7. Linton A. Swift, *A Social Worker's Creed* (New York: Family Service Association of America, 1946); this is a one-page document that was prepared for distribution to member agencies.

Right to Self-Determination

Most of us agree in theory that people should be allowed to make their own decisions, but it becomes remarkably difficult to respect this right when clients appear so determined to defeat their own best interests. On a purely pragmatic level, however, social workers have learned that it does no good to force a certain course of action on others; the plan is sabotaged to protect against unwanted interference.

A belief in the right of self-determination affects the policies and practices of social work in every setting and with every method. In all encounters between workers and clients, the clients have the greater stake, for it is they who must live with the outcome; therefore, the final decision is theirs to make. In order to make the best decision, however, clients must be made aware of the range of choices available to them and the probable consequences of each course of action. Social workers also are obliged to offer clients all pertinent information and help in making use of available resources. It occasionally happens (in protective services, for example) that a worker is faced with the need to act because a client is a danger to self or others, even though the appropriate action is rejected by the client. In such cases, and they are relatively rare, the worker's judgment is properly subject to review by a supervisor or by the courts. The importance of this principle—that the right to make decisions lies with the client or group served by the social worker—cannot be over-emphasized. Without it, social work "help" becomes social work "coercion."

Practice Competencies

Developing the competencies to put beliefs into practice is the essence of becoming professional. Common sense, good intentions, and a natural sensitivity to the feelings of others are necessary but not sufficient to insure practice competence. In addition to general aptitude, professional education and supervised experience are required to help a social worker translate professional values into practice skills, and to develop the judgment to apply them wisely. In broadest terms, the basic competencies in social work practice are: skill in communication, development and use of relationships, and understanding of the dynamics of human behavior. Many other skills are pertinent to the diverse settings of social work practice, but all of them are grounded in the generic principles that undergird all of social work.

Historically the MSW was the only professional degree in social work, but a change has occurred during the last twenty years. With the rapid expansion of undergraduate social work degree programs and the development of doctoral-level education, the field of social work has begun haltingly to move toward establishing a coherent educational continuum, from BSW to MSW to DSW or Ph.D. In this relatively short span of the profession's life, BSWs have become full members of the National Association of Social Workers and have become firmly established in all areas of clinical practice.

Important as education is, in the final analysis social work's fate hinges less on the implied status of academic degrees than on the ability of degree holders to demonstrate their competence. In the simplest terms, this means that social workers must be able to demonstrate that what they do actually makes a difference in the lives of clients. In the years ahead, social work will prosper to the extent that (a) methods become increasingly more effective, (b) performance is seen by the public as competent and reliable, and (c) goals are realistically tied to what social workers know and can do.

For the individual social worker, the goal of practice excellence requires a commitment to continuous learning (from journals, books, workshops, courses, colleagues, and most of all from practice itself) from the first social work course to the last day of practice. But workers cannot be expected to move practice beyond what is known. For the profession, in the long run, the answer to achieving new levels of competence lies in giving priority—for the first time—to research. Such research should aim not only at evaluating practice as it is now, but at looking for ways to improve our present methods and service delivery system.

A CHANGING MANDATE FOR SOCIAL WORK

Practice will almost surely change in many ways during the decade of the 1980s as social work attempts to meet clients' needs in a society that appears to be backing away from human service commitments in order to facilitate national priorities concerned with defense and inflation. Unfortunately, governmental retrenchment does not conveniently result in a decreased need for services, and the all too familiar problems that social workers have always addressed will still demand solutions. Agency structures, service delivery systems, and funding patterns will almost surely change in many ways to adjust to the limitations of a less affluent society, but the distinctive mix of characteristics, values, and competencies that binds social workers together will remain. The chapters in this book describe the creative blend of unity and diversity that is the essence of social work and that, paradoxically, is the source of both its greatest weakness and its greatest strength as a profession.

SUGGESTED READING

Bartlett, Harriet M. *The Common Base of Social Work Practice*. New York: National Association of Social Workers, 1970.

Cooper, Shirley. "Social Work: A Dissenting Profession." *Social Work* 22 (September 1977): 360-367.

Eaton, Joseph W. "Science, 'Art' and Uncertainty in Social Work." *Social Work* 3 (July 1958): 3-10.

Levy, Charles S. "The Value Base of Social Work." *Journal of Education for Social Work* 9 (Winter 1973): 34-42.

Schorr, Alvin. "Who Promised Us a Rose Garden?" *Social Work* 20 (May 1975): 200-205.

Siporin, Max. *Introduction to Social Work Practice*. New York: Macmillan, 1975.

2

THE HELPING ART
OF SOCIAL WORK

ALAN KEITH-LUCAS
Professor Emeritus, School of Social Work
University of North Carolina, Chapel Hill

Social work is concerned with helping people. This help may be given to an individual, a family, a group, or a whole community. The purpose of the help is to enable people to cope with the difficulties of living in society, to make decisions about their lives that they can live with, and generally to enjoy lives that are as full as possible in today's world. The help cannot always achieve these ends, but it can often make them more possible; it can alleviate despair and confusion, and can help people do something about circumstances instead of being overwhelmed by them.

Part of the help that social work offers may be of a material nature, such as money to live on, housing, training for a job, or treatment for a handicap; but part has to do with using these things wisely, gaining the courage to undertake new courses of action, planning ahead, straightening out conflicting feelings, and gaining control of one's life. Both kinds of help are often needed if a social service is really to be of help.

BASIC APPROACHES TO HELPING

There are, basically, two approaches to the problem of helping others. They can be called the "therapeutic" and the "co-planning" approaches.

The Therapeutic Approach

Social workers have traditionally espoused a therapeutic approach with people who are in trouble or who do not seem able to manage their own lives. Such an approach says to the client, in so many words, "There is something wrong, either with you or with your situation, or most likely with both. Let us see if we can find out what it is and put it right." Social workers who espouse this approach tend to use medical terms such as "diagnosis" (although "assessment" is more popular at the moment), "treatment," and "therapy." Some of the terms even seem to have a military flavor, for example, "intervention," "preventive strategy," and "target groups." The focus is on "combatting" something that is wrong.

The therapeutic approach can be very helpful when deep-seated problems are preventing someone from operating in anything like a normal way, or when the situation is such that outside intervention is required for the protection of the individual or of society. We all use this approach to some extent. Clearly, it is essential for us to assess correctly what is happening to our clients. But social workers have long known, as have some physicians, that unless the person who is being treated really wants to get well and begins to work on getting well himself, a great deal of what one does to or for a person, however appropriate the treatment, goes to waste or has a very temporary effect. One must help people to use what one has to give.

If this is forgotten—and it sometimes is, in our enthusiasm to solve other people's problems and even in our need to use our specialized knowledge of human relationships and so to be truly "professional"—we tend to see all human problems as arising from personality deficiencies that need to be treated or changed. In some cases this is true, of course; and, indeed, probably all of us could do with a bit of straightening out. But in terms of a practical solution to a problem, this psychological emphasis may be unnecessary, even wasteful and presumptuous. It is not our job to cure everybody's emotional quirks, even if we could, but to help people cope with what is bothering them in society.

The therapeutic approach can also be degrading to those in need. For many years, social workers treated all clients who needed public financial assistance as problem personalities. We demanded a great deal of social information from them in order to understand them, and we constructed elaborate "case plans" to help them. It took the welfare rights movement of the 1960s for some of us to realize that many of these people were perfectly capable of managing their own lives if they could be assured of a minimal income.

The Co-Planning Approach

There is increasing evidence that thousands, if not millions, of people are in trouble—sometimes quite serious trouble—simply because the world has become too complicated for many quite ordinary people to manage without some help. One far-seeing social worker has even suggested that in a few years everybody—not just the sick, the poor, or the oppressed—will need help with at least three things: how to deal with large organizations, such as hospitals, school systems, or the government; how to play roles for which they have not been prepared, such as single parent or retiree; and what lifestyle to adopt.[1] Help with these problems of living in a rapidly changing and depersonalized society may become routine, necessary, and universal.

Many of the people who are facing problems they cannot solve alone are quite ordinary people. They may be less educated than others or at a disadvantage because of their age, race, or sex. On the other hand, they may not. They may simply be up against problems that most of us have had the good fortune not to encounter, or they may be lonely and lack the support of family members and friends. Along with the addition of new problems, such as drugs, inflation,

1. Edward Loewenstein, "Social Work in a Post-Industrial Age," *Social Work* 18 (November 1973), pp. 40-47.

and unemployment, we have lost a number of supports that we could rely on in the past: the multigenerational extended family, the closely knit community, even many of the resources of the farm or garden.

What people overwhelmed by problems of living need is what has been called a co-planning approach. They need to be asked not "What is wrong?" but, "Given the difficulty you are encountering, what do you want to do about it, and how can I help you do it?" They need to be treated as responsible people, not as sick or weak people whom we need to prescribe for, influence, manipulate, or control. Some of them may indeed be sick, and treatment for their illness may be part of the plans we help them make; but the more we work with people, taking a co-planning approach, the more we find that groups whom we used to think totally incapable of handling their own problems, such as children and the retarded, can become actively involved in finding solutions if they are given the right kind of help. Even the seriously mentally ill have a well part to them.

The Components of a Problem

How does one decide where the emphasis should be put in working with a particular client? A model that some workers have found useful involves seeing any situation as composed of three components, which can be drawn as a column representing the extent of the problem, as shown in the first column in Figure 2.1. These components are the *culture,* or what is usual or traditional in the group to which the client belongs; the *pressures* the person is under; and the client's *personal make-up.* In a case of child abuse, for example, the culture would encompass such features as traditional child rearing practices that allow corporal punishment, and the tacit assumption so prevalent on television that one can solve all problems physically, by hitting or shooting the other person. Pressures, for an abusing parent, might include loneliness, a difficult child, 24-hour-a-day parenthood, crowded living conditions, or severe marital or financial problems. Personal make-up would encompass the psychological factors that tend to make people deal with their problems in this particular way instead of going into a depression or developing ulcers or drinking or taking drugs. Such personal factors might include having been abused as a child oneself, or having an unusual need to assert one's authority.

All of us have a break-point, the time at which we lose the ability to manage our affairs adequately, although for many of us this point may

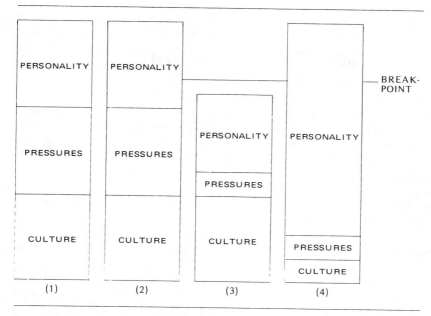

Figure 2.1.   Schematic representation of a problem.

never be reached. All of us, for instance, have the virus within us that causes pneumonia, but we only get pneumonia when we put our systems under too much strain. All of us are potential child abusers or mentally ill patients, or are subject to any other misfortune to which humans are prone; but as long as our break-point is above what we are facing, we can live full and useful lives. However, if the break-point falls below the sum of our problems, as it does in the second column of Figure 2.1, symptoms and actual illness will appear. That is why even child abusers can be loving parents at other, less stressful, times.

As social workers, our job is to help bring the column representing the extent of the problem down below the break-point of the client. If we are sensible, we will work with whatever part of the problem (i.e., personality, pressures, or culture) is most easily changed and thereby reduce the column to manageable size. Often, the most easily dealt with is social pressures. Changing personality is much more difficult, takes longer, and is more expensive. Simply by reducing social pressures we may arrive at the situation, shown in the third column of Figure 2.1, in which the family will be able to live happily together even though personality problems and the cultural milieu remain the same.

But suppose the situation is, as shown in the fourth column of the figure, one in which personal pathology is the greatest part of the problem. In such a case, no amount of work on the social pressures will bring the column down below the client's break-point; thus there is no alternative to working on the personality problem. Or, we may decide that the sensible thing to do is to work on all three components of the problem, reducing each a little, until the family can manage.

But giving the right kind of help is not a simple business. There is not only the question of the *what,* but also the question of the *how.* Most people have had the disconcerting experience of being willing to help, even of knowing quite precisely what was needed, and then of finding one's help ignored or twisted somehow, so that either nothing happened or what did happen was the opposite of what one intended. Fortunately, there are some insights that social workers have acquired about helping that serve as guides for beginning practitioners. These insights may sound simple, but they are in a very real sense the key to successful helping.

GIVING AND TAKING HELP

Helping Takes Place in a Relationship

The first thing that a social worker must understand is that helping takes place within a relationship, between someone or some group of people being helped and someone who is offering help. If the relationship goes wrong, the difficulties may be just as much due to worker as to client. When our efforts are not successful, we are all inclined to place the blame on the persons being helped. We call them weak or stubborn or stupid when they do not make good use of what we have to offer. We even say that someone is "past helping." But maybe we have offered our help in such a way that the costs of taking help are greater than the rewards. The world is full of bad helping, most of it very well intentioned, but given with so many strings attached or such demands for the impossible that it cannot be used.

The Fear of Taking Help

This brings us to a second insight. Most people are afraid of taking meaningful help—any help, that is, that will really make a difference. This idea may surprise some who see people, every day, with their hands out, so to speak, demanding to be helped. What such observers do not realize is that to demand help on one's own terms is often a way of warding off the help one really needs but does not dare accept. It keeps the helper at bay, as it were, and forbids deeper probing. The most demanding person is often the most afraid.

The fear of taking meaningful help is a very natural one. It is a fear of risking oneself that we all have to some extent. We can understand why this is so if we look at what taking meaningful help demands of the person who seeks it. Suppose you are the person who is troubled. You need, first, to realize that you are up against something you cannot handle alone, which is not a pleasant discovery. We all like to think of ourselves as self-sufficient. Next, you have to tell someone about it, and that is a dangerous thing to do. You do not know how the other person is going to use this information. The person in whom you confide may respond to your self-disclosure by blaming you or by laughing at you, or may use the acquired knowledge to punish you or gain power over you. The helper also becomes, in a sense, the superior because, for the moment at least, you are dependent on him or her.

Finally, in order to make real use of help, a change in your way of handling things is required. And that is the most frightening thing of all because it involves giving up the old, the familiar, and the known, however difficult it may have been, in favor of the new and the untried, which sounds better but may actually leave you worse off than before. Many people in unsatisfactory situations are very obviously in this bind. There are invalids who would sincerely like to get well, but who find it hard to give up the secondary gains of dependence in favor of responsibilities that they are afraid they could not manage and from which their illness now protects them. Very few people are "content" to live on public assistance, but there are thousands who are afraid to do without it, and many of them are justified in their fears about their ability to make it on their own in our economy. What is perhaps not so generally recognized is that this principle operates in nearly every helping situation. Most of us would rather cling to a known evil than take a leap in the dark, not knowing quite where we might land.

It is, therefore, not surprising that people go to considerable lengths to avoid taking help. We have already mentioned the technique of demanding help on one's own terms. Other methods, which are sometimes difficult to detect, include projecting the problem onto someone else ("It is not I but my husband [or child, or neighbor, or employer] who needs to change"); agreeing with everything that the helping person suggests and carrying out instructions mechanically, so that when something goes wrong it is the fault of the helper, not the client; and getting the helper to do all the work, to find the job, to write the letter, to talk to the landlord. People often look as if they are eager for help and grateful for it, too, but do no moving on their own. They remain completely passive; the helper is the one who is active.

Choosing to Be Helped

A further important insight is that one cannot *give* people help. One can only make it possible for them to choose to be helped. But this choosing is of a particular kind.

There are actually two types of choice that people exercise. One is the kind of decision one makes when one chooses between wearing a red shirt or a blue one. This can be called *alternative choice*. Such freedom in decision-making is pleasant to have, and citizens in a democracy are usually given as much of it as possible. However, alternative choice is limited in many ways. One may possess only one shirt, or not be able to find the shirt one really desires in the stores, or be restricted by a dress code or lack of money. As a matter of fact, too wide a selection may be frustrating—too many possible lifestyles, for instance, or sports in which one could engage, or electives in a college. But unless the choice is symbolic of something else, as wearing a black shirt might be, or wearing no shirt at all, this kind of choice has little significance for helping.

There is, however, a kind of choice that can be exercised even when alternative choices are denied. A prisoner cannot choose what to wear, what to eat, what kind of work to do, or where to live. But even prisoners still have four options among which they can freely choose: (1) They can accept and use imprisonment to learn a trade and perhaps even to decide not to continue their criminal behavior; (2) they can fight against imprisonment by trying to escape or by filing briefs for a new trial; (3) they can evade the reality of their experiences by retreating into fantasy or doing something merely to pass the time; (4) they can be overwhelmed and shattered by what has happened. This kind of choosing is sometimes called *commitment choice*. It can be said that the goal of the social worker is to help the client move from one of the last two alternatives, which are essentially passive, to one of the first two, which are active.

Negative Choices

We want our clients to deal with their problems constructively. We would like to deny them potentially negative choices and influence them to do what seems sensible or moral. Yet, in order to make a true commitment, there must be freedom of choice. If people could not be bad, they could not be good either. The word would have no meaning. In order to say yes and mean it, one has to be able to say no.

This kind of choice cannot be made for one by another person. The client may appear to share the worker's commitment to a particular course of action, but if it is not truly the client's own decision, if the client has been "conned" or persuaded into doing something for which he or she is not ready, the verbal commitment will not hold up. Some way of undoing it will be found: becoming accident-prone or developing an allergy that makes its accomplishment impossible; "forgetting" what he or she agreed to do, or not showing up for further appointments.

There are still other reasons we cannot eliminate the negative choice. There are some situations that ought to be fought against. It also sometimes happens that when a person stops evading a situation or being overwhelmed by it, the first reaction is an apparently negative one. We should remember, too, that a person who is struggling against something is much nearer to accepting and using it than someone who is doing nothing at all about it. We can, and should, help the client understand the likely consequences of making a negative choice. We would be unfair if we did not do so. But we cannot make the choice ourselves. The attempt to make others choose what we see as desirable is the source of much bad helping in the world.

Establishing a Helping Relationship

What we can do is to set up a relationship in which a person can, as far as is possible, lose the fear of change and develop a commitment to doing something about the problem. But here, we need to look carefully at what we mean by a *relationship*. A relationship is often thought of as something one sets out to get with someone else. It is sometimes said that one must "establish a relationship," or a "rapport," with a client before one can begin to help. But the helping relationship is something one gains as the result of helping someone, rather than a preliminary to helping. To concentrate on establishing a good relationship with clients, even if this is done to facilitate helping, often makes it more difficult for help to take place. It disarms clients, and because they want to please, they do not feel free to express their real feelings for fear of offending the worker or appearing not as estimable as the relationship implies. It also makes it harder for the social worker to confront clients with unpleasant truths that need to be faced, for fear of spoiling the relationship. Finally, and most important, it keeps the attention of both parties on the state of the relationship and not on the help that is needed.

Characteristics of a Helping Relationship

A helping relationship with social work clients has certain characteristics that distinguish it from a relationship between friends. It is not necessarily a pleasant relationship, although it may be and it generally ends up that way. But it may also include confrontation and the facing of painful realities. Indeed, sometimes clients do not begin to change until they get angry enough to do so. In some situations social workers have to help clients express their anger about their situations, and sometimes the way to do this is to draw anger onto oneself, where it can be handled. This is particularly true in situations such as child abuse, where the abusing parent needs help but at the same time would much prefer to be left alone. The social worker comes as the bringer of bad news and is likely to be treated initially with anger and hostility by the reluctant client. It is only by accepting and working through these negative feelings that progress can be made.

The social work relationship also has a single primary purpose: to help someone. If the social worker has any other objectives, even the most laudable ones such as a concern for justice, or morality, or the good name of the agency, the relationship is likely to suffer. These desirable secondary objectives may well be fulfilled as a result of the help given, but if the social worker starts with them as the first priority, the goal of helping will be endangered. And often, in trying to help, the worker gets distracted by personal needs, such as the need to be liked, or to succeed, or even to be the one who gives the help. A social work relationship must be concentrated on the client's need for help, and on nothing else.

Negative Emotions

A helping relationship is one in which negative emotions can be expressed safely; that is, without incurring blame or losing the concern of the helping person. This can perhaps best be shown graphically by likening a person in trouble to a vehicle which is, for some reason, standing still. This vehicle has an engine. Although the engine may not be very strong, due to exhaustion or debility, there is still some forward thrust, just as there is in all living creatures and in nature as a whole. Yet the vehicle is not moving.

There are two possible reasons the vehicle is stalled. There may be an obstacle in the way. In this case, the sensible thing to do is either to remove the obstacle or to find a way around it. Obstacles, in this sense, may be lack of money, lack of education, ill health, a handicap, or an unfavorable environment. But even if all obstacles are removed, many people still cannot move forward. They are held back by what are known as negative emotions, of which the most usual are fear, despair, and overwhelming rage. In our analogy, we can think of these emotions as acting somewhat like a spring against which the engine pushes. Actually, they are inside the "vehicle," but for the sake of clarity we will think of them as if they were outside it.

One's natural tendency is to want to push the vehicle, to add to the strength of the engine, especially as one cannot see the spring against which it is acting. This produces a temporary forward movement but only tightens the spring. When the pressure is taken off, the vehicle quickly returns to its former position or regresses even further. What one actually needs to do is to uncoil the spring. This can be done only if the negative emotions are identified and discussed and seen as the unreal things they often are.

Only in a helping relationship is such a process likely to occur. People having difficulties usually seek out sympathetic friends who try to cheer them up or reassure them, but who are unlikely to help them look at their fear or despair or anger. Such help is not easy to give because none of us like dealing with the negative emotions of others; and indeed we often feel a strong inclination to ignore them entirely or explain them away. We are afraid that by discussing negative feelings we will encourage them or make them worse. Indeed, the clients' negative emotions can be exacerbated if the worker, in a misguided effort to give support, reinforces them and allows them to be used as an excuse for dysfunctional behavior. This distinction between helping clients look at their feelings and joining them in those feelings may become clearer in our later discussion of sympathy and empathy.

The role of negative emotions is particularly crucial during a crisis. People in crisis are facing something that they perceive as a serious threat to their comfort, their security, or their aspirations. Such an event might be the death of a spouse, the birth of a retarded child, the unexpected loss of a job, or even something quite natural such as becoming an adolescent or being retired. Facing a crisis generally involves at least three stages. The first stage is characterized by shock and disbelief, and often involves the person's moving mechanically through a habitual schedule of activities even though such behavior makes little sense. There may be attempts to solve the problem by making small adjustments, but whether these are undertaken or not, the period of shock is often followed by a protest against fate and the people involved in the crisis, even a loved person whose death is being mourned. The person had no right to leave, or should have taken better care of him- or herself.

At this point two things can happen. One may achieve a mastery of the situation which is sometimes better than one's condition before the crisis occurred. Having to face adversity does sometimes ennoble people. Or one may sink into despair, for which the only solution is detachment from the problem, persuading oneself that one doesn't care or can do without what really matters to one.

Why are some people able to achieve mastery of a situation while others are overwhelmed by it? Part of the explanation undoubtedly lies in differences in personality and in prior life experiences. But there is another important factor that has been found to be even more significant. This factor is the extent to which the protest is understood and allowed expression. If we try to make people "look on the bright side of things," if we do not allow them their grief or anger, we may unwittingly condemn them to despair and detachment or force them to express their protest in unacceptable ways when the next crisis occurs in their lives. For example, children who adjust too easily in foster homes, because it is expected of them, frequently have an exaggerated reaction of grief and rebellion during adolescence.

We can visualize the path between despair and mastery as being blocked by a wall. There are no holes in the wall. To help people move from despair to mastery, we must help them climb over the wall (i.e., reactivate the protest) in order to deal with feelings that were repressed but not extinguished.

REALITY, EMPATHY, AND SUPPORT
IN THE HELPING RELATIONSHIP

The Worker's Use of Reality

In the helping relationship something new happens. Essentially, this is the introduction of a *reality* that the client must recognize and deal with. The reality may be a law, a budget, the actual facts of the situation, the likely consequences of a course of action, the resources that are available, the rights of the client, the authority, if any, of the worker, the constraints of an agency's policy, or even what is considered reasonable or customary in our society. In presenting this reality, the social worker does not soften the facts or deal in false reassurances in order to protect clients from unpleasant truths. Even with children this is important. More children are harmed by not facing tragic realities, such as the death or disinterest of parents, than are damaged by having to come to terms with what is happening. The truth itself is usually not nearly as bad as one's fears and fantasies about what the truth might be. The social worker must also avoid justifying the reality by explaining that it is really fair or good for people. The point is not whether it is a good reality, but that it is really there. If one is to help clients cope with reality, one must look at it through their eyes and be on the same side of it as they are. If worker and client are on different sides of the reality, no progress can be made.

The Worker's Use of Empathy

Reality alone can be harsh and brutal. We need to help our clients deal with the reality we present. One way we do this is by expressing our understanding of what the reality means to the client and our appreciation of what the client is going through. This is called *empathy*. It is not the same as sympathy, at least as that word is used here. To sympathize is to feel the same as the other person feels, to weep with the other, to get angry about the same things; in short, to share the other's feelings. It is often comforting for people to know that someone else agrees with them, but the knowledge does not help them to face reality. Empathy needs also to be distinguished from *pity*, which always implies some superiority on the part of the person who offers it.

Empathy is somewhat of a paradox. It demands both thinking and feeling, objectivity and subjectivity, at the same time. If the understanding of the worker is purely intellectual, its impact on the client is that of someone who really does not understand and is cold and insensitive. At the same time, the empathic person remains rooted in reality and does not get caught up emotionally in the other person's problems.

Empathy has been called an act of the loving imagination. It is a faculty that can be sharpened through training but probably cannot be developed in someone who does not have some natural ability in this area. Rigidly intellectual people and their opposites, those who are "all feeling," have some difficulty with it. Empathy can also be conveyed long before one understands the complexities of the client's problem. Some of the most useful empathy is quite tentative. The sentence sometimes used to express empathy is, "I know that it must hurt," rather than, "I know how it hurts"; and much of it may deal with quite small problems, such as having to wait for an interview or not having the house tidy when a social worker calls.

The Worker's Use of Support

For help in facing reality to be successful, it is necessary that empathy be accompanied by *support*. Part of what is required is material support, the tools to do the job. Material support may mean finding money, or knowing where to get medical care or training for an occupation. But support also means moral support, which is the assurance that one does not have to face one's problems alone. The social worker will be there to help.

The important thing about the social worker's support is that it must be unconditional. However badly one's clients behave, whatever their decisions, the social worker still cares about them. This is what makes it possible for clients to risk changing. They know that they will not be deserted. Nor will they be blamed or depreciated. The helper has made an absolute commitment to them.

Reality, Empathy, and Support Must Go Together

These three elements or factors—reality, empathy, and support—are necessary to nearly every helping situation. They go together. Any one is useless without the others, and when something goes wrong in a helping situation, the cause is usually a weakness in one of the three. Maybe the social worker could not face reality or was afraid to share it with the client. Perhaps the worker's empathy was restricted: "I can understand your feeling like this, but not like that"; or, more likely, empathy had slopped over into sympathy. Or the support was conditional on the client's behavior: "I will care about you as long as you do what I approve of."

The Need for Self-Discipline

Despite the paradox in empathy and the total commitment involved in giving support, most people find reality the hardest of the three to convey. It is much easier to reassure than to face up to things. One does not like to be the bearer of bad news. We all like to shut our eyes and hope that problems will go away. We feel protective toward people in trouble. Sometimes the worker shrinks from the client's reality because it is dangerously close to the worker's reality.

Empathy and support are not easy, either. Sympathy, and even pity, are more natural responses than is empathy. We may not want to suffer what our client is experiencing. Our moral standards sometimes limit our support. That is why it is essential to develop the professional self-discipline that requires putting oneself entirely at the service of the client, regardless of one's own feelings about the person. At first, disciplined behavior may seem restrictive, preventing one from being the spontaneous, warm person one would like to be. But in social work, as in any art, there are ways of behaving that must be learned and impulses that must be curbed. True professionals, like true artists, have acquired self-discipline as a sort of second nature and, with it, are then free to be as spontaneous and human as they wish without impairing their helpfulness.

PERSONAL QUALITIES OF THE HELPER

There are important personal qualities that go along with good helping. Perfection is not one of them. The most dangerous helpers of all are the people who have solved their own problems and forgotten what it cost them to do so. Being too virtuous, too calm, or too competent intimidates people. A good helper is a very normal person with a normal array of faults. Good helpers get angry or impatient, at times, and occasionally fail to understand. Obviously, good social workers cannot be extremely neurotic or out of touch with reality; equally obviously, one might hope that they would be honest, fair, reasonably competent and hard working, and have a sense of humor. There are, however, three qualities that are particularly valuable in this field. They may surprise some people who think of social workers as "bleeding hearts," or, alternatively, as bossy, interfering people who tell one what to do.

The first of these qualities is *courage*. Any idea that social work is a sentimental and unchallenging profession, particularly for a male, is way off the mark. It takes considerable personal courage to face reality, to deal with anger, even to court it sometimes, and to risk oneself in a relationship with another. Many social work failures come from not being brave enough, from a fear of "getting in too deep" or not being able to handle clients' reactions to the reality one has brought them.

The second important characteristic is *humility,* in the real meaning of the word: not thinking too little of oneself, but knowing that one lacks the omniscience to prescribe what is good for other people. One is lucky if one knows what is good for oneself. Humility means not insisting on one's own way, treating clients with respect, and seeing them as people to be worked with and not things to be worked on. It means not thinking one has all the answers. It means, also, not having to be the one who made all the difference in another person's life, and being willing to refer the client elsewhere when this is indicated. It means being able to learn from one's clients as well as from books or teachers. It means being willing to help rather than control or direct. It means being able to admit that one does not know something or has made a mistake. It even means using simple words rather than high-sounding professional jargon.

The third important quality is *concern*. Concern goes much further than liking and includes people one does not like. Liking and disliking are rather selfish emotions. We dislike people who threaten us or who do not like us, or who remind us of despised parts of ourselves that we have learned to control. Extremes of either liking or disliking are possible barriers to helping. Paradoxically, the hardest people to help are those whom one dislikes the most and those whom one likes too much. With the first, an insensitive worker is likely to be punitive and a sensitive one is apt to overcompensate; with the second, one tends to protect or indulge. Social workers who believe that liking all clients is obligatory are almost sure to feel guilty fairly often. There are bound to be people, clients included, whom one cannot like, and in some cases for good reason. But one can care what happens to people, likable and unlikable, and this is the essence of concern. Someone is in trouble, is angry, sad, undecided, afraid, desperate. Regardless of personal characteristics, he or she is a person in need. Social work is there to help.

SUGGESTED READING

Benjamin, Alfred. *The Helping Interview*. 3rd ed. Boston: Houghton Mifflin, 1981.

Brill, Naomi. *Working with People*. Philadelphia: J. B. Lippincott, 1973.

Compton, Beulah, and Bert Galaway. *Social Work Processes*. 2nd ed. Homewood, IL: Dorsey Press, 1979.

Egan, Gerard. *The Skilled Helper*. 2nd ed. Monterey, CA: Brooks/Cole, 1982.

Eriksen, Karen. *Communications Skills for the Human Services*. Reston, VA: Reston Publishing, 1979.

Garrett, Annette. *Interviewing: Its Principles and Methods*. 2nd ed. New York: Basic Books, 1972.

Glasser, William. *Reality Therapy*. New York: Harper & Row, 1965.

Kadushin, Alfred. *The Social Work Interview*. New York: Columbia University Press, 1972.

Keith-Lucas, Alan. *Giving and Taking Help*. Chapel Hill: University of North Carolina Press, 1972.

Mahoney, Stanley C. *The Art of Helping People Effectively*. New York: Association Press, 1967.

3

THE KNOWLEDGE BASE
OF SOCIAL WORK

NORMAN A. POLANSKY
Professor, School of Social Work
University of Georgia

Social work practice is a blend of art and science. It is a helping relationship requiring affective skills, as Keith-Lucas discussed in the previous chapter; at the same time, it is a problem-solving process requiring cognitive skills and mastery of a knowledge base. In order to be first-rate practitioners, therefore, social workers must be generally well informed on a wide range of subjects. Sooner or later, they are likely to use nearly everything they have ever learned. For instance, a client has just been discharged from a mental hospital after a manic episode. How is her "judgment" at this point? Well, she just bought a used sofa and chair in good condition for $300. Was this a reasonable act? Another client is an auto mechanic who has come for marital counseling. He is willing to talk but is psychologically naive. Can the worker speak his language? "You always seem to go at things with your wife the hard way. Are you too proud to put an extender on your ratchet wrench?" A third client has a child of 14 months who is not yet toilet trained. Is that unusual? Which agency or church will give immediate cash assistance to a family that is new in town and destitute? The information needed is enormously varied; it does not limit itself to a single field of discourse, as in an academic discipline such as economics or geology. Social work knowledge, like life itself, cannot be neatly defined and categorized, nor can it be so highly abstract that it fails to speak to the specific needs of individual clients.

Indeed, it is tempting to contrast our field with the behavioral sciences by remarking that whereas they deal in theories, we work with facts. But the distinction does not hold. Social work needs theory, too. Karl Marx once commented that his aim was not to understand the world but to change it. Yet, oddly enough, for all action-oriented groups including social work, the need for theory is made more, not less, pressing because they are trying to change real things for real people. Indeed, a specialized knowledge and theory base is essential for any occupation that calls itself a profession. Does social work qualify?

THE PROFESSIONALIZATION OF SOCIAL WORK

Few modern students have heard of Abram Flexner, even though he may have played a role in whether they are alive. Flexner surveyed the state of medical education in the United States early in the twentieth century and found much of it appalling. A large proportion of schools of medicine were free-standing institutions, of which some were privately owned and run for profit, answerable only to themselves. Faculties too often consisted largely of local physicians who augmented their incomes with a bit of teaching, and who were not necessarily chosen because they were competent. There was little medical research being done, except by a few centers in the northeast, so that recommendations about treatment were generally more opinion than science, and advances came slowly. Flexner's report was widely disseminated and had much to do with changing medical education toward the level we now expect. Quality of personnel, facilities, and curriculum are now monitored by the universities to which medical schools are attached and by national accrediting bodies. Faculties are expected to combine scientific inquiry into causes of disease with the objective testing of new methods of treatment. Nearly all training programs in medicine are highly selective and intellectually demanding. Graduates are thought to have qualifications fully shared by no other group of practitioners, and are expected to police each other's practice and observe self-imposed rules of ethics. Such criteria form the basis on which society has granted medicine full acceptance as a profession.

There was great interest when Flexner cast an appraising eye on the emerging field of social work, in a speech delivered at the National Conference of Charities and Corrections in 1915, asking, "Is social work a profession?"[1] Based on Flexner's criteria of the caliber of systematic knowledge being imparted to newcomers to the field and the extent to which this body of knowledge was exclusive to social work, his answer was in the negative. Nowadays, we do not ask whether a given occupation is or is not a profession. Using professions such as law and medicine as prime examples of the "ideal type," we judge the degree to which other occupations fit the image. Greenwood saw it as a question of where social work falls on a continuum of occupations, ranging from professional to semiprofessional to subprofessional.[2] Greenwood's criteria for determining placement on the continuum include the following:

(1) the basis for a systematic theory; (2) authority recognized by clientele of the professional group; (3) broader community sanction and approval of this authority; (4) a code of ethics regulating relations of professional persons with clients and with colleagues; and (5) a professional culture sustained by formal professional associations.[3]

From Greenwood's sociological perspective, our having professional status is very much a matter of achieving respect and prestige; that is, "authority" in the eyes of clients and "community sanction and approval." Most social workers are far too busy in their day-to-day

1. Abram Flexner, "Is Social Work a Profession?" in *Proceedings of the National Conference of Charities and Corrections* (Chicago: Hildman Printing, 1915).

2. Ernest Greenwood, "Attributes of a Profession," *Social Work* 3 (July 1957), pp. 45-55.

3. Ernest Witte, "Profession of Social Work: Professional Associations," in *Encyclopedia of Social Work*, ed. Robert Morris (New York: National Association of Social Workers, 1971), p. 973.

work with clients to invest much thought in problems of professional prestige. However, there is no question that the reputation for kindliness and absolute integrity of nearly all social workers has given us a certain form of respect in the society. And our expert-prestige has clearly grown during the last forty years as our skills, and the knowledge on which they are based, have gradually advanced. As one who has been active in social work during most of those forty years of professional growth, I believe that the key to greater prestige for the occupation—if it matters—lies in maintaining our values and continuing to develop practice knowledge and skills.

One way a profession fosters its status is to create a mystique of privileged information and exclusive domain. Only members of that profession, supposedly, can perform certain services, and the quality of those services can be assessed only by colleagues. Such claims are not of great moment to our field. It is more important that our knowledge be useful than that it be exclusive. However, we are aware that the work we do requires a high level of expertise and that there is a continuing need to fill gaps in what we know. We turn, therefore, to the nature of social work knowledge and how it has been and is being accumulated.

THE FUNCTION OF SOCIAL WORK THEORY

A good theory performs several important functions. First, it helps reduce the chaos of raw experience. So much bombards the worker in first impressions of a client—age, sex, body build, hair color, clothing, father's occupation, mother's apparent depression during the client's infancy, and on and on. How can one group these observations into larger units that make sense? Which facts are critical for understanding and helping? Which can safely be disregarded? A good theory helps one to organize one's perceptions in terms of concepts and to set priorities among them.[4]

Theory makes it possible to take intelligent action on behalf of the client. This is especially so when the theory is "dynamic." By dynamic theory we mean one concerned with change, or tendencies to change. In contrast to purely descriptive systems that pigeonhole

---

4. Norman A. Polansky, "Theory Construction and the Scientific Method," in *Social Work Research: Methods for the Helping Professions*, rev. ed., ed. Norman A. Polansky (Chicago: University of Chicago Press, 1975).

things according to structural commonalities, dynamic theory deals with relations among events: "If A happens, B will happen; if A does not occur, B will not." Examples of dynamic theories (which, unfortunately, are not always true) are: "Frustration leads to aggression"; and "Anxiety leads to use of defense mechanisms." Having a reliable and extensive dynamic theory aids the practitioner because it heightens his or her ability to predict. And, being able to predict events is the first step toward controlling them on behalf of one's clients. Possession of a theory that leads to valid predictions facilitates control, and rational control is the mark of a scientifically based practice. A civil engineer designing a bridge, for example, must be able to calculate how strain will be communicated through the structure, in order to build in a safety margin that will bear the weight of loaded trucks. A caseworker, too, needs a theory to estimate whether the client's attachment to the worker will bear the strain of a confrontation regarding how the client is mishandling a child. Will the confrontation provide a painful, but helpful, advance in treatment? Or will it arouse so much anxiety or anger that the family will break off contact, putting the child in jeopardy?

Over a lifetime in practice, an intuitive worker may have acquired enough wisdom by trial and error to be able to make such an estimate without having a formal theory. But it is inefficient to have to learn all one's trade from scratch, without profiting from the accumulated experience of those who have gone before. Theory condenses and summarizes the learnings of previous generations of clinicians. And it does so in a form that makes it possible to make predictions in specific, concrete instances by reasoning from general principles. In a highly parsimonious theory, the condensation is such that there are not too many concepts, postulates, and laws to learn,[5] for, surprising though it may seem, a parsimonious theory is geared to minimizing memory strain. Thus it becomes possible to stay on top of what is happening and make quick deductions about what to do. No wonder Kurt Lewin, the founder of Group Dynamics, used to say, "There is nothing as practical as a good theory."[6]

Disciplines that are made up of doers rather than knowers—of caseworkers and engineers rather than social psychologists and physicists—never evolve their *practice theory* logically and systemati-

    5. Polansky, "Theory Construction and the Scientific Method."
    6. Alfred J. Marrow, *The Practical Theorist: The Life and Work of Kurt Lewin* (New York: Basic Books, 1969).

cally. Clusters of observations and principles are set down, each more or less isolated from the others. Some of the early ideas of clinicians, concerning what works, are wrong and need later correcting. Only gradually do the nuclei of ideas grow, so we can begin to envision how larger wholes may be put together. It would be misleading to imply that there is now in existence a neatly comprehensive set of precepts that covers all of social work. The matters we deal with are far too complicated for that! There are semiskilled factory jobs that can be learned in six weeks; a worker is able to perform them for another twenty years with few changes. There are disciplines, such as dentistry, whose practitioners spend 90 percent of their time on work that requires high skills, close attention, and energy, but that is completely routine. Social work is not like that. What practitioners in our field lose in a sense of mastery, we gain in the stimulation of continuing puzzlement.

TYPES OF SOCIAL WORK
PRACTICE THEORY

The nuclei of theory we do have can be grouped under three headings: therapeutics, pathology, and general theory. It is amusing to reflect on the nonlogical order in which these nuclei have evolved.

Therapeutics has to do with the nature of the helping process. In addition, it concerns principles developed around the application of particular technologies. For example, one would think that with the enormous accretion of knowledge in physics and chemistry, a method for spraying insecticides on crops could be invented by a computer. Not so. A professor at my own university has made a major contribution by devising a spray that puts an electrostatic charge on each droplet of insecticide, ensuring that at least some of the solution will cling to the underside of the leaf. No new laws of physics are involved, but development of this machine has required a blending of scientific laws and specific knowledge of farming practices, along with patient experimentation. Analogous types of creativity in social work are called "practice theory" and "social treatment."[7] For example, Kadushin has summarized principles of social work interview-

7. James K. Whittaker, *Social Treatment: An Approach to Interpersonal Helping* (Chicago: Aldine, 1974).

ing;[8] working with clients in groups involves the general laws of group dynamics,[9] but goes beyond them.

Theory about therapeutics is apt to emerge first in a clinical field. This is because the demand by a new worker confronted with a case is "Quick, tell me what to do." You would think the workers' first question would be, "What's wrong here?" Logically, this is the prior question, but, psychologically, "What do I do?" takes precedence.

Nevertheless, it soon becomes evident that if one has no theory of what is wrong, one's attempts at curative action are likely to be misdirected. Theories about *pathology* begin to emerge as failures in therapeutics make people stop and think. William Morse of Michigan used to say that politicians evidently believe delinquency is soluble in water; faced with an increase in delinquency, they always build another swimming pool! If delinquencey is not water-soluble, or recreation-distractible, it is hard to escape the conclusion that some new approach, based on a clearer understanding of causation, is indicated. So we have studies of the causes of delinquency, of violence, of chronic poverty, of child neglect and child abuse. Along with others, social workers have done many such studies; I have contributed some of them myself.[10] With improved understanding of pathology, we move more intelligently toward cure.

Once again, if life were neat and logical, one might ask, "Is this the efficient way to go about building knowledge?" If we had a theory about human behavior that was inclusive enough and valid enough, we could observe a symptom and logically deduce from *general theory* not only what has gone wrong, but what needs to be done about it. Fields such as physics and chemistry are aided by such cognitive maps. Social workers are still very far from developing a powerful overarching theory, and, given the openness of our practice system, we may never do so; but we wish social workers and behavioral scientists well who are currently involved in theory-building efforts.

Unfortunately, when social work was begun, few laws of human behavior had been advanced, and some of them were perhaps mis-

8. Alfred Kadushin, *The Social Work Interview* (New York: Columbia University Press, 1972).

9. Sue Henry, *Group Work Skills in Social Work: A Four-Dimensional Approach* (Itasca, IL: F. E. Peacock, 1981).

10. Norman A. Polansky et al., *Damaged Parents: An Anatomy of Child Neglect* (Chicago: University of Chicago Press, 1981).

leading. For example, Darwin's classic work on the origin of the species led to a strong interest in heredity as a cause of social problems. Tracts were written about "hereditary paupers," as if one inherited a fate such as poverty along with hair color! Looking back, it is easy to recognize other excesses, ideas, and programs that now seem silly, judgmental, or both. Why were such erroneous actions seized upon? Mistakes were made simply because, although psychology and sociology were in their infancies, the clients were there, their needs were desperate, and something had to be tried.

Only fragments of a valid general theory of human behavior exist today, but the clients are still there. Social work has borrowed heavily from the Freudian theory of personality,[11] from group dynamics,[12] and from the sociology of institutions.[13] But the knowledge available from the "pure" scientists does not begin to meet our everyday needs. Social work has to fill the gaps with learnings from its practical experiences, findings from the small amount of research that goes on in our own field, and ideology. Our ideology is a combination of general beliefs held about the nature of humankind, which have not really been tested, and prescriptions that emerge from our values. An example of a general belief is our conviction that people like to make their own decisions (certainly not universally true). The prescriptive role of values may be seen in the rule that clients are to be handled humanely and honestly. It has not been proved that this decent style solves problems better, but we wish to work this way and have no intention of reconsidering it.

So, the theory currently in use is necessarily a mélange of a therapeutics, pathology, and general theory, augmented by inductions from practice and infused with ideology. Practice, under these conditions, although it resembles medical practice a half century ago, is not as "unscientific" as some fear. If that were so, there would be other fields in similar difficulties. For example, fifteen years ago, dentists encouraged people to brush up and down, and some recommended scrubbing the gums with a hard brush to "toughen" them. Now, plaque has been discovered, and we are urged to brush

11. Norman A. Polansky, *Integrated Ego Psychology* (Chicago: Aldine Publishing Co., 1981).

12. Dorwin Cartwright and Alvin Zander, eds., *Group Dynamics: Research and Theory*, 3rd ed. (New York: Harper & Row, 1968).

13. Herman D. Stein and Richard A. Cloward, eds., *Social Perspectives on Behavior* (New York: Free Press, 1958).

horizontally with a soft brush, at the gumline, also formerly a no-no. The practice of social work is scientific to the extent that it is based on general laws that have been established, and to the degree that we stand ready to change it by using the scientific method to evaluate what we accomplish. Evaluative research, as it is called, is a very important facet of social work research,[14] and contributes to the theory of therapeutics. Practice also shifts in response to advances in general theory, as one would hope. An inspiring example, during my own lifetime, was the speed with which social workers closed down their infant nurseries in favor of infant foster care in response to Spitz's findings on "institutionalism."[15] A number of my friends who directed traditional children's institutions busied themselves at putting their own agencies out of business.

SOME INTELLECTUAL ANCESTORS

Social work, today, stands on the shoulders of socially conscious thinkers, writers, and activists who came before us. It is instructive to recall a few of the many pioneering men and women who have contributed to the development of social work's theory and knowledge. Some of them are ancestors we have in common with related disciplines such as sociology, economics, psychology, and law, for we all started out together, many as branches of philosophy. For example, when Abram Flexner's critique of our field was delivered before the National Conference of Charities and Corrections in 1915 (now renamed the National Conference on Social Welfare), not only were penologists and social workers there, but also large numbers of sociologists, who, in those early days, held their own national meeting in conjunction with ours. Over time, however, the distance between allied professions has grown, as each has carved out its own area of expertise. Only social work, like philosophy, has remained a generalist field.

It was well into the twentieth century before the slow movement of the social sciences out of philosophy was accomplished. For example,

14. Ruth E. Weber and Norman A. Polansky, "Evaluation," in *Social Work Research: Methods for the Helping Professions,* rev. ed., ed. Norman A. Polansky (Chicago: University of Chicago Press, 1975).

15. René Spitz, "Hospitalism: A Follow-Up Report," *Psychoanalytic Study of the Child,* vol. 2 (New York: International Universities Press, 1946).

my first sociology course at Harvard in 1938, "Social Problems," had emerged only a few years earlier out of the curriculum of moral theology.

Why study our history? Most important, the successes and failures in ideas and programs from our past are instructive for practitioners today. As Santayana warned us, in his famous epigram, "Those who neglect history are doomed to repeat it." Our social work past is also fascinating in its own right. The people who helped shape social work as we know it today were not only talented and dedicated, they were also a colorful lot. I like to say that history is the final sewer into which all good gossip flows, and anyone who does not enjoy gossip is out of place in social work. In writing about some of these giants from our past, I am indebted to an excellent chapter by MacDonald.[16]

Social Polemicists and Pamphleteers

Our intellectual ancestors include a series of fiery British polemicists and pamphleteers concerned with arousing the British conscience to the terrible conditions of the poor in eighteenth- and nineteenth-century England. Jonathan Swift's *Gulliver's Travels* (1726) was not written primarily to entertain children; it was, in part, a telling parody on the injustice of British government. Daniel Defoe was famous among my pretelevision generation as the author of *Robinson Crusoe* (1717). However, our mothers kept from our youthful eyes his *Moll Flanders* (1683), a book starkly depicting the risks and realities in the life of a working-class girl in seventeenth-century England; and we were also totally unaware that Defoe, at great personal risk, was a crusader who pamphleteered vigorously on behalf of the poor in his society. Charles Dickens, the most popular British novelist of his time, used his great ability as a storyteller to bring to the attention of the British middle and upper classes a vivid picture of what life was like for adults and children in the nineteenth-century London slums (e.g., *Oliver Twist*, 1838). So influential was Dickens in the United States, as well as in Britain, that a crowd would gather in New York to meet the weeky boat from England bringing a new installment of his latest novel for newspaper publication here. A man of action as well as letters, Dickens persuaded a number of wealthy acquaintances to

16. Mary E. MacDonald, "Social Work Research: A Perspective," in *Social Work Research*, ed. Norman A. Polansky (Chicago: University of Chicago Press, 1960).

invest in some "model tenements" in which he took an active personal interest. Judging from the concentrations of social pathology that so many of our public housing projects have become, it is hard to realize that the tenement was, initially, a great step forward. For one thing, there was an inside toilet on every floor. But in social work, as in medicine, there is no such thing as a dosage without a potential side effect that might prove noxious. Compared with open sewers, dirt floors, and the like, tenements were a decided advance in nineteenth-century England.

In the United States, Samuel Clemens comes to mind, writing as Mark Twain. Our recollections of the later Twain as humorist, lecturer, and New York *bon vivant* may cloud the messages he delivered in *Huckleberry Finn* (1885), which was a satire on the heartland of the United States in the nineteenth century. Huckleberry's adventures with slavery and its evils, with murderous feuds among civilized families, and as the child of a drunken, abusive father whom no law could touch have left permanent records in our memories. We have had later muckrakers and reformers, but few so adroit at sneaking his point past a middle-class guard as Twain. More typical, perhaps, was the fate of Upton Sinclair, the crusading reporter who wrote *The Jungle* (1906). The book was intended as a terrible indictment of the cold, the filth, and the dangers in the lives of packing-house workers. It aroused national attention, but relief for that immigrant underclass was slow in coming. Congress responded with legislation closer to its self-interest: inspection of the meat in interstate commerce, and pure food and drug acts.

Scholar-Reformers

More closely related to the knowledge-building process is another group we can term the "scholar-reformers." In contrast to the literary and reportorial styles of the polemicists, they collected data in an organized fashion. While it was sometimes not clear whether the conclusions the scholar-reformers drew and publicized came inductively from their scholarly studies or whether the studies were undertaken in order to hammer home reformist convictions previously arrived at, they sought to persuade others by a weight of factual evidence, rather than by sheer argumentation. John Howard (1826-1890) began as sheriff of a county jail in England, where he saw men acquitted only to be returned to prison because they were unable to pay for the food they had eaten while awaiting trial. He made other staggering observations and devoted the remainder of his life to detailing prison conditions in Britain, as well as throughout Europe, including numbers incarcerated, their food, living conditions, and the like. Howard died from a fever contracted while he was studying military prisons in Russia. It is no wonder that an organization for penal reform is named for him.

Dorothea Lynde Dix (1802-1887) was a magnificent reformer of the same genre. After retiring from teaching because of "poor health" in midlife, she volunteered at a local jail and was astounded to discover mentally ill people confined there for lack of any other arrangement. Her concern aroused, Dix began to investigate the care of the insane, the retarded, and epileptics, first in her native Massachusetts and then throughout the pre-Civil War United States. Dix found treatment of the insane to be a national disgrace. Some were locked in garrets; some were kept in pits in back yards, into which their food was thrown. Occasionally, psychotics used poor judgment about weather and wandered into freezing temperatures, unclothed. From this behavior, it was concluded that they were immune to the cold, and despite such evidence as fingers and toes dropping off from frostbite, many mentally ill persons were provided no heat or protection from the elements. Traveling through the rough countryside by horse and stagecoach, undergoing tremendous hardships, Dix collected convincing statistics and horrifying case examples. Because the average locality could not afford proper care for its small number of insane, Dix turned in 1854 to the federal government for help. She petitioned Congress for a national program for the insane, pointing out that available local facilities could not care for even a fourth of the cases she had located. Congress passed the required legislation, but it was vetoed by President Pierce on the grounds that it was a violation of state/federal separation of powers, a denial of federal responsibility that continued well into the twentieth century. Dorothea Dix was also largely responsible for creation of the state mental hospital systems that, in our own day, have themselves needed massive reform. However, there was no question at the time about the urgent need for such hospitals. They were truly "asylums" when first built. In fact, they are still needed for large numbers of patients who are now being prematurely "deinstitutionalized" without the provision of adequate protection in local communities to which they are returned.

Another potent scholar-reformer was Beatrice Webb (1858-1943). Born just before the founding of the Charity Organization Society movement, out of which modern social work developed, Webb served an apprenticeship as a rent collector in a model tenement. Alas, like other well-meaning students who have come later, she was repelled from that commitment by the dreadful smells of poverty. She persevered, however, to join Charles Booth's survey research staff. Politically involved and very astute, Webb, in partnership with her husband Sydney, made an exhaustive study of the history and functioning of the English Poor Laws, dating from the time of Elizabeth I. Presented to a Royal Commission and to the Parliament in 1909, the Webbs' conclusions led to a general overhaul and liberalization of English Poor Laws. The Webbs were very much in the tradition of marshaling statistics and historical trends that, presented to reasonable people, would move them to make the necessary legal changes. Such an approach, of course, assumes a level of rationality and goodwill among political leaders that is not always present.

A truly fascinating English figure was Charles Booth (1840-1916). Booth was a "self-made millionaire," via trade and shipping, who became interested in the plight of London's poor and in the various debates about causes of poverty. A very intelligent and active man, he decided there really was no credible information about the poor—their numbers, lifestyle, source of earnings, and so on. To remedy this situation, Booth financed and personally directed a monumental survey of London for nearly ten years, collecting data through direct interviews with knowledgeable local informants. His interview data and statistical information emerged in seventeen volumes, *The Life and Labour of the People of London,* from 1891 to 1903. Beatrice Webb, as noted earlier, was one of his assistants. So, this self-made man became also a self-taught researcher and the founder of the social survey movement. One thinks of Booth, Howard, Dix, and the Webbs as people who shared one great gift, at least: Each was capable of a "passion," of becoming fascinated.

The survey movement played a prominent role in United States social work of the early twentieth century. Not all those doing surveys were full-time researchers. For example, Jane Addams (1860-1935), founder of Hull House and the most famous of all our great settlement workers, shrewdly had herself appointed sanitary inspector of her area of Chicago. This was not considered a politically strategic position by most people, but in her hand it provided excellent leverage for forcing delinquent landlords and businessmen to clean up unsanitary conditions that were threatening the health of the people in the Hull House neighborhood. From this small post in politics, Addams went on to active involvement in the Progressive wing of the Republican party, even seconding the nomination of Theodore Roosevelt at the Bull Moose convention of 1911. Later, however, she fell from grace with the party and with the public because of pacifist views during World War I. Almost from the beginning, however, along with political action, those who operated Hull House also busied themselves with collecting systematic data on their Chicago neighborhood to guide service programs. Thus this great settlement had, in addition to its many other commitments, a series of excellent publications called the "Hull House Maps and Papers."

Among many distinguished Hull House residents were Grace Abbott (1878-1939), an early chief of the Children's Bureau; and Sophinisba Breckenridge (1866-1948), of a distinguished and political Kentucky family, first woman to be admitted to the Kentucky bar. While teaching at the School of Social Service Administration at the University of Chicago, Breckenridge directed numerous studies of the history of public welfare in the United States from colonial times onward, written in a style reminiscent of the Webbs'. Edith Abbott (1876-1957), sister of Grace, was dean of that school from 1924-1942. Harry Hopkins (1890-1946), President Roosevelt's right-hand man during World War II, was also a former settlement house resident. Herbert Lehman (1878-1963), an enormously wealthy governor and senator from the state of New York, acquired much of his intimate knowledge of the poor from his years as a resident. Although the great era of settlement houses is past, fact gathering and muckraking still continue to occupy a place in their programs. Now, as then, it is a social work responsibility not only to care for the soft underbelly of the social class structure, but also to arouse the society to the fact that it is there.

The intellectually disciplined passion of the Hull House group seems a good place to end this section. Given this heritage of service, it is not without good cause that we social workers boast that we "come from a proud line of snoopers, busy-bodies and folks addicted to minding other people's business."[17] In research, we have moved in more recent times from broad, large-scale surveys such as Booth's, which were aimed at alerting the entire society to the plight of the

17. Norman A. Polansky, "Introduction," in *Social Work Research: Methods for the Helping Professions*, rev. ed., ed. Norman A. Polansky (Chicago: University of Chicago Press, 1975), p. 6.

poor, to studies with more limited foci. The professionalization of social work, the shift from amateurs to career altruists, has required studies that provide intellectual tools for practice.

CODIFYING AND TRANSMITTING PRINCIPLES OF PRACTICE

Universities have acquired such a dominant role in organized research that one is likely to overestimate the academic influence on practice fields. Where, after all, are beginning hunches about therapeutics and pathology for social work most likely to arise? Probably the most important questions occur to practitioners, who are directly and continuously involved with helping clients. The exigencies of a case press the worker to try something different; the flood of information makes a pattern that suggests a "cause" of the person's troubles. At least until very recently, most practice theory emerged from those directly engaged in it. Universities serve, primarily, as the repositories of knowledge gained from other disciplines and from practice, and are entrusted with the important task of transmitting that knowledge efficiently to newcomers. In social work, the ideal faculty member combines teaching and research with continuing expertise in practice. We are not alone in this expectation. One asks no less of those teaching surgery, trial law, or agricultural engineering. The demand for a high level of practice skill is what distinguishes the professional school faculty from arts and sciences.

A major task in the professionalization of a field is that of *codifying* the knowledge it has been accumulating. Much of the knowledge we have acquired came to us by incidental learning. For example, the student new to a college town does not, typically, set out on his first walk determined to find a dry cleaner. Yet, when he needs something cleaned, he recalls having seen a cleaner's in the block opposite the coffee shop. We all pick up information and store it, even when we have no immediate use for it. At least some of the information that later may seem highly significant for helping people was initially stored simply as incidental. But, typically, there are other bits and pieces of knowledge that have been gathered more intentionally.

It is a major milestone in the development of a field when someone has the vision and ability to bring these pieces together into the beginnings of a whole. Often, when it is done well, the book is called a textbook, and lends its name to a whole new field. While the book may become heavily used in educational programs, some textbooks actually were written by authors who had in mind people already practicing the occupation. Thus the great textbook writers serve a real function in systematizing and codifying knowledge for the field. The first influential textbook for casework was Mary Richmond's *Social Diagnosis*.[18] Richmond laid down principles for conducting the "social investigation" of the client's family in order to arrive at a proper diagnosis and treatment plan. The warm and colorful personality of this half-Gypsy mother of modern casework is well concealed behind her review of the rules of evidence. But, she did firmly ground a principle that many of us think irrefutable: Treatment must be geared to diagnosis. A comparable job was done for the field of social group work by Grace Longwell Coyle. Her book, *Group Work with American Youth*,[19] did not appear until 1948; the other great early text in that field, *Social Group Practice,* published in 1949, was written by Gertrude Wilson and Gladys Ryland.[20]

It is typical of the greatest textbook authors that, in addition to compiling much of "what is known," they provide the profession another service. The outlines and, indeed, the chapter headings that are used provide what one may call an *analytic mapping* of the field of discourse. If the occupation finds its social niche, survives, and grows in numbers of practitioners and wisdom, its accumulating knowledge becomes much greater and has to be differentiated into segments to be studied sequentially. The chapter headings of the pioneer forecast the textbook title of the codifier, who does the same job in one segment for the next cohort of newcomers. The process may then continue until practitioners "know more and more about less and less." At some point, it becomes essential to return to first principles and devise a reunification of the whole. Hence the books labeled "introductory" actually require great skills at synthesis but do not always show it. The reader will now understand why this elderly professor believes it is the introductory courses that ought to be taught by senior faculty—provided they have kept up!

18. Mary E. Richmond, *Social Diagnosis* (New York: Russell Sage Foundation, 1917).
19. Grace L. Coyle, *Group Work with American Youth* (New York: Harper & Row, 1948).
20. Gertrude Wilson and Gladys Ryland, *Social Group Work Practice* (Boston: Houghton Mifflin, 1949).

The codification and transmission of knowledge is epitomized in the textbook, but occurs in many other places as well. Various editions of the *Social Work Encyclopedia,* under the auspices of the National Association of Social Workers, contain a large number of summary papers on selected topics relevant to our work, each of which attempts an authoritative and up-to-date review. Professional journals also contain review articles. Even more important, journals are filled with articles reporting advances in practice knowledge in every aspect of our work. As they ought to be, a high proportion of these articles are written by professionals who are currently engaged in direct practice. Those of us who serve on editorial boards welcome contributions from practitioners because they are probably the best available source of innovative treatment tactics and the best indication of what workers are actually encountering in modern practice. Each such article begins with references, which the student might regard as merely an obligatory ritual. It is, however, more than that, for the author has to help the rest of us recognize where his or her contribution fits into what is already known. For people hard at work in agencies far away from university libraries, reviewing the literature may seem an imposition, but without such reviews a coherent knowledge base for social work cannot be achieved.

FORMAL RESEARCH

Finally, there comes a time in the evolution of a profession when it is recognized that the accretion of theory by experience, by incidental learning, and by serendipity may work, but it takes a long while. Consequently, some individuals are assigned full time to the task of producing knowledge as full-time researchers. There is a discipline, *social work research,* which I know from having been in, more-or-less continuously, for over thirty years. As compared with such fields as psychology, medicine, or industrial chemistry, the numbers of social work researchers have always been pitifully small. Unfortunately, research has not been given high priority in our action-oriented field. The financing of research has also always been a problem, especially since research often competes with direct services to clients for limited funds. But the aim of such endeavor is clear: It seeks to speed the process of accumulating and integrating knowledge into valid practice theory.

Social work research harnesses the "scientific method" toward the ultimate goal of helping clients. The set of precepts and logical rules that have evolved into the scientific method will be discussed in the next chapter, so I will not dwell on them here. Formal research, up to the present time, has played a small but useful role in social work. However, the 1980s and 1990s may bring an increase in research activity in all areas of practice, as more social work researchers are trained at the doctoral level and as the field becomes more convinced of the significant gains in practice knowledge that can be made through systematic and disciplined inquiry.

Among their fellow scientists, social work researchers are labeled as "applied" rather than "pure." This is a distinction with pejorative implications that tends to exercise the unsophisticated but that is not truly meaningful. As Tamara Dembo, a distinguished social psychologist with whom I worked (in a very junior capacity) under Kurt Lewin, expressed it to me: "All problems sufficiently pursued lead back to *fundamental* questions."

Newcomers to the field are typically more aware of fundamental social work issues than those who, having given up hope of solving such issues, have now repressed them. Whether one's research is merely specific and limited or contributes to the goal of building integrated theory for the whole field depends more on whether the scientist retains the visions held as a newcomer than on technical skills. Contact with students helps to recover the sense of place, of where we are going. But in social work research, at least no one suffers the perplexity that has afflicted some social scientists regarding "relevance." Unlike sociology, we have no need for a book asking, "Knowledge for what?"[21] Our question is, "Knowledge for whom?" Its answer is given throughout this volume.

SUGGESTED READING

Ganter, Grace, and Margaret Yeakel. *Human Behavior and the Social Environment: A Perspective for Social Work Practice.* New York: Columbia University Press, 1980.

Levine, Murray, and Adeline Levine. *A Social History of Helping Services: Clinic, Court, School and Community.* New York: Appleton-Century-Crofts, 1970.

21. Robert S. Lynd, *Knowledge for What? The Place of Social Science in American Culture* (Princeton, NJ: Princeton University Press, 1939).

Mass, Henry S., ed. *Social Service Research: Reviews of Studies*. Washington, DC: National Association of Social Workers, 1978.

Polansky, Norman A., ed. *Social Work Research: Methods for the Helping Professions*. Rev. ed. Chicago: University of Chicago Press, 1975.

Turner, Francis J., ed. *Social Work Treatment: Interlocking Theoretical Approaches*. 2nd ed. New York: Free Press, 1979.

PART II

POLICIES AND PROGRAMS OF MODERN SOCIAL WORK PRACTICE

The first part of this textbook presents a large landscape for social work practice. Even though social work cannot be defined accurately by the settings in which social workers offer help to people, social work concentrates on specific population groups. In general, these groups are those who are disadvantaged in American society. For example, Americans are concerned about the welfare of all children, but social work concentrates its attention on children who do not have families, or children who live in families with no income, or children who have physical or emotional handicaps. Americans are concerned about the welfare of all older people, but social work concentrates its attention on those older people who are poor, or who have social problems adjusting to older adulthood because of illness or lack of social resources.

Although some would argue, with good authority, that America has been slow in developing social resources for the disadvantaged, a large number of social programs currently exist. These programs have been shaped over many years by social welfare leaders, many of whom were also outstanding social workers. Often these social programs began as voluntary activities of churches and private associations, and frequently they began as charitable acts by local governments. Gradually many of these varied programs have been brought together under comprehensive state and federal laws. Always these programs are directed at the disadvantaged in American society. They are the resources that social workers employ in helping the disadvantaged. These resources may be thought of as tools of the social work trade. A carpenter uses specific tools in skillful ways to build a home; a social worker uses social programs in skillful ways to help the disadvantaged.

In Chapter 4, Pfouts and Fink discuss how the most recognizable social programs developed in America. This chapter provides more than historical perspective on American social welfare because it shows clearly how public resources consistently emerged in five social welfare fields of service: children, children in schools, medical resources for disadvantaged, criminals, and older people. In each of these fields of service there are persons with social disadvantages, and, over time, it is in these fields of service and with these disadvantaged people that social workers have concentrated their helping activities. Pfouts and Fink show that despite the expansion of social resources, the greater professionalization of social agencies, and an increasing federal commitment to social welfare, social work practice continues to concentrate its energy within these five service fields.

Identifying the particular emphasis of social work practice, and showing how public commitment to serving the disadvantaged has grown since the 1900s, raises two other issues that social workers must face. The first issue is that of the relationship between services to help the disadvantaged and what goes on in the rest of society. The second issue concerns which specific programs operate today. The first issue is often called a "social policy" question. In Chapter 5, Dobelstein shows the relationship between social programs and social expectations. This type of discussion is important to social workers, because if social workers do not understand the broader social purposes for the programs with which they help clients, they may well use these programs inappropriately. If, for example, the broader social purpose for income maintenance programs for children is to produce strong families, social workers will give helping attention to all the family members, not just the children who receive public aid. The social purposes, or the public welfare policy purposes, of the social programs provide guidance for the way the programs are used in social work helping activities.

Dobelstein, in Chapter 5, and Hoshino, in Chapter 6, then go on to display the exact characteristics of today's social programs. Dobelstein discusses housing programs and social programs for older people and Hoshino concentrates his attention on income maintenance programs. Hoshino discusses these programs within a broad framework that has been identified as "public welfare." The Social Security Act of 1935, as amended, is the locus of public welfare programs that either provide cash income directly to disadvantaged people or provide in-kind resources that help the disadvantaged protect their modest income from larger disabling social forces.

Hoshino gives important details about the administration of public welfare programs. Because federal, state, and local governments all have some responsibility for carrying out these programs, each of these governments has some say in the way the programs are offered to people. The program to aid dependent children (Aid to Families with Dependent Children, or AFDC) is one of the most difficult to understand, and Hoshino provides students with insights into this most important program. Hoshino concludes Chapter 6 and Part II by pinpointing the emphasis of social work practice in the 1980s. The personalized social services that have developed from the public welfare focus provide the present focal point of social work helping activities. This idea developed by Hoshino is repeated by Turner in the Epilogue of this text.

Part II expands the idea that social work is a complex profession that attempts to do many things in many different environments, with many different responses. Despite such complexity, it is still possible to identify the unifying trends and directions. While the materials on public policy, social programs, and fields of social work practice activity may seem to oversimplify the social work mission, they provide some of the foundation knowledge that social workers must have, as Polansky states in Chapter 3.

4

DEVELOPMENT OF SOCIAL PROGRAMS IN THE UNITED STATES

JANE H. PFOUTS
Professor, School of Social Work
University of North Carolina, Chapel Hill

ARTHUR E. FINK
Professor Emeritus, School of Social Work
University of North Carolina, Chapel Hill

In every historical period, a nation's social agencies reflect both the society's value system and the extent to which an economic surplus is available to support the needs of deprived and dependent people. As societies move from preindustrial, through industrializing, to fully industrial status, public recognition of individual rights and needs expands, and the agency system expands to accommodate these new priorities.

In the seventeenth and eighteenth centuries, when settlers were struggling to create a viable society in the new world, the needs of "unfit" and nonproductive members were necessarily given scant attention. Consequently, agencies to minister to their needs were few and poorly funded. By the second half of the nineteenth century, however, the process of industrialization was well under way, and the nation's economy had prospered to the point where the society was willing and able to deal with social abuses that it had formerly tolerated. Throughout the nineteenth century, an ever increasing range of services was offered to needy groups, particularly through the efforts of the private sector. The twentieth century has been characterized by the growth of public entitlements and services for previously excluded groups, and for the middle class as well as the poor. This growth has been particularly rapid since World War II, a period during which the United States became the richest and most powerful of the Western democracies. In the 1980s, what began over 200 years ago as a rudimentary system of local charity has become a vast and complex agency system, delivering money and services that directly affect the lives of millions of citizens. This chapter describes the development of six types of agencies in which social work has played and continues to play an active role. The areas of practice are as follows: services for dependent children; services in educational, medical, psychiatric, and correctional settings; and services to the aged.

SERVICES FOR DEPENDENT CHILDREN

All societies, no matter how scant their economic surplus, make an effort to provide for the survival of their children. In the United States, this concern was expressed early in our national life, and has been from the beginning a central focus of social welfare activity.

Institutional Care

During the time of the colonies, a movement began to protect homeless children from the evils of the almshouse by providing separate institutions for their care. The first instance on record is that of the Sisters of the Ursuline Convent; brought from France to New

Orleans in 1727, the nuns provided a school for young girls who had been orphaned by wars with the Natchez Indians. A second institution, and one that is still in operation, was the Bethesda Home for Boys (located near Savannah, Georgia), which owed its existence largely to the zeal of the celebrated English preacher, George Whitefield. The third, and the first to be organized and supported by tax funds, was the Charleston Orphan House, built in 1794. Three more institutions quickly followed: John de la Howe Industrial School in South Carolina (1797); St. Joseph's Female Orphan Asylum, under the auspices of the Catholic Church in Philadelphia (1798); and the Asylum for the Care and Education of Destitute Girls, established by St. Paul's Episcopal Church in Baltimore (1799).

Throughout the next century, more than 400 children's institutions were established, and by 1925 there were 1400 in operation throughout the United States. Most of these institutions were under the auspices of denominational groups or fraternal orders. A few were endowed by private philanthropists and occasionally an institution originated as a state, county, or city facility and was supported by tax funds. In some places, provision was made for minority groups, such as black orphans in Philadelphia (1822) and destitute American Indian children in Buffalo (1845); but in our segregated society, the needs of minority children generally were ignored. Following the Civil War, numerous homes were established, mostly with tax funds, for the orphans of fathers killed in the conflict.

A new development of the early nineteenth century was the provision of care, in institutions other than almshouses, for children with special disabilities. These institutions usually were initiated by concerned groups of private citizens, but not infrequently they were later partially subsidized by public monies. Such was the case with the first permanent school for the deaf, established in Hartford in 1814, and the New York Institute for the Instruction of the Deaf and Dumb, founded in 1818. The first school for the deaf to be established directly by a state legislature was in Kentucky in 1823.

The nineteenth century was also the time of the first concrete expressions of concern for the welfare of blind children. In 1832, an institution was opened that subsequently was to become known as the Perkins Institution and Massachusetts School for the Blind. Later, it was designated to serve the needs of blind children throughout New England and was supported by appropriations not only from Massachusetts, but from all of the New England states. The first institution for blind children to be funded wholly by taxes was established in Ohio in 1837. Virginia followed Ohio's lead by opening an institution for blind and deaf children in 1839.

By the middle of the nineteenth century, another group, now termed the mentally retarded, had begun to receive specialized institutional care. The first venture was authorized and funded by the legislature of the Commonwealth of Massachusetts and began operation in 1848. Within three years, the appropriation was doubled and the school became the Massachusetts School for Idiots and Feeble-Minded Youth.

Delinquent youth became a subject of welfare concern in 1825, when the House of Refuge for young offenders became the first institution of its kind in the country. New Yorkers, who in 1817 had formed the Society for the Prevention of Pauperism, had become so concerned about the lack of separate facilities for incarcerated juvenile offenders that in 1824 they renamed their organization the Society for the Reformation of Juvenile Delinquents. The following year, with the aid of a land grant from the city and an appropriation from the state legislature, the society opened the House of Refuge. A group of Philadelphia citizens, following the New York plan, opened the Philadelphia House of Refuge in 1828; later, it received funds from both the city and the state.

Foster Home Care

The Children's Aid Society

Although institutions for children continued to proliferate throughout the nineteenth century, thoughtful people increasingly questioned the wisdom of warehousing children in large, regimented, isolated asylums. Some of these institutions were adequately financed and well run, but others were uncomfortably reminiscent of Oliver Twist's fictional "home away from home," so poignantly described by Charles Dickens. Most disturbing of all was the knowledge that regardless of how well run an institution might be, many very young children were living, year after year, in a world where the family bonds so important to normal development were missing.

By the middle of the nineteenth century, a movement was in progress that addressed these concerns. The essence of the new type of assistance was to place children in foster families rather than in institutions. The leader of the effort was Charles Loring Brace. During his training for the ministry, Brace directed a children's mission in New York City, where he saw firsthand the misery of large numbers of neglected children who were forced to live by their wits in the streets and alleys of the city. In 1853, the mission was renamed the Children's Aid Society, and almost at once Brace began to carry out his long-cherished plan for removing vagrant and destitute children from the streets of New York by transplanting them to suitable homes far from the city slums. As originally conceived, Brace's plan was based on an assumption that the children would earn their keep by doing a share of the work in their foster homes. For its part, the Society would bear the expense of getting the children to the new homes and, if necessary, returning them to their families or placing them elsewhere. Through the efforts of Brace and the Children's Aid Society, many New York children were transported, with a minimum of preparation, to farms and small towns as far away as Michigan, Wisconsin, and Minnesota.

The abrupt mass migration of hundreds of children was inspired by a human desire to rescue them from intolerable circumstances, but the "child savers" lacked an understanding of the intricacies of foster home placement. The leaders of the movement believed that the chief problems were the logistics of gathering children and transporting, housing, and feeding them. Not much thought was given to the preparation of parents for the move, or to the psychological problems created when children were abruptly separated from family and friends and had to adjust to a totally different milieu and unfamiliar people. Also, since foster home investigations were cursory at best, there was always the danger of exploitation by the new family.

Despite all the shortcomings of the scheme, which were due to ignorance rather than to design, its lasting significance lay in its radical departure from indenture, the almshouse, and institutional care. It was an important step, albeit an imperfect one, toward adapting services to meet the children's needs, rather than simply warehousing them. Very quickly, Children's Aid Societies spread throughout the northeast. In 1860, an agency was founded in Baltimore for the purpose of finding homes for destitute children. Within three years, organizations had been formed in Philadelphia and Boston. Other societies were organized in Brooklyn (1866), Buffalo (1872), Pennsylvania (1882), and Rochester (1895). Social workers in these agencies gradually learned a great deal about the meaning of separation and loss to a child being placed in foster care, and about the ways in which this powerful process can become a constructive experience for both foster children and their families of origin.

Foster Care as a Public Program

Only a decade or two passed before a number of states had recognized their responsibilities for the welfare of children and had begun to seek means of care other than indenture and institutionalization. Massachusetts was the first state to make a beginning in that direction; in 1869, it provided a visiting service to all children released from state institutions. This contact with otherwise virtually unsupervised young people convinced government leaders that the state should assume the cost of boarding many of the children in private homes. Ten years later, the practice of depositing children in city and town almshouses was outlawed in Massachusetts; in 1882 provision was made for state payment of board for all destitute children under 10 years of age, an example followed by New Jersey in 1899.

Pennsylvania's approach combined the principle of foster care with the services of a voluntary agency. When a state law, passed in 1883, imposed on local communities and counties the responsibility for protecting children, no consideration was given by the statute to the provision of adequate care. Fortunately, the Pennslyvania Children's Aid Society had been organized as a child-placing agency the year before, and it immediately offered to assist local authorities by working with them on the development of a program of boarding homes. Many of the larger counties availed themselves of the Society's services, and payment was made out of county funds for the boarding homes that the Society secured.

In the years since these beginnings, foster care has been a service under both private and public auspices. However, as funds have become increasingly available from local, state, and federal sources, foster care services have tended more and more to be placed within the public sphere. The Social Security Act of 1935 and its subsequent amendments broadened the range of governmental services to children in foster care; however, at the same time, through its AFDC provisions, it placed increasing emphasis on the desirability of keeping poor families together through AFDC payments and other services on behalf of the children.

What we have seen, in this historical sketch of provisions for dependent children, is a shift in preferred solutions from the almshouse to the institution, to foster care, and finally to parental care supported by AFDC payments and services. However, while care of all children in their own homes is the ideal, it is not always possible in this imperfect world. Therefore, in the 1980s, foster care and—to a much lesser degree—institutionalization continue to be the best answers yet devised to meet the needs of a minority of children who cannot remain in their own homes because of severe deficiencies in the children or in family life.

SCHOOL SOCIAL SERVICES

In contrast to the children's services already described, social services within the educational system have existed only since the first decade of the twentieth century. Originally referred to as "visiting teacher" services, such programs are now called "school social services." With the school acting as host agency, these social services developed in response to changes within the educational system that were caused by a rapidly changing society.

Shifts in educational philosophy and practice in the early years of the twentieth century were hastened by a rising school population, more stringent attendance laws, and increasing numbers of immigrant children who needed to be "Americanized" within the schools. Before the days of compulsory school attendance, there was no great concern for children who did not achieve academically or who caused trouble in the classroom; it was easy to expel them or allow them to drop out of school. It was not the system's responsibility to adapt to the individual, but the individual's responsibility to conform to the system. The advent of compulsory attendance (which concurrently placed on the state a requirement to furnish instruction to all children) created new problems, especially those of large, heterogeneous classes and a tendency toward greater regimentation. The child with special needs stood a good chance of being lost in the system.

Teachers (and teachers of teachers) were, at the same time, being influenced by new knowledge from other disciplines. From psychology, there emerged concepts of individual differences. Sociologists were reporting on the nature of the social order and the ways that personality is modified by the environment. Social workers, from their daily practice, were contributing information about the individual's capacity to adapt to the environment and about the ways in which the environment could be altered to meet the individual's needs. As a result of these and other contributions, greater educational attention was focused on the individual child. Large classes and regimentation, stressing subject matter and pressuring children to fit a mold, began to yield to a philosophy that emphasized individual needs.

Thus the shift in education involved enlarging the emphasis, from subject matter alone to the inclusion of a growing concern for the emotional factors that are related to learning and that, indeed, often impede learning. With this realignment of objectives came a revised definition of successful teaching. A teacher's success was to be measured by the extent to which individual children realized their own potential for growth.

The School as a Host Agency

Earlier, we referred to the school as a host agency. A school is not designed to serve as a social agency, any more than is a hospital, a court, or a prison. A hospital is a medical agency, a court is a judicial agency, and a prison is a correctional agency. To accomplish their purposes more fully, however, an ancillary social service function is added. Thus, as host agency for social services, the hospital engages in medical social work, the court dispenses probation, and the prison authorizes parole. So it is with the school. As an educational agency, the school engages in social work for the purpose of helping students make full use of what the institution has to offer.

During the period from 1906 to 1907, school social work was introduced in three cities: New York, Boston, and Hartford. In New York, the immediate impetus came from two social settlements that had assigned visitors to school districts in order to keep in closer touch with teachers of children from the settlement neighborhood. The initiating group in Boston was the Women's Education Association, which established the position of home-and-school visitor in one of the Boston schools. In Hartford, the suggestion that schools serve as a host agency for social services came from the director of a psychological clinic. At first, the social worker, who was known as a "special teacher," assisted the psychologist by gathering case histories. Later, the assignment included carrying out the psychologist's recommendations.

Influence of the Commonwealth Fund

The subsequent development of school social services gave substance to much of their early promise. Following the pioneering efforts of private agencies, public school authorities began to introduce visiting teachers into tax-supported school systems (Rochester, New York, was an early instance). The greatest impetus, however, came from a visiting teacher demonstration project inaugurated by the Commonwealth Fund. There were 30 approved centers, located in 23 states, that served as bases for the project. The Commonwealth Fund supported these 30 demonstrations for their first five years, beginning in 1921. In the ensuing three years, the Fund's attention was concentrated on training teachers for the work.

Of the original 30 projects, 21 were continued as ongoing services of school systems after the conclusion of the demonstration period, but the contribution of the Commonwealth Fund went far beyond the boundaries of those communities. Within the next decade, as the conviction mounted that more social services were needed in the schools, increasing numbers of both rural and urban school systems inaugurated similar programs. From then until now, communities in ever-growing numbers have utilized school social services, and the services themselves have continued to expand. The original approach was limited to direct work with children and their parents, but it was soon extended to include consultation with teachers and principals. Later, services were extended to include consultation with school administrators on matters of curriculum (e.g., offering more vocational courses to meet career goals of students who are not college bound). The next move, and a quite contemporary one, was to forge closer links between the school and the community. In some communities, for example, parents and civic leaders of minority groups are brought into the schools to collaborate with school social workers in shaping the educational experience to meet the needs of minority children more satisfactorily. Another facet of this latest move is for school social workers to act as facilitators in the process of engaging parents as volunteers to assist classroom teachers. Thus school social services, which received their original impetus from community forces, have come full circle, back to the community, more than a half century later.

MEDICAL SERVICES

Like school services, medical social work did not begin to take form until the first decade of the twentieth century. As Ida Cannon recorded in her historical volume *Social Work in Hospitals,*[1] the immediate precursors to medical social work were as follows:

(1) services provided for the aftercare of the insane in Germany, France, England, and America
(2) services furnished by lady almoners in London hospitals
(3) nursing, especially the visiting nursing service provided by Lillian Wald and Mary Brewster in New York City
(4) fieldwork training of medical students at the Johns Hopkins Medical School and Hospital

On two successive days in October 1905, social workers were introduced into medical settings in the Boston area—the Berkeley Infirmary (no longer in existence), and the Massachusetts General Hospital, where Dr. Richard C. Cabot, a member of the hospital staff, took leadership by creating the Social Service Department. In addition to being in charge of the outpatient department of the hospital, Dr. Cabot was a board member of the Children's Aid Society of Boston and a consultant to the state Industrial School for Girls. Cabot was firmly convinced that hospital social workers were needed, both to provide a link between the patient and all available sources of help and to connect the hospital with the social forces and helpful agencies of the community. He envisioned the social worker as an interpreter of the hospital to the patient and of the patient to the hospital. As a physician for both rich and poor patients, Dr. Cabot believed that rich people needed social services when they were sick almost, if not quite, as much as poor people.[2]

Dr. Cabot deplored the increasing impersonality of the hospital and the proliferation of medical specialties; yet, from a current perspective, the hospital of his time was a relatively uncomplicated

1. Ida M. Cannon, *On the Social Frontier of Medicine* (Cambridge: Harvard University Press, 1952).
2. Richard C. Cabot, *Social Service and the Art of Healing* (New York: Dodd Mead, 1928).

institution. Today, the sick person is in danger of being lost in the medical maze—a highly compartmentalized hospital with a confusing array of clinics and specialized departments, elaborate equipment, and an endless flow of patients and staff. It is clear that Dr. Cabot's reasons for introducing social work to medical host agencies in 1905 are equally valid and even more urgent today.

Social Services in Hospitals

Since Dr. Cabot's time, the medical knowledge explosion and increasing specialization have resulted in physicians' being better informed about specific illnesses and less aware of the patient as a person. To fill this gap, medical social workers seek to understand the meaning of illness to patients, their family relationships, and their community resources. With benefit of this knowledge, the physician and other care providers can do a better job of restoring patients to health, and the social worker is able to help families cope with the fears and problems accompanying both hospitalization and discharge of a parent, spouse, or child.

As a result of this collaborative professional process, patients and their families receive better service, and health providers acquire an orientation to the patient as a member of a larger social system that is of permanent value in their future practice. Thus, although service to patients has always been the major focus of medical social work, there has also been, from the beginning, a strong commitment to clinical teaching. As early as 1913, medical social workers at Massachusetts General participated in the teaching of medical students at the Harvard Medical School and of student nurses in the hospital's training school. Medical social workers of the 1980s continue to do a great deal of clinical teaching with regard to particular cases, as well as some teaching and lecturing on the psychosocial aspects of illness. They also serve as consultants to other professional colleagues, participate in program planning, and, to a lesser degree, are involved in policy formation and research.

Medical Social Work in the Community

Today, medical social workers also engage in a broad range of activities outside hospital walls. In addition to providing direct services to patients who remain at home, these specialists serve as hospital liaisons and consultants to health and social agencies and the community as a whole.

Perhaps the force that has been most instrumental in moving medical social work into the community is the accelerating trend toward comprehensive health care. This approach has been described as providing medical care when patients need it, where they need it, and to the extent that they need it. It may be provided in a hospital, a clinic, a physician's office, a group practice center, a patient's home, or a long-term care facility. A good program is characterized by continuity of care, family-centered service, and coordination of activities. If, as is likely, comprehensive health care expands in the future, it will place increasing demands on medical social workers; but even if it does not, helping to deliver traditional health services almost surely will be one of the most rapidly expanding and challenging areas of social work practice in the remaining years of the twentieth century.

MENTAL HEALTH SERVICES

Throughout the nineteenth century, our society's answer to deviant behavior was institutionalization. In a fascinating review of that period, Daniel Rothman shows that institutions were always the place of *first* resort—the preferred solution to problems of poverty, crime, and insanity. Rothman describes a system in which philanthropists and other concerned laypersons urged families to put their deviant members in institutions as soon as symptoms appeared.[3]

In the nineteenth-century mental hospital, according to Albert Deutsch, the emphasis was on restraint and isolation. Not infrequently, the mental hospital was far removed from population centers, and access was difficult. Increasingly, as the century wore on, the mental hospital became the repository for society's rejects—the violent, the old, the weak, and those with whom the family could not cope.[4]

The brilliant insights of Sigmund Freud and the work of his students and associates effected a dramatic breakthrough. Their analyses of the structure of personality opened new avenues of approach to the treatment of deviant behavior, and a new orientation in diagnosis and

3. Daniel J. Rothman, *The Discovery of the Asylum: Social Order and Disorder in the New Republic* (Boston: Little, Brown, 1971).

4. Albert Deutsch, *The Mentally Ill in America*, rev. ed. (New York: Columbia University Press, 1949).

treatment became possible. Freud's dynamic concept of personality was to modify, if not eventually replace, the older static view, as many American psychiatrists—although not psychoanalysts in any sense of the term—came to espouse this more dynamic view during the first quarter of the twentieth century.

The change from custodial care to individualized study and treatment revolutionized the kind and quality of care accorded mentally ill persons in many institutions and clinics. It found its first expression in newly opened psychopathic hospitals, neurological clinics, and hospital social service departments. Psychiatrists, who were becoming increasingly aware of the effect of emotional experiences on personality development, were realizing that environmental pressures on the individual were also factors to be reckoned with. The early psychopathic hospitals concentrated on studying, diagnosing, and treating forms of mental disease that appeared to have a hopeful prognosis. As part of this process, psychiatrists gathered material on the life histories of patients. Gradually, this assignment was delegated to fieldworkers who functioned under the psychiatrists' direction.

The first employment of a psychiatric social worker in a hospital was in the neurological clinic of Massachusetts General Hospital in 1905, under the direction of Dr. James J. Putnam, a colleague of Dr. Cabot. Soon thereafter, a social worker was employed in the psychopathic ward of New York's Bellevue Hospital, and state hospitals in New York and Massachusetts quickly followed suit.

Substantial impetus was given to psychiatric social work in 1913 when the Boston Psychopathic Hospital opened its social service department under the leadership of Dr. Ernest Southard and Mary C. Jarrett. Hardly had this project started when World War I began, and by the time the United States entered that conflict in 1917, it was clear that psychiatric social services were urgently needed in military hospitals. The practical difficulty was that there were not enough psychiatric social workers to meet the emergency needs. As a result, plans were made to enlarge the training facilities at Boston Psychopathic Hospital. Eventually an arrangement was effected whereby an emergency training course was given under the joint auspices of Smith College, the National Committee for Mental Hygiene, and the Boston Psychopathic Hospital, with Mary Jarrett in charge of the program. It is generally believed that the term *psychiatric social work* was coined by Southard and Jarrett. In their book *The Kingdom of Evils*,[5] they expressly state that this branch of social work was a new emphasis, not a new function, that had grown out of ideas and activities that already existed in scattered form. In this respect, the development of psychiatric social work was not unlike that of medical social work.

Out of the eight-week training courses directed by Mary Jarrett in 1918 came the establishment, within a year, of a permanent graduate school of psychiatric social work at Smith College. Schools of social work that had been established earlier (e.g., New York School of Social Work, Pennsylvania School of Social and Health Work, Chicago School of Civics and Philanthropy) began to prepare students for the new field of psychiatric social work. Within the decade, there was not a school of social work in the country that did not pay its respects to the psychiatric point of view; for some (Smith College, for example) it constituted the cornerstone of the curriculum. Caseworkers who trained in these schools drew upon a common base and utilized their knowledge and skills in a variety of agencies that offered psychiatric services. In the mental hospital setting, they became—as they remain today—integral members of the professional treatment team (psychiatrist/clinical psychologist/psychiatric social worker) whose services were directed to the treatment of mental illness and the restoration of sound mental health.

Today, psychiatric social work extends far beyond the traditional settings of hospitals, outpatient clinics, and child guidance clinics. Workers have moved into the community, where they are a central part of the service delivery system of community health clinics, and into a variety of aftercare facilities such as halfway houses and day hospitals. They also are employed as specialists by nonpsychiatric agencies, and some are moving into private clinical practice. Because psychiatric social workers, more than any other group of mental health practitioners, use a psychosocial approach in work with clients, they are particularly well suited to meet the need for community-based services in today's era of deinstitutionalization.

The Commonwealth Fund and Child Guidance Clinics

Once again, our discussion would not be complete without mention of the pivotal role of the Commonwealth Fund in expanding

---

5. E. E. Southard and Mary C. Jarrett, *The Kingdom of Evils* (New York: Macmillan, 1922).

the scope of social work practice. Within a few years of its organization as a private foundation in 1918, the Commonwealth Fund called upon representatives from fields such as psychiatry, psychology, education, the juvenile court system, and social work to formulate a new plan for child welfare services. These representatives were familiar with the work of the psychological clinic established by Lightner Witmer at the University of Pennsylvania; with the Chicago Juvenile Psychopathic Institute, founded by Dr. William Healy; and with the Henry Phipps Psychiatric Clinic of Johns Hopkins Hospital in Baltimore, under the direction of Dr. Adolph Meyer. In November 1921, the Commonwealth Fund undertook a five-year experimental program to explore some of the root problems of juvenile delinquency. The program included, in addition to the visiting teacher demonstrations discussed earlier, a mandate for the psychiatric study of juvenile delinquency and the development of appropriate treatment methods based on that study.

A number of organizations already in existence were utilized to help carry out these projects. The New York School of Social Work was in a strategic position to offer courses for psychiatric social workers, to provide fellowships for training students, and to establish a psychiatric clinic for studying and treating children with special problems. The National Committee for Mental Hygiene, through its newly formed division on the prevention of delinquency, was asked to establish demonstration child guidance clinics in selected locations.

Early in 1922, the first demonstration child guidance clinic was opened in St. Louis, with a staff of one psychiatrist, one psychologist, and one psychiatric social worker. Children with behavior difficulties were referred by schools, institutions, juvenile courts, and individual families. Since three-fourths of the referrals came from juvenile courts, it was soon realized that if a truly preventive service were to be offered, it would have to be provided long before children reached the juvenile court. At the same time, it became apparent that more social workers were needed in the child guidance clinics. Accordingly, the ratio of staff personnel was changed to include one psychiatrist and one psychologist for every three psychiatric social workers.

Community Mental Health Services

In 1908, widespread interest in the treatment of mental illness was aroused by the publication of Clifford Beers's book, *A Mind that Found Itself.*[6] The author, who had become mentally ill several years

6. Clifford W. Beers, *A Mind that Found Itself* (New York: Longmans, Green, 1908).

earlier when he was an undergraduate student at Harvard, wrote a shocking exposé of his experiences as a patient in both private and public mental hospitals in Connecticut. Beers spent the rest of his life working in the mental hygiene movement that he helped to create. One of the objectives of the mental hygiene movement was to educate the public concerning mental illness. As a result of its efforts, public awareness of Freudian concepts, which began to develop early in the twentieth century, was widespread by the time of World War II. Still, the country was not prepared for the high rate of failure among men who took the Selective Service psychological examinations for entry into the armed forces. Not only were many found unfit for duty because of mental or emotional difficulties, but, of those who did serve, an astonishing number proved unequal to the demands of military life. By the end of the war, more than 380,000 individuals were reported to have been discharged because of psychiatric disabilities.

In the postwar period, the nation and the Congress were determined to provide appropriate service for these disabled veterans. Under the aegis of a revitalized Veterans Administration (VA), a national program of services for veterans was established, including hospitals and community-based clinics. This massive program influenced the future direction of mental health work in two important ways. First, the extensive services offered by the VA's outpatient clinics demonstrated the value and practicality of psychiatric treatment at the community level. Second, with the sudden need for a greatly expanded cadre of professional workers, VA facilities were committed to training programs in psychiatry, clinical psychology, and psychiatric social work. The VA training programs eventually resulted in the addition of thousands of trained professionals, to the nation's pool of mental health workers.

The period since the postwar influence of the VA has been characterized by developments that have emphasized our national awareness of the importance of good mental health and the advantages of offering services within the community. A national network of community mental health centers has been established, underwritten by federal legislation (e.g., National Mental Health Act, 1946; Community Mental Health Centers Act, 1963; and the Comprehensive Health Planning and Public Health Service amendments of 1966). The overall effect of these federal laws and complementary state legislation has been to educate the public to mental health problems, encourage community use of local facilities, and further the training of professional mental health workers.

Advances toward reliable methods of "curing" mental illness have been discouragingly slow; but improved methods of treatment (especially chemotherapy in the treatment of schizophrenia) have resulted in extraordinary reductions in the number of psychiatric hospitalizations and length of patients' hospital stays, with a corresponding rise in the need for community-based mental health facilities. The national response to this newest need has been inadequate in both size and quality; but, imperfect as it is, it is a far cry from the insane asylum of a century ago.

CORRECTIONAL SERVICES

Another area of social work practice that calls for some degree of historical perspective is that of correctional services. To appreciate how far we have come in our attitudes toward correction, we need to have some understanding of where we started.

In early America, the local jail was supplemented by the state prison or penitentiary. In the late eighteenth century, one type of correctional facility—the Pennsylvania system of round-the-clock solitary confinement—owed its origins to the somewhat questionable application of the views of the Society of Friends on the creative powers of silence. Another type—involving confinement at night and congregate labor in prison shops during the day—developed first in Auburn, New York, in the early nineteenth century. The first House of Refuge for young offenders was established in the 1820s, and the first reformatory for offenders between the ages of 16 and 30 opened in the 1870s. Other early milestones included the creation of the juvenile court and the beginnings of probation and parole.

The Juvenile Court

Illinois enacted the first juvenile court law in 1899. The fundamental premise of this pioneering legislation was stated by the law itself:

> that the care, custody, and discipline of the children brought before the court shall approximate as nearly as possible that which they should receive from their parents, and that as far as practicable they shall be treated not as criminals but as children in need of aid, encouragement, and guidance.

The Illinois law provided for separate and private informal hearings; protection of court records from publicity; detention of children separate from that of adults; appointment of a probation staff; and establishment of one jurisdiction for all cases involving delinquent, neglected, and dependent children up to the age of 16.

Within recent years, there has been increasing recognition that the child affects and is affected by other family members, and that a family court that provides a range of useful judicial and social services for the family unit, rather than for the child alone, makes a great deal of sense in terms of rehabilitation. It is, of course, essential that family courts be structured as judicial, not social, agencies, even though certain social services must be provided if the courts are to achieve their maximum usefulness.

In addition to ensuring informality, privacy, and individualized treatment, the juvenile court has an obligation to safeguard the legal rights of children, just as adults' rights are protected in the legal system. Two landmark cases involving juveniles reached the Supreme Court during the 1960s: *Kent v. District of Columbia* (1966) and *Gault v. Arizona* (1967). The essence of the Court's decisions in these two cases is that children do not surrender their constitutional rights because they are juveniles. They are entitled to counsel, they must be given notice in writing of the charges against them, they have a constitutional privilege against self-incrimination, they have the right to confront witnesses and the right of appeal, and their counsel has the right of access to records. The importance of due process in juvenile court cases was clearly expressed by the Supreme Court in the *Gault* decision: "Unless appropriate due process law is followed, even the juvenile who has violated the law may not feel that he is being fairly treated and may therefore resist the rehabilitative efforts of the court personnel."[7]

In the years since the *Kent* and *Gault* decisions, there has been a critical reappraisal of custodial facilities for juveniles. The tragic plight of the nation's incarcerated children, depicted by reformers such as Wooden in his powerful book *Weeping in the Playtime of Others*,[8] has aroused public concern and sparked legislative and judicial activity. A number of states have either closed or upgraded their juvenile

7. *In re Gault,* No. 116, *United States Law Week,* May 16, 1967, pp. 4399-4423; in writing his opinion, Justice Fortas drew on *Standards for Juvenile and Family Courts* (Washington, DC: Children's Bureau, 1966) and Stanton Wheeler and Leonard S. Cottrell, Jr., *Juvenile Delinquency: Its Prevention and Control* (New York: Russell Sage Foundation, 1966), p. 33.

8. Kenneth Wooden, *Weeping in the Playtime of Others* (New York: McGraw-Hill, 1976).

correctional facilities on order of the courts, and community-based services such as halfway houses and group homes have been expanded. Emphasis in juvenile correctional work now is being placed on a fair trial, followed by rehabilitative efforts within the community, rather than incarceration—except for the most serious offenses. Overall, there has been great progress, but as Wooden reminds us, there are still far too many "throwaway" children locked up in reformatories that are a national disgrace.

In the 1980s, juvenile justice appears to be moving in two quite different directions. On the one hand, a number of cases involving the rights of children have been brought successfully before the courts by child advocacy groups, and children today have greater legal protection than they have ever had before. On the other hand, a law-and-order backlash, coupled with widespread disillusionment with the juvenile court system, threatens to undermine or destroy the special protections now given to children, because they are children, by the juvenile court.

Probation

One of several dispositions available to the courts—whether of juvenile or adult criminal cases—is probation. Although probation was characteristic of the juvenile court from the beginning, this type of disposition predated the juvenile court by many years, appearing first as a voluntary service. In 1841, a Boston shoemaker named John Augustus served, at his own request, as surety for a drunkard. Augustus continued to provide supervision for many other offenders over a period of years.

In 1869, the Commonwealth of Massachusetts made legal provision for an agent of the State Board of Charities to appear in criminal trials involving juveniles and, when necessary, to find suitable homes and make periodic supervisory visits. Probation for adult offenders was undertaken officially in Boston in 1878 (37 years after Augustus began his voluntary work), and within two years it was made legal throughout the state. Between that time and the present, every state has adopted adult probation; and since establishment of the juvenile court, every state has made provision for juvenile probation.

Correctional Institutions

Modern theory presses more and more for community-based correctional services, but our present state of knowledge about human behavior does not permit totally abandoning the three most common correctional institutions: the training school, the reformatory, and the prison. Only juvenile status offenders, a group who formerly were incarcerated, have in recent years been reassigned to community facilities. These minors once were sent to training schools as a result of having committed "status offenses" (acts not commonly subject to punishment if committed by adults, but punishable if one's status is that of a juvenile) such as truancy, sexual promiscuity, or ungovernable behavior. Social workers believe that treating status offenders differently and apart from juveniles who have been convicted of more serious crimes is desirable. However, for community-based treatment to work, the program must offer truly rehabilitative services, not simply local incarceration.

Another social work conviction is that despite realistic limitations, effective help can be given to inmates of more restrictive facilities to enable offenders to deal with incarceration and to plan constructively for their release. Social services can also help to ameliorate prison conditions that lead to individual exploitation and mass rebellion. However, while social workers are actively engaged in probation and parole work across the country, prison systems (particularly adult facilities on the state level) employ relatively few trained social workers within prison walls. Perhaps an expansion of correctional social work services within these facilities will occur if prison conditions continue their present trend toward being ever more overcrowded and explosive.

Parole

Preparation for parole actually begins before the offender is ever committed to a correctional facility. Treatment received at the hands of police, jailers, prosecutors, and judges creates an impression that influences the offender's attitude toward officials and agencies long after the prison sentence has been completed.

The parole officer's job is similar to that of the probation officer, in that both require skill in helping offenders learn to take advantage of personal and environmental resources in order to bring about desirable changes. Similarly, utilizing community resources is as vital in the work of parole officers as it is for probation officers. When an offender is discharged from parole, the worker must be certain that the individual is ready to move forward without further help. If the institutional experience has been constructive and parole supervision has helped the parolee accept personal responsibility for feelings and behaviors, the parole officer may feel fairly comfortable about the parolee's ability to proceed without further help. Realistically, however, it is difficult for parole officers to be as helpful as they would like; case loads may be unmanageably heavy, and parole workers often are relatively untrained in comparison to social workers in other specialized areas.

Other Correctional Programs

Many facilities now have legal provision for some form of work release program, either for educational purposes or for restricted employment. Such programs help prepare prisoners for freedom while enabling them to conserve or develop working habits and earn income for themselves and their families.

Under work release programs, selected prisoners work at jobs in the community during the day and return to the institution at night. Wages are earned at the prevailing rates. Part of the earnings is charged against the prisoner's maintenance costs, part is committed to the support of dependents, and the balance is held in trust until the prisoner is discharged from the correctional institution.

The months immediately following discharge are considered the most critical in the offender's adjustment to life outside the institution. It is at this stage that intensive help can be most useful. The work release program is one step in that direction, and the prerelease guidance center, or "halfway house," is another. The purpose of the prerelease guidance center is to provide a living and working experience as part of the completion of the sentence. The center offers vocational rehabilitative services, along with personal and group counseling. Most of these programs are publicly sponsored, although some are under the auspices of voluntary religious, fraternal, or civic groups.

The movement toward deinstitutionalization that is currently reducing the populations of psychiatric hospitals, retardation centers, and children's institutions is also influencing the correctional field. Alternatives to imprisonment, such as probation, parole, and community-based facilities, are increasingly being used for offenders as preferable to warehousing people in large, isolated, overcrowded, violence-prone prisons.

SERVICES TO OLDER CITIZENS

Most European countries, and especially Great Britain, were alert to the special needs of their older citizens at least a generation before the subject became popular in the United States. With disappointingly few exceptions, social workers were part of this general neglect, as evidenced by the paucity of social services available to the aged until the 1930s, except in a few family service agencies and institutions for the aged. Hardly a paper on any aspect of aging appeared in social work journals, or on the agenda of annual meetings of professional organizations, before 1935. The plight of the elderly finally became tragically apparent during the Great Depression, when the high incidence of poverty among the aged, the helplessness of elderly people on relief rolls, and the widespread displacement of older workers in agriculture and industry led to legislative proposals for old age assistance and insurance, a movement finally culminating in the Social Security Act of 1935.

Older people had already begun to advocate for themselves before passage of the Social Security Act when, for example, they rallied behind the Townsend Plan for old-age pensions. In the 1940s, they continued to work on their own behalf through organizations such as the American Geriatrics Society (1942), the Gerontological Society (1945), and the National Retired Teachers Association (1947). These groups were followed in the 1950s and 1960s by the American Association of Retired Persons (1958), the National Council on Aging (1960), and the National Council of Senior Citizens (1962). Finally, recognition of this nationwide social obligation was highlighted significantly when three different presidents hosted White House Conferences on Aging in 1961, 1971, and 1981.

As the nation began to understand the problems facing older members of the society, there came a national conviction that it was desirable to offer elderly citizens a wide range of services and programs. Most of these services deal with problems that affect all human beings, but that are particularly severe for the aged, such as deficits in money, health, housing, and family networks. The family service agencies traditionally have worked with family members, including, of course, the family's older members. More recently, however, the creation of public welfare departments has made possible still more extensive and intensive services to aging persons.

Most of the services offered by these agencies, and others such as medical social service departments, focus on helping older people remain in their own homes. For example, friendly visits from a volunteer may be the greatest need of a homebound older person who lives alone and desperately needs occasional contact with other human beings. Not infrequently, a homemaker service permits a fragile older person to continue living at home by carrying out essential household tasks that the older person can no longer perform. In other cases, older people may need the protective services of a public welfare department or family service agency. It has been estimated that between 5 percent and 10 percent of all persons over 65 years of age are unable to manage their own affairs and have no relatives or friends to help them. They may live under hazardous conditions, be confused, be ill in body or mind or both, constitute a possible danger to themselves or others, or be subject to exploitation. They may need not only medical and nursing care, but legal services to conserve their financial resources and protect their legal rights, perhaps related to guardianship or even commitment to a custodial institution. The primary goal of the social worker is to keep the older person in the familiar home setting through the use of these auxiliary services. Alternative forms of care are resorted to only if they are deemed essential and appropriate to the individual's needs.

For elderly persons who require medical care, a range of facilities and services has been established. Hospital care is one of these resources, of course, but no community hospital can provide indefinite bed care. In recent years, therefore, hospital personnel, public health workers, visiting nurses, social workers, and community leaders have been developing what are known as home-care programs. These programs are designed to serve the patient who is not acutely ill enough to require the concentrated technical facilities of the hospital but who is unable to visit outpatient clinics or physicians' offices for treatment. The programs provide for readmission to the hospital when necessary, followed by a return to home care upon discharge from the hospital.

Two other types of facilities for the medical or nursing care of long-term patients have, thus far, proved woefully inadequate to the task—institutions for the chronically ill, and nursing homes. The services offered by these facilities must be updated and improved if they are to meet the needs of an aged clientele that is particularly vulnerable to exploitation.

In Chapters 5 and 6, Dobelstein and Hoshino describe other significant acts of federal legislation that deal with aspects of aging: the Social Security Act of 1935, with provisions for old age assistance and old age insurance; the Social Security amendments of 1965, which added Medicare and Medicaid; and programs developed under the Older Americans Act of 1965. This strong legislative response of the federal government has come about, in large part, because older people have learned that they must speak up for themselves. They resent being merely tolerated by those who are younger, and they resent being stereotyped as feeble, sick, "on the shelf," or ready to die. Their resentment is justified. They have served their country through major wars, they have contributed to our productive system, they have raised their families; now they insist on continuing to be a useful, viable part of the economy, to take their stand politically, to cherish their families and friends, and to remain in the mainstream of American life while strength and spirit endure. After a slow start, much progress has been made, and it will increase in future years. If for no other reason, public interest in the problems of the elderly is likely to continue because of the "graying of America." Men and women who are aged 60 or older are members of a larger, better educated, and more articulate pressure group than in the past, and their influence will increase as their numbers continue to grow during the 1980s.

SOCIAL AGENCIES IN THE 1980s

We have taken a look at the beginnings of social agencies, and we have discussed their present status; but what of their future? It seems safe to predict that most social workers in the years ahead will continue to work through agencies, although the current movement of a minority of practitioners into the private sector will probably also accelerate. The traditional client groups (children, the sick, the deviant, the aged) will still be around; but service priorities will depend, as they always have, on a combination of social work's professional judgment, economic conditions, and the relative ability of various client groups to convince society of the legitimacy of their claims for service.

Agencies will continue to require the professional services of generalist workers who are now being prepared in bachelor of social work programs, along with the more specialized services of workers who have attained the master of social work degree. It is also likely that social workers will have to adapt to service delivery systems that differ from traditional programs in ways that are only dimly apparent today. Whatever the differences, change is inevitable. As society moves in new directions, so will the agency system. What will not change, regardless of agency structure, are the needs of people and the basic values and competencies of the social work profession that have marked agency practice from its inception.

SUGGESTED READING

Blenkner, Margaret. "Social Work and Family Relationships in Later Life with Some Thoughts on Filial Maturity," in *Social Structure and the Family: Generational Relations,* ed. Ethel Shanus and Gordon Strieb. Englewood Cliffs, NJ: Prentice-Hall, 1965.

Davis, Ann. *The Residential Solution.* New York. Tavistock, 1981.

Fanshel, David, and Eugene Shinn. *Children in Foster Care: A Longitudinal Investigation.* New York: Columbia University Press, 1978.

Goldstein, Joseph, Anna Freud, and Albert J. Solnit. *Before the Best Interests of the Child.* New York: Macmillan, 1979.

Hancock, Betsy Ledbetter. *School Social Work.* Englewood Cliffs, NJ: Prentice-Hall, 1981.

Murphy, Patrick T. *Our Kindly Parent the State: The Juvenile Justice System and How It Works.* New York: Viking, 1974.

Ross, Judith W. "Social Work Intervention with Families of Children with Cancer: The Changing Critical Phases." *Social Work in Health Care* 3 (Spring 1978):257-272.

Showalter, David, and Charlotte Williams Jones. "Marital and Family Counseling in Prisons." *Social Work* 25 (May 1980):224-228.

Stanton, Alfred H., and Morris S. Schwartz. *The Mental Hospital: A Study of Institutional Participation in Psychiatric Illness and Treatment.* New York: Basic Books, 1954.

Troll, Lillian E., Sheila Miller, and Robert Atchley. *Families in Later Life.* Belmont, CA: Wadsworth, 1979.

Vladeck, Bruce C. *The Nursing Home Tragedy.* New York: Basic Books, 1981.

Wicker, Tom. *A Time to Die.* New York: Quadrangle/New York Times, 1975.

5

PUBLIC WELFARE POLICY
A Background for Understanding Welfare Services in the United States

ANDREW W. DOBELSTEIN

**Professor, School of Social Work
University of North Carolina, Chapel Hill**

The day was Thursday, October 24, 1929. "Black Thursday," as it was to become known, began on Wall Street with the same uncertainty that each trading day had brought for several weeks—bullish pessimism. By the end of that fateful day, 12,800,000 shares of stock had been traded, and New York was in financial panic. Selling continued at a feverish pace for the next five business days, and by then the entire nation was in a state of panic. Banks closed; thousands of depositors stood in lines, attempting to withdraw their savings before the money was gone. Fortunes were wiped out overnight. As the new year began, financial conditions had become even worse; each of the next three years brought greater distress than its predecessors. By 1932, when Franklin D. Roosevelt was elected president, almost one-third of the nation's labor force were unemployed, and many who had jobs were earning wages at less than a subsistence level. Soup lines were common. The popular song was "Brother, Can You Spare a Dime?" Large segments of the population were demoralized and frightened. The country was in the depths of the most serious economic crisis it had ever experienced. It was called the Great Depression.

On January 17, 1935, President Roosevelt proposed that Congress enact new and startling legislation. What he called an "Economic Security Act" was an effort to pull together a number of emergency programs that had been initiated during the previous two years to cushion the blows of the Great Depression. But the resulting legislation, called the Social Security Act, had much more far-reaching effects. It charted a new course for public welfare policy in this nation. Before its enactment, each state had been responsible for creating and carrying out its own welfare policies and programs. This historic responsibility had been firmly restated in 1854 with President Pierce's veto of federal legislation to aid the mentally ill, when Pierce reaffirmed the view that the federal government had no responsibility under the Constitution to provide for the welfare of the poor or disabled. Now, just eighty years later, President Roosevelt was taking exactly the opposite position:

> The establishment of sound means toward a greater future economic security of the American people is dictated by a prudent consideration of the hazards involved in our national life. No one can guarantee this country against the dangers of future depressions, but we can reduce those dangers. We can eliminate many of the factors that cause economic depressions, and we can provide the means of mitigating their results.[1]

When he signed the Social Security Act on August 14, 1935, Roosevelt further stated:

> This law, too, represents a cornerstone in a structure which is being built but is by no means complete. . . . It will act as a protection to

---

1. Ben Levin, *The Selected Addresses of Franklin Delano Roosevelt* (Cleveland, OH: World, 1943), p. 27.

future administrations against the necessity of going deeply into debt to furnish relief to the needy. . . . It is, in short, a law that will take care of human needs and at the same time provide for the United States an economic structure of vastly greater soundness.[2]

The Social Security Act did, indeed, become a cornerstone of social welfare policy in the United States. Half a century later, it remains the basis of resources and direction for most of the significant welfare policies of the country.

How was President Roosevelt able to turn the nation completely around in its views toward public welfare? How was it that a federal government that in 1932 had no responsibility for public welfare seemed in 1935 to have it all? What does the example of the Social Security Act tell us about public welfare policy in the United States? We must answer these questions before we consider the question of greatest relevance to beginning social work students: Why must social workers study public welfare policy?

WHAT IS PUBLIC WELFARE POLICY?

The development of the Social Security Act, even in the brief way it is presented here, can tell us a great deal about public welfare policy in the United States. At least three characteristics of all public welfare policy are evident in this example. Public welfare policy is (a) a reflection of the times, (b) a political process, and (c) a battle among competing "truths."

A Reflection of the Times

Public welfare policy always reflects the times during which it is formulated. In the example of the Social Security Act, it is clear that had it not been for the Great Depression—and the concomitant growth of public sentiment that only a political unit with the scope and power of the federal government could alleviate suffering of such magnitude—there might be no Social Security Act today. Similarly, if Michael Harrington had not galvanized public sentiment in 1962 over hidden poverty in an otherwise affluent society, with his book *The Other America*,[3] there might have been no Economic Opportunity Act in 1964.

2. Levin, *The Selected Addresses of Franklin Delano Roosevelt*, p. 28.
3. Michael Harrington, *The Other America* (New York: Harper & Row, 1962).

When citizens identify circumstances that adversely affect their lives, they seek solutions in the form of public policies. Such policies are, as President Roosevelt said, governmental actions designed to address the "hazards of our national life." In short, they are a reflection of the times.

A Political Process

There is no doubt that policymaking is a political process. Indeed, a variety of political actions shape the process at every turn. Although welfare experts and liberal reformers certainly played an important part in making the Social Security Act a reality, their actions were necessarily circumscribed by the political arena in which their ideas had to be translated into legislation. President Roosevelt had organized a Technical Advisory Committee (100 of the outstanding welfare leaders of the time) to advise him on matters of social security legislation, but it was the Committee on Economic Security (composed of cabinet members and chaired by the first woman cabinet member, Secretary of Labor Frances Perkins) that actually drafted the legislative proposals. Then, when Congress enacted the legislation, it took into consideration not only the recommendations of the Technical Advisory Committee but the political pressures applied by such groups as the popular Townsend movement. Francis Townsend and his army of angry retirees marched on Washington in the mid-1930s in much the same militant fashion as the civil rights workers who came to Washington with Dr. Martin Luther King, Jr., in 1963. In the same way, the Townsend followers sought $200-per-month retirement pensions. Even after passage of the Social Security Act, it was two years before the intense political controversy receded, following a favorable Supreme Court ruling on the constitutionality of the act in 1937.

Thus public welfare policy develops through a lively process in which a number of desirable social objectives are considered, rather than as a stately march of liberal reforms toward an ultimate good. Some options are chosen; others are not. The activity takes place publicly, with many diverse groups and individuals contributing to the debate. Ultimately, the decisions are made by public officials—legislators, court justices, administrators, governors, and the president. It is crucial to recognize the centrality of politics in the creation of our welfare policies. These political factors help explain why policies change so rapidly, and why we so often seem to develop policies that do not deal effectively with social welfare problems.

A Battle of Competing "Truths"

In a society as complex as ours, there can be no clearly "right" or "wrong" public welfare choices. We would prefer, of course, to be able to classify policies unambiguously, if only for the sake of simplicity; we could welcome them if they were "right" or change them if they were "wrong." But that seldom happens. In the first place, it usually takes a long time to assess the results of a given policy; in the meantime, conditions in society continue to change. Even if the policy seemed "right" when it was enacted, it is never quite as satisfactory over time as was anticipated, because policymakers cannot forecast the future. In the second place, the policymaking process is made even more complex by the fact that the "right" way to do things, which seemed so self-evident at one time, gives way under changed circumstances to other "right" ways to do things. It is inevitable that new beliefs and ideologies will arise within the society to invalidate the "truths" of earlier times.

The retirement provisions of the Social Security Act seemed "right" in 1935. The program required people to save a small portion of their income for their retirement years, to supplement their personal savings or pension plans. The federal government would act as banker, holding the money for millions of workers and then returning it, with interest, when the workers retired. But ten years later, the federal bank account that held the retirement funds had begun to swell alarmingly, and it was feared that if all that money were held until all of the contributors retired, so much of the nation's funds would be controlled by the federal banks that the very foundation of our economy would be weakened. So a new "truth" began to emerge.

The new "truth" held that the nation's economy would be damaged by collecting all of the retirement funds in advance. The federal government was empowered in 1947 to collect only enough money from employers and employees to pay for the nation's retirement needs five years into the future. This action kept individual contributions to the federal account at a low level, even though payment levels were rising. But then, about fifteen years later (in the 1960s), a curious thing happened. The old "truth" reemerged! Policymakers began to realize that low birthrates, inceased longevity, and high inflation meant there would not be enough money, at some future time, to pay retirement benefits to all who would be applying for them. Again, great debates occurred, this time about the original intent of the Social Security Act. Finally, Congress undertook a series of steps to save the retirement program, and in 1977 began to intiate the sharp increases in individual contributions that have continued into the 1980s.

Thus people who state dogmatically that this or that public welfare policy is "right" or "wrong" are arguing much too simplistically. Reasonable people may disagree reasonably over the nature of any social problems and the steps that should be taken to redress them. Providing income support to children and families deprived of parental support, which was institutionalized in the Social Security Act's program of Aid to Families with Dependent Children (AFDC), is a case in point. Should AFDC mothers be required to work to support their children, or should they be encouraged to stay at home and take care of their children personally? An impressive accumulation of research on the subject has failed to provide a definitive answer, and the question has continued to be the subject of heated debate among reasonable people since 1935. Consequently, the AFDC program has become a tangled web, reflecting both "truths" simultaneously. This is because both views are "right" and, as those who are familiar with AFDC will quickly admit, both views are "wrong."

If there is no "truth," how do policymakers decide which of many options to select? In recent years, *economic analysis* has been a useful tool. When a range of policy options is being debated in the political arena, an analysis of the potential economic impact of each proposal helps decision makers choose the option that will produce the outcomes they prefer. During the debate over the Social Security Act, Secretary of the Treasury Henry Morgenthau informed President Roosevelt that the contribution rates proposed by the Committee on Economic Security would be inadequate to keep the system self-supporting after 1950. As a result, the president ordered the committee to recompute its calculations and revise the rate schedules—the day before he presented the proposal to Congress! Because Roosevelt was committed to the principle that the system should be self-supporting, he used economic analysis to choose an alternative that would realize that goal.

In 1974, Congress created a special agency to provide it with economic analyses of the public welfare proposals it wished to consider. The Congressional Budget Office (CBO) prepares, upon request, extensive economic evaluations of proposed legislation to show how enactment might affect various groups of citizens. Impact analyses of this type are often used by members of Congress to help them decide which of several policy alternatives has the greatest chance of achieving the public goals they seek. When President Reagan proposed major reductions in the funding of welfare programs early in his administration, the CBO analyzed the proposals to show the potential effects of the cuts. A summary of the CBO analysis of the possible impact of proposed reductions in income maintenance programs is presented in Table 5.1. The analysis indicated that working women who were close to the poverty line would be most adversely affected by the reductions. In light of ensuing budget implementations, the CBO's projections appear to have been accurate.

Despite policymakers' increasing reliance on economic analysis, it is important to emphasize that economic analysis does not substitute for the political process. Rather, political decision makers use the information resulting from economic analysis to support and explain their policy choices. The facts of the CBO's analysis of the Reagan budget did not dissuade the president or his budget director from the course of reducing federal expenditures. What the analysis did was to show them what the impact of their choices was likely to be on various segments of the population.

Summary

The process of formulating public welfare policy is generated by aroused public concern about specific social problems. But various groups within the society may identify a similar concern in different ways. Relatively few people may be strongly interested in a particular social problem, but, unless they constitute a very powerful group, they may not be able to accomplish their goal of translating their concern into public policy. A recent example can be seen in the increasing numbers of parents who send their children to private schools. These parents believe they should be excused from paying certain portions of local school taxes because they are already supporting education through the private sector. Despite their efforts to explain their position, the problem is viewed quite differently by a much larger group of citizens who themselves attended, or whose children attended or are attending, public schools.

The process of formulating public welfare policy is complex. David Easton called it the "black box" of politics because the activities are so

TABLE 5.1 **Estimated Income Changes for Poor and Near-Poor Families Resulting from Reductions in Income Maintenance Programs**

Family Categories	Number of Families as of Fiscal 1980 (in thousands)	% of Families with Income Losses of		% Decline in Income for Families Losing More than 5%
		More than 5%	Less than 5%	
All poor and near-poor families	16,505	3.9	47.3	16
below 50% of poverty	1,469	4.7	52.1	18
50% to 99% of poverty	6,430	3.1	66.6	15
100% to 149% of poverty	8,606	4.4	32.0	16
All families below 150% of poverty with an aged head	5,284	.1	40.5	
Families with a nonaged female head				
below 50% of poverty	831	4.3	56.1	13
50% to 99% of poverty	2,667	5.2	70.1	
100% to 149% of poverty	2,261	11.7	40.1	15
Families receiving AFDC at some time during the year				
with some earnings	888	42.0	37.8	13
without earnings	3,434	9.9	59.7	16

SOURCE: U.S. Congress, Congressional Budget Office, "Staff Memorandum" (14 April 1981), Tables 3, 4, 5, and 7.

wide ranging and difficult to categorize, even if one is able to observe them directly.[4] Usually, policymaking is a protracted process. It begins with a period when an idea germinates; it develops and takes shape as various groups respond to it. Frequently the process lacks a specific beginning, and often there seems to be no ending. Indeed, passing a law may mark only the beginning of a longer process of amendments and changes that cover a span of many years, as in the case of the Social Security Act. Finally, there is a diverse array of participants in the process, all of whom have differential access to the many policymakers and all of whom have various points of view about the problem. The process is a very uneven one.

What has all of this to do with the beginning social work student? Social welfare programs, which more often than not are implemented by social workers, are the result of public welfare policies. The policies that we carry out were established by some body of policymakers in response to specific public problems and concerns. Because the process of formulating public policy is so uneven and complex, it is necessary to understand the intent of the policymakers in order to implement programs as they were meant to be carried out. A social worker who is responsible for activities within a specific program often must trace the program back to the problem from which the program derived. The important relationship between knowledge of public welfare policy and application of practice skills is shown in Figure 5.1. As you read the remainder of this chapter, look for examples of how understanding the development of the policy might help you implement the program.

TRANSLATING PUBLIC WELFARE POLICIES INTO PROGRAMS

We have seen that public welfare policies grow out of public concerns, public problems, and social issues. But how do policies become programs that can benefit those in need of service? The first step is to give the policy some legal authority, that is, translate the policy into some type of law or some type of pronouncement that has the force of law. This process provides different types of policies with respect to the amount of authority behind them. After policies are

---

4. David Easton, *Politics and Policy* (Boston: Little, Brown, 1957).

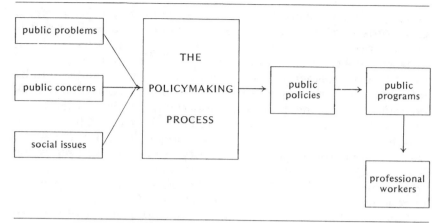

Figure 5.1.   The policymaking paradigm.

translated into binding public statements, there must be machinery to implement them. This implementing machinery is what we call "programs."

Types of Policies

Public welfare policies take four characteristic legal forms: statute law, case law, executive order, and administrative policy. Each form is described briefly in this section.

Statute Law. Statute law is produced by legislators at the several levels of government—local, county, state, and federal. This written law is the foundation of the entire legal system of our country. Statute law is a very powerful form of public policy and is, therefore, considered by policymakers to be a desirable way of establishing policies. Unfortunately, statute law is also difficult to produce, because a majority of legislators must come to some agreement before a law can be passed. In actual practice, many compromises are necessary to produce most laws, and public policies that are embodied in statute law often are not very decisive. They are also difficult to change as times and public needs change. The Social Security Act is public policy in the form of statute law.

Case Law. Case law is public policy produced by the judicial branch of the government. Case law can produce forceful public policies because the judicial system can mete out penalties for noncompliance and because Americans show great deference to court orders. Although case law commands great authority, it is infrequently available as a resource for policymakers. In most instances, the courts cannot initiate action; they can only be moved to act by disagreements that are brought to them for settlement by interpretation of existing statute laws. Because the courts rely heavily on tradition in making their legal interpretations, most case law tends to reaffirm the status quo. There have been some cases, however, in which the courts have broken new legal ground and caused repercussions throughout the country. A historic example is the Supreme Court's school desegregation ruling in *Brown* v. *Board of Education* (1954), which changed, and continues to change, patterns of economic and social behavior on all levels of society.

Executive Order. Executive order can be a powerful form of policymaking because governmental executives (most often, the president or the governors of the states) control both public funds and the actions of workers in the administrative branch of governmental units. A disadvantage of the executive order is that, although swift and to the point under most circumstances, it may not have a strong base of political support and therefore is open to review and revision, if not invalidation, by other policymakers (usually, legislators). On the other hand, executive policies can serve lasting purposes, particularly if other policymakers are unable or unwilling to tackle a controversial political issue. A good example of executive order as social policy is Executive Order 11135, signed in 1956 by President Eisenhower, which banned racial and sexual discrimination in federal hiring. This order continues to be a useful device for minimizing sexual discrimination in hiring, a subject that few federal laws have addressed.

Administrative Policy. Administrative policy is the result of decisions made by the agencies that have been mandated to implement public policies. Administrative policy may take the form of instructions issued by the agency on how programs should be conducted, or of regulations that forbid carrying out programs in certain ways. When federal agencies engage in this type of policymaking, both the proposed and final rules are published in the *Federal Register;* when properly formulated, these policies have the same force as statute law. Administrative policies are likely to exist as a necessary part of all public welfare programs; they are often derisively referred to as "bureaucratic red tape."

Programs

Once a public policy has been given legal form, it must be translated into action through programs. The programs created to implement public welfare policies are of particular interest to social workers because it is these programs that social workers often are hired to carry out.

Many policies create their own programs, and it may be possible to distinguish policy from program only on the basis of the degree of specificity. In other cases, the distinction may be much more pronounced. Indeed, although all welfare programs are the result of welfare policies, not all policies produce specific programs. For example, President Eisenhower's executive order banning discrimination in federal hiring was turned over to the Department of Labor, which created several programs to implement the order. Even when policies do prescribe programs, the programs may lack sufficient specificity and may have to be re-created in a form that permits implementation. The Social Security Act mandated creation of a retirement program, but a federal administrative agency (the Social Security Administration) had to design a detailed and specific program of activities to meet the intent of the act.

Another distinction between a policy and a program stems from the fact that a policy reflects a philosophy and carries an intention about how things should be. A program, according to classic administrative theory, is designed to achieve the philosophy and intent of a policy—not to set philosophy as part of its creation or implementation. While this distinction exists in theory, it is often not sharply drawn in practice. In fact, programs sometimes attempt to set a philosophy that is clearly not a reflection of the policy under which they operate. Invariably, developing a program in such a way as to be completely contrary to the philosophy of the policy leads to trouble. A situation of this kind occurred when the Nixon administration sought to limit federal expenditures for social programs. In 1973, President Nixon instructed the Department of Health, Education and Welfare to order its regional offices to disapprove state welfare plans that provided social services to persons with incomes above the poverty line. This program revision was contrary to the philosophy of welfare policy, as expressed in Title IV of the Social Security Act, which established the AFDC program. Senator Russell Long opened hearings in the Senate Finance Committee to explore the extent to which program administrators were promoting programs that were inconsistent with the public policy intentions of the Congress. After much controversy and debate, the Senate proposed, the Congress accepted, and President Ford signed into law the first social services law under the Social Security Act. One of the provisions of Title XX, as this legislation is known, specifically prohibits federal program administrators from taking it upon themselves to define what constitutes a social service, thereby clarifying in no uncertain terms the philosophy of the Congress with respect to these social services.

Here we see a reason for social workers to understand how public policy is formed and implemented. It is not enough to have the relevant practice skills and professional ethics. Professionals must have a complete understanding of the programs with which they deal, but, equally important, they must understand the policies that support the programs. To the extent that policies reflect a philosophy, professionals must carry out the programs in such a way as to be consistent with the philosophy. Further, to understand the philosophy of any given policy, it is necessary to understand the public concerns and social problems from which the policy developed. Only when the entire policymaking paradigm is understood can meaningful services be provided to clients. Put another way, providing services to clients does not take place in a vacuum. The work takes place within the total context of the problems addressed by the policies and the programs designed to deal with them. Let me clarify this point by giving an example from social work practice.

The Elderly Nutrition Program was developed in 1973 as part of the Older Americans Act. Originally passed by Congress in 1965, the Older Americans Act was legislated to deal with a number of serious problems associated with growing old. Specifically, the act's declared purpose was to provide specific services that older people could use to help them live with respect and dignity in a society where they were increasingly being forced to live isolated and lonely lives. The Elderly Nutrition Program provides a hot meal to older people who are unlikely to prepare nutritious meals for themselves—not because they are poor, but because they are not motivated or able to fix adequate meals as a result of living alone or being socially isolated. Professionals who administer this program need to understand the philosophy expressed in the Older Americans Act and the social problems that the policy was designed to alleviate. Without this understanding, it is easy to offer the program incorrectly. If nothing more than a hot meal is provided, the service is not in keeping with the intent of the law. The philosophy behind the Older Americans Act demands that the meal be provided in an environment that reflects respect and dignity for older people. The recipients must be made to feel welcome, as if they were attending a family dinner.

The philosophy of the Older Americans Act further suggests that the meal is a means to an end, not an end in itself. Older people are offered an opportunity to eat together, in a group, because sociability and education are philosophical goals of the policy. This philosophy must be expressed in every aspect of program operation. If the professional does not understand the philosophy, the most outstanding menu-planning skills and the greatest ability to feed large numbers of people economically and efficiently will not suffice to provide a successful program.

Many programs fail precisely because the professionals who are responsible for carrying out program activities do not understand this principle. Programs cannot be separated from the intention and philosophy of the policies that created them. Nor can programs be separated from the social problems that the policies were designed to correct.

THE PHILOSOPHICAL BASES OF PUBLIC WELFARE POLICIES

How can we trace a specific program to the philosophy and intent of the policy? To do this successfully, we need to look at the broad social purposes that public welfare policies serve in American society. These purposes reflect general philosophies or public attitudes, often unstated, about our country's welfare problems. By examining these purposes, it is possible to distill four general philosophies underlying American public welfare policies: redistribution of resources, intervention in the free market, promotion of the public good, and achievement of social justice.

Redistribution of Resources

One of the philosophies common in public welfare policies reflects public support for the redistribution of resources. Redistribution can be thought of as a Robin Hood approach—taking from the rich and giving to the poor. The intent of redistributive policies derives from a variety of motivations that, taken together, reflect a public philosophy that the nonpoor have some obligation to help the poor and that both governmental and voluntary charitable organizations should provide legitimate opportunities to achieve this goal.

Although there is general agreement that redistribution is an appropriate intent of public welfare policy, the philosophy can become much less straightforward in application. Probably no one would disagree that the very, very rich should be expected to help the very, very poor. But as discussion moves from the extreme ends of the continuum toward the middle, disagreements arise. How rich must one be to be required to give some of one's "wealth" to the poor? As a college professor, I may think there are many who can better afford to help the poor than I; but others may think my obligation is clearly greater than their own. And how poor should one be to benefit from the redistribution of wealth? People who work, but who perhaps have low-paying menial jobs and excessive medical expenses, may think they are more worthy of benefits than are those who do not try to support themselves, even though the working poor are likely to be better off economically than the nonworking poor. From this dilemma surfaces one of the most contestable of welfare philosophies: Should benefits be available to those who do not want to work?

Another controversy arises in connection with welfare policies that seek to redistribute resources. Should the redistribution be in the form of money or of resources in-kind? Providing money is consistent with a free market economy; in any welfare reform debate, there are likely to be advocates for "cashing-out" welfare—an argument recently advanced in debates over the Food Stamp program. Other people advocate for redistributing resources in-kind. They believe that because of economies of scale, it is cheaper to provide benefits in-kind than it is to give the recipients cash. Proponents of benefits in-kind say, further, that this method provides assurance that resources are used to meet the intended need. This argument, too, has recently been used in connection with the Food Stamp program. Restricting the use of Food Stamps to certain products, some say, guarantees that the resource will not be spent on alcohol, tobacco, or other luxury items. A further argument in favor of the redistribution of resources in-kind is that this method permits the setting of certain standards. In the case of public housing, for example, using public funds to build adequate housing units for the poor is viewed as superior to giving money to recipients who can find housing in the private sector only in slums that are unfit for decent living.

Intervention in the Free Market

Public welfare policy often is based on the philosophy that it is necessary for the government to intervene (or interfere, as some would call it) in the operation of the free market economy. The free market system assumes, essentially, that millions of individual consumer decisions are matched with millions of individual production decisions in a manner that works best when there is no interference or manipulation by governments. This assumption is a modern translation of the *laissez-faire* doctrine of Adam Smith, which states that most of the time, for most people, the economic system is self-regulating.

For some people at some times, however, the free market system is *not* self-regulating. The Great Depression was one of those times when the economic system clearly did not work very well when left to operate freely. Likewise, for the millions today who are unable to be self-sufficient because they are too young, too old, handicapped, or unable to find a job, the free market system does not work. Therefore, the argument goes, under certain conditions the government must step in, either to restore the system to a level of functional activity or to intercede on behalf of those who are unable to be self-supporting under prevailing market conditions. This philosophy gives rise to public welfare policies that call for governmental intervention in the free market without challenging the basic philosophy of the economic system. Such public welfare policies are often referred to as *residual* policies, because they deal with the parts of the system that, unassisted, do not function smoothly.

Notwithstanding the social convenience of this philosophy, some of the most durable of all our public welfare programs have derived from residual policies. For example, the AFDC program was predicated on the assumption that if financial aid were made available to dependent children in families without breadwinners, the children would develop in normal home environments, become productive members of society, and no longer need government support. For the most part, programs such as AFDC, which carry out residual policies, are presumed to be temporary. Indeed, most of the programs originally legislated under the Social Security Act were viewed as temporary measures; those that did have permanent features, such as retirement insurance, did not depart in their basic orientation from existing schemes. Rather than charting a plan for a different kind of economy, residual welfare policies are based on the philosophy that the present economic system should be retained.

Of course, most citizens are aware that our economic system actually operates only relatively freely. It is clear that government intervenes in the free market in many ways, which gives a mythical air to talk of residual public welfare policies. Oil depletion allowances are made to compensate investors for potentially diminishing returns as oil reserves are depleted. Farmers are paid subsidies in order to keep certain farm prices at an acceptable level. Special governmental interventions, such as guaranteeing the loans needed by the Chrysler Corporation to avoid bankruptcy or creating Amtrak to ensure operation of the nation's railroads, are undertaken to preserve certain sectors of the so-called free market economy. Such activities are not usually considered public welfare programs, yet they are the result of a mix of two public welfare philosophies—intervention in the free market economy and promotion of the public good.

Promotion of the Public Good

Promotion of the public good is a fundamental reason for the very existence of governments. Most modern political philosophers agree with Thomas Hobbes that the first order of government is to ensure the public good. Political philosophers think in terms of preserving the peace and ensuring public safety as examples of the public good, but citizens in maturing societies tend to want ever greater numbers of public services as part of the public good, or as their rights of citizenship.

Highways and public schools are examples of public goods that are provided by government because it would be uneconomical for private enterprise to undertake such vast projects. Occasionally, private philanthropists promote a public good, as, for example, when Andrew Carnegie and his heirs initiated the public library system in Pittsburgh. In most cases, however, the philosophy states a governmental responsibility to promote those programs that benefit the whole society. Immunization programs, public health inspections, and licensing of child-care facilities are examples. In fact, extensive governmental support of child-care programs was provided during World War II to promote a public good. Under the Lanham Act, care for children was made readily available by offering attractive federal subsidies, thus enabling more women to work in the war effort. Old Age Retirement (Title II of the Social Security Act) is another example of a public welfare policy based on the philosophy of promoting the public good. In this case, the goal was economic security in retirement and old age. The policy was considered a general public good because, by contributing to their own retirement during their working years, citizens would relieve future generations of the cost of caring for them when they no longer worked.

Harold Wilensky and Charles Lebeaux have called public welfare policies that promote the public good "institutional welfare."[5] Because the policies are promotional in nature, they create new institutions to ensure continuity. Unlike residual policies, institutional policies carry the presumption that they will be continued indefinitely because they contribute to the improvement of the social and economic orders.

Achievement of Social Justice

For people in the United States, one of the most compelling philosophies underlying public welfare policies is that of achieving social justice, or setting things right. Centuries ago, Aristotle pointed out that there is a fundamental difference between treating people *equally* and treating them *fairly*. Today, social scientists make the same distinction by differentiating between *horizontal equity* and *vertical equity*. Horizontal equity refers to the equality principle of "like treatment for like people in like circumstances." Vertical equity, in contrast, evokes the principle of "to each according to need."

Brown v. *Board of Education* (1954) is an example of public welfare policy based on the principle of horizontal equity. The Supreme Court's decision clearly affirmed that "equal but separate" treatment is not necessarily fair treatment; it can, in fact, lead to gross injustice. An example of vertical equity is Head Start. Here, the philosophy states that children from culturally deprived backgrounds need special treatment if they are to be able to make equal use of formal education. Government loans to minority businesses are in the same category, as are efforts to establish bilingual educational programs in many parts of the country.

5. Harold Wilensky and Charles Lebeaux, *Industrial Society and Social Welfare* (New York: Free Press, 1965); see especially Chapter 6.

Summary

Redistribution of resources, intervention in the free market economy, promotion of the public good, and achievement of social justice are four major philosophies underlying public welfare policies in the United States. Each philosophy can be linked to specific public welfare policies that, in turn, generate specific public welfare programs. Examples of these linkages are shown in Figure 5.2. In examining them, it becomes clear that the meaning the society has to the individual citizen is crucial in determining what kind of policy that person prefers as a solution to a particular social problem. For instance, if you think that poverty is caused by a breakdown in the economic system, you might want to support a residual program such as AFDC. If, on the other hand, you believe that poverty is the result of fundamental defects in our economic system that cause resources to be distributed unfairly, you might prefer to support redistributive and social justice policies that mandate sweeping tax reforms. Thus the policies created to correct social problems are a result of how the public initially states the problems. In the final analysis, what the majority of people believe to be true is a potent force in shaping the welfare programs that social workers implement.

EXAMPLES OF PROGRAMS DERIVED FROM PUBLIC WELFARE POLICIES

It would be impossible to discuss in this chapter all of the public welfare programs that exist at the present time in the United States. One reason is that some programs are difficult to categorize as "public welfare" rather than some other form of governmental policy. In addition, more than 300 federal programs require cooperative activity by state and/or local governments, and they often reflect different welfare features from place to place. Another problem is that, despite federal leadership in funding, welfare policies and programs are not the sole province of the federal government. The states have unrestricted authority to develop welfare programs, and the authority of local governments is restricted only by their articles of incorporation. The several hundreds of welfare programs initiated by state and local governments have not been catalogued in any comprehensive way. To add to the confusion, there are innumerable voluntary programs, including such examples as hot lines, rape

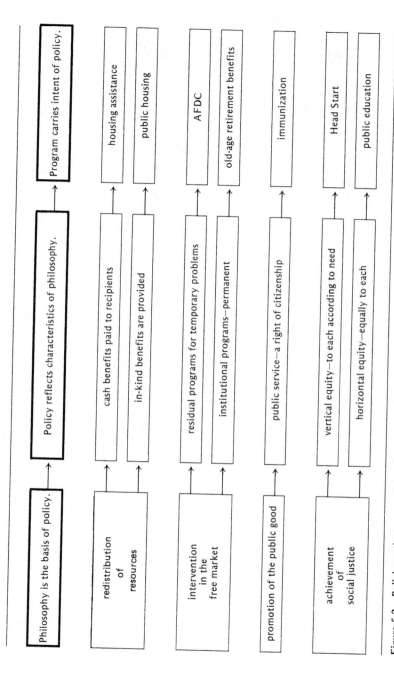

Figure 5.2. Policies and programs that reflect philosophies.

counseling centers, emergency food and clothing distribution centers, and transportation programs. The United Way of America has estimated that it funds more than 150 kinds of activities in the private sector, and the exact number of programs, including those operated by church and civic groups and private foundations, is easily in the tens of thousands.

It is virtually impossible to catalogue and describe all of these programs, yet social workers must have some understanding of the most important of them. In this chapter, we are most concerned with the public programs, those funded by the federal government or by the states and local communities. These programs can be divided into three major types: income maintenance programs, housing programs, and programs to assist the elderly.

Income Maintenance Programs

Almost all of the income maintenance programs are provided under the authority of the Social Security Act, which was originally legislated in 1935. The Social Security Act has been discussed earlier, and there is an extensive discussion of some of its provisions in the following chapter. Briefly, the income maintenance programs are as follows:

(1) Old Age, Survivors, and Disability Insurance (commonly called "social security"), Title II
(2) Unemployment Compensation (also referred to as "unemployment insurance"), Title IV
(3) Aid to Families with Dependent Children (AFDC), Title IV
    (a) AFDC money payments, Title IV-a
    (b) Child Welfare Services (payments for foster care), Title IV-c
    (c) Child Support Enforcement (enforcing child support payments from absent parents), Title IV-d
(4) Supplemental Security Income (SSI), Title XVI
(5) Health Insurance (Medicare for the elderly), Title XVIII
(6) Medical Assistance (Medicaid for children and the handicapped), Title XIX

Until 1982, Title XX to the Social Security Act provided federal funds for social service programs. Although not an income maintenance program, Title XX became an important companion to those programs when it was legislated in 1974. Under President Reagan's block grant programs, which accompanied his drastically revised federal budget in 1982, Title XX became part of a greatly reduced block grant for general social service programs.

The income maintenance programs within the Social Security Act are the nation's most significant and comprehensive social programs. This is because maintaining an income is a crucial problem for those in our society who are too young, too old, too sick, or too handicapped to work. Of all Americans over the age of 65, 97 percent receive income maintenance support. The income maintenance programs were designed to provide a basic income floor to protect people from the economic and social hazards that accompany poverty.

Housing Programs and Programs for the Elderly

In addition to the income maintenance programs, Americans also enjoy special housing programs and programs designed for the elderly. In the remainder of this section, we will look at the problems that led to public policies in these two areas and then at some of the specific programs that have resulted from the policies.

Housing Programs

The Problem

One of the oldest national public welfare laws was the Housing Act of 1933, but this yearly legislation was intended more to stimulate the economy by aiding the construction industry than to help the poor. It was to be many decades before housing legislation began to reflect a concern for the needs of the poor, the disabled, and the elderly. In 1937, the Housing Act was expanded to include construction of public housing through grants and loans to private contractors; but low income public housing was never a popular part of the act, and when it came up for renewal after World War II, the public housing sections were almost deleted.

The Policy

Most of the housing programs within the framework of public welfare policy in the United States are based on an economic theory of housing called the "trickle-down" philosophy, which holds that construction of new housing units can be afforded only by the affluent. They invest where land values are relatively low, usually on the fringes of cities. After some years, as land values begin to rise in that location, the affluent sell their homes and reinvest where land values are still low, thus protecting their capital while making a profit (accelerated in recent years by inflation). The slightly less affluent buy the older houses with a somewhat smaller investment of capital. After a few more years, the second generation moves on, passing the original housing on to a third, still less affluent generation. The process continues until the original housing has practically no market value and frequently is inadequate or unsafe, when it becomes housing for those who have little or no capital to invest.

The trickle-down philosophy has been defended on the grounds that it is the most economically efficient method of developing housing in the free market. As a result, most efforts to stimulate the production of housing units have taken the form of incentives to individual citizens to develop new units. For example, income tax incentives are given to homeowners in the form of exemptions for property taxes and interest payments on mortgages, and depreciation allowances are given to owners of income-producing housing. For people who can afford to invest in the construction of larger, multifamily housing units, the government provides incentives through low-interest loans and mortgage insurance. Housing assistance to the poor traditionally has been in the form of direct rent subsidies, which are applied by the recipients toward rental of units developed by the private sector.

The Programs

Four of the programs developed under the Housing and Community Development Act of 1974 are Public Housing, Housing Assistance, Housing for the Elderly and Handicapped, and the Farmer's Home Loan Program. They represent governmental efforts to provide for the housing welfare of the poor, the disabled, and the elderly.

Public Housing. This is one of the most visible and controversial welfare programs currently administered under the Housing and Community Development Act. In the Public Housing program, construction of housing units is federally funded by tax-free municipal bonds, and the housing units are managed by local housing authorities. The program is designed to aid people whose incomes are too low to enable them to find housing in the free market. Eligibility is determined by an established income ceiling, and no renter is charged more than 25 percent of net income for rent. According to the Congressional Budget Office, about 29 million low- and moderate-income families were living in the United States in 1980. Public Housing served about 1 of every 30 of these families.

Because rents can be no more than 25 percent of family income under this program, Public Housing is a substantial financial saving. This fact gives rise to one of the most widely held criticisms of the program: The means test of eligibility acts as a disincentive to economic advancement. For example, suppose the value of the annual Public Housing subsidy for a family of four, with a net income of $4200, is $2000. If the family's earnings were to increase by $800, to the level of $5000, it would lose $2000 in benefits because it had exceeded the eligibility level, even though it was still well within the income class called "poverty level." Thus an increase in income of $800 would result, for this family, in a net loss of $1200, plus the necessity of competing for housing in the open market.

Public Housing has also been criticized because the units can be constructed only where local citizens will permit them to be located. As a result, human nature being what it is, Public Housing units usually are found only in physically deteriorated neighborhoods. Some critics also assert that Public Housing contributes to the development of social problems by "social loading"; that is, by packing together people who need large amounts of social amenities but have the least financial capacity to generate them. Despite these problems of eligibility, poor location, and social loading, most people today believe that providing decent housing for low-income citizens is an important part of our public welfare policy.

Housing Assistance. Housing Assistance (Section 8 of the Housing and Community Development Act of 1974) was established to provide financial support to low-income renters. Under this program, the amount of rent charged for a standard rental unit in the free market is compared to the amount of money the low-income person can afford to pay. The federal government makes up the difference in the form of a cash payment to the landlord. The median income of families participating in the Housing Assistance program in 1980 was about $5000; if this subsidy were "cashed out," it would amount to about $1800 for a family of four with an annual income of $4200. Although the Housing Assistance program is relatively new, approximately 344,000 low-income families received help from the program in fiscal 1979.

There are two features of the Housing Assistance program that are generally considered distinct advantages. First, because participants can "afford" housing in the free market (when given the subsidies), they can be scattered wherever housing is available, rather than being concentrated in one location, as is the case with Public Housing.

Second, the program does not compete with the free market; it attempts to support the private sector.

To see how the Housing Assistance program can work, consider an older person who has rented a house for years, but, because of the limitations of a fixed income, has been unable to meet the rental increases needed to keep the property in good repair. Before Section 8 was enacted, the landlord had to choose between maintaining the property by raising the rent and forcing the elderly tenant out of the home or keeping the rent constant and allowing the property to become run-down. Under Section 8, the landlord can charge a reasonable rent to the tenant, at the same time maintaining the property in good condition through a federal supplemental rent subsidy.

Housing for the Elderly and Handicapped. This program was incorporated in the Housing and Community Development Act of 1974 (Section 202) as Congress came to realize the dilemma facing many elderly and handicapped citizens. These people were being forced to sell their homes because they were no longer able to keep the structures in good repair, but they were unable to find suitable new housing in the free market. To encourage personal independence, the federal government intervened in the free market economy by encouraging the construction of housing units at affordable prices for the elderly and handicapped.

Section 202 provides direct federal loans to nonprofit, private organizations to develop multifamily housing units or rehabilitate existing units for the use of elderly or handicapped persons. The units may be rented only to individuals or families 62 years old or over or to individuals with permanent handicapping conditions. The housing developed so far under this program consists mostly of smaller clusters of rental units than is the case in Public Housing projects. Thus the smaller clusters are more likely to be scattered throughout a city than to be concentrated in a single location. In many ways, Housing for the Elderly and Handicapped is similar to Public Housing, except that nongovernmental organizations are the primary sponsors rather than a local Public Housing authority.

Farmer's Home Loan. This program, as originally legislated, was directed primarily toward assisting middle-income rural families to buy homes by providing low-interest loans over long periods of time. Since 1974, however, the program has been expanded to include the rural poor. An important feature of the Farmer's Home Loan program is that in addition to assisting the rural poor to buy homes, it helps those who already own their homes but lack sufficient capital to make repairs or improvements. Most of the nation's housing units that lack indoor plumbing are located in rural areas and are owned by poor people.

The Farmer's Home Loan program has been particularly helpful because it operates in areas where Public Housing units usually are not built and where available housing is widely scattered. The program has contributed substantially to the housing inventory in many rural areas, and its newest features are helping to bring inadequate rural housing units up to acceptable living standards.

Programs for Older Adults

The Problem

The United States has always been a youth-oriented nation. We think of our country as "young"—ambitious, courageous, aggressive, and occasionally impulsive. Our economy has flourished on "planned obsolescence"; we want new cars, new appliances, and new homes. These attitudes have been reflected in our treatment of elderly citizens, to whom we have historically accorded little respect. However, the nation itself is aging. In 1980, according to the Bureau of the Census, there were almost 25 million Americans who were aged 65 or older—about 10.5 percent of the population. Partly because of the growing political influence of these citizens, the national attitude toward this group has begun to shift to one of respect and empathy. With our growing national interest in the well-being of older Americans has come a better understanding of their problems and potential.

The most significant of our new insights about aging is that older people's needs, interests, and desires do not differ from those of their youth. We have discovered that older people who liked to work before they reached the magic age of 65 often want to continue to work. Some older people like to live in "retirement villages"; others prefer neighborhoods with residents of all ages. Some like high-rise apartment complexes; others prefer to live in one-family dwellings, perhaps in the homes where they have spent most of their lives. Older people enjoy making love; they attend theaters and concerts, read books, join in lively debates of current issues, travel, and participate in sports. In short, older people cannot be stereotyped. Their interests and capabilities are as broad as the society itself.

With this new national perspective on aging comes the realization that older Americans should have the same opportunities to participate in the society as anyone else. To achieve this goal, however, they need protection from exploitation, abuse, or adverse economic conditions such as runaway inflation. The problem, therefore, is how to see that older Americans have access to services that will ensure their ability to continue to live full and independent lives.

The Policy

Designing a welfare policy to benefit a group of citizens on the basis of age alone, crossing the traditional welfare boundaries such as income, health, and minority status, was a new undertaking for the nation. The idea was not so much to create services as it was to encourage this group of citizens to utilize existing resources. For example, many older people needed day-care services if they were to remain in the homes of their adult children rather than move to rest homes, but almost all day-care services were designed for children. Under the new policies for older adults, the idea was advanced that traditional day-care services could be useful to older citizens as well.

Following the first national White House Conference on Aging, in 1961, Congress began to look closely at the special problems of the elderly. Among those problems were needs for more adequate income, housing, and health services; in addition, there was a pervasive negative public attitude toward the aging as a group, and a resultant tendency to exclude them from the benefits of social programs that many people believed could be overcome only by legislation. Thus the Older Americans Act of 1965 was intended to identify older adults as people with special needs and to help them get their fair share of existing resources.

The Programs

The Older Americans Act of 1965 is too broad and comprehensive to be considered here in its entirety. Therefore, only two of the programs administered under the act are presented in this section: Coordination and Planning, and the Elderly Nutrition Program.

Coordination and Planning. This program (Title III of the Older Americans Act) is a major effort to coordinate all existing resources for the benefit of older adults. Implicit in Title III is the view that the needs of older people, and the resources available to meet their needs, differ across the nation. Initially, therefore, no specific national objectives were set. Each community was to coordinate and plan its own programs. It was recognized, however, that certain localities might find it too difficult to work cooperatively with one another in identifying and meeting needs. Therefore, a multijurisdictional organization was mandated at the substate level. The federal government was to provide 90 percent of the funds necessary to set up the substate Coordination and Planning bodies. These Area Agencies on Aging (AAA) are the focal point for identifying the needs of older people and locating appropriate resources. The remaining 10 percent of AAA funding comes from nonfederal sources, usually in the form of state or local revenues. In-home personal care, chore services, and transportation are but a few examples of programs that have been developed across the nation by local communities—often without additional federal funding.

The Elderly Nutrition Program. This program, legislated in 1972, was the first major departure from the welfare strategies embodied in the Title III programs of the Older Americans Act. Rather than encouraging local planning and coordination, the Elderly Nutrition Program (ENP) provides a specific service that is offered nationwide. We saw earlier in this chapter that the intent of the ENP is to provide a nutritious hot meal daily to all older persons, regardless of income level, who have difficulty preparing their own meals, for whatever reasons. The ENP also specifies, however, that the meal must be served in a central location in order to provide companionship. The staff at each ENP site must ensure that transportation is available and must offer a program of nutritional education, a social program, and personal social services for those who need them. In addition, each meal site must have a council, composed of participants in the program, to plan activities and determine how the program is to be operated at that site. If it wishes, the council may request that those who can afford to do so make a donation toward the cost of the meal. The donations are used according to the decision of the council. If all of these requirements are met, the federal government pays the full costs of meal preparation and service.

Experience with the Elderly Nutrition Program has contributed further to our understanding of older people in contemporary America. First, it has become obvious that many older people, if left to their own devices, lead isolated and lonely existences. Bringing them together for meals has broken down one of the strongest fears connected with aging—that of being alone. Second, the program has reminded us that many of today's older people grew up in communities where helpfulness and neighborliness were the norm. When they are brought together through ENP, they have the opportunity to help one another with interpersonal and social problems and to feel cared for and needed again.

SUMMARY

This overview of public welfare policy has emphasized the complexity, variation, and scope of the contemporary public welfare system of the United States. Besides pointing up the progress that has been made, the overview should also provide insights into the formidable problems facing advocates of social welfare reform. Taken together, our welfare programs form a crazy quilt of vastly differing eligibility requirements and benefit levels. Some programs are open to everyone of a particular age group, regardless of income; others are available only to people with low incomes who have passed a means test of eligibility. Eligibility requirements themselves pose a dilemma. In most cases, eligibility for one program does not make the recipient ineligible for benefits from another program; on the other hand, because different programs are means tested at different income levels, not all recipients are equally eligible for all programs. In addition, some programs (for example, Public Housing) are designed so that an increase in income that pushes the recipient above the income eligibility line may cause a loss of benefits that is many times greater than the gain in earned income. Another complex and cumbersome feature of our welfare system is that the administrative networks developed to carry out our welfare programs reflect a confusing mix of political philosophies and program designs. No single program is entirely responsible for distributing benefits to any single group of people, and some clients undoubtedly receive many benefits from several programs while others receive few benefits from few programs. All of these variables make the task of rationalizing public welfare into a unitary system very difficult indeed.

Despite the serious problems existing in today's welfare policies and programs, the multiplicity and magnitude of coverage is truly impressive. Our welfare programs may be unequal for some and lavish for others, but, for the most part, people who need assistance—whether with money, food, housing, health care, or social services—have an excellent chance of obtaining what they need. Overall, the United States has shown tremendous social progress in the past four decades, and the end is not in sight.

SUGGESTED READING

Axinn, June, and Herman Levin. *Social Welfare: A History of the American Response to Need.* New York: Harper & Row, 1982.

Dobelstein, Andrew W. *Politics, Economics and Public Welfare.* Englewood Cliffs, NJ: Prentice-Hall, 1980.

Dolgoff, Ralph, and Donald Fedlstern. *Understanding Social Welfare.* New York: Harper & Row, 1980.

Gilbert, Neil, and Harry Specht. *Dimensions of Social Welfare Policy.* Englewood Cliffs, NJ: Prentice-Hall, 1974.

Morris, Robert. *Social Policy of the American Welfare State.* New York: Harper & Row, 1979.

Skidmore, Rex A., and Milton Mackelay. *Introduction to Social Work.* Englewood Cliffs, NJ: Prentice-Hall, 1982.

6

PUBLIC WELFARE PROGRAMS
Federal, State, and Local

GEORGE HOSHINO
Professor, School of Social Work
University of Minnesota

In previous chapters, the antecedents of contemporary public welfare and social work were traced in broad perspective: the Elizabethan Poor Law in England and the United States; voluntary organizations such as the Charity Organization Societies and settlement houses; programs for the care and protection of certain vulnerable groups such as children or the mentally ill; the origins of social insurance in England and the United States; and the emergency measures of the Great Depression, which culminated in the Social Security Act in 1935. What today is called "public welfare" in the United States is a product of that evolutionary process, a process that is still in a state of development. Indeed, recent events have altered the public welfare system and the role of social workers within it in drastic ways. Fundamental changes are in the making as the public policy process, described by Dobelstein in Chapter 5, is being played out in the 1980s in the public welfare arena.

PUBLIC WELFARE DEFINED

What is public welfare? A broad definition might encompass all social welfare provided under governmental, or public, auspices. Such a definition would embrace a vast array of public social policies under which direct benefits and services are provided to individuals or families. Under this rubric can be included six areas of social welfare, five of which are traditional and well established: (1) income maintenance (both in cash and in-kind); (2) health care (both physical and mental); (3) education; (4) housing; and (5) employment. The sixth area is the newly emerging field of personal social services, which includes the range of programs in which most professional social workers are involved. In fiscal 1978, governmental expenditures for welfare under this broad definition totaled $394 billion, nearly 60 percent of all governmental expenditures and 19.3 percent of the gross national product.[1] Slightly more than three-fourths of all public funds for welfare purposes came from the federal government; the remaining portion was contributed by state and local governments. Public expenditures accounted for 70.4 percent of all social welfare expenditures, public and private, and about two-thirds of the private expenditures went into health programs. These figures clearly demonstrate the extent to which the public sector dominates the social welfare scene today.

At the other extreme, a very narrow definition of public welfare is implied in the way the word "welfare" is commonly used, with a pejorative connotation (as in "those people on welfare!"), to mean public relief—the cash and in-kind assistance programs of state and local welfare departments. Welfare, in this sense, usually refers to the programs of Aid to Families with Dependent Children (AFDC), Medical Assistance (Medicaid), and a wide assortment of assistance programs offered by state, county, and municipal governments. All of these progrmas are means tested and heavily stigmatized. This popular definition of welfare, however, is too narrow for our

1. Alma W. McMillan and Ann Kallman Bixby, "Social Welfare Expenditures, Fiscal Year 1978," *Social Security Bulletin* 43 (May 1980), p. 5.

purposes. It does not include important welfare programs such as school meals, Housing Assistance, and Low-Income Energy Assistance; and it does not include some immense, federally administered programs. Nor does it encompass the broad category of personal social services provided by welfare departments (either directly or through purchases in the private sector) to children, families, the aged, the physically and mentally handicapped, and other vulnerable groups.

In this chapter, we will use the term *public welfare* to refer to the network of federal/state/local public welfare services, and our focus will be on *local welfare departments and the programs they administer.* Because a number of federal programs are carried out by local departments, they too will be discussed, as will programs within the voluntary sector with which the public services interact. Before we can begin, however, we must look briefly at the provisions of the Social Security Act of 1935 and its subsequent amendments that constitute the country's most fundamental and comprehensive social welfare legislation.

The Social Security Act had three distinct components that directly shaped the public welfare system of the United States:

(I) cash transfer payments
  (A) social insurance
    (1) Old Age, Survivors, and Disability Insurance (OASDI); administered by the Social Security Administration
    (2) Unemployment Compensation; administered by the states
  (B) public assistance
    (1) Supplemental Security Income (SSI); administered by the Social Security Administration
    (2) Aid to Families with Dependent Children (AFDC); administered by the states
(II) health care payments
  (A) Health Insurance (Medicare) for the aged and disabled; requires no test of need; administered by the Health Care Financing Administration
  (B) Medical Assistance (Medicaid) for children and the aged, blind, and disabled; requires a test of need; administered by the states
(III) personal social services
  (A) Title XX program of grants to the states for social services
  (B) child welfare provisions of Title IV (AFDC)

As the major public welfare programs of the United States are discussed, the massive impact of the Social Security Act will become increasingly apparent.

FEDERAL PUBLIC WELFARE

The federal government's responsibilities for health and welfare are discharged mainly through the U.S. Department of Health and Human Services (DHHS). The DHHS was established in 1979 when President Carter created a cabinet-level Department of Education, thus removing educational services from the former Department of Health, Education and Welfare (DHEW). The DHEW had been established in 1953 to consolidate in one cabinet department the federal government's major health, education, and welfare responsibilities. Before 1953, those activities had been handled by such groups as the Federal Security Agency (established in 1939), the many New Deal agencies of the Roosevelt administration, the Social Security Board (originally created to administer the public assistance, unemployment compensation, and old-age benefit programs of the Social Security Act), the Children's Bureau (established in 1912), and the Public Health Service, which dates back to 1789.[2] Perhaps the major impetus for the eventual creation of DHEW was the establishment, during the Great Depression, of a number of federal agencies to administer specific emergency programs such as the WPA and CCC work relief projects. These programs were later abolished, as more permanent programs took their place or as their need abated with the coming of World War II. From that time on, however, the federal government remained firmly committed to major responsibilities in the field of social welfare; and federal activities have, until recently, tended to expand regardless of which political party was in control of the executive or legislative branches of the government.

Today, DHHS is a huge department, spending by far the greatest portion of the federal budget for its social welfare programs. In fact, the DHHS budget exceeds that of any other cabinet department, including the Department of Defense, largely because of its social security and public assistance operations. In addition, there are

2. In 1789, the First Congress enacted legislation providing for a deduction of 20¢ per month from the salaries of seamen to pay for medical care. Thus one could say that national health insurance is as old as the Republic.

various social welfare functions scattered among other federal departments, including the Department of the Interior (Bureau of Indian Affairs), the Department of Housing and Urban Development (Public Housing, Housing Assistance), the Department of Labor (Work Incentive Program and various youth and human resources projects), the Department of Education (school meals), and the Department of Agriculture (Food Stamps).

Federal departments discharge their welfare responsibilities in a variety of ways. Some programs are administered, and benefits and services are provided directly, by a federal agency; others are administered through a complex system of grants to the states or localities, which, in turn, provide the benefits and services. The District of Columbia's Department of Human Resources operates the District's welfare programs in much the same manner as do state or county welfare departments, and its programs and relationship to DHHS are essentially the same as those of the states.

Some federal services are provided directly through specialized administrative units of the government, such as the Social Security Administration. Another example is the Veterans Administration, which has an extensive network of hospital and outpatient health and social service programs for veterans and certain of their dependents. Similarly, the Bureau of Indian Affairs provides direct services to American Indians who are under federal jurisdiction, although these persons may also qualify for state or county assistance of various kinds.

Social Security Administration

By far the largest and most significant of the programs directly administered by the federal government are those of the DHHS's Social Security Administration, which has a network of regional and district offices that reaches into almost every locality in the nation. It is at the district office of the Social Security Administration that U.S. residents have their first contact with social security. Claimants go to the district office to file their claims to benefits when they reach retirement age, become disabled, or are widowed or orphaned by the death of a breadwinner.

Old Age, Survivors, and Disability Insurance

At the end of March 1981, 35.8 million people received the OASDI payments that are popularly called "social security." Of that number,

23.9 million were aged 65 or over. This group included 17.6 million retired workers, 6.2 million survivors and their dependents, and .1 million "special age 72" pensioners (noncontributors who automatically qualify for minimum benefits by reason of age alone). Another 11.9 million beneficiaries were under age 65; this group included 2.1 million workers who had taken early retirement, 2.8 million disabled workers, and 7.0 million survivors and their dependents.[3] In fiscal 1978, the Social Security Administration distributed the impressive sum of $117.4 billion in cash payments to recipients of OASDI.[4]

The magnitude and significance of OASDI are indicated by the facts that over 90 percent of the nation's labor force is covered by social security and about three-fourths of the aged population receive OASDI payments. For most elderly citizens, OASDI is the largest source of income; for about 16 percent, it is the only regular income. The influence of the Social Security Administration even reaches beyond the confines of the United States, because some beneficiaries reside in foreign countries. Indeed, so pervasive is the system that many parents obtain Social Security numbers for their newborn offspring. The Social Security number has become, for better or worse, the universal identification symbol for countless transactions, including student records at large educational institutions.

In July 1982, OASDI benefits to retired workers averaged 55 percent of the worker's last monthly paycheck. Monthly payments averaged $406 for a single person and $695 for a couple. The maximum amount anyone could receive was $729 per month. As both Harrison and Dobelstein have pointed out in earlier chapters, this massive pension plan faces severe funding problems caused by such factors as inflation (benefits are tied to the cost of living), recession, and the growing number of pensioners relative to the population's work force. Proposed solutions to the current funding difficulties include the following: (a) borrowing from general revenues to supplement insufficient payroll contributions; (b) slowing the growth of benefits and capping future cost-of-living increases; (c) gradually raising the age of eligibility for full benefits from 65 to 68 years; (d) bringing all workers in the country into the system, including the three million federal employees now under a separate system that pays higher benefits. Neither the president nor the Congress wants to take the

3. "Current Operating Statistics," *Social Security Bulletin* 44 (August 1981), p. 1.
4. McMillan and Bixby, "Social Welfare Expenditures," p. 5.

politically unpopular step of cutting back on retirement benefits, and the aged themselves are determined to retain their hard-won gains. Nevertheless, economics and demography dictate that a series of remedial steps must be taken to keep the system solvent. The battle over how to solve the problems of OASDI will continue to rage throughout the 1980s. Demographers predict that funding problems will abate in the 1990s but will reemerge in the 2020s. At that time, the baby boom generation will be retiring, and the heavy burden of their support will fall on the shoulders of a relatively smaller work force born in an era of declining birthrates.

Supplemental Security Income

Since 1974, the Social Security Administration has operated the Supplemental Security Income program, a major federal assistance program for the needy aged, blind, and disabled. SSI replaced the adult public assistance categories of Old Age Assistance, Aid to the Blind, and Aid to the Permanently and Totally Disabled. Prior to 1974 those programs, although federally authorized and funded, had been administered by the states through their public welfare departments.

In April 1981, 4.1 million beneficiaries received SSI payments. Of that number, 1.8 million were aged, .1 million were blind, and 2.3 million were disabled.[5] In January 1982, the basic SSI benefits for persons living in their own homes were $264.70 per month for individuals and $397.00 for couples.

In many states, a system of supplementary payments operates in conjunction with SSI. Although a state may elect to have the Social Security Administration disburse its supplemental benefits, thereby being relieved of administrative costs, eligibility for state supplements is determined by the state or local welfare department. Thus considerable complexity and some confusion are introduced into the SSI program in states that have supplemental payments.

SSI represents a significant step in this country's movement toward a comprehensive system of providing adequate and dignified protection against income interruption and poverty. Although SSI is a means-tested program and the "take-up rate" (the proportion of eligible persons who apply for and actually receive benefits) is still little more than 50 percent, the program holds far less stigma than was associated with the state-administered adult categories of assistance that SSI replaced, or than is still associated with the state-adminis-

5. "Current Operating Statistics," p. 35.

tered AFDC program. SSI eligibility requirements and benefits are considerably more liberal, and two of the most punitive Poor Law features of the former programs—property liens and relatives' responsibility—are notably absent.

SSI is intended to supplement OASDI benefits, but it can also be viewed as a guaranteed minimum income. As such, it is the first national program of its type for selected groups of the population, and it represents an approach that could be extended to other groups; in particular, to needy families with children. Some of these families are covered by AFDC as the result of the death, disability, continued absence, or unemployment of a parent. Others, however, are excluded from AFDC and many other kinds of income maintenance, either because state law disqualifies the two-parent family or because the family is part of the group known as the "working poor."

In Chapter 5, Dobelstein pointed out that public welfare policy is the "black box" of the political process. Congressional enactment of SSI is an interesting example. Originally, SSI was but one element of a major welfare reform bill, called the Family Assistance Plan, introduced by the Nixon administration. The Family Assistance Plan was proposed to replace AFDC and Food Stamps, and to extend coverage to the working poor. The plan as a whole failed to pass the Congress, but SSI was enacted.

Health Care Financing Administration

In a major DHEW reorganization in 1977, responsibility for the two federal health care programs of Medicare and Medicaid was assigned to the newly created Health Care Financing Administration.

Medicare

As part of the nation's system of social security, Medicare is a form of health insurance that covers the aged and the disabled who are eligible for Disability Insurance. Medicare provides payments for hospital care and for posthospitalization skilled health care in a nursing facility or at home (Part A, Hospital Insurance). Beneficiaries can, in addition, elect to pay a monthly premium, matched by the federal government, which covers outpatient hospital care, physicians' services, medical supplies, and home health visits (Part B, Medical Insurance). In fiscal 1978, Medicare payments totaled $25.2 billion.[6]

6. McMillan and Bixby, "Social Welfare Expenditures," p. 5.

Medicaid

Through a federal program of grants to the states, Medicaid pays for the health care of categorically eligible individuals (i.e., persons who receive AFDC and SSI benefits). Medicaid also covers the health costs of the medically needy (i.e, persons whose incomes are greater than the level that would qualify them for AFDC or SSI but who need assistance in meeting heavy medical expenses).

Interaction of Federal with State and Local Programs

Federally administered programs such as OASDI, SSI, and Medicare are significant for local public welfare workers because many beneficiaries of federal assistance are in need of other services and aid that are available only on the local level or are purchased in the private sector by the local welfare department. Medicare, for example, does not cover nursing home care, but Medicaid does. Consequently, the largest part of all welfare department expenditures is for Medicaid payments to the providers of health care, and most is for nursing home care. Similarly, OASDI, SSI, and Medicare provide basic maintenance and medical care; but many beneficiaries need other supportive and protective services to remain in their own homes or in community care rather than being institutionalized. Supplementary services are also needed to combat the isolation, loneliness, and exploitation that some aged and handicapped citizens might otherwise experience. In some cases, clients of welfare agencies are unaware of, or reluctant to apply for, benefits available to them through the Social Security Administration. In such instances, agency workers help their clients apply for and secure their federal entitlements. Thus federally administered programs constitute a major component of the network of social welfare services within which local welfare deparments operate and about which local staff must have knowledge.

Other Federal Welfare Programs

In addition to administering programs of direct benefit to citizens, such as OASDI, SSI, and Medicare, the Department of Health and Human Services is responsible for a variety of programs that provide funds to the states for certain categories of problems. These include programs in the areas of crippled children's services, maternal and infant care, alcoholism and drug addiction, mental health, and child abuse and neglect. Among the largest of the programs are two we have already mentioned: federal grants-in-aid for AFDC and Medicaid. A third is the program of social service block grants. Finally, there is Low-Income Energy Assistance, which provides financial assistance to low-income persons for heating or cooling their homes. In most localities, this program is administered by community action agencies.

The Department of Agriculture administers the Food Stamp program, a major income maintenance program for low-income individuals or families. This program is financed solely by the federal government, but eligibility is determined by state or local welfare departments. Criteria for eligibility are much broader than for AFDC or general assistance; the working poor, who constitute a large proportion of families in poverty, use Food Stamps as a major source of income supplement.

In all of the programs that combine federal with state and local responsibilities, the federal role is to establish standards and criteria, review and approve state or local plans, survey state or local operations to ensure compliance with federal regulations, and provide guidance and technical assistance to state or local staff. These functions are exercised through a system of regional offices, the field staffs of which act as liaison between the states and the federal offices in Washington, D.C.

The greatly expanded federal activity in the area of social welfare since enactment of the Social Security Act in 1935 has come about largely as a result of the efforts of special interest groups and lobbies. Much of the categorical legislation is the culmination of lobbying efforts on behalf of such groups as the aged, the disabled, children, juveniles, alcoholics, and drug addicts; for such causes as mental health, family planning, and the prevention and treatment of domestic violence; and for a variety of health programs.[7] Typically, statute and administrative laws contain detailed program specifications with which states and localities must comply. Moreover, many categorical programs are also entitlement programs, that is, an

7. Early federal grants to the states were in the form of land for such purposes as education. In the early 1800s, Dorothea Dix campaigned for better care of the mentally ill, resulting in passage of congressional legislation to fund mental hospitals. President Pierce's veto established a precedent that governed federal-state relationships until the Sheppard-Towner Act of 1921 authorized federal grants for maternal and infant hygiene.

expenditure by a state automatically obligates the federal government to reimburse the state for a specified proportion of the expenditure.[8]

The Newest "New Federalism"

The Reagan administration, which took office in 1981, was determined to reverse the trend toward an ever-expanding federal role in social welfare by curtailing federal financing, reducing federal participation in state and local programs, and shifting responsibility back to state and local governments. Particular targets were the categorical health and welfare grants-in-aid. The strategy was to consolidate the many health and welfare grants into a small number of "block grants," to cut back and cap federal appropriations for each block grant, and to eliminate detailed federal regulations and guidelines. Block grants were to be allocated among the states according to each state's proportion of the national population, and the requirement of state financial participation, or matching, was to be eliminated. Thus not only would federal initiative, direction, and funding be reduced, but the political influence of special interest groups and lobbies would be blunted. The states also could reduce or eliminate their own participation in various programs if they wished.

Under heavy pressure from President Reagan, Congress did sharply reduce federal spending for health and welfare. Congress, however, was also feeling the pressure of constituents, and as a result enacted seven block grants instead of the four recommended by the president: Social Services; Community Services (to support community action agencies in combatting poverty); four health block grants (Maternal and Child Health, Preventive Health Care, Alcohol/Drug Abuse and Mental Health, and Primary Health Care); and Low-Income Energy Assistance. At the same time, other legislation sharply curtailed programs that had little support among middle-class taxpayers, such as Medicaid, AFDC, and Food Stamps. Both the Congress and the president decided not to tackle the problems of the most popular entitlement program, OASDI, until after the 1982 elections.

In his State of the Union message to Congress on January 26, 1982, President Reagan outlined his plan for a "new federalism." The plan

---

8. Similarly, the principle of individual "entitlement" is built into the social security system to guarantee claimants' rights.

would turn back to the states responsibility for administering and funding AFDC, Food Stamps, and some forty other programs of health, education, housing, welfare, and social services that previously has been federally aided. In return, the federal government would assume total responsibility for Medicaid and would establish a trust fund to assist the states during the transition period. The "new federalism" clearly ran counter to virtually all other welfare reform proposals of the last half century. For example, both the Nixon and Carter welfare reform plans would have abolished AFDC and covered the working poor through a federally administered system of income transfers to families with children.

It is too early to evaluate the "new federalism," but initial reaction seems cautious. Although state and local officials would welcome the takeover of Medicaid by the federal government and the relaxation of federal control of state-administered programs, they are considerably less enthusiastic about the prospect of assuming total responsibility for costly programs such as Food Stamps and AFDC without a firm commitment of federal aid. Viewed from a historical perspective, the "new federalism" proposal is but one phase of a continuing national controversy over the concept of *federalism* (the respective roles, functions, and relationships between federal and state governments). That controversy dates back to the writing of the Constitution and even earlier, to the time when the colonies rebelled against a strong central government and created a federal system. Indeed, the entire history of public welfare policy in the United States is very much a history of the playing out of the drama of federalism—a dynamic, ever-changing concept that is continually reshaped by society's needs, attitudes toward government in general and the federal government in particular, and political tides. Within this historical perspective, it seems clear that block grants, the "new federalism," and other Reagan administration proposals represent an overt and determined effort to redirect federal domestic policy in fundamental ways. The Reagan proposals reverse the historical trend toward expansion of social welfare, particularly the trend toward an expanded federal welfare role that began with the Great Depression and the subsequent enactment of the Social Security Act of 1935.

STATE PUBLIC WELFARE

We saw, in Chapter 4, that by the time of the Great Depression most states had some structure of boards, commissions, or bureaus to administer or supervise a collection of programs such as old-age pensions, widows' pensions, correctional facilities, children's institutions, and almshouses. State boards of charities and corrections existed in most states. A few states had departments of welfare—an outcome of reform movements of the early 1900s—that were designed to reorganize state operations more rationally, efficiently, and responsively. Most responsibility for welfare services still remained with the localities and private charities. With the advent of the emergency relief programs of the Great Depression, however, every state had to develop machinery for working cooperatively with federal agencies such as the Federal Emergency Relief Administration and the Works Progress Administration. The passage of the Social Security Act marked the establishment of a permanent program of federal grants to the states for public assistance, child welfare, and other social services. As a result, a clearly discernible and fairly uniform pattern of organization began to emerge among state programs.

Certain characteristics of state departments of public welfare can be attributed to federal requirements for organization and administration as a condition of receiving federal funds. Among the more significant were the requirements for a single state agency to administer or supervise programs, a merit system of personnel administration, machinery for handling grievances and appeals, and uniform standards and policies throughout the state. The states also were required to submit reports and adopt methods necessary for proper and efficient administration.

Because the original Social Security Act required a state to have a single agency for administering or supervising federally aided programs, two distinct patterns of organization and administration emerged: state-administered systems and county-administered, state-supervised systems. The general trend is in the direction of state administration, and the majority of states now follow that pattern. Various combinations exist, however. In Pennsylvania, for example, public assistance is administered directly at the state level, but child welfare services are the function of county child-care services. The names given to agencies also vary: "Department of Public Welfare" is common, but some agencies are called "Department of Pensions and Security," "Family and Children's Department," "Department of Social Services," or "Department of Social Welfare." Moreover, there is a trend toward consolidating services such as welfare, corrections, health, and mental health into umbrella organizations that bear such titles as "Human Services Department."

Despite differences in titles and patterns of organization, state departments of public welfare throughout the country have much in common. In all states, public welfare is one of the largest (if not the largest) departments, in terms of both budget and personnel. Executive and administrative staffs operate from headquarter offices, along with program specialists such as public assistance, social services, and child-care consultants. Executive and administrative staff members communicate with the governor and other state executives, work with the legislature, and coordinate departmental programs with activities of other state agencies. They also oversee field operations, including the programs of local departments and other welfare institutions and community facilities. Together with the specialist staff, the executive and administrative staffs develop policies, plan programs, engage in research, evaluation, and training, work in liaison with their federal counterparts, and supervise and consult with county and local agency staffs.

LOCAL PUBLIC WELFARE

Welfare services must be available where people live; therefore, whether as a branch unit of state government or as part of a county or city government, there exists in every locality in the United States a public welfare department or its equivalent. Local departments range in size from the huge bureaucracies of New York City and Los Angeles County to two- or three-person operations in sparsely populated rural counties that in some cases cover thousands of square miles. There are enormous variations in structure and activity among the more than 3000 local departments of public welfare, but it is possible to identify some general functions and a common core of programs.[9]

The functions of local public welfare departments can be classified within three categories: (1) to assist certain groups of individuals and families who have insufficient personal resources to maintain a decent standard of living; (2) to provide help to persons who have problems in social functioning; and (3) to protect and care for those who are unable to care for themselves because of age or physical or mental disability. Local public welfare programs are of two general

9. The *American Public Welfare Dictionary,* published annually by the American Public Welfare Association, contains a list of federal, state, and local public welfare agencies, their addresses, and the programs they administer.

kinds: those having to do with economic assistance and those having to do with personal social services. In the category of economic assistance are such programs as AFDC, Medicaid, Food Stamps, general assistance, and, in some states, supplementary SSI benefits. In the category of personal social services are a diversity of therapeutic and rehabilitative services to families, children, the aged, the physically and mentally handicapped, alcoholics, and drug addicts. Thus, in addition to administering AFDC, Medicaid, and general assistance, a public welfare worker typically determines eligibility; provides child welfare services such as protective services, foster care, and adoption; offers family planning services; provides protective and supportive services to the aging; and operates services for groups of people who have a wide range of social and psychological problems.

Interactions with Other Agencies

The local public welfare department is linked to the private social welfare sector, to other related public systems, and to the proprietary and profit-making sector (for example, nursing homes and day-care centers). These linkages occur through an intricate network of affiliations and relationships.

All local welfare departments operate an information and referral service where citizens can inquire about local services and be referred to appropriate community resources. The welfare department may refer its clients to such community services as a Family Service Agency, private or sectarian child-care centers, family planning clinics, legal aid clinics, rape crisis centers, vocational rehabilitation, the State Agency for the Blind, or state employment services. Cases involving abused or neglected children are handled by welfare departments, in some instances in conjunction with the juvenile court. Under current law, most adult recipients of AFDC must register with the Work Incentive Program (WIN) for job training and placement. Other agencies frequently contacted by welfare departments include the State Worker's Compensation and Unemployment Insurance offices, the state crippled children's programs, child guidance clinics, and community mental health centers. All of these agencies, in turn, are sources of referral to welfare departments. For example, juvenile courts refer youths for supervision or children for foster care or adoptive placement, and local Family Service Agencies refer their clients who are in need of financial assistance.

Most public welfare departments purchase substantial portions of the services they offer from other public or private agencies rather than provide all services directly. In most localities, for example, the welfare department contracts for such services as family planning, foster and institutional care of children, and day care. Most nursing home care is purchased from private nursing homes with Medicaid funds. Indeed, it is not uncommon for a local welfare department to purchase a large part of its services from the private sector, and for a private agency to receive much of its funding through the tax monies used by public agencies to purchase its services. This situation has created considerable concern and controversy over questions of accountability and performance within the private sector, and it has been charged that unequal patterns of treatment exist within this dual system for various economic, racial, or religious groups. Some people are apprehensive that the autonomy of private agencies will be compromised; others fear that the function of the public agency will be reduced to that of an intermediary, serving primarily to channel tax funds to the private sector. Despite these problems, the public-private relationship continues to be an important element of local welfare departments' operations, and it must be viewed as part of the public welfare system.

Local departments of public welfare also provide indirect services that, although not serving specific clients directly, promote their general well-being. For example, welfare departments establish and enforce standards by serving as licensing agencies for such facilities as foster homes, nursing homes, and day-care centers. Community educational and informational activities, on topics such as the problems of neglected and abused children and the services available to them and their parents, constitute another indirect service.

Financial Assistance Programs

In terms of dollar expenditures, financial assistance (i.e., Medicaid, Food Stamps, AFDC, general assistance) is by far the largest of all programs administered by local welfare departments, as well as one of the most controversial. Although most references to "welfare" by the general public are really to AFDC, what is too often overlooked is that cash payments to AFDC recipients have been surpassed by Medicaid payments to the providers of health care (nursing homes, hospitals, physicians, dentists, pharmacists) and are rivaled by expenditures for Food Stamps. In 1978, for instance, total payments for Medicaid were $18.0 billion; for AFDC, $10.7 billion, for Food Stamps, $5.6 billion; and for general assistance in which the federal government did not participate, $1.2 billion.[10] By the end of 1981, the cost of Food Stamps had skyrocketed, due to elimination of the purchase requirement that enabled more people to use the stamps, the increased cost of the hypothetical market basket of food on which the value of the stamps is based, and increased unemployment.[11] Similarly, expenditures for Low-Income Energy Assistance rose sharply, from $200 million in 1977 to $1.8 billion in 1981.

Aid to Families with Dependent Children: A Welfare Dilemma

AFDC is a federally aided program of cash payments to the specified caretakers (usually, mothers) of needy children who are dependent because of the death, disability, or continued absence of a parent. The program is means tested and is available only to specified groups of families. In most states, AFDC excludes intact, two-parent families—a particular hardship in periods of high unemployment— and it usually excludes the working poor, even when their incomes are inadequate for subsistence. Although AFDC is literally the last line of defense against destitution for the poorest of the nation's children, it has serious shortcomings and has been the target of much public criticism. Paradoxically, the program has been attacked for encouraging dependency and family break-up at the same time that it has been assailed as being too restrictive and punitive. It has also been accused of rewarding those who do not work and penalizing the working poor.

Widows and their children constituted an important segment of AFDC recipients in the early years of the program, but in recent decades the case load has consisted increasingly of families headed by divorced, separated, deserted, or unwed mothers. Racial minorities have been disproportionately represented, with slightly over half of the recipients being non-Caucasian. In the early 1980s,

10. *Social Security Bulletin: Annual Statistical Supplement, 1980,* pp. 207, 232, 234; and McMillan and Bixby, "Social Welfare Expenditures," pp. 5-6.

11. Robert J. Fersh, "Food Stamps: Program at the Crossroads," *Public Welfare* 39 (Spring 1981), pp. 9-14.

however, there has been a discernible trend toward greater numbers of better educated, Caucasian recipients, and of smaller family units.

Because the states have wide discretion in determining eligibility, and almost total discretion in establishing standards of need and levels of payment, AFDC has been characterized by sharp contrasts among and even within states. For example, in October 1980, the average monthly AFDC payment per recipient was $99.79 nationally, but the range among states was from highs of $160.70 in Alaska, $149.33 in California, $142.20 in Wisconsin, and $137.24 in Washington to lows of $38.95 in Alabama, $35.80 in Texas, $29.70 in Mississippi, and $13.03 in Puerto Rico.[12] It should not be forgotten that many families have other resources to supplement AFDC, such as earned income, child-support payments, and an unknown amount of unreported income; some, however, do not. In addition, many AFDC recipients are eligible for in-kind benefits such as Food Stamps and Medicaid, which add substantially to the family's total income. Nevertheless, regardless of how income is figured, the general picture is of a standard of living that reaches the official poverty line in only a few states and descends to abysmally low levels in many states with high proportions of racial minorities. Moreover, AFDC allowances for earned income and personal assets are much less generous, and application procedures are more detailed and demeaning, than those of SSI.

To understand the persistence of a major public assistance program for families with children throughout the decades following World War II, a period when the United States was the ultimate in affluent industrialization, it is necessary to look beyond the program itself to the larger context within which it operates. The families who receive AFDC (as well as the working poor who are still excluded from it) are those whose adult members are unable to compete on equal terms in the job market. This condition stems from a variety of reasons— disability, inability to find a job, the need to remain at home to care for young children, lack of education and job skills, and racial/sexual/age discrimination. At the same time, these are the people who are not protected by the nation's universal maintenance programs. Thus AFDC can be viewed as a victim of the "creaming" phenomenon. That is, although the number of beneficiaries and the level of benefits for income maintenance programs have increased enormously as

12. "Current Operating Statistics," p. 43.

successive groups have been lifted out of (or prevented from dropping into) poverty, coverage has been selective. The recipients of universal income maintenance have been the worthy or impotent poor—the aged, the blind, the disabled, the survivors of deceased workers, and the temporarily unemployed—who receive the benefits of OASDI, Unemployment Compensation, and SSI.[13] Meanwhile, AFDC goes on; it has not withered away, as was the hope when the program was created.

With the expansion of income maintenance programs, the nation's poverty population became one of women, children, and minorities who do not fit the favored categories. Women and minorities also have been overrepresented in the secondary labor market—those dead-end, low-paying, unskilled jobs that do not offer the fringe benefits of paid sick leave, health insurance, unemployment compensation, and social insurance. The minimum wage paid in the secondary job market offers little protection to an unskilled worker with several children. Even if the worker is fully employed, the large family's income remains below the poverty line. Social insurance programs have little impact on childhood poverty because eligibility is based on a substantial prior work record. Further, social insurance programs ignore the causes of most AFDC eligibility—marital separation or desertion, and unwed parenthood. Finally, social insurance ordinarily pays benefits only when the recipient is not working (i.e., is unemployed, deceased, retired, or disabled) and thus excludes most of the working poor. The only recourses left to poor families with children are Food Stamps and AFDC, and even AFDC excludes most two-parent families and single-parent working families, regardless of their financial condition.

PUBLIC WELFARE REFORM

The inadequacies of the AFDC program have led to repeated calls for welfare reform. Suggestions have been made for tighter federal standards (such as mandatory minimum benefits), complete federalization of the program, and a new system of income supports.

13. Even the terminology differentiates individuals served by OASDI and Unemployment Compensation from those receiving public assistance. The Social Security Administration calls the former "claimants" and "beneficiaries" and the latter "applicants" and "recipients."

One proposal that received serious consideration was the Nixon administration's Family Assistance Plan (FAP), which would have established, in effect, a national minimum income level for families with children, including families of the working poor. Although the minimum level was very low ($1600 per year for a family of four), FAP would have extended coverage to thousands of families who were excluded from AFDC and would have raised the income levels of AFDC families in many states, particularly in the South. Theoretically, payments would not have been lowered in states where benefits were higher than the proposed minimum, because state supplements would have been allowed much as state supplements are allowed with SSI. As the FAP bill moved through the Congress, amendments were proposed, including one for a higher minimum income level. In the end, however, the FAP bill was defeated, although, as noted earlier, SSI was enacted and signed into law by President Nixon.

The Carter administration's plan for welfare reform was introduced by President Carter in a message to Congress in August 1977. President Carter proposed the abolition of AFDC, SSI, and Food Stamps and creation of a single federal system, which he called the Better Jobs and Income Program (BJIP). BJIP included a component of "work creation" in the form of an expanded Comprehensive Education and Training Act (CETA) program and a two-tiered income security program. The latter would have divided the poor into two categories, or tiers, for purposes of determining eligibility and benefits. The upper tier, who would not be expected to work, included the aged, the blind or disabled, single-parent families with children under 7 or with children 7 to 13 when jobs and day care were not available, and two-parent families with one parent incapacitated. The basic national benefit for an upper-tier family or four without income would be $4200. For the aged, blind, or disabled, the basic benefit would be $2500 for an individual and $3750 for a couple. Those in lower tier, who would be expected to work and would receive lower benefits, included families with children aged 14 or older and single persons and childless couples who were neither aged nor disabled—but only if they could not find work. A lower-tier family of four would receive $2300 if a job were available; if a job were not available it would receive $4200. Single persons and childless couples would receive $1100 and $2200, respectively, if no jobs were available. For those who were expected to work, the first $3800 of annual earnings were to be disregarded in computing benefits; the remainder of earnings would reduce benefits at the rate of $1 for each $2 of earned income, and benefits would phase out at $8400 of earnings. As an additional work incentive, the earned income tax credit, which at that time allowed a 10 percent tax credit on earnings up to $4000, would have been expanded and liberalized.

The Carter BJIP proposal would have altered the nation's public welfare system in fundamental ways. It viewed welfare, in the sense of income maintenance, as a direct federal function rather than as a state or local responsibility, with or without federal aid. Coverage would have been extended to previously excluded groups, particularly to two-parent families and the working poor. On the other hand, the Carter proposal retained some traditional welfare features such as a strong emphasis on work and on making benefits conditional on work, classification of the poor into categories of deserving and undeserving, and use of a means test to determine eligiblity. It is of interest that despite the sweeping changes proposed by Carter, almost no thought was given to the possibility of making basic changes in the nation's social insurance system or of instituting some type of universal family allowance system—a system that has been adopted by virtually all other industrial countries of the world. Moreover, the Carter proposal would have continued the inequities of variable state supplements, just as SSI does.

Although BJIP initially received considerable congressional support, particularly from states seeking fiscal relief from the burden of welfare payments and from traditionally liberal groups of citizens, equally strong opposition was voiced with regard to the plan's overall thrust and to particular details, such as the level of payments. In the end, BJIP failed in Congress primarily because its cost was feared in the face of growing national concerns about inflation and because the Carter administration became increasingly preoccupied with a series of international crises.

Ronald Reagan, who succeeded Carter, entered the office of president with the announced intention of curtailing welfare costs, particularly the federal government's share. Although the Reagan administration considered converting AFDC into a block grant to the states, a specific bill was not introduced for that purpose. Instead, the AFDC law was amended to restrict eligibility; and the subsequent "new federalism" proposal, to return total responsibility for AFDC to the states, moved away from earlier trends toward a greater federal role or complete nationalization of income maintenance. Although the outcome of the "new federalism" remains in doubt as this chapter is being written, what is not in doubt is that welfare reform—particularly as it concerns AFDC—will continue to be one of the most significant and hotly contested issues on the domestic policy scene throughout the 1980s.

HEALTH INSURANCE REFORM

Like welfare reform, medical assistance and national health insurance have been persistent topics of controversy. The fact that the original Social Security Act did not contain any provisions for health insurance is somewhat surprising, when one considers that health insurance is one of the oldest forms of social insurance. Today, the United States stands virtually alone among the industrialized nations of the world in not having some kind of national health system for its population. It was not until 1965 that health insurance for the aged, in the form of Medicare, was incorporated into the Social Security Act (along with Medicaid, to replace a more limited federal-state program of Medical Assistance to the Aged).

Medicaid is a more comprehensive program than Medicare, in terms of the kinds of health care services it pays for, but it is more restrictive in its coverage. That is, Medicaid serves only SSI and AFDC recipients and people who are classified as medically needy, while Medicare covers those who are eligible for Disability Insurance and anyone who is elderly. Since Medicaid's beginning in 1966, the program has grown at an explosive rate as ever greater numbers of people have been forced to resort to welfare to meet medical expenses, particularly for nursing home care. In addition, medical costs have skyrocketed, imposing an increasingly heavy financial burden on state budgets and leading to growing demands for health insurance reform. Major proposals have called for a greater federal sharing of Medicaid expenditures, or for complete nationalization along the lines of the "new federalism" proposal. There has also been continued interest in some form of national health insurance program.

National health insurance bills, in fact, have been introduced in successive Congresses for many years, including one sponsored by the Nixon administration. The Carter administration, too, favored national health insurance; but beyond a general proposal for a catastrophic program (i.e., to cover major medical expenses), no specific bill was submitted to Congress and no proposed bills were supported by the Carter administration. Presumably this was because the administration was concerned about the inflationary effects of such a proposal. The Reagan administration did not favor national health insurance, but did propose the complete takeover of Medicaid by the federal government as part of the "new federalism."

Over the years, the various proposals for national health insurance have differed in purpose, comprehensiveness, coverage, cost, financing, method of payment, administration, and effect on the health care system. They have ranged from suggestions for a system of graduated tax credits for health care costs to extending Medicare to the entire population. A health service bill, for example, would have established a national health service to provide for all persons, without charge, a full range of medical, dental, and mental health services from fully salaried health professionals. Some plans have emphasized protection against the costs of catastrophic illness by proposing to supplement Medicare and the basic coverage of nonprofit or commercial health insurance plans. Proposals have differed in their emphasis on prevention and primary care or on specialized and heroic hospital care, and in whether payment should be by fees for service or some other arrangement. Some plans have relied on the existing private health industry to provide health care, while others would virtually eliminate it. Cost sharing would be required by some proposals, while deductibles or copayments would be absent from others.

How to deal with Medicaid is another subject of difference among the proponents of national health insurance. Some would abolish it, some would greatly reduce the need for it, and some would nationalize it. If Medicaid were to be nationalized, as President Reagan has suggested, the result could be a consolidated federal health care payment system for the beneficiaries of both Medicare and Medicaid. The Health Care Financing Administration already has the structure for administering Medicare and overseeing the states' administration of Medicaid. Under the "new federalism," this agency could become the focal point for a federal system of financing health care that would be rivaled only by the Veterans Administration— although, of course, the VA system is a health service rather than a health care financing system.

Despite numerous attempts and some near successes, the immediate propsects for enacting any kind of national health insurance appear dim. Nevertheless, because health care costs continue to rise and because the beneficiaries of a national program would include the middle class as well as the aged and the poor, national health insurance undoubtedly will remain a major domestic policy issue for some time to come.

THE PERSONAL SOCIAL SERVICES

In earlier sections, the personal social services were discussed briefly in connection with other topics. I have reserved a fuller discussion of this topic for a separate section, however, because it is a subject that is of particular importance to the profession of social work.

Throughout the history of public welfare, financial aid has been accompanied by some kind of rehabilitative function—whether the moral guidance of the poor relief officer, the social casework of the Charity Organization Society, or the social services offered through public assistance programs. This principle of tying services to financial aid was sanctioned by Congress with enactment of the Social Security amendments of 1962. In that action, Congress authorized federal funding of social services to the recipients, former recipients, and persons likely to become recipients of public assistance. The premise was that services provided by professional workers would lead to a reduction in case loads and a corresponding decrease in expenditures for public assistance. This "services strategy," as it was called, failed. For example, instead of decreasing, AFDC expenditures continued to rise, and the problems of administering this massive, complicated financial aid program overwhelmed attempts to build a viable service program. By the late 1960s, funding for social services had become what some called "back-door" revenue sharing. In 1972, a decade after its enactment, Congress ended the "open-ended" grant-in-aid service program and imposed a $2.5 billion ceiling on federal payments for social services.[14]

14. The $2.5 billion ceiling on federal expenditures for social services was imposed by the General Revenue Sharing Act of 1972 and carried over to Title XX in 1974. The Social Services Block Grant Act of 1981 reduced federal authorization for Title XX to $2.4 billion for fiscal 1982.

It is not surprising that differences of opinion arose over the services strategy. One view held that services should be tied to financial aid because service is an integral part of aid. The opposite view was that determining eligibility and providing services are inherently different functions that should be performed by different kinds of staff; the former by nonprofessional workers trained in the specific procedures of determining eligibility, and the latter by professionals trained to deal with personal, family, and social problems. Those who favored separation of the two functions argued further that assistance should not be conditional on behavior or service requirements. Moreover, the separatists claimed, determining eligibility is an investigative function that introduces an adversary element, thus precluding a truly professional relationship. Finally, separatists advocated dissociating services from financial aid in order to make services available to a broader population than that of public assistance case loads.

By 1970, general sentiment had swung in favor of separation, and in 1972, separation was mandated by DHEW. DHEW required agencies to have at least (a) separate staffs for the two functions, (b) separate supervisory and administrative structures, and (c) separate accounting systems. In 1973, the establishment of SSI completed the separation process as far as older people were concerned, because SSI is administered by the Social Security Administration and adult social services are provided by local welfare departments.

In 1974, Congress amended the Social Security Act by abolishing the service provisions of the public assistance titles and creating, in a new Title XX, the Grants to the States for Services, thus providing for what are commonly called the "personal social services." The personal social services encompass a variety of supportive, therapeutic, and facilitative services to individuals and families. Activities take the form of *soft*, or relationship, services such as social casework and counseling, and *hard*, or tangible, services such as day care, domestic assistance, meals on wheels, and residential care. All of these services can be distinguished from other well-established areas of social welfare (e.g., income maintenance, health, housing, education, employment), and they are clearly emerging as an important component of social welfare in all of the industrialized nations. Albert Kahn has described a threefold classification of personal service functions: (1) socialization and development; (2) therapy, help, and rehabilitation (including social protection and substitute care); and (3) access, information, and advice.[15] Still, despite the efforts of Kahn and others, the personal social services—whether conceived as a system, as discrete programs and services, or as the collective and individual activities of staff—remain broadly and imprecisely defined.

Likewise, there is little consensus about the kind of training needed to work in the social services. Staff who are currently providing services include a variety of professional, semiprofessional, and paraprofessional workers—family therapists, adoption workers, vocational counselors, homemakers, day-care workers, case aides, and residential staff—whose training ranges from high school education or less to graduate professional education.

Title XX's recognition of the personal social services as a distinct and separate component of a system of social security for all Americans is significant in its immediate consequences for the social services, its symbolism and potential for future development, and its implications for the social work profession. Prior to Title XX, there was little opportunity to develop a separate, viable system of personal social services. Such activities had been adjuncts to public assistance or human resources programs, rather than services needed in their own rights. With the Title XX separation, a clearer conception of personal social services is emerging, as is a delivery system for providing them.

Minnesota and the state's largest county, Hennepin, are examples. During the 1970s, Hennepin County separated services from

15. Alfred J. Kahn, *Social Policy and Social Services*, 2nd ed. (New York: Random House, 1979), p. 16. Title XX defines social services in terms of five goals: (1) achieving or maintaining economic self-support to prevent, reduce, or eliminate dependency; (2) achieving or maintaining self-sufficiency, including reduction of dependency; (3) preventing or remedying neglect, abuse, or exploitation of children or adults unable to protect their own interests, or preserving, rehabilitating, or reuniting families; (4) preventing or reducing inappropriate institutional care by providing for community-based care, home-based care, or other forms of less intensive care; and (5) securing referral or admission for institutional care when other forms of care are not appropriate, or providing services to individuals in institutions. Title XX services must be directed toward one or more of these five goals and may include, but are not limited to, services for "children, the aged, the mentally retarded, the blind, the emotionally disturbed, the physically handicapped, and alcoholics and drug addicts."

assistance by creating two departments: the Department of Economic Assistance, to administer AFDC, Medicaid, Food Stamps, General Assistance, and other maintenance programs; and the Department of Community Services, to provide family and child services, mental health services, services to the elderly, and other personal social services. In 1979, the Minnesota legislature enacted the Community Social Services Act "to establish a system of planning for and providing community social services administered by the boards of county commissioners of each county under the supervision of the commissioner of public welfare." The act consolidated into a single financing formula a state social services block grant and an integrated local service delivery system. It tied together the funds and administrative responsibility for most of Minnesota's personal social services, including Title XX, mental health and retardation, child welfare, and services to the aging, to drug addicts, and to alcoholics. Because the counties have wide discretion under the Community Social Services Act to plan and provide services, different patterns of organization and operation have evolved across the state. Yet, despite the differences, there is emerging a clearly identifiable, free-standing system of personal social services in every Minnesota county.

A similar development is taking place in other states, and the trend appears to have been further encouraged by enactment in 1981 of the Social Services Block Grant Act. At the same time that the federal legislation reduced federal funds for personal social services, it gave almost complete discretion to the states to plan and provide services, in contrast to the detailed regulations and guidelines that were characteristic of former social services legislation. Consequently, the states are giving greater attention to planning and developing more efficient and effective systems. Many states are following the trend toward consolidating personal social services into some kind of local delivery system, either county or state administered.

SOCIAL WORK'S TURF IN THE 1980s

Until a few short years ago, public assistance was viewed as an important area of social work practice; today, it is seen as a separate career line. The relatively few professionally trained social workers in

AFDC and Medicaid programs work mostly at the administrative level, and there are even fewer professional social workers in the SSI program. Recent developments in the personal social services may someday be viewed as the nation's first significant steps toward a universal and free-standing system that is justified by its intrinsic merits and available to the poor and nonpoor alike. If, at some future time, national health insurance replaces Medicaid and a guaranteed minimum income for families with children replaces AFDC, it is conceivable that local welfare departments could become social service agencies in which public assistance is a residual function and the personal social services are the primary function.

The future of social work, therefore, appears to lie in the personal social services. Social welfare is the province of social work; indeed, it may be the only area in which the profession can claim unique competence. Future developments will depend on the profession's capacity to identify, conceptualize, and train personnel for the personal social services. This will mean systematic description and analysis of the programs that make up the system, more precise conceptualization of the social service function, and delineation of the tasks involved. It will mean, in addition, clarifying the generic and specialized knowledge and skills needed for the various service roles. Finally, it will mean developing formal and in-service training programs to impart the knowledge and skills to workers.[16]

It is now clear that providing basic social welfare services such as income security and health care does not diminish the need for personal social services. Rather, the contrary seems to be the case. The guarantee of income and health care for the older population, for example, has stimulated a need and demand for new and expanded programs of supportive, protective, residential, and socialization services. Social work is not the whole of the personal social services, of course, any more than is medical practice the whole of health care. At the present time, many social workers are pessimistic about the future because the personal social services are vulnerable to federal and state cutbacks in funding, as are all social welfare programs.

16. A "Proposed Policy Statement: Personal Social Services" was defeated by the 1981 Delegate Assembly of the National Association of Social Workers. It called for a nationwide system of personal social services, built around federal leadership and financial support, that would result in a free-standing, integrated, and identifiable entity in every locality in the United States under professional leadership of and service provision by social workers.

Nevertheless, the personal social services constitute an emerging and increasingly important field in which the social work profession should play a pivotal role and in which the identity of the profession may, at long last, clearly emerge.

SUGGESTED READING

Amidei, Nancy, "Food Stamps: The Irony of Success." *Public Welfare* 39 (Spring 1981):14-21.

Burke, Vincent J., and Vee Burke. *Nixon's Good Deed: Welfare Reform.* New York: Columbia University Press, 1974.

Derthick, Martha. *Uncontrollable Spending for Social Services Grants.* Washington, DC: Brookings Institution, 1975.

Fersh, Robert J. "Food Stamps: Program at the Crossroads." *Public Welfare* 39 (Spring 1981):9-14.

Gibelman, Margaret. "Are Clients Served Better When Services Are Purchased?" *Public Welfare* 39 (Fall 1981):26-33.

Hoshino, George, "Public Assistance and Supplemental Security Income: Social Services," in *Encyclopedia of Social Work,* pp. 1150-1156, ed. John B. Turner. Washington, DC: National Association of Social Workers, 1977.

Hoshino, George. "Separating Maintenance from Social Services." *Public Welfare* 30 (Spring 1972):54-61.

Kahn, Alfred J. *Social Policy and Social Services,* 2nd ed. New York: Random House, 1979.

Kamerman, Sheila B., and Alfred J. Kahn. *Social Services in the United States.* Philadelphia: Temple University Press, 1976.

Mott, Paul E. *Meeting Human Needs: The Social and Political History of Title XX.* Columbus, OH: National Conference on Social Welfare, 1976.

Moynihan, Daniel P. *The Politics of a Guaranteed Income: The Nixon Administration and the Family Assistance Plan.* New York: Random House, 1973.

Pray, Kenneth L. M. "Public Funds in Private Hands?" *Proceedings of the National Conference of Social Work, 1937.* Columbus, OH: National Conference of Social Work, 1937.

U.S. Congress, Congressional Budget Office. *Low-Income Energy Assistance: Issues and Options.* Washington, DC: Government Printing Office, 1981.

U.S. Department of Health and Human Services. *Annual Report.* Washington, DC: Government Printing Office, published annually.

PART III

SOCIAL WORK METHODS OF PRACTICE

Part III of this text is about social work methods. Social work methods are understood best as a series of activities, or the ways that social workers help people. If the social programs are the tools of helping, social work methods are the ways those tools are used. To the extent that carpenters have to learn how to use hammers and nails to build their products, so social workers must learn how to connect the programs with people in such a way the programs will improve the lives of people. To make these connections, social workers use different methods, or different approaches, depending upon the type of people with whom they may be working, the kinds of problems the people may have, the settings, or the field of service in which the social worker is located, and the social programs with which the social worker is working. In this regard, social work methods bring together both the skills and the art of social work practice as discussed in Part I.

When social work first began as an organized profession, there was very little known about social work methods. Social work methods then were whatever one happened to do in order to accomplish the results sought. Mary Richmond, who is considered to be the founder of modern social work, first tried to summarize social work methods in her book *Friendly Visiting Among the Poor,* published in 1899. This book and her book *Social Diagnosis* (1916) were the first and only social work textbooks for many years. But as social work matured as a profession, and as more social science knowledge was applied in the act of helping people, social work began to develop more specific ways of helping, and the idea that social work had definable methods of helping began to emerge. With the emergence of social work methods came greater specialization among social workers in the ways they helped people. Whereas originally social workers did whatever seemed necessary to achieve the results, as social work practice methods became more defined, social workers became identified by the methods they used to help people, rather than by what they tried to accomplish. Thus, rather than the terms "social work" and "social workers," the terms associated with the profession were "caseworkers," "group workers," "family workers," and so forth.

In recent years, there has been a lot of discussion about whether the methods of social work practice are the most important parts of social work. As important as these discussions are, the fact remains that social workers do different things, and they do them differently. These differences are reflected in the methods by which social workers undertake their missions. The purpose of Part III, therefore, is to acquaint social work students with these different ways of doing things. The purpose is not to divide the practice of social work into neat components, because what much of the debate over methods has taught is that social work methods are compatible, and that social workers usually use a combination of methods in professional social work practice.

The first social work methods that emerged in social work practice were social casework and social group work. Social casework was quickly associated with the way Mary Richmond practiced social work. Hers was a one-by-one or case-by-case approach to helping. She dealt with one person or one family at a time. It was not long before this case-by-case method was called "casework." Because Mary Richmond applied social science knowledge to her work, and because she wrote about what she was doing, most of early social work was identified as casework. But at the same time, social workers were helping people in groups. They were teaching principles of citizenship and helping socially disadvantaged persons integrate into the mainstream of American society in groups. It is not surprising, therefore, that this kind of helping method became known as "social group work."

Chapter 7 discusses and explains the casework of helping as it is practiced in social work today. Although some of specific methodological techniques of social casework have become sharply refined, Lois Taber and Richard Taber show that the casework method of helping is most useful when dealing with individualized, or one-at-a-time, helping efforts. Even so, as Chapter 7 shows, casework helping efforts have become greatly sophisticated, to the extent that there are highly specialized helping activities within social casework. The greatest influence on the casework helping process has come from the widespread application of Freudian psychology and Freudian methods in social casework helping. Although Taber and Taber identify many skills that social caseworkers possess, these skills are not learned only by reading about casework methods. Casework skills, like other social work skills, are developed as the knowledge presented about the methods is practiced. Therefore, the case studies presented in Part IV should be used in conjunction with all the chapters in Part III.

Social group work is discussed and explained in Chapter 8. Sonia Abels and Paul Abels present a lively and provocative view of this social work method. Like social casework, social group work has developed so much specialized knowledge that the many subdivisions of social group work practice seem to tear it apart. Yet the common thread of group work practice is the idea of a group of people who are being united, regardless of the benefits that may or may not accrue to each person who is a member of that group. Because groups are the fundamental form of social organization, social group work has greatly expanded the scope of social work practice, and, in part, social group work practice explains some of the diversity in social work as identified in Part I. Again it is important to study the case studies in Part IV along with Chapter 8.

Community organization has less definition as a social work method than either casework or group work, and this is the main point made by P. Nelson Reid in Chapter 9. The roots of community organization go back to Mary Richmond's days, even though there continues to be difficulty in specifying the scope of community organization. This difficulty stems from trying to think about helping "communities." Here, as Reid points out, there are many different views about what constitutes a "community" and even if that problem could be solved, one seldom helps a community, as such. Thus the organizing idea of this method has had greater meaning than the idea of community. In this view, organization can take place around a variety of socially desirable objectives, from groups of disadvantaged people to social service structures and programs. Thus there is often great overlap between community organization methods and a wide variety of social planning activities, including social program coordination and planning, fund raising, and even efforts to develop socially healthy communities, however they may be defined.

In Chapter 10, Jane Pfouts explains family social work. This is one of the newer social work methods, one that may seem similar to both casework and group work. Its distinctness as a method derives from the unique focus on the family unit, a uniqueness made possible as greater knowledge about the family has been integrated into all of social work. Pfouts cautions that the family cannot be defined by its form, but by characteristics of a family system. When variations in these characteristics are so great as to place the family system in a disadvantaged situation, then family social work is directed toward getting these variations into the range of acceptability. For example, when variations in parental roles causes children to fail in school, family social work provides the assistance to reduce these variations and return the family unit to one that can nurture and support growth and development. Because family social work is such a new social work method, great judgment is necessary in deciding exactly how social workers assist families in each situation.

Chapter 11 explains case management. Case management may seem to be less a social work method than an administrative tool, but Peter Johnson shows why this is not the case. The need for a social work method to assist people in organizing and using all the resources available to them came from efforts to get mentally handicapped individuals out of institutions and back to as normal lives as possible. Many and varied services were required to do this social work task, and as a result social workers had to develop some activities that would equip them to meet this helping expectation. Johnson's discussion shows that case management methods are required in all the varied fields of social work as more and more social programs are available. In this way, case management is a natural progression in the refinement of social work's way of helping, made necessary by the great social policy and program developments that were discussed in Part II.

As you read this section, keep in mind that the methods of social work change as greater and greater amounts of knowledge are applied to social work helping activities. In this view social work methods change in their importance as the profession of social work changes, and since American society is constantly changing, social work will change as well. The social work methods discussed in Part III are the social work methods of the 1980s. They may not have been the methods of the 1950s, nor might they be the methods of the twenty-first century. But these methods are the way today's social workers go about helping the people they serve.

7

SOCIAL CASEWORK

LOIS R. TABER

Social Worker (retired)
Veterans Administration Hospital

RICHARD H. TABER

Social Worker
Family Service, Philadelphia, Pennsylvania

Contemporary social work practice draws less distinction among the methods of helping than it used to. Ten years ago, social work was closely identified with the method of social casework, and to a lesser extent with social group work and community organization. But even though social work methods are likely to be used interchangeably in the practice of social work, much of what is known about helping people is still found in the application of method skills.

At first, social casework gave definition to the whole profession of social work. As social work began to develop a professional status in the early 1900s, the idea was to assist persons with their problems one at a time, or, as Mary Richmond said, on a case-by-case basis, and the name "casework" was given to this particular set of activities. To this extent knowledge and social casework skills have always influenced the development of social work, so that even today social work is practiced with many more methods and skills. The principles of social casework remain a fundamental part of what all social workers need to understand.

Social workers have long held convictions about the worth of the individual. All social workers believe that each person has a right to find satisfaction in life, and that society has some obligation to help each person during times when problems seem insurmountable. Social casework grew as these commitments to individual self-realization became more explicit in America. Particularly in the 1960s and 1970s, people angered by the constraints of poverty and frustrated by institutionalized social injustice sought new avenues for self-realization. Frustrated by the inability to control their own lives, belittled by the impersonal nature of large institutional structures, bewildered by the disruption of supportive family and social networks, many people sought the individualized assistance of social casework.

One of the important objectives of all social work practice is to assist persons in making meaningful connections with these positive sources of strength. Most persons who come to the attention of social workers are those who have found themselves unable to cope with a significant aspect of their lives—their jobs, their children, their close personal relationships—at precisely the time they are separated from their support structures. The combination of these two forces precipitates a "problem" for which social casework assistance is often requested. The exact character of the problem may be difficult to categorize, as each problem is unique to each person. It could be the difficulty a college student experiences in separating from home, or it may be the isolation and loneliness felt by a person after the death of a spouse. The problem may be that of a juvenile delinquent who is trying to change his way of living, or it may be that of a young woman concerned about her mothering ability.

Part II of this text outlined the types of social work services that are likely to be available to persons seeking help. In any of these settings there will exist efforts to personalize the service and provide individual attention to a problem. The settings may differ, depending upon the type of problem and the purpose of the organization. In some settings, such as a family service agency, the social caseworker carries the major burden of providing the service to the client. In larger, institutionalized organizations, such as hospitals, for example, the social caseworker is only one of the many professional persons providing different kinds of services. In such a setting the social worker's role may be that of assisting the client in keeping all the parts of the help together and preventing confusion.

ORIENTATION

Objectives

The purpose of social work with individuals is to offer a means by which a person is enabled to obtain a higher level of social functioning through an interpersonal transaction or face-to-face, person-to-person encounter.

The method utilized by social work in this endeavor, social casework, is an enabling process through which one individual (the caseworker) helps another (the client) to take steps toward achieving some personal or social goal by utilizing the resources available to the client,[1] resources inherent in the strength of his personality, the social system in which he lives, or the social provisions supplied by the community, including the agency through which he is receiving help. It is not a method imposed upon an individual, but is offered as a means by which he can make use of the caseworker's knowledge and expertise to gain strengths to move more productively in the social situation in which he finds himself having difficulty.

Whatever the problem presented to a caseworker, her objective is to help the person learn how to deal with it and thus to provide a means by which he can increase his capacity for coping with other life stresses. The objective is not toward personality change, although changes in attitudes and feelings may result from this contact. The applicant may become less critical of himself, increase his ability to communicate and relate to others, and learn how to handle hostility and aggression so that they serve him rather than become his master. He may feel greater self-confidence and find new values and aims. These gains depend on the quality and substance of the relationship

---

1. For the sake of clarity, the client will be referred to throughout this chapter as male; the caseworker will be referred to as female.

that develops as client and caseworker interact in their joint endeavor, whether the contact is of short or extended duration.

It is the purpose of casework with individuals to facilitate their engagement in social relationships when their effective participation with others has reached an impasse.

Relationship

Whatever factors contribute to the client's increased ability to cope with his problem lie within the framework and quality of the relationship between caseworker and client as they work together. This relationship is based on the concept that all human beings have the capacity for growth and for the realization of their unique personalities through relationships with others, and that they can gain satisfaction through their participation with others as social beings. It is further acknowledged that learning and growth take place through creative interaction with others provided there is a climate of mutual respect and confidence in the participants' integrity and provided the challenges met are related in some measure to their individual capacities. This is especially true of the interaction that takes place between client and caseworker. The caseworker does not manipulate or control, but helps the client find his own values and aims through an orderly process that enhances his capacity for self-determination.

Preparation for Practice

For this endeavor to be productive, the caseworker needs to prepare herself by gaining knowledge of the human condition from other disciplines—that is, from the behavioral sciences, psychology, sociology, learning theory, anthropology, and systems theory; by understanding the social forces that affect and are affected by individuals; and by developing the self-discipline and skills necessary to help the client take steps to increase his ability to function more adequately. Her skills are learned through the experiences she encounters in her work and through a training process that includes periodic case conferences with a competent supervisor or teacher. Through this process she learns to understand how she can use her strengths productively and come to terms with attitudes and feelings that color her perceptions or interfere with the client's willingness to use her help. She learns to assess where her own values can strengthen those of the client or where they could jeopardize the attainment of the client's own purposes.

She brings her own unique personality to her work and as she incorporates her professional knowledge she moves more spontaneously and surely in a variety of situations and with a variety of clients.

It is recognized that people have been helped by many different approaches, and by many different individual styles of working. Since there is no one basis for understanding human behavior, nor one theory of casework practice, a worker must choose what is of most value to her. What is of crucial importance is that she have a reliable framework upon which to base her practice. From such a base, she can offer the troubled client a steady source of strength upon which he can rely. In times of stress, when people feel confused and vulnerable, they look for support and guidance more than at any other time in life. What a troubled person needs is someone outside of his immediate situation who is strong enough to bear the feelings he expresses without criticism or prejudgment. The helping person needs to be secure enough in her role to interact with the client by means of genuine, honest, and commonsense responses and input.

The necessity for acquiring competence in helping with the complex nature of people in difficulty has led to the professionalization of social work. Like other professions, social work is based on a code of ethics and values, a set of standards for practice, bodies of knowledge and tested principles leading to methods that serve its purposes. As a professional person the social work practitioner is responsible for maintaining standards held by the profession and confirmed in statements of purpose and performance by the National Association of Social Workers, which receives sanctions for the implementation of social purposes from society as a whole.

Social casework as a part of the larger social work profession surfaced in response to the problems encountered when social workers attempted to help individuals caught in difficulties resulting from the impact of an industralized society. The first theoretical exposition of a methodology for casework was formulated by Mary Richmond in 1917. Influenced both by the scientific method and by the medical model of that era, she advocated careful history taking as a means of arriving at a causative factor, which would then be the target for effecting change. Her contribution lay in the development of a systematic approach to the study and diagnosis of problems. It was she who set forth some of the principles upon which social casework is based, not only the necessity for a careful appraisal of environmental influences, but also an obligation to individualize each client, to recognize his right to determine his own life, and to place great value on the client-caseworker relationship.

In each succeeding era theories and practice reflected a response to human needs within the framework of the value system and scientific knowledge of the day. As in other professions, a variety of theories emerged. Insights from Freud and the ego-psychologists led to a psychosocial diagnostic base for practice, later refined to include problem-solving and crisis-intervention modalities. Differing from these was the functional school, which utilized the concepts of Otto Rank in the development of a philosophy and implementation of casework as a service related to specific functions of an agency.

All of these approaches continue to contribute to casework practice today and have been augmented by the adoption of new models such as those based on existential and systems theory. These diversities have served not only to broaden the range of modalities open to caseworkers for their practice, but also to enrich the social worker's knowledge of human behavior and understanding of the dynamics of the helping process.

In the 1970s knowledge from philosophers, social scientists, and physicists introduced a new dimension to social thought; rather than reasoning in a linear cause-and-effect manner, we now think in terms of action and reaction, a process of constant change within the reciprocal relationship between individuals, and between people and their environment. In social work this shift in emphasis to interactional components of behavior has resulted in expansion in the use of multiple interviewing, such as in marital counseling, family therapy, and peer-group counseling. These latter modalities are discussed in separate chapters. In this chapter we concern ourselves with components of social casework as it deals with individuals and their interactions with others and with systems in which they are involved, through the one-to-one relationship of client and caseworker.

Impetus for Service

The impetus for the coming together of client and worker as agency representative occurs when there is a perceived need for service. Perception of need may come from one or more of three sources:

(1) The client may come to the agency as a result of his own perception of need for assistance, such as for financial help, adequate housing, foster

home placement, or counseling when he experiences feelings of anxiety, depression, or helplessness, often following an incident in which the person feels caught, as in a family quarrel or a threat to job security.

(2) The client may come to the agency as a result of perception of need by another person or institution, such as a family member, an employer, the court, a school principal, or a hospital whose staff is concerned about his behavior or his reluctance to use its services.

(3) The client and worker may come together as a result of the worker's or the agency's perception of need, such as in outreach services, case finding, or referral within a multiservice agency. For example, a worker in a high-risk area may perceive a child's need for service by observing the child's behavior in school or in a youth group.

Regardless of the source of impetus toward service, what most clients have in common is that they are having difficulty negotiating a social system. In the case of children, it may be the family or school system. In the case of teenagers, it may be a peer system or the judicial system. Adults may be having difficulty with a health service system, an employment system, or a social service system, including the system of which the worker herself is a part. In most cases the worker helps the person to participate and contribute more effectively in the system in which he is experiencing difficulty. In some cases her efforts are focused on helping a person extricate himself from a system that is destructive to his social functioning, such as to change his place of employment, to dissolve a marriage relationship, or, in the case of a child, to remove him from his current living situation.

One of the central parts of the helping process is to make a series of decisions in collaboration with a client and/or significant others about the extent to which the social system or the individual will be the target for change. In some cases the most appropriate form of help may be intervention in the social system, such as in changing the interpersonal climate of a classroom or hospital ward or family.

In other situations it may be inappropriate and a violation of a client's rights or wishes to intervene in the system, thereby depriving him of the self-enhancing opportunity to handle his own problems. People begin to act differently as they have an opportunity to sort things out, share feelings that may have been unexpressed for years, and gain in understanding of the causes of their own behavior as well as that of others. The flow of energy in the relationship may be the most important—the feeling that one is accepted and acceptable. The relationship may provide the client with an opportunity to model more appropriate behavior. It can provide a feeling of safety and security that is the springboard for the client to risk attempting new and more effective behaviors as he leaves the office and faces the day-to-day world—yet knowing that whatever the results of the new behavior, he can return to discuss them with the worker and find acceptance for his failures as well as his successes.

In any event, it is the individual client who approaches or is approached by the caseworker, and it is their relationship that serves as the milieu in which they will function together. Whether it takes one or more interviews, the process through which they attempt to achieve their purpose depends on an orderly, rational structure that makes problem solving possible and that determines the parameters of their relationship.

We will proceed to outline one possible model for the helping process applied to work with and on behalf of individual clients.

THE CORE HELPING PROCESS

The formulation by Max Siporin (*Introduction to Social Work Practice*) of important elements in the helping process has proven useful. The components include (1) engagement, (2) exploration, (3) planning, (4) intervention, (5) evaluation, and (6) disengagement. These will be discussed as far as possible in sequential order. In actual practice they often overlap.

Engagement

Whatever the circumstances and feelings surrounding the encounter of client and caseworker, each has his unique personality and way of expressing himself, his own outlook on life, and the goals he wishes to achieve. Each has had different life experiences and, as they often have come from quite different backgrounds, each has found different ways of coping with problems. It is partly because of these factors that their coming together holds the promise of new learning and understanding of themselves and others. Its likeness to other relationships encountered in life—such as parent-child, husband-wife, teacher-pupil—lies in its reciprocal nature, each influencing the other as they interact in achieving their individual and social purposes. Its difference from other relationships is that its purpose is to achieve changes through a disciplined process in which one person makes use of another to achieve his goal.

In this respect they meet as equals, each with different roles and responsibilities. The caseworker's role requires that she be professionally responsible and committed to offering what can best be used by the client. The client's role requires that he make the problem understandable to himself as well as to the caseworker and that he take responsibility for whatever steps are required.

When a person arrives at the decision to seek or to accept outside help, the anxiety that the problem itself has produced may be compounded by two feelings: uncertainty of trusting another when he exposes what he perceives as weakness, and the fear of what may result from his new experience. However difficult the circumstances that propelled him to take action and whatever the discomfort he feels in his situation, at least these elements in his situation are familiar. To change his ways and to engage in talk with a strange person are often difficult.

It is the worker's attitude of acceptance and willingness to see a client as a whole person with strengths and weaknesses that enables the building of the interpersonal relationship that is the beginning step of their work together. Relationship happens when there is emotion shared between two people and they come to have ongoing impact in one another's lives. As any two strangers come together and interact, there are feelings and questions. Will I be accepted by this other person? Will the outcome of our contacts be what I am hoping for? Can this other person be trusted? Will I be "put down," judged, laughed at? In a worker-client interaction these feelings and questions may be intensified.

In situations where an individual comes to social workers for help, the asking for help is an admission that one cannot make it on one's own. In a society that places emphasis on independence and self-reliance, this admission of need for help may be experienced by the person as a step backward, toward dependency. Consequently, feelings run high. The client may be anxious about the worker's response to his request for help. He may be angry with himself or angry with those who in his perception have caused him to come to the agency. However, he comes too with the hope that he will be helped and with a readiness to mobilize his energy toward a solution and views the worker and the agency in a positive way.

In situations in which the contact has been initiated by the worker, or in which the client comes to the agency under pressure from an authority such as court or school, he may be angry toward the worker, suspicious of the worker's motives, or fearful of what she may do. However, frequently he is relieved that someone has been concerned about him and provided him with a means whereby he can obtain some understanding and help in his predicament.

Meanwhile, the caseworker will also be wondering whether she can help the client or whether her personal biases will interfere with her perceptions and responses. Will the client's anger stir her own to such an extent that she will be unable to deal with it, or will the client's distress be so great that she may be overwhelmed and lose perspective? Will the client's problem be so similar to her own that her perception of the client as an individual will be distorted, or will the client's experiences be so different from hers that she cannot identify or empathize with him? However, the caseworker knows that she can rely on the self-discipline she has gained through understanding of herself and she can use the skills she has developed through professional education as well as through her experience. Her greatest assets are her genuine concern and willingness to put herself at the disposal of the client.

Most clients have experienced stressful relationships in their growing-up years or have been embittered by circumstances over which they have had no control. It may take some time before a person can trust the worker, since these experiences have not been conducive to trust in others. However, until he learns to trust the worker, there can be no benefit derived from their contact. No amount of good intentions can take the place of the client's belief and trust in the worker. This basic ingredient provides the greatest incentive for change.

It is the worker's skill in "tuning in" to the heightened feelings of the client that is essential to the development of their relationship. It is often useful to help a client verbalize what his feelings are about coming to or being approached by the agency. This can be done by a direct question or by commenting on one's perceptions of his nonverbal communications. The client may respond and talk about feelings, thus giving him an opportunity to reduce his anxiety or vent his anger or frustration. The client may deny the emotion perceived by the worker. In either event the worker sets the stage in terms of making it clear that the interview situation is a place where there is concern for feelings as well as for facts. While it is true that feelings need to be expressed, overindulgence in their expression may cause a client to react by feeling he has opened up too much of himself, and he may then feel guilty and exposed. Or he may release feelings that he cannot manage. The caseworker's task is to keep these expressions within bounds by focusing on the reality of the situation and by dealing with the specific problem facing the client. A full description about what happened can help lessen the client's anxiety and enable him to proceed with what, if anything, he wants to do about it.

The first step has to do with the worker's skill in listening and the ways in which she elicits information. She needs, first of all, to be receptive to the client's telling his story in his own way, being sensitive to both verbal and nonverbal communications that reflect feelings, anxieties, and tensions. If the client is unassuming and tentative in his presentation, the worker will want to encourage him by introducing leading questions, at the same time permitting him time to organize his thoughts. If he comes across strong, with anger and vituperation, the worker must accept his blowup to a point, but know when to cut into his harangue by playing back the content of the client's outburst. Throughout, the worker communicates her strength by her own composure and willingness to wait until the client is ready to go on.

By whatever means the client manages to tell what troubles him, the very telling brings a new sense of himself as a person able to communicate and share with another.

Most people present their problems as caused by external circumstances. If the "other" were different, he would be different. The perceptive worker understands that people find it difficult to see their part in a problem situation, let alone share their knowledge of it with someone else. At the other extreme is the client who blames himself entirely, as if he were the sole perpetrator of all that has happened. In either case, if these attitudes persist, the worker cannot be of immediate help. Overcoming the impasse is dependent upon the worker's skill in helping the client see something of the relationship between what has happened to him and what he has done to contribute to his dilemma.

When she listens and asks questions, the worker has no stake in the rightness or wrongness of the issue. She accepts the client's view of the situation and does not belittle its meaning or importance, however bizarre or superficial it may sound. She knows that when a person asks for help, even though he is motivated to do something about it, he will have ambivalent feelings about accepting that help; that he both wants and does not want to meet the challenge it represents and to take on the responsibility for its solution. The client's resistance can be expressed in a variety of ways. He may block in answering a simple question, argue about some point that is brought up, or treat his situation in an offhand or humorous manner when in reality it is serious. Recognizing that people need their defenses for purposes of stability and integrity, the worker does not try to cut through at once but continues to listen and to provide the means by which he can deal with his ambivalence. She may want to know, for instance, how it happened that the client decided to do something about his problem at this time and what he hopes the worker can do to help him. Before the end of their first interview, there needs to be some expression on the part of the client that he is willing to do his part in working on the problem. It is his, not the worker's, problem that is at stake.

The question that both worker and client must address at this point is whether there is a resource in the agency services that is usable and useful to the client. It is a process of clarification of client needs and agency resources. The consequence of this phase of the engagement process is a decision that ongoing service is or is not appropriate. Often when the agency does not have the resource that is needed, the applicant is referred elsewhere. Thus the worker needs to have a thorough familiarity not only with her agency's resources, but also with other sources of assistance in the community. The worker must also be clear about the restraints imposed on her by the policies and procedures of the agency and by the resources available. She must help to make them understandable to the client in down-to-earth language. When the agency cannot provide service because of eligibility standards or waiting lists or lack of money, the resultant discussion can be a difficult responsibility, as workers want to respond to need.

As the agency representative the worker also makes clear to the client what responsibilities are his in this undertaking. Thus in an agency that gives financial assistance, the client will need to produce evidence of need; or in a foster placement agency, the prospective foster family will need to reveal facts and attitudes that make it possible to determine whether it can offer an appropriate home for a foster child.

When worker and client come to an agreement on goals for work together, plans can be made for ongoing service. The agreement should stipulate the frequency and duration of further contacts and the immediate tasks to be undertaken by both worker and client. A client should leave the initial interview with more than a casual "See you next week" on the worker's part, which leaves the client wondering why and what he should do in the meantime. For instance, the purpose of an encounter may be stated in broad terms, such as a mother's desire to improve her relationship with her child; the mother's task in this regard might then be that she write down the details of a disturbing incident for discussion in the following interview, and the worker's task that she contact the child's school to learn how the school views the child. Having definite objectives, however immediate and tentative, and tasks to be accomplished, both persons leave the transaction with a sense that positive movement will take place and both have assumed some accountability for what is to happen. The very articulation of the problem and the decision toward action in themselves constitute the beginnings of mastery and heightened motivation for continuing work together.

Exploration

In any responsible professional enterprise the first step needs to be the gathering of facts that define the parameters of the problem; thus it is important to explore any attempts the client has already made to solve the problem or answer the question. Consequently, the worker focuses the interaction on understanding how the difficulty first surfaced and respects the fact that solutions have been tried and have failed. In addition, she explores those areas in which the client has been successful and the ways in which he has learned to handle other problems. Thus they can understand what coping capacities the client has at his disposal. It gives both client and worker clues as to the nature of his personality strengths and how he takes advantage of opportunities open to him. The problem facing him at this point is one for which his usual ways of coping have not proved adequate to handle either internal or external stresses.

Social workers tend to believe that behavior is motivated and that its precipitants can be understood. Interventions made on the basis of limited facts and faulty judgments can be a disservice to the client and sabotage any effective help that may be given. The emphasis on the facts to be gathered varies widely according to the theoretical framework of the worker. Psychotherapeutically oriented workers may tend to emphasize historical data, whereas existentially oriented workers may focus much more on the "here and now."

The worker gathers facts through skilled interviewing techniques, and by her responses she guides the clients in offering appropriate data. Simple responses such as nods let the client know that the information is understood and related to the topic under discussion. Rephrasing a statement may encourage a client to think through what he is sharing. Feelings as well as facts are important to understanding behavior. If the client is not verbalizing feelings, the worker may wish to reach for feelings with statements such as, "How did you feel when that happened?" or "From what you are saying, I'm wondering if you're not angry about that." Reflections may also be made about nonverbal communication such as muscle tension or facial expressions. In so doing the worker transmits not only her acceptance of the client as a feeling person but also her respect for his autonomy in the problem-solving relationship.

The extent of exploring and confronting must be judged in relation to the strength of the relationship and the resilience of the client. It is often important to "reach for the opposite." If the client is talking primarily on a rational, intellectual plane, the worker may encourage verbalization of feelings, or if the client is caught up in emotional expressions she may want to ask questions that focus on the client's thinking on the issues being discussed.

As a result of this exploration the worker can make an assessment for purposes of judging what can be offered to the client for further work on his problem. Her assessment consists of determining the strengths the client has at his disposal as well as the environmental supports and opportunities available to him, including his family.

To determine the client's strengths, worker and client need to judge how pervasive and inhibiting the problem is to other areas of his life. As the client talks, the worker will be thinking about whether his anxiety is heightened or lessened through discussion of reality issues and whether the feelings surrounding his predicament are appropriate, keeping in mind that anxiety is always present in a new undertaking. In this, she will be sensitive as to whether the client's responses to her questions are appropriate and logical or whether there is an inordinate amount of emotional overlay. She will be thinking about whether or not the client's actions seem to be in tune with his values and intellect. She will be aware of the stresses operating from environmental conditions and how they affect the client, how he relates to friends and family and group associations, and whether he takes advantage of the resources available to him. This helps in understanding the supports the client has at his disposal and gives a clue as to his ability to interact socially. How he uses others and how he takes hold of what the caseworker offers indicate where his potential ability lies in being able to cope with the present problem. The worker can thereby assess the severity of the problem, its relation to the client's total life experience, and the appropriateness of its being dealt with in the particular agency or institution in which she functions. She can discuss her assessment with the client and thus have a basis for making plans about what seems most appropriate to do in tackling the problem.

In this whole process it is hoped that what helps the client most is that the caseworker engages him in a discussion of his hopes and expectations and encourages his full participation. By revealing the feelings and attitudes that surround his problem he is able to see the problem more realistically. By exploring related facets, he gains a better perspective on how the problem relates to his present and past life, and he begins to face the problem with a greater degree of objectivity. He begins to feel that the worker understands and accepts him and he senses he can rely on the worker's expertise—"she knows what she is about." At the same time it conserves and strengthens his feelings of self-worth and mastery. Its intent is to free the client so that the choices he makes will lead to actions that take him a step forward in fulfilling his aims.

Planning

When the worker and client have gained a shared understanding of the problem and have identified factors that have impeded the client's ability to cope with it, they will need to explore what resources can be of assistance and formulate a plan of action. The plan should identify specific goals agreed upon by both worker and client. The worker must be genuinely convinced about the right of a client to choose a course of action freely. She will give an explanation about what the agency has to offer and what would be entailed in working together on the problem that has been presented.

Resources outside of the agency may be considered more appropriate in meeting client needs, in which case the worker would suggest alternative sources of help. The selection of resource would be dependent on an evaluation as to whether the resource is one that will indeed further the client's aims and purposes.

Often workers can help clients find needed resources from their own social context. A client may determine with a worker that he needs experiences in which he can achieve success in order to help him feel more positive about himself. She may then work with his teacher or parent or recreation leader to help them set up, or help him set up, such activities. There may be a neighbor or friend who can supply immediate needs or stand by as a stablizing influence for a very troubled person.

In many instances the resource needed is not present in either the client's current social context or the agency to which the client is looking for help. In this case the worker may want to help the client link up with sources of such help. In addition to established health and welfare agencies, there are a variety of mutual aid organizations such as Alcoholics Anonymous, Parents Without Partners, fraternal organizations, and political clubs.

When worker and client agree on an appropriate external resource, a referral is made. The way the referral is made depends on the nature of the problem and the capacity of the client to carry through with it. The referral may be made on one level by a simple suggestion on the part of the worker, which is easily followed through by the client. At another level the worker may need to take time to prepare the client by talking through fears, apprehensions, and lack of knowledge. The worker may "pave the way" by contacting the other agency and sharing information so the work can be done more expeditiously. A highly agitated or depressed client may need to be escorted to a psychiatric facility. The principle here is that the client be encouraged to do as much as is feasible for himself.

The influence that the worker has with the client comes largely from her knowledge and expertise about community resources and from the authority of her position as agency representative, especially in crisis situations. The worker's effectiveness in helping the client take stock, sort out alternatives, and choose a course of action is critical in providing linkage services. In doing this she is aware of the possibility that the client may have feelings of frustration that need to be expressed. Often clients have gone from agency to agency in attempts to find a solution. The handling of feelings can free a client so there is positive motivation for seeking help elsewhere.

In making a determination for plans to utilize the agency, particularly with a multipurpose agency or institution, there will be a number of resources from which to make a selection. The worker's responsibility in these situations is not only to determine if, when, and how much of the agency's resources can be offered, but also to help the client make the best possible use of them. To do this the worker must gather appropriate data and give clear information about available resources, policies, and procedures. Her attitudes should convey to the client that he has a right to avail himself of these resources. She will use her casework skills in helping him overcome barriers to the use of the resource (e.g., in meeting eligibility standards or in overcoming doubts, fears, or feelings of shame) while at the same time making clear to him what responsibilities he must assume. Her success in obtaining the needed resource will be dependent on their maintaining positive working relationships with other staff, or, in some settings, on her ability and skill in confronting those in authority.

When the client-worker relationship is the important resource, planning may involve setting priorities. The worker may, for instance, see deficits in patterns of child rearing or household management, while the client is focused on more specific goals, such as getting the electricity turned back on or having his child's classroom changed. Realistically, these are of crucial concern and the worker will help him attempt to meet the needs that require immediate attention. Whether or not these needs can be met depends on the realities of the other social systems. The outcome of these endeavors may be successful or unsuccessful, but the sharing of mutual tasks in the effort gives worker and client a beginning sense of value in each other's contributions to their undertaking. Through the experience of coping with these realities they may later wish to move toward dealing with some of the underlying factors that brought about the client's predicament.

In another context, if worker and client decide to focus first on marital problems, the worker can use this agreed-upon plan to pull the client back into this focus if he should begin to spend a lot of time talking about his relationship with his employer. Here flexibility, of course, is important. If the employment situation has become increasingly stressful and the verbalization is not an effort to avoid the focus on the marriage, then it may be appropriate to alter the plan since this may in reality be putting stress upon the marriage. The important thing is that the work is purposeful and both worker and client are clear about the goal toward which they are working.

As they progress, each of the parties should know what is expected in behavioral terms, since it is through behavior, whether by the spoken word or by action, that persons give expression to their aims and move toward achieving them.

Because of the increased awareness of the importance of accountability and clearer goal definition, many social workers have found it useful to set forth a plan in the form of a contract. The contract is the result of negotiation between worker and client and spells out goals and tasks to be performed. Such a contract can help to make clear to the client that change in social functioning does not take place within the interview situation. Change takes place as the client takes steps to interact with others in new ways, or to alter his patterns of negotiating with the systems he faces day to day, or as systems are altered in ways that enhance his functioning. The contract itself gives a base for talking about what has and hasn't been done and why and serves as a vehicle for making choices, including choices as to what mode or modes of intervention to take.

Intervention

Intervention is activity on the part of the worker to bring about change so that the client can participate more effectively in the social system in which he is involved. In addition to the actions taken by the worker in obtaining resources and setting the stage for future working on a client's problem, intervention may be undertaken with significant others, in advocacy for change, or within the client-worker relationship itself.

Intervention with Significant Others. The nature of the influence process when a worker intervenes with significant others within the client's social system is usually dependent on the extent to which she can find common ground with them so that together they can enlarge their understanding of the needs and/or problems confronting the client and find ways of helping to alleviate the attendant stresses.

It is important that a worker respect the feelings, attitudes, and beliefs of those involved in this endeavor. A common mistake of caseworkers, particularly of beginning workers, is to overidentify with their clients to the extent that they have little tolerance for what are perceived as "uncooperative" persons such as parents, teachers, and neighbors. Time may be needed to establish good working relationships so that goals and outcomes may be clarified in the change effort.

When a caseworker serves in a "host" setting, such as in a school or hospital, she is one of many staff members who are committed to rendering an overall service. In such a setting she may serve as interpreter, mediator, or facilitator in situations where there is a breakdown in communication between a client and a staff member or when there is some obstacle in the effective functioning in carrying out the purposes of the setting. By intervening, the worker hopes to ease attitudes so that responsibilities will be understood and taken by both the client and significant others in order to meet their common purposes.

In collaborative undertakings, such as when a teacher seeks the help of a caseworker because she is concerned about a pupil's behavior, the success of their combined efforts is dependent on the extent to which they can trust and respect each other's expertise in their common task. For both teacher and caseworker there is a reduction in anxiety when a responsibility is shared. Likewise, there is an opportunity to enlarge their knowledge about the pupil's behavior and the problems with which he is attempting to cope. The teacher may be encouraged to experiment with alternative ways in which she can help the pupil to feel that he is achieving, which in turn may lessen the pupil's need to compensate for failure by negative behavior. At the same time the pupil is encouraged to come to grips with what he is doing and to take positive steps to avoid the pitfalls that are defeating his purposes. Thus in this as in other collaborative undertakings, the worker uses her skills to help both participants increase their effectiveness in reaching their goals.

Intervention as Advocacy for Change. When there is evidence that the needs of a client or group of clients are not being met, a caseworker has an obligation to take an advocacy role in pressing for changes, either within the setting itself or in the larger community. She may elect to do this independently or in participation with the client when appropriate.

Within the setting itself, because she has the meaningful contacts with clients and understands their needs from firsthand knowledge, she can bring to staff or administration whatever changes she sees as desirable to provide the best possible service. These may concern such simple matters as providing appropriate reading material in a waiting room or such complex matters as doing away with outmoded procedures that interfere with flexibility in practice or outreach to clients. They should be given full consideration by all staff members involved in the effort. Changes so implemented require judgment as to their effectiveness and their influence on other services.

The changes that a worker perceives as necessary within the wider community can be related to housing codes, institutional arrangements, lack of municipal services, and the like. Here the worker may participate with other groups who have the same concerns, such as a welfare rights organization, or she may work through her professional association, the National Association of Social Workers. The overall purposes of any such changes are to help service delivery systems become more responsive to clients and their needs.

Intervention Within the Client-Caseworker Relationship. Within the client-caseworker relationship the inputs of the worker are forms of intervention that are designed to result in movement toward the desired goal. These inputs represent the responsibilities that a worker assumes for guiding, motivating, and educating in the client-caseworker relationship. The worker may become a truly important person in the client's eyes. Her verbal and nonverbal messages are studied by the client for signs of approval and disapproval. The worker must be aware of her own values, attitudes, and feelings so that she can be clear that she is helping the client to change as he wants, rather than as she wants.

Each interview should take a client one step forward in mitigating or resolving his problem. The worker's responsibility is to keep the client focused on the task upon which he is embarked, without fostering his dependency but rather strengthening his sense of autonomy.

How a worker can intervene depends on her perceptions of the client's way of dealing with life situations. Some act without giving much thought beforehand; others reflect before taking a step until they are sure it will work. Still others are so introspective that they are unable to get beyond self-analysis to take action. Others are so highly emotional that they need considerable venting of their feelings before they can act. What the worker attempts to do is to help each client build on or modify his usual coping abilities so that he can integrate thought and feeling sufficiently to be able to take the action that will further his aims.

The worker keeps in mind that no one finds change easy, even when it is desired, and least of all when it requires changing oneself and one's ways of relating to others. Since change represents the unknown, there are strong tendencies to maintain the status quo or to see problems as caused by factors outside of one's own control. There are resistances to accepting one's own responsibilities. Therefore, both client and worker respect the fact that progress is not even and that there will be ups and downs.

Most people mobilize their energies to take specific actions when they result in tangible rewards. In the casework effort, a client may be motivated by the attainment of immediate needs, such as financial assistance or benefits received from undertaking a new approach with spouse or child. Another client may find benefit in understanding aspects of his personality that he has not understood before. Moreover, the client may be benefited by the lessening of anxiety or the assurance of the worker's continued support. This is true particularly when a client has experienced severe emotional deprivation or has low self-esteem. Motivation may result as well from being challenged, or from increased competence gained through making choices that lead to productive actions. Whatever the means by which a client's motivation is stimulated, it is the caseworker's responsibility to use this knowledge of the client by bringing into the helping process those techniques of intervention that will increase the client's competence.

The worker's skills revolve around her ability to know when to be supportive, to empathize, to relieve anxiety; when to question, to stimulate, to confront; when to clarify a point or to interpret behavior. She will need to know when it is important to provide information and knowledge or to share her own experience and point of view, and how to reward the client's efforts and competence. The undertaking upon which they are embarked is a new and different experience from others in which the client has engaged. It is one that offers a means by which the client can learn to take more responsibility for his actions and anticipate or learn to deal with the consequences of the choices he makes.

Each client needs to proceed at his own pace. For some, it is important to set time limits for the accomplishment of a specific task. For others, a time limit can impose undue anxiety, so that the client is immobilized. No amount of pressure can substitute for a client's own motivation and readiness to progress; nor can a client be prompted to develop his own capacities by a caseworker's desire to provide a prescription that the client should follow. A worker may point out realities or suggest alternatives, but the client's own view of what he can do is the primary motivating force, and it should be respected as such. The worker encourages him to experiment or to take risks, but she must be ready to support and help him bear the consequences of his efforts. Both can reveiw what has happened and think about alternatives. The important element is that the client participate in discussion and make the decisions as to what he can do and/or think about in the interim between appointments. The worker stands by to handle the feelings and attitudes that accompany any change.

Evaluation

As worker and client approach the completion of their contract, the worker initiates an evaluation process. Evaluation involves reexamination of the objectives set out in the plan and a review of the progress that has been made toward those objectives. The advantage of having objectives that were limited and definable in behavioral terms during the planning is clear here. This look at the history of the helping process is often useful in helping the client to realize how far he has come. He can take pride in what he has been able to accomplish and thereby feel more confident in himself and his capacity to participate effectively in the systems in which he lives.

It is important that the evaluation include a review not only of what progress was made, but also of how the movement took place. Progress did not take place through magic. Worker and client together need to evaluate what happened. What activities of client or worker seemed most helpful? Which ones failed? Why? What might have been done differently? Dealing with such questions will, it is hoped, (1) reinforce client gains, (2) help the client to be more conscious of the problem-solving process so that he can apply it again when new difficulties arise, and (3) provide the worker with important feedback so that she can grow in her own effectiveness as a helping person.

Failures as well as successes in reaching objectives must be reviewed, though this is often painful for worker and client. Why were attempts at problem solving blocked? How might it have been done differently? Were objectives realistic? Their expectations may have been too high or the needed supports inadequate. Whatever the reasons, the worker must have the courage to face the full impact of the meaning this has for them both, since both have invested themselves in the effort. For the client, in particular, the feeling of failure can compound the sense of inadequacy that prompted him to seek help. A review of the realities that made their endeavor unproductive can serve to place the problem in perspective without undermining the client's feeling of self-worth or adequacy in other areas of his life. A sharing of their disappointment and the worker's emotional support for the strengths that are required for the client to "live in his circumstances" must not be overlooked; indeed, this in itself can be a strengthening experience.

The evaluation process often leads to discussion of problems that were not the focus of the initial contract. The client may have had concerns that could not be expressed in the beginning—perhaps because it was too risky to share them with a stranger at that time. The worker may have perceived problems the client was not ready to deal with because other concerns were more pressing to him. If the worker and client have been involved in a process that has led to movement in a desired direction, and if trust has been developed, then it is only natural that these other concerns be raised. In this instance worker and client will reinitiate the process of problem definition, exploration, and assessment, and establish a new contract. Otherwise the helping process moves into the stage of disengagement.

Disengagement (Termination)

Disengagement occurs when (1) the objectives set out in the contract have been accomplished, (2) further progress does not seem possible, or (3) external reasons—such as the worker's leaving the agency—intervene. In the disengagement process client and worker withdraw from their relationship.

This does not mean that the change process ends. If they have been successful, the client and/or significant others in his life have developed their problem-solving resources to the point where continuing progress can be made in the client's efforts to negotiate the significant social systems in his life.

Disengagement needs the worker's careful attention because the ending of a relationship can bring with it feelings of loss that may reactivate other feelings of loss the client (or worker) may have encountered at other times in his life. Feelings of anger, uncertainty, and insecurity are common, particularly if the contact has been intense or has lasted over a period of months. In these situations it is important that the client be prepared early for disengagement. By bringing up ending several weeks before the actual date of their last contact, worker and client have an opportunity to talk over feelings. Referral to another resource in the community may be appropriate, or reassurance that the client may return at a later time. If the client is one who has had difficulty trusting people and has come to trust the worker, it may be necessary for the worker to help him to find others whom he might trust. Workers have also found it useful to increase the interval between contacts as the end approaches, so that the client can feel increasingly confident of his problem-solving capacities as he moves away from dependence on the relationship.

CONCLUSION

In this chapter we have discussed some of the objectives and components of the casework process, as well as the roles that caseworkers generally assume to be necessary in working with and on behalf of clients so that they can utilize the opportunities available to them when there have been breakdowns in their abilities to function adequately in the systems in which they are involved. In so doing, we hope that these considerations can serve as basic principles upon which casework practice can be implemented in the various settings in which caseworkers function. Although each setting differs in its purposes and requires certain specialized knowledge to achieve those purposes, the worker's essential skills and knowledge can be enlarged or refined according to the needs of each setting.

The presentations in the following chapters cannot hope to cover the full gamut of services, but will introduce important areas of practice, pointing out some of the changes that are taking place. There is considerable overlap in the delivery of these services, with a variety of agencies performing similar functions. However, the fields of practice considered here revolve around services to families and children, adolescents and aging persons, as well as to those in the specialized areas of schools, corrections, health, and mental health. The changes that are taking place present a challenge to the social worker to keep an open mind and develop flexibility in the uses she makes of her practice, as well as to experiment with and incorporate new concepts and methods as they emerge and are tested for their reliability and serviceability.

SUGGESTED READING

Aptekar, Herbert H. *Basic Concepts in Social Casework*. Chapel Hill: University of North Carolina Press, 1941.

Bartlett, Harriet H. *The Common Base of Social Work Practice*. New York: National Association of School Workers, 1970.

Benjamin, Alfred. *The Helping Interview*. Boston: Houghton Mifflin, 1969.

Briar, Scott, and Henry Miller. *Problems and Issues in Social Casework*. New York: Columbia University Press, 1971.

Faatz, Anita J. *The Nature of Choice in Casework Process*. Chapel Hill: University of North Carolina Press, 1953.

Hamilton, Gordon. *Theory and Practice of Social Work*. New York: Columbia University Press, 1951.

Hollis, Florence. *Social Casework: A Psycho-Social Therapy*. New York: Random House, 1964.

Kadushin, Alfred. *The Social Work Interview*. New York: Columbia University Press, 1972.

Kanfer, F. H., and H. Phillips. *Learning Foundations of Behavior Therapy*. New York: John Wiley, 1970.

Keith-Lucas, Alan. *Giving and Taking Help*. Chapel Hill: University of North Carolina Press, 1972.

Lowe, C. Marshall. *Value Orientations in Counseling and Psychotherapy: The Meaning of Mental Health*. San Francisco: Chandler, 1969.

Meyer, Carol H. *Social Work Practice: A Response to the Urban Crisis*. New York: Free Press, 1970.

Parad, Howard J., ed. *Crisis Intervention: Selected Readings*. New York: Family Service Association of America, 1965.

Perlman, Helen Harris. *Perspectives in Social Casework*. Philadelphia: Temple University Press, 1971.

Pincus, A., and A. Minahan. *Social Work Practice: Model and Method*. Itasca, IL: Peacock, 1973.

Reid, William, and Laura Epstein. *Task-Centered Casework*. New York: Columbia University Press, 1972.

Rich, Margaret E. *A Belief in People*. New York: Family Service Association of America, 1956.

Richmond, Mary E. *Social Diagnosis*. New York: Russell Sage Foundation, 1917.

Roberts, Robert W., and Robert H. Nee. *Theories of Social Casework*. Chicago: University of Chicago Press, 1970.

Robinson, Virginia. *A Changing Psychology in Social Casework*. Chapel Hill: University of North Carolina Press, 1930.

Rokeach, Milton. *The Open and Closed Mind: Investigations into the Nature of Belief Systems and Personality Systems*. New York: Basic Books, 1960.

Siporin, Max. *Introduction to Social Work Practice*. New York: Macmillan, 1975.

Smalley, Ruth E. *Theory for Social Work Practice*. New York: Columbia University Press, 1967.

Timms, Noel. *Social Casework, Principles and Practice*. London: Routledge & Kegan Paul, 1964.

Towle, Charlotte, *Common Human Needs*. New York: American Association of Social Workers, 1952.

Whittaker, James K. *Social Treatment*. Chicago: Aldine, 1974.

8

SOCIAL GROUP WORK

SONIA ABELS
Professor, Department of Social Work
Cleveland State University

PAUL ABELS
Professor, School of Social Work
Case Western Reserve University

This chapter presents an overview of current perspectives on social work with groups. It provides a selected panorama of the variety of groups in which social workers participate. Brief case examples present an account of the social worker and the group in action. The small social group is a response, a counterforce to increased depersonalization, accelerated mechanization, and blatantly indifferent institutions. There is a growing recognition that groups provide a vital context, not only for individual growth and social change, but for enriched relationships among people and between people and their social institutions. This growing importance of the group in people's lives has particular significance for the field of social work as agency-established and self-help groups become more widespread.

HOW THE GROUP WORKS

The small group aids as a mediator between the individual and society. People learn through groups to accomplish certain life tasks and work for desired ends. Starting with the family, it is the group that offers security and opportunity. Often, people join with others for economic, political, religious and/or social-cultural reasons. The group becomes the means, or tool, that people can use on their own behalf and for others. This central concern around which people organize becomes the "point of concentration," for the group.

Mothers Against Drunk Drivers organized to combat drinking and driving. Members of Parents Without Partners meet in groups to have fun, meet new people, and share experiences with others in the same boat. Alcoholics Anonymous meetings are held worldwide, with members attending meetings three to four times a week to help them gain control over their drinking and their lives. The local Democratic or Republican caucuses meet to get candidates elected and influence legislation. Parents Anonymous is an organization where parents meet to figure out ways to improve their parenting and to end abuse of their children. Members of religious orders join for communion and reinforcement of religious commitments. The dynamics of these groups are similar. Members of each share purposes, common interests, group structures, patterns of interaction, and group norms. All groups, from their beginnings through termination, move through periods that call for new demands on relationships within the group and with the environment.

The difference between any group and groups in which there is a social worker, is the difference between what a group can do on its own, and what it accomplishes with the added skills, knowledge, and assistance that a social worker brings. The social worker's activities and roles are shaped by social work's purposes, the practice perspective of the worker, and the social agency. These activities are associated with helping members aid each other in achieving individual and collective purposes.

The central concern, or point of concentration,[1] of all social group workers, no matter what their theoretical orientation, is the interaction between and among the members in the group, and the way group purposes shape these interactional patterns. In this context, social group work is a social work process in which the worker helps the members use each other, and the group, to strengthen their social interactions and achieve their goals.

The Differences a
Social Worker Might Make

In a single-parent group a new member felt ignored by other members and stopped coming after the third meeting. The group members were not unpleasant; rather, they sometimes responded this way to new members. The new member required greater reaching out than was normal for this group. A social worker might have entered the process (the patterns of interactions) between members and the new recruit to help ease the uncomfortable feelings that arose.

Social workers, in thinking about how to intervene, might generate several assessment hypotheses that would shape their practice: (1) some members might feel uncomfortable that the person stopped participating after three meetings, (2) some might feel relieved, (3) others might not care, (4) and some might feel uneasy about the group's procedures relative to new members. Several hypotheses might also be generated around how the person who withdrew felt: He or she might feel (1) rejected, (2) relieved, (3) unconcerned, or (4) isolated from other single parents.

The worker's professional orientation and the agency's theoretical orientation most likely shape the direction and focus of the worker's intervention in this group. In most cases a social worker's orientation has been developed through his or her educational experiences.

Contemporary Group Work
Professional Orientation

Currently, three dominant group work perspectives, or models, influence social work practice with groups in a general way:

1. R.D. Vinter, "The Essential Components of Social Group Work Practice," in *Individual Change Through Small Groups*, ed. P.H. Glasser, R. Sarri, and R.D. Vinter (New York: Free Press, 1974), pp. 9-33.

interactional, treatment, and social goals. Obviously there are no absolutes and there is overlap among the different perspectives. Pappell and Rothman (1966), in a comprehensive review, refer to these models as "social goals," "remedial" (treatment), and the "reciprocal" (interactional).[2]

Within each perspective, there are distinct underlying structures identified in the above discussion of the single-parent group.

(1) The major focus of the *interactional* model is mutual aid— helping members work on enhancing relationships among themselves and the systems of which they are a part in order to achieve their desired ends.

Within this framework, the worker in the single-parent group might point out to the group what occurred. The new member came three times and dropped out. The worker might also express concern about this pattern of interaction and ask the group members their thoughts about the experience. The members might choose to discuss the issue, describe the ways they were treated when they joined, or move to make their membership policy clear.

The worker operating within an interactional framework expects the members to decide if they want to work on this issue. If they chose not to, the social worker would not press a demand, as the issue is apparently unimportant to the group. The worker's decision relates to his or her confidence in the group's decision-making process, the quality of the contract between the worker and the members, and the awareness that only those concerns that belong to the members can shape the group's work. Further, the worker knows that the serendipitous nature of human experience initiates fresh perspectives on relations with new members.[3]

(2) The major orientation of the *treatment* approach is change of the individual. In utilization of this perspective, the worker's focus is on pointing out what occurred according to the assessment of individual and group functioning. The worker might facilitate the creation of specific group conditions that foster the ability of group members to help each other become more sensitive to the meaning of entry in new situations. Further, the worker helps the group understand the consequences of adhering to one value (that is, the

2. C. Papell and B. Rothman, "Social Group Work Models—Profession and Heritage," *Journal of Education for Social Work* (1966), pp. 66-77.
3. W. Schwartz and S. Zalba, *Social Work with Groups* (New York: Columbia University Press, 1975).

value of a closed group versus an open group and its impact upon the persons who had withdrawn) as opposed to another value. The worker demands that group members work on this issue whether or not the *group* has concern with the issue. This intervention reflects the treatment orientation focus on the social/psychological growth of individual members in the group.

A derivative of the treatment framework is the behavior approach. The leader applies behavioral principles to alter either the group's pattern of behavior—such as helping them learn to give clear, unambiguous messages about acceptance or non-acceptance of new members—or the new members' behavior, for instance, by teaching them to enter more assertively. Depending upon the sophistication of the group, this decision to apply behavioral principles could be made by the worker and the agency, or by the worker, agency, and group members collectively.

(3) In the *social goals* perspective, the focus is shaping the values of the members toward appropriate social action, such as active citizenship. Group effectiveness, vitality, and responsibility are emphasized. The worker attempts to enable the group to function responsibly in its purposes, within the agency and in the community. This is done by confronting the group about its attitudes and behavior, recognizing group functioning, and using legitimate agency limits and authority.

In the single-parent group, the worker would confront the group about its responsibility to the community and the treatment of individual members and expect them to reach a socially correct value decision. The social goals perspective aims at development of individuals in groups as mature, responsible citizens.

Historically the social goals approach was the primary group work orientation. Its philosophy and methods derived from the progressive education movements of the early 1900s. "The club is a school in human relations," wrote Grace Coyle, a group work pioneer.[4] This type of group found its home in the settlements, neighboring houses, and YMCAs of America. As the methods of working with these groups became more specific, groups began to be used in medical and psychiatric settings, child guidance work, and related forms of personality treatment. Its early roots included strong egalitarian, democratic, and participatory underpinnings. The early group

4. G.C. Coyle, *Group Work with American Youth* (New York: Harper & Row, 1948).

reflected a strong concern with fulfilling democratic goals in a quickly urbanizing society and amid growing big-city alienation. Its value orientation provided the nucleus from which all subsequent group work approaches emerge, and it had strong impact on the evolution of contemporary social work principles and values. Its theorists were instrumental in initiating small group research, leading to current understanding of group dynamics. The heritage of these early contributions was built upon by subsequent group workers such as Wilson, Ryland, Knopoka, Kaiser, Northern, Hartford, and Pernell, whose viewpoints are very much alive within the dynamic social goals approach. Others, such as Trecker, Kendelsberger, and Lindeman, incorporated the social goals perspective into the area of agency administration.

Each of the three perspectives or models takes into account both individual and group interaction patterns; these three represent social group work's major perspectives.

OUR PERSPECTIVE

The discussion of approaches in this chapter is guided by the interactional approach developed by William Schwartz as articulated in "The Social Worker in the Group."[5] However, this approach has been influenced significantly by the other group work perspectives and our own theoretical interests.

The central concern of this approach is that the group is an enterprise of mutual aid, focusing on specific issues with which the group has agreed to meet. The worker's function is to mediate the group's transactions among and between members and between the group and the social agency of which they are a part, and with their environmental systems. Just as the group is the mediator between individuals to achieve their own purposes, the worker mediates to help the individual use the group, and the group to use its social institutions. These patterns are illustrated in Figure 8.1. In our view, this perspective mirrors the purposes of social work identified in the curriculum policy statement of the Council on Social Work Education, which says, in part, "The fundamental objects of social work concern

5. W. Schwartz, "The Social Worker in the Group," in *Social Welfare Forum* (New York: Columbia University Press, 1961), pp. 146-171.

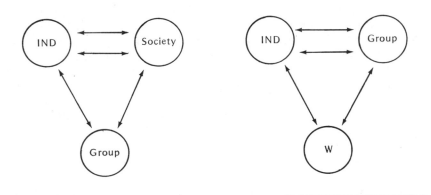

Figure 8.1.   Interactional patterns of social group work.

are the relationships between individuals and between individuals and social institutions."

STARTING WITH GROUPS

Organizing

Groups begin in various ways. In friendship groups, members who have known each other for many years may approach the agency for a meeting place and/or a worker. Neighborhood groups often recruited by the agency include social groups for older persons, classes, athletic teams, street clubs, teen clubs, social action groups, and, as in the following case,[6] a gang:

> Since I did not know anyone who could introduce me to the gang members and since I learned that the Byzantines, the gang I had been sent to work with, did not frequent any of the community centers in the area, I elected to use the "hanging around" method. After a few nights of walking around the neighborhood, I was able to pick out a candy store, a restaurant, and a street corner where an unusually large number of boys seem to congregate all hours of the day and night. I gradually found that many of the boys were members of the Byzantines. I in-

6. This case example and the others used in this chapter are taken from the authors' notes.

stalled myself as a fixture in these places. I listened openly with a friendly air to the boys' conversations, and it was not too long before some of the friendlier ones would nod to me, or look over in my direction to catch my smile when they had made a particularly biting or humorous contribution to the conversation. The restaurant had pinball machines and video games. I would put in a couple of quarters and ask the nearest boy to play with me. I was thus able to start a casual conversation with him about the newest video games. After a while, although the majority of the boys remained suspiciously aloof or indifferent, there were two or three boys with whom I had become quite friendly. Our conversations, at this early point, had to do with the coming baseball season, basketball, rock music, the best video games, and a TV rock station.

After a month in the neighborhood I had my first opportunity to explain something of my role when I heard two fellows discuss their difficulties in getting jobs—even at the temporary help places. I offered to help them, and I used this situation to invite the boys to the agency. Meanwhile, I had established contact with the teen job development program and the vocational guidance office to see if they could help in job finding for the boys, or at least in some job support. I knew it was almost impossible to find jobs for teens, but there were some city jobs opening in the summer that I hoped I could steer the boys to. The boys came to the center, and began to call me their social worker.

Other groups formed at the request of some authority or third party are initiated by such persons as parents, teachers, or physicians, who believe a group might benefit children experiencing emotional difficulties, or children in school who seem to have trouble with peers or parents with seriously ill children. A juvenile court judge may decide to refer probationers to a youth group; a mental health hospital might decide to start a ward discharge group to help its patients make the transition to a halfway house. The halfway house might decide to organize its members as a group to help them learn to work together to share common concerns of employment and living in the house. One such situation is illustrated by this first meeting of adolescent boys in a treatment center:

During the past few weeks I'd been trying to get together a discussion group, where we could discuss the concerns the boys had around Oakdale, their school, and the general community. In the past week, many of the boys talked about dating, asking girls for dates, what they called the Oakdale stigma, and their anxiety about the reaction of the girl's parents.

With this information, I felt that the time was right to start a discussion group focusing on dating and its various consequences for the boys. The boys seemed enthusiastic, hoping to get from the group some ideas on the ways to approach the girls in an effort to get dates for the various high school functions.

The Meeting

Some groups are formed to offer benefits that individual treatment might not provide. The worker with a group of boys in a Mental Development Center notes:

> These boys had no friends. There was no contact with other children their own age outside their brief time in special classes. They had little control over most things in their lives and no opportunities to test themsleves out with persons outside the family or within their institutional relationships.
>
> Some of the activities of this group revolved around trips. As they travelled, members assumed names of powerful characters. This seemed to give them a feeling of power and control, something they had very little of in their usual relations with others.

At times groups come already formed, with their own structures and ongoing programs. They want a place to meet and/or the assistance an agency might provide. The agency might recruit additional members, or the group may recruit on its own. In two support groups for single parents, one preformed group requested that the agency assign a social group worker and indicated that it would determine its own membership. In the second support group, the agency assigned members it considered appropriate and encouraged the group to recruit new members as well.

Some groups maintain an open membership, which means anyone wishing to join may (within the group's limits—such as interests, age, attendance). Some groups accept recommendations for new members from the agency, but maintain veto power. Conflicts around admissions policies can take several paths:

- The group wants to determine its own membership; this may conflict with a policy that the agency interview all applicants and determine membership assignments.
- The agency wants to recruit for the group, but the group indicates that it will do its own recruitment.

- The group wants to recruit members that do not meet the agency's eligibility criteria.

- The group wants to close its membership, but the agency has an open membership policy.

- The group or the agency maintains a policy of discrimination against a class of persons (for example, concerning ethnicity, race, sex, or sexual preference).

The group's autonomy on determination and selection of membership is important to both the agency and the group. Much is at stake in these conflicts. Relations between the agency and the group can remain productive if decisions on admissions policy are based on an adequate inquiry process, open discussion, and full participation. If consensus is unachievable, there are three options. The group may choose to leave, the agency may decide it will not serve the group, or one of the parties accepts the other's policy. When the agency, group, or worker becomes oppressive in shaping decisions about admissions, confidence in the process among the members, the worker and the agency erode.

In some agency practice, when a group accepts use of agency facilities it must accept "open" membership practices as well as other policies. In one example an advisory group to one agency's program made a decision that the agency did not support. Because the agency used its authority to reject the group's decision, almost all the members of the advisory group withdrew.

In some groups, membership is not always clear and may shift continually. Group work practice with single room occupants (SRO), as the next example illustrates, requires a great deal of membership flexibility.

In one SRO, the worker went through the halls of the residence slipping notices of a first meeting under the doors of potential members too fearful to leave their apartments:

I began the meeting by introducing myself. I explained that I was a social worker for St. Luke's Hospital and that I had been working here for about four weeks. The reason I was here was that the Hospital had found out, through working in other buildings that were similar to this in some ways, that people were often interested in some kind of group or recreation program. . . . Then a man walked in who was quite drunk and started to yell, somewhat incoherently, about the boys dying in the mud, etc. and how we just sit around. I felt uncomfortable, and when he left, I said that I hadn't really known what to do, and I was wondering what would happen if this happened in the recreation room. Mrs. V. said that people should not be let in if they were drunk, and there should be no drinking in the room. I asked if everyone agreed, and there was general agreement.[7]

While there is a wide range of beginning patterns, certain commonalities exist. In each group new relationships develop, while roles are formed and reformed, rules and norms established, goals and purposes discussed, and the means and intended ends identified and articulated. The transition from nonmember to member initiates an accommodation process that calls for modification of behavior as the person interacts with a number of new people.

Concerns Faced at Group Formation by Individuals and Group Members

As members initiate their lives together as a group within a social agency, questions and feelings directly related to this start-up experience arise. These are important factors to be considered by the worker. Figure 8.2 identifies the concerns faced by individuals and group members at group formation.

THE HELPING CONTRACT

The member is helped to overcome group formation concerns by the realization that there are common rules of behavior that are generally adhered to in most groups. From the group's inception, members and worker engage in clarifying their specific contract as it relates to purposes, goals, responsibilities, and the process to be used in achieving their objectives.[8] While this dynamic contract shifts and changes as the group evolves, it is a particularly vital integrating process in the beginning of the group's life.

Particularly in nonvoluntary groups, it is essential that the worker clearly define the limits on what he or she will report to others about the members and what activities are likely to get them into trouble. This is an important part of the worker's commitment. It does not mean that the worker promises confidentiality in order to buy

7. J. Shapiro, "Dominant Leaders Among Slum Hotel Residents," *American Journal of Orthopsychiatry* 39 (1969), p. 644.

8. B. Seabury, "The Contract: Uses, Abuses and Limitations," *Social Work* 21 (1976), pp. 87-88.

	Task	Social-Emotional
Individual	"What do I want?" "What can I give the group?"	"My role?" Will I be liked? Will I like them? Will the worker like me? Will he or she help me? Do I like him/her? How much does this group mean to me?
Group	"What do we want to do together?" Purpose Expectations Rewards "How?" Activities Structure (control) Members	"How to deal with stress?" "Can we function?" Will we be permitted? Will the leader let us?

Figure 8.2. Concerns faced at group formation by individuals and groups.

confidence, but that the worker levels with the group about what he or she can or will do. Furthermore, when conflicts do arise, the worker will attempt to work them out with the members. The worker may say something like the following:

> I'll try to tell you how I work with the court. And the rest of you think about whether the idea is correct, OK? I don't tell the court what we talked about. If you break the law, I'll try to get you to straighten it out. If it's really bad I'll go with you to court. I'll do what's right to protect you and to protect other people.

Often agreements on goals and actions are forgotten, ignored, or altered. There are many reasons for this, including testing the worker's readiness to follow through, new information (about each other, interests, environmental demands) leading to change in group focus, and wide variation in the members' capabilities to function in the particular group. The worker understands these dynamics and agreements are reexamined with the members. The group contract is dynamic; it is always changing. Decisions surrounding the changes come through dialogue among members and with the worker.

Contract: An Aid to Group Directing

Although the contract negotiation process starts with the initial worker-member encounter, an agency's contractual obligations are often known or assumed in advance, through its community image, its functions, and its programs as described in bulletins or newspaper articles. Once the worker and the members mutually decide upon the group goals, means, and programs, the worker can rightfully expect group members to work on the issues that brought them together.

The worker's ability to help the group focus on specific concerns is essential to the group's success. A clear work focus releases the energy of both members and worker so that they can carry out their parallel functions. The members' functions are to aid each other in the mutual enterprise; the worker's function is to nurture mutual aid behavior by supporting members' shared interests in group tasks.

In this process of focusing upon goals, purposes, and objectives, efforts are directed toward clarifying the means by which mutually agreed-upon goals are to be achieved. Some means will be known; others will be discovered by the members and/or the worker. Clarity is required about those things that might be out of bounds. For example, parents participating in a treatment group might want the worker to report on their child's behavior. It is crucial that the worker understand the parents' real request, and explain the boundaries (they may not understand what is happening to their child). The worker could recognize the parents' concern and indicate that he or she cannot provide the information, but could offer to set up a meeting between the parents and the child-care staff.

In working with a nonvoluntary group, clarification of appropriate behavior is essential. In group work with parents who abuse their children, the worker must make clear that abuse is not permissible and must expect that the members support the principle with each other. In a women's correction facility, a cottage group's policy was that violations be reported by the violating member to the total group. The worker was obligated to remind a woman who broke the furlough rules that she was expected to report it to the group. The violating member preferred that the correction worker take responsibility for applying the appropriate restrictions for the violation, rather than reporting it to the group. The worker reminded her that the worker was also responsible to uphold the terms of the contract of the group.

Clarifying boundaries is an attempt to set ground rules for appropriate and acceptable behavior. Some issues are sticky, as often no hard-and-fast rules exist. When group members tell a worker they are about to engage in illegal activity, it seems probable that they may be ambivalent and want help. Gang workers report that their group members frequently report challenges to fight to their workers so that face-saving options can be considered.

Contract: An Aid to Engaging Members in the Work of the Group

---

The process of helping members focus and decide on things to be done is the beginning of real work. This requires an engagement of members around their common ground. The demand for work in the group comes from environmental factors. For example, a group of parents tries to effect change in a hospital policy that limits children's access to health care, or members of a single-parent social support group may desire competence in dealing with the divorced spouse. In some situations, the worker serves as a conduit for the demand to work by asking the group to examine its process and invest some energy, thought, and feeling in the tasks at hand. Group work theorists stress the importance of relationships and the centrality of trust and confidence if help is to occur.[9] The mutuality of decision making implied in the contract quickens this process. In essence, the worker says, "I know it takes time to feel confident in this process, in me, and in each other. Can we try out that trust in this small, safe area that we have agreed to work on? If this works, we can move on to increasingly significant areas." Empathic commitment by the worker is articulated throughout the dynamic process of contracting.

The kind of contract developed beyond the quintessential shared purposes of member, worker, and agency depends on several factors:

(1) members' age and ability to reason
(2) individual and group purposes and goals
(3) agency-worker relationship with the group
(4) agency and worker's commitment to democratic practice principles
(5) distribution of power among agency, worker, and group
(6) value principles that guide agency practice

9. G. Konopka, *Social Group Work: A Helping Process* (Englewood Cliffs, NJ: Prentice-Hall, 1963).

(7) sensitivity of the agency and worker to the issues faced by vulnerable populations, including minorities and women
(8) voluntary/nonvoluntary structure of the group membership
(9) confidence of worker and group in the value of this mutual aid enterprise

The basis of contract is mutual commitment, trust, and hope. Commitment to work toward the achievement of desired ends is possible through the mutual cooperation that occurs in the contracting activity.

SETTING THE CONTEXT FOR HELPING

The worker's helping behavior is carefully observed by the members in the early stages of the group's life. The ways in which the worker responds to the members are assessed carefully by members. Members wonder: What are we doing here? How safe am I? Can this worker and the others members understand me? What are the expectations? The worker is part of the members' environmental context, and any action on his or her part may have important consequences for the members. The worker's intent is to model respectful behavior toward members even when they behave poorly or provocatively. In the following example, this occurs in the first meeting of a probation group. Chris Santiago is the worker:

> The boys sang in unison. "Beat it . . . Beat it . . . Chris Santiago. Beat it . . . Beat it . . ." Everyone claps. Chris calls . . . "Settle in, settle in. It's not easy for any of you and I'm not finding it too good either." Torrence comments, "If you don't find it so good, why don't you leave?" Chris says, "I can, but you can't and that one we talk seriously on. You may not want to come to this group, you may not even like it, but you have to come."

The concept of reciprocity, in which respect is returned for respect—or, in other terms, "an eye for an eye"—often gains respect from some members. The worker operates under a different moral framework, offering respect even under conditions in which members do not act respectfully. This "odd" behavior continually puzzles some groups and confronts them with an ambiguity with which they must come to terms. Faced with a worker who confronts members with a belief that they are worthy of value, without using his or her position to control, reject, or to punish, forces members to experience the worker differently than expected. The worker consistently offers positive regard. This does not mean that the worker is uninvolved. Santiago does confront; he limits inappropriate behavior and demands focus and work by the members on the temporal tasks of the group. Yet he, *the worker*, responds differently, respecting members under all conditions.

This respect for persons is also exemplified in demands for participatory decision making, a natural expectation in most social work groups. The worker attempts to help the members clarify and understand that participatory processes are part of the group's mutual commitment. It may take a while before this orientation is reflected in the members' ability to make shared decisions, but it is in this context of participatory decision making that the basic values of social work translate into worker actions. In the following excerpt, we see the worker introducing ideas about what life in the group might be like and what would have to take place in order for the group to achieve authentic participation:

> Roberto, standing up again on the chair, "Is this what we gonna do? Talk about pee and Pleaser's you know what?" Chris is uncertain as to Roberto's motivation. "Sit down Roberto and I'll try to tell you how I work with the court. And the rest of you think about whether the idea is correct. OK? If you break the law, I'll try to get you to straighten it out. I'll tell the court if it's really bad. I'll do what's right to protect you and to protect other people." John looks at the worker and the other, "Man what's the value in talking here? You're a regular fink reporter." Pey shaking his head looks at Roberto. "This group sucks." Some of the others nod in agreement. The worker responds. "Cut the . . . You know the real place. You're playing the old con game, and I'm not guilty. You broke the law, you got probation because they thought it was better and they sent you to this group. And, this group is a helping group. If you break the law and it can be fixed legally we'll do that and talk about it here, all of us know what to do and then we'll do it."

Earlier we reflected on group work's historic emphasis on mutual aid. Mutual aid is the core for all social group work practice. The combined creative intelligence of the group far outweighs the ability of the worker, and group participants accept ideas more readily from those with similar life experiences. Being in the same boat adds primacy and vitality to mutual aid obligations. Members of the group bring knowledge of their own experiences. It is this richness of "present knowledge" that strengthens the members' ability to act upon their own, or the group's, purposes.

For example, in a battered women's group, the knowledge that others have gone back and forth to their husbands and then finally found a way to move out of the battering situation gives both hope and knowledge to other women. It is this sharing of others' experiences and the expression of this knowledge that gives members the expanded knowledge base for their own decisions. Group workers recognize that persons learn their behavior primarily through experiences with others. The consequences of these associations and social experiences create and sustain new behaviors. Recent research on social networks and support groups provides substantial evidence on the significance of continuity and reciprocity of social relationships for human development.[10] As Kurt Lewin's research demonstrated, the presence of a peer group increases the probability that people will maintain the commitments previously made in primary groups.

The small group is an important vehicle for sustaining and supporting new behaviors. In studies of loss, unemployment, life-threatening illness, abuse, or mental illness, the availability of a support group significantly correlates with the ability to survive. Thus the small group becomes an important tool in the hands of the capable social worker.

THE DEVELOPMENT OF THE GROUP: THE FIRST TRANSITIONAL CONTEXT

Groups develop in stages, moving from one stage to the next. These transitions contain the dynamic elements of each group. The beginning transitional context in groups shapes the group structure. Group structure is the way the group organizes itself to work. The processes of forming this structure constitute a significant point of concentration for the worker. It is structure that promotes and enhances optimal possibilities for mutual aid. The worker's role at this stage is significant in the group's development. Some studies indicate that the more active the worker is in the early stage of the group's development, the more likely it is that the group will turn to the

10. For example, see M. Hammer, "Social Networks and Schizophrenia," *Schizophrenia Bulletin*, 4, 4 (1978); A.H. Collins and D.L. Pancoast, *Natural Helping Networks* (New York: National Association of Social Workers, 1976).

worker for assistance and answers rather than use its own membership resources.[11] Bion, for example, notes what he calls the "emotionality" in groups: a tendency for groups to depend upon authority as a way to avoid work on its own primary tasks.[12] The continual looking to the worker as the authority becomes problematic. When group members give greater value to knowledge based on the position of authority, later group development can be impeded. Fostering a structure that enhances group mutuality challenges the group toward a form of interdependence.

Structuring the role of the worker in ways that support the demand for the group to do its own work facilitates development of the group's own mutual aid system. If dependency upon the worker is reinforced in the structural stage of group life, similar expectations may develop in later transitions.

During the transition from outsider to member, the dynamics of member interactions shape and modify the group's structure. Individual and membership interests are processed with attempts to synthesize individual interests with group interests. The individual, group, and worker agendas are modified and examined; roles are developed and swapped, and, finally, if the group is to work, a collective image is formed. Individual agendas consistent with membership and group interests are accepted and reciprocated. For example, within a group of parents who had abused their children, an individual agenda might be making a friend, but the group's agenda is improving the quality of parenting and ending the abuse. Clearly there is a synthesis between the two agendas. In a single-parent group, an individual agenda might be "making out," whereas the group agenda is helping members deal with relationships with the opposite sex. Agenda differences that lead to conflict may impede the group's development.

The worker's intervention, spotlighting the conflicting agendas as obstacles to the group development, provides members an opportunity to determine their own strategies for conflict resolution. The worker seeks to help the members find synergistic solutions in which no one need sacrifice a point of view. It is in the development of the common ground, the common concern, that ways to work together are found. The members' encounters with conflict as they search for the common ground make group development a reality.

11. S. Henry, *Group Skills in Social Work: A Four-Dimensional Approach* (Itasca, IL: Peacock, 1981).

12. W. R. Bion, *Experiences in Groups* (New York: Basic Books, 1961).

Out of this conflict and the group's work, bonding among the members occurs.

COHESION/GROUP BONDS

For the group to function at its best, members must feel a positive attraction, a sense of shared interest, and the belief that this enterprise is worthy of energy and investment. This attraction is called "group cohesiveness" and it can be an important factor in the group's ability to achieve its purposes over time. Strong cohesion make it more likely that the group will accomplish its tasks. The reason that cohesive groups are more successful seems to be that the energy focused on group maintenance can be redirected to the accomplishment of major tasks. Furthermore, strong cohesion indicates that the group's structure and norms are accepted by the members.

Three prerequisites must exist before strong group bonds are developed. First, the interactions take place among people who like each other. Second, the group seems to be accomplishing its tasks and purposes. Third, the agency and worker have positive interactions with the group.

Another value of cohesiveness lies in the group's collective response to external threats. In a situation of common fate, members and the worker have potent influence upon each other. But sometimes cohesiveness, if associated with increased uniformity and diminished diversity, dulls the group's ability for creative solutions. The worker helps the group develop a balance of cohesiveness with respect for diversity. That is, as conflict occurs, either among the members' interpersonal relationships or within the group's purposes and tasks, the worker challenges the members to encounter the obstacles so that the group can move forward in its endeavor. Meeting this challenge, and discovering that conflict can be dealt with and a consensus reached without violation of individual integrity or destruction of membership relationships, informs the group of its power of growth and survival. The group's ability to confront obstacles reinforces reasons for the group's existence and gives an idea of what the members and the group can be if they work together and accomplish their goals.

The social work may be viewed as a symbolic representation of the members' relationships with each other and the worker. Group is an abstraction. The group in reality does not exist beyond the concrete relations among members. What does exist are the members and their relationships with each other and with people and institutions outside the group. The group is symbolic in the sense of value members give it. Some group members may consider the group a force in their lives, while others may not give it the same order of value. The group's value for its members depends upon how often it meets, the frequency of association outside the group, the press of competing relationships, access to external resources, and the group's external image. Within the group, if relationships deepen, members are valued, and reciprocity and equity are supported, the group's symbolic representation takes on powerful significance for the members.

Group Conflict

Conflicts in groups are created by environmental stresses or intermember differences in value orientations. Such conflicts often raise concerns as to who should be in or out of the group. Workers facing such conflicts require clarity about their own perspectives on group membership. In some groups membership decisions are out of the members' hands. Such groups are prone to conflict and, in these situations, the worker helps the group confront ways in which it can respond to these external stresses.

In a group in which a member is disruptive or nonproductive, the group determines procedures it needs to decide whether the member should remain or be dismissed. Some membership decisions are determined by the nature of the contract the group has with the agency. In the following excerpt, we see efforts to influence the worker to put a member out of the group. This is a parents' group in a housing project, the purpose of which is to help the parents help each other learn parenting skills.

Parent/Conflict Record

At the end of the second session, Mrs. Green offered to drive me to my office. Mrs. Holmes was gone when the offer was made. By the way the remaining members were grouped, I concluded that Mrs. Green wanted to speak to me in an official or semi-official capacity.

She expressed herself as concerned about Mrs. Holmes' effect on the group. Nobody liked her and she made trouble. I wondered what Mrs. Green wanted to do. As a committee person, Mrs. Green felt that it was her responsibility to do something—she didn't know what—she wondered about the exclusion of Mrs. Holmes.

I thought the exclusion was a drastic measure and that we ought to be careful of how we used it. I reviewed what we knew about Mrs. Holmes from what Mrs. Holmes had told us before, during and after the meetings. I stressed particularly that she had been deserted twice by a person from whom she had a right to expect consideration and protection. I touched on other incidents in Mrs. Holmes' life as she had related them to us, and then concluded that Mrs. Holmes knew she wasn't liked. Sometimes when people know that, they do and say odd and upsetting things.

In this situation the worker intervenes by encouraging Mrs. Green to see that part of the task of this particular group is to assist people like Mrs. Holmes, and that if Mrs. Holmes is excluded from the group, the group is not achieving its goals.

GROUP TASKS/WORKER TASKS

There are two categories of tasks present in the relationship between the group and the social worker. The group has a set of tasks to accomplish so as to achieve its goals and maintain itself as an autonomous group. The worker's tasks relate directly to helping the group with its tasks. Both sets of tasks—the worker's and the group's—operate throughout the group experience, often changing from moment to moment. Sometimes the group works on its goals, or on mutual aid, or on the obstacles that impede work. As the group is engaged the worker carries a set of functions different than those of the group. For example, in the example of the probation group given above, Santiago's task is to help the group members help each other meet the requirements of probation. Santiago cannot meet those requirements, nor can he do the work the members must do to help one another. That work belongs to the group.

Figure 8.3 identifies the group and worker tasks. The possibility for carrying out these tasks rests on the availability of and access to a variety of social and economic resources, both within and outside the group, that may be relevant to the group's goals and purposes.

ASSESSMENT

Assessment in group work practice is an attempt to figure out what's going on as the group members engage in their work together. This is an ongoing process requiring the worker to pay attention,

The Group Tasks	The Worker Tasks

Task accomplishment
  The group works to achieve its
  specific goals and purposes.
	Identifying the common ground
	
	Focusing the work of the group
	  Partializing

Group maintenance
  To find ways for the members to
  respond to each other in the context
  of mutual aid. To function construc-
  tively and to maintain itself over
  time in order to accomplish its
  purposes.
	Identifying obstacles and challenges group
	  to work
	    Empathic reaching and responding
	
	Contracts
	
	Fostering mutual aid

Autonomous functioning
  To achieve relative control of the
  ways the group reacts to its
  immediate environment. To
  develop and maintain viable
  relationships with its environment
  so that it can function as an
  autonomous group.
	Engaging group in exploration and discovery
	  Providing relevant information
	
	Stimulating utilization of resources—members,
	  worker, agency, environment
	    Advocacy
	
	Helping members use and give feedback
	
	Helping members gain access to other systems
	
	Lending a vision of hope

Figure 8.3. The group/worker tasks.

listen, and respond appropriately. Assessment is active, often simultaneous with the worker's activities of helping the group. In Mary Richmond's terms, assessment translates into asking the members the question, "What's going on here?"

A worker might ask some of the following questions as a means of assessing the group:

(1) *What does the member want from the group?* "Mr. Lane, it is sometimes helpful to ask the others in this hospital burn group how they manage their personal relationships with their wives."

(2) *What are the group's purposes and goals?* "Last week everyone complained that this group of single parents was unclear about what it wanted to do. Perhaps we can figure out what's making it difficult to clarify what this group wants to do."

(3) *What is the task the group is working on?* "There seems to be a lot of ill feeling in this battered women's group that we ask people to leave the shelter after two weeks, and yet everyone knew this was the policy. What's going on?"

(4) *What is the group's structure?* "Mr. Jamison said to one member in the group of parents, 'It's time you listened to the other members as well as telling us what we should do.' "

(5) *What is the nature of the contract the worker has with the group?* "Sure, it's frightening to talk about your children's leukemia, yet everyone wanted to. What happened?"

(6) *What are the ways in which members interact with each other that cause problems for other members?* "Each time this group sits down to talk about what you're going to do about the landlord, everyone starts to yell at Mrs. Heller, telling her it's her fault that the landlord doesn't do anything. What's happening?"

(7) *What is each member's role in the group?* "What does the group expect from its members in this burn group?"

(8) *What kind of relationship do the members have with the worker?* "I'm sorry you did not tell the entire group that you were not going to participate in the demonstration. We forgive you, knowing you're no more perfect than the rest of us."

(9) *What are the group ties with other groups and organizations?* "It certainly was disappointing that the union was unable to provide this group with money to lobby at the State House. Maybe some of the other unemployed persons' groups can join us in raising funds."

(10) *What sociocultural factors are relevant to understanding and working with this group?* In an interracial group: "How come you all didn't show last week for our swim at the Recreation Club?" "Hey, worker, don't you know the membership is restrictive?"

Assessment aids the transitions in the group by smoothing those rough spots that might delay the movement of the group from one stage to the next.

PROGRAM

One unique aspect of social group work is the use of programs and activities as a medium to achieve group its purposes. The combination of verbal and nonverbal activities has a vigorous tradition in group work practice: music, art, literature, games, drama, movies, dance, psychodrama, role play, cooking, puppets, and all forms of program activities. These activities enrich group life, aid in group development, and help the group achieve its goals. For example, in an urban community mental health center, the members (identified as persons with chronic mental illness) participate in all sorts of program groups for the purpose of social rehabilitation. Each group is formed around a different activity: current events, Black awareness, feminist consciousness raising, creative writing, music, poetry, and jogging, to mention a few. In these social rehabilitation groups, a program is designed to achieve a specific focus. For example, the purpose of the current events group was to help the members focus on public events, discuss newsworthy issues with each other, and relate the news to their own life experiences. Each member brought in a current event topic, described it to the other members, and took responsibility for leading a specific discussion. This simple program reflected the mutual contractual agreements among agency, members, and group worker. It is important that a program introduced either by the worker or members reflects the contractual agreements and elements that lead the group to its desired intentions.

Program serves the group, and needs to emerge out of the life of the group. Program is not a substitute for the group's work or tasks, but rather a tool of these tasks. For example, members of an agency staff group were concerned that they were not listening to each other. Through assessment, they discerned that the problem was that they were habitually not listening. They planned a program to improve their listening skills. Staff members kept journals, noted when they listened or did not listen, the activity at the point of listening/not listening, who was speaking, the topic under discussion, and the time. They compared notes with each other to enrich the data base and stimulate discussion. The program helped them become more skilled in listening to each other, and improved their ability to listen to clients.

In a probation group, the initial program consisted mainly of talking and jabbing at each other, verbally and physically. The worker's proposed contract was for the group members to talk about ways that they could help each other meet the requirements of probation. At first, talking seriously was impossible, as members were not confident enough in themselves, each other, or the worker to talk about their concerns. Programs such as pool, food, or sports fit the group's life at that particular point in its development. These programs were not a substitute for the members' working on the issues that brought them together, but helped set the stage for the transition to mutual aid to take place. The value of the use of certain programs—such as music, games, or dance—in order to achieve specific goals is an important part of the group worker's knowledge.

Program relates to group life—not only the members' particular interests as they see them, but the problems to be resolved. Program often helps members generate a new perspective on factors blocking group transition. In a hospital discharge group, for example, program may practice activities of preparation for life out of the hospital, or any anxieties about leaving. Program could include role play about conflict with the bank, check writing, asking directions to the bank, and rides on buses to help members learn to move around the city.

In a Parents Anonymous group, the worker, noting the members' discomfort during a discussioin of the stress of parenting, suggested that stress often was a factor in child abuse. She asked the members to identify the most stressful times with their children, and to share with the others their effective ways of dealing with the stress. One parent said he learned to juggle; he liked to do it, and it made his kids laugh. The other members asked him to juggle, which he did, using doughnuts. Then everyone tried. The discussion soon led to the members' deciding to search out new ways to deal with loss of control with their children and bring the ideas to the next meeting.

In some groups, a committee plans the program, while other groups spend part of their meetings to plan activities for the following week. The worker's role in program depends upon a number of variables. Initially, the worker may play a central role in program development, consistently focusing on ways to involve members in the process. Ideally, the worker's ideas are soon seen as neither more nor less valuable than those of the members. The worker needs to consider just how much responsibility for program development each takes: If the worker does the deciding, members quickly realize this is the worker's group. For example, in an older adult program, members stopped coming to an arts and crafts group that made painted wreaths. The worker had decided upon the craft, rather than proposing the wreaths as one possibility and seeking out the participants' interests in holiday crafts.

Rules of thumb related to programming are as follows:

(1) Program connects to the work of the group.
(2) Program fosters the members' ability to work together.
(3) Program activities reflect the contractual agreements with members. Hidden agendas, such as learning how to share, are not artificially incorporated within the program activities; if they are seen as problems in the group they are opened as items to be dealt with.

It is essential that the group has some success for itself. Some groups set long-range goals that demand resources of funds, time, and people that may be beyond its initial capability. In one such situation, a group of parents of children with learning difficulties hoped to change the state educational laws so that their children could have equal access to education. The worker was able to help this group engage one aspect of the problem—public awareness. The group began publicizing the children's needs in the local press and inviting politicians to its meetings. Further steps included a membership drive to recruit other interested parents and supporters. In time the group developed the necessary resources to influence educational policies.

At times, groups propose programs that appear unrelated to the task at hand, such as a party or a trip. Doing things that are fun together is often requisite to group maintenance, since one of the groups' tasks is to maintain itself over time. The change in pace, the party, may make it possible to return to work with renewed vigor. Programming is every activity of the group, planned or unplanned, that has significant consequences for the members relative to individual and group purposes.

In the following excerpt, we see how a worker develops programs from an unexpected event, with far-reaching consequences:

> We went up to the nursery school to use the record player and they practiced teaching one another and teaching me. After a while they found some old hats. Amy and Ruthie started to burlesque an old couple dancing—Amy the man, Ruthie the woman. They were just fooling around and I decided to structure it a bit by telling them they were out celebrating their 15th Anniversary and hadn't danced together since they were dating. Eventually Amy pushed Ruthie down and picked another partner and Ruthie started bawling, "Don't leave me, I'll be good," etc., and doing this on her hands and knees.

HELPING THE GROUP WORK:
THE TRANSITION TO ACTION

The group's ability to direct its energy toward work is contingent upon the period of time it will be meeting as a group. In short-term groups, the work focus cannot wait for the building of relationships. The demand for work is present at the start. In short-term groups, such as an intake group of adult children and their parents at a nursing home, there is only one meeting. The purpose of such a group would be to help the parents and their adult children relative to placement decisions. This one meeting requires extraordinary emphasis on mutual aid, and maximum encouragement of the group participants to ask the questions that reveal the ambivalence present in these decisions. In this situation, the worker structures the meeting in such a way as to help the group work. The design must foster the group members' utilization of each other's knowledge in their inquiry process—knowledge about the nursing home, expectations, and knowledge of shared feelings of concern, apprehension, guilt, and sometimes relief.

Long-term groups require more time for testing the contract's limits and developing trust. It takes time for relationships to mature and for shared mutual commitment to emerge. During these transitions, interactions among the members change and the group balance shifts, freeing energy for the work of the group.

As the members move through their group experience together, a sense of security within the group and with each other begins to emerge. The members search for ways to assemble their needs and perspectives, and the worker and other members help turn these into forms of action. Individual behavior patterns learned over time are sometimes modified to strengthen the group's competence to work on its tasks, and mutually satisfying ways of communicating are developed. It is unlikely that a group can achieve its purposes unless this balance develops.

In the interactional approach, helping depends upon the ability of the members and the worker to communicate with each other and with environmental forces in a goal-directed and constructive manner. Communication is a vital part of the approach. The more the communication styles of the participants are nonthreatening and helpful, the more the participants feel that others are empathic to their needs and concerns.

Empathy is the ability to tune in to the nature of the other's experience and to respond appropriately to the person's feelings and thoughts. It is the ability to understand the meaning of the verbal and nonverbal forms of communication. To recall a portion of the record on single room occupancy:

> One man, large and disfigured, squeezed my hand hard; he would not let go. I guess my face showed a flash of panic and I tried to jerk my hand away. Another tenant, seeing my need, came over and whispered to me, "You just gently ease your hand away and talk to him." It worked.[13]

The fact that a member helped the worker is as important to the group as the worker helping a member. It is important to the self-image of the participant and to the members' recognition that

13. Shapiro, "Dominant Leaders Among Slum Hotel Residents," p. 644.

they have something to offer and that the worker will listen. Part of the helping process is the ability of the worker to communicate humanness and to express his or her own set of feelings relative to the particular experience. In the probation group the worker tells of his dislike of being called derogatory names:

It's 4:20 p.m., and Chris [the worker] hurries to the meeting room. This time he remembers the ice and carries with him potato chips and Fritos. Pey is the first member to arrive and laughs at Chris. "I told you you were some 'spic,' only 'spics' eat Fritos." Chris nodded, "Pey put these on the table, open them and pour them into a bowl while I do the same with the chips." He added, "I like all sorts of chips, I even like you and I don't know what you are, and if I did I would still call you by your name." Pey asked, "You want to know what I am man? You really want to know?" Chris, laughing, said, "Cut it Pey, I asked you a real question and you come back with Sesame Street." Pey's laughter filled the hall. "I'm half Irish and half Polish." Steve said to Pey, "What I really meant to say was, 'I don't like you calling me a spic.' " Pey turned around and began to talk to some of the others as they came in.

Building on the work of Schwartz, Laurence Shulman developed a series of worker action concepts directly related to assisting the group with conflicts in communication. These include concepts such as amplifying or tuning down a communication, for example, helping a more timid member to be heard by the group, reconstructing a member's hostile comment into phrasing more acceptable to the group, helping the members direct their messages to the proper person, or focusing their communication more concretely.[14]

As the worker continually mediates the group processes, the point of concentration is the demand for work and a focus on tasks. As obstacles arise, the worker helps members examine and break the problems down into parts with which they can deal. These worker skills take time to grow into a natural helping style. This development begins with the worker's awareness and sensitivity to what is happening in the life of the group, and the worker's own set of responses and feelings about these encounters.

The heart of the interactional approach is not only mutual aid, member helping member, but also changes in member behavior, resulting in changes in worker behavior. The group's character as a system includes the worker. Overall stability coexists with a constancy

14. L. Shulman, *The Skills of Helping Individuals and Groups* (Itasca, IL: Peacock, 1979).

of change in the internal process of the group. This process of change is circular, one in which engagement, commitment, and action are thematically present throughout the life of the group. The members engage each other in goal-directed activity, make commitments to respond to events in some fashion, and take action to fulfill these commitments. The consequences of these actions in turn reshape future engagement.

TERMINATION

Strong feelings about past experiences and prospects for the future mark endings and separations as transitional contexts that can be dealt with only in the present, although their content is past and future.

A group that has met for six weeks to learn to cook gourmet food may end the experience with a lavish dinner, gales of laughter, and light promises to see each other shopping for artichokes. Accompanying the laughter might be comments such as, "I'll never make the dish on my own"; "I wish this weren't over, it was so good"; and "Henry, let's get together for lunch sometime and we can talk about how you doubled the salt in the sausage, and we had to throw it out." Clearly, the members had a good time; some learned to cook, some enjoyed being with others, and all felt a general sense of sadness about the change in their Tuesday schedule. In this experience the focus was learning to cook, with members helping each other.

Contrast this with another group that has also met for six weeks. These are single parents in their first year of divorce. It is evident that their state of being differs significantly from that of the cooking group. Their purposes for joining the group were different. They were to help each other deal with the pain of divorce and to figure out with the other single parents effective ways to deal with the pain. At the end of the six weeks, their comments are similar to those of the members in the cooking group, but at a different level of intensity.

The group knew from its first meeting that it would end after six weeks, and the worker, at the third meeting of the group, spoke with the members about the approaching ending. At the final meeting one member said to the worker as they discussed what they found helpful in the group, "I think you should have scheduled this group to last ten weeks rather than six." This statement reflects some feelings about endings. Another member told the group, "I can't stand any more endings. Here I developed real attachments to some of you, and it's already over. It seems to me that's what my life is like, beginnings and endings. It's like when I was a child and my mother went off to work—what a miserable time that was, let me tell you . . ." So the litany proceeded.

These ending transitions appear more troublesome for the members and the worker involved here than they did for the cooking group. They are more troublesome because the content requires a greater level of involvement, a higher intensity due to the expectations and demands that members share feelings, concerns, and experiences with other members. The worker consistently helped the members aid each other in dealing with the terror of their losses of the previous year.

It is not unreal to suggest that many groups focus on issues that have to do with loss. Endings for such groups lead to a good deal of stress. For example, cottage groups in residential care face constant experience with loss. Children in residential treatment centers initially encounter their own grief. They mourn the loss of family and friends, lack of control, and loss of the normal day-to-day life outside the institution. These children learn that grief is an ongoing theme. Workers they care about come and go; students in field placement stay six months to a year and then leave. The children remain.

At the day camp for children considered retarded, the camp counselor talked with the children about the fact that the following week camp would be over. One child came over to the counselor and said, "You'll be lonely." Another child took the clay statue he had made and smashed it with his foot, saying, "That's mine." A young adult with Down's syndrome at a camp with his group for a weekend talked about his life, of being unable to marry, get a job, or live a normal life. The camp, his group, and his being away from home elicited feelings of loss. In a group for burn victims, members often spoke of their disfigurements and of the feeling of being unlovable. Women who have had radical breast surgery have been helped by other women sharing their own initial sense of loss and their feelings about their femininity.

Just as the starting process in groups brings strong feelings, so do endings. Beginnings and endings are transitions that require awareness of the impact on the group. While beginnings are often seen as hopeful, a new start, termination elicits a wide range of feelings about loss and hope. Termination is real, and often the easiest forms of endings raise early feelings of loss. In some sense the worker's job is to be unafraid of these intense feelings. These feelings depend upon the kind of experience members have had among themselves and with the worker, and their pregroup history. The worker helps by expressing feelings about the termination and soliciting perspectives, not by making promises that cannot be kept, such as promising members to call or write, when in fact this rarely occurs. Workers often promise that they will be in touch with group members because they care about them and fear the negative feelings that emerge at termination. Group members facing termination of the group, or loss of the worker, often feel hurt, angry, and resentful toward the worker; they often have a sense of rejection and betrayal. Children's responses to endings take varied forms: attacking the worker or the other members, blaming the group for not following through on its plans, ignoring the worker, or sometimes very clearly telling the worker of their deep sadness. Adolescents often tell the worker that he or she is unimportant to them, and might as well leave. All these undisguised feelings of loss emerge as group members end their relationships with each other and with the worker.

The worker can help by identifying feelings of loss, and by helping the members focus on the mutual enrichment gained from each other, as well as next steps. Programs that focus on the termination process, both the sad and joyful aspects, can aid the members to use each other. Discussions, a celebration, and revival of memories through pictures, stories, music, literature, dance, and poetry can serve as a medium for the work of termination. The human experience is loss. Shakespeare, at the end of *Macbeth,* reminds the audience that grief must be spoken of. The small group is an excellent context for speaking of and sharing grief.

GROUP WORK IN TRANSITION

In order to grow, a profession must change. This is particularly true for a profession that recognizes the importance of an ecological perspective and deals with social change and its impact on people. The end of world War II ushered in an era of rapid industrial growth, and also changes in views of the role of government as a provider of human services. Services to veterans, large international aid programs, displaced persons, new towns, and a rapid population increase all aided the growth of the social work profession.

The use of groups for treatment within the armed forces led to acceptance of group therapy and social work groups, particularly in psychiatric and mental health settings. This was followed in the 1960s by a strong community and advocacy orientation in group work, stimulated in part by the civil rights movement, the War on Poverty, the influx of large sums of money to deal with adolescent groups, and equal opportunity jobs and education programs. Neighborhood groups were organizing to bring services to formally disenfranchised people.[15]

The need for competent staff stimulated graduate and under-graduate programs in social work, with increased growth in social group work. Group work's systems perspective—in practice and in ecological theoretical underpinnings—is relevant in an era of rapid change.

Concurrent to this development, the National Association of Social Work was established. It was formed in the mid-1950s from various social work professional associations, including those concerned with psychiatric social work, medical social work, and group work. This unified organization enhanced social work's ability to present a strong forum for lobbying, fund raising, and social action. Its theoretical perspective reflected the one-to-one counseling approach and slowed the theoretical advancements developed by the group work chapters. For example, a single NASW journal replaced *The Group,* and the number of articles devoted to social group work was limited.

While group workers created new and exciting services in the poverty program, the platforms for sharing these ideas shrunk. At the same time, other groups, such as nurses, psychiatrists, and psychologists, discovered the group and developed their own form of "group therapy." These "new" approaches appeared in numerous new journals that sprung up in the 1970s. Recognizing the need for social group work to express its contributions, Pappel and Rothman began a new journal, *Social Work with Groups.* Beginning with its first issue in 1978, it became a catalyst for revitalizing group work. They also initiated and supported the first conference of the Committee for the Advancement of Social Work with Groups in 1979. Cleveland was selected as the conference site in order to honor Grace Coyle, a founding group worker, who had been professor of social group work at Case Western Reserve School of Applied Social Sciences (SASS). Chaired by Paul Abels, a member of the SASS faculty, the conference drew more than 400 people from the United States and Canada. These conferences continue to be held annually. The fragmentation of

15. S.L. Abels and P. Abels, "Social Group Work's Contextual Purposes," *Social Work with Groups* 3 (Fall 1980).

communities by urban renewal, high mobility rates, and the destruction of friendship patterns by profound unemployment has given group work another task, to strengthen and connect people with each other.

SELF-HELP GROUPS
AND SOCIAL NETWORKS

Self-help groups are voluntary, small group structures connected for mutual aid and for the accomplishment of a specific purpose—usually peer-related support. Some groups, such as Alcoholics Anonymous, can become large networks. The expansion of the self-help movement can be seen as an outgrowth of bureaucratic and professional neglect, the liberating movements of minorities and women, and the realization of many people that helping each other is another way of receiving help. Shatan, who has worked with Vietnam vets, notes, "The men sit on packing crates, filing cabinets, and radiators in a ramshackle downtown office building. They have been listening to each other since December, 1979, under the auspices of the Manhattan Chapter of the Vietnam Veterans Against the War. 'In the absence of patterns tailor made for us,' explained one veteran, now coordinator of the rap groups, 'we had to structure our own solutions.' "[16]

The success of programs such as AA, the desire to transcend social fragmentation, and an underground awareness that voluntary associations strengthen the very fabric of the democratic society stimulated the growth of self-help groups. These groups are an expression of hope, of a belief in oneself. The groups tend to share collective responsibility and minimize hierarchical structures.

For example, parents of handicapped children wanted help for their children, but they also wanted help themselves in dealing with their children. They were eager to find out how other parents were dealing with the same problems and how to help their children at home. Often they expressed their resentment of diagnostic prescriptions for their problems, and frequently they felt guilty about asking physicians for more information and help. They wanted to meet among themselves in order to share the real-life circumstances of their experiences.

16. C. Shatan, "The Grief of Soldiers: Vietnam Combat Veterans' Self-Awareness Movement," *American Journal of Orthopsychiatry* 43 (July 1973), p. 64.

Within the social work profession, group work functions in a manner that supports self-help. While group work projects potential hierarchical issues—the group worker as expert, organizer, or the central person in the group—the countervailing theme in group work practice emphasizes mutual aid, people helping each other. Many self-help groups seek ways to use the professional without giving up their autonomy and self-help character. A number of programs melding the professional and the self-help group have developed and are models for how this partnership can function.

CONCLUSION

We have described group work as a social work process, which suggests that all of the values, knowledge, and skills of the profession are brought to bear on helping people in the group to develop their potential, enhance their social relationships, and accomplish their goals and common purposes with other members. In our orientation to social group work we suggest that there is a constant exchange between worker and group that enhances their use of each other to accomplish their mutual goals. In social group work, the point of concentration is always on ways in which the members can help each other. There is not just "a worker." All the participants are workers, who, with the added skills of the social worker, can learn to help each other. The group with worker, at its best, is an ever-evolving testament to mutual aid. Social group work as mutual aid is an endeavor undertaken in the hope that people working together on their own behalf can gain control over their lives.

9

COMMUNITY ORGANIZATION

P. NELSON REID
Director, Department of Social Work
North Carolina State University

Social work is a profession concerned with the responsibility of people to and for one another. It is concerned with the character and boundaries of that responsibility and, to an extent, with the actual carrying out of that responsibility in a systematic fashion. The organization of this responsibility between persons through economic, political, and social transactions is the main business of "community," and the concept and actuality of "community" have figured importantly in social work since its inception as a profession in the nineteenth century.

Social work is an overtly "moral" profession in pursuit of what one might call the "right order of relationships" in society. Early writers as diverse as Jane Addams and Josephine Shaw Lowell agree on the necessity of social work to make community work. Lowell, borrowing her vision of the community remade by social work from Abram Hewitt, says,

> Here are the rich and there are the poor, separated by the great mass of honest, hardworking, prosperous, well-to-do people. The problem is to reduce the number of the poor by finding channels of occupation for them so they do not feed and prey upon the product of the industrious. The problem is to take the idle rich . . . and to develop in them the sense of trust, that they hold these profits which have been taken from the earnings of the great mass . . . (for you know perfectly well that whatever the rich have has to be earned day by day by those who work) to develop in them a sense of trust and so to organize the channels of communication between those who are consumers otherwise of the fruits of human industry, and those deserving laborers who have drifted out of the ordinary channels of occupation; to bring these two agencies together and make them useful to each other so that the great working class may accumulate still more, and not to be shorn of their proper earnings, as they otherwise will be, by the consumption of the poor and rich.[1]

Addams is concerned with the development of a social ethic that supports the concept of social responsibility beyond the family at the community level:

> Certain forms of personal righteousness have become to a majority of the community almost automatic. It is as easy for most of us to keep from stealing our dinners as it is to digest them. To steal would be for us to fall sadly below the standard of habit and expectation which makes virtue easy. In the same way we have been carefully reared to a sense of family obligation, to be kindly and considerate to the members of our own households and to feel responsible for their well being. . . . If the fulfillment of these claims were all that a righteous life required, the hunger and thirst would be stilled for many good men and women, and the clew of right living would be easily in their hands.[2]

In the nineteenth century, when social work as a professional matter was conceived and initiated, the ideas of rational control over society and the ability of human will to promote progress were quite

1. W. R. Stewart, *Philanthropic Work of T. S. Lowell* (New York: Macmillan, 1911), pp. 154-155.

2. J. Addams, *Democracy and Social Ethics* (Cambridge, MA: Harvard University Press, 1964), pp. 1-2.

powerful. Social work is an expression of this faith in rationality and will. But the twentieth century, in which social work has endured adolescence and exhibited a modest maturity, has not dealt kindly with rationality, will, or progress. While the human social possibilities seemed boundless in the late nineteenth century, the twentieth century has seen the emergence of a profound skepticism and an overriding concern with the failures of social life. Disorganization, decline, insecurity, breakdown, conflict, and annihilation are the unfortunate control words and concepts of our own time. Governments, certainly Western governments, and the quasi-public social professions such as social work, rarely exhibit any coherent vision for a more perfect future. Our public life is well captured in Oakeshott's oft-quoted statement of 1951, which he made, ironically, upon his succession to the Harold Laski Chair of the London School of Economics:

> In political activity . . . men sail a boundless and bottomless sea; there is neither harbour for shelter nor floor for anchorage, neither starting place nor appointed destination. The enterprise is to keep afloat on an even keel; the sea is both friend and enemy; and seamanship consists in using the resources of a traditional manner of behavior in order to make a friend of every inimical occasion.[3]

Dealing with adversity as it develops, and without grand hopes or expectations, is surely characteristic of American public life, and probably private life as well. But optimism is not extinguished and there is still a strong current of feeling in American life that if something is wrong it ought to be set right. In 1953, Robert Nisbet, a sociologist of considerable note, published *The Search for Community,* in which he argues that history, at least in its recent industrial form, has destroyed the "primary associative areas of society." Behind the "preoccupation" of people with community is

> the growing realization that the traditional primary relationships of men have become functionally irrelevant to our state and economy and meaningless to the moral aspirations of individuals. We are forced to the conclusion that a great deal of the peculiar character of contemporary social action comes from the efforts of men to find in

---

3. D. P. Moynihan, *Maximum Feasible Misunderstanding* (New York: Free Press, 1974), p. 8.

large scale organizations the values of status and security which were formerly gained in the primary associations of family, neighborhood, and church.[4]

Nisbet, unwilling to languish in despair, proposes the creation of new social institutions that would replace or replicate the decaying or defunct traditional social units. He saw in this the remaking of history by human will. The older revolution of middle classes that gave us free men and free markets sought to create circumstances in which autonomous individuals could propser, free from the oppressions of class, kinship, and community. But the emphasis on individualism was destructive to traditional social cohesion, so that now, according to Nisbet, we must develop intermediate social systems that allow "autonomous groups" to prosper.

While Nisbet's prescription has not been terribly influential, his sense of the failure of community is widespread, and the idea that new associations and relationships among people in communities are necessary to solve problems is everywhere accepted. The idea that community exists imperfectly and that a mechanism exists for improving it through the formation of new alliances and associations, or the rearrangement of old ones, is the foundation of community organization in social work. Whatever might be said about the diversity of things that go on under the general category of community organization, that they are all problem solving, concerned with making a more perfect community, and optimistically interventionist—believing that a technology of change exists and is applicable—cannot be disputed. Beyond this rather general common set of assumptions and focus, the divergence of concepts, purposes, and methods is very apparent.

STRANDS OF COMMUNITY ORGANIZATION

In the history of professional social work in the United States it is possible to distinguish two major and two lesser strands of thought and action within the larger area of community organization. Each of these strands has a somewhat separate origin and each major strand has been dominant over the other at one time or another in the

---

4. R. Nisbet, *Quest for Community* (New York: Oxford University Press, 1953), p. 49.

history of social work. These strands have been described by a number of writers in community organization and have been labeled variously. Rothman, as a notable example, identifies social action, social planning, and locality development as the three "models" of community organization practice. But perhaps more descriptive is the identification of the two major strands as (1) resource development and (2) interest group development and the lesser strands as (3) community treatment and (4) community development. Resource development is that activity related to the development and support of social welfare services. It encompasses fund raising, social service planning, and the development of networks of support for social welfare programs. Interest group development consists of the processes of organizing groups expressly for the purpose of political or social influence and changing the balance of interests that are influential in a community. Community treatment refers to those overtly "capacity"-development or problem-reduction activities represented by self-help groups, neighborhood improvement, or other community activities designed to benefit the participants in a socio psychological way or to increase the ability of groups to function. Community development is made up of those activities concerned with the transfer of technology, the development of a community economic base, or the development of political structures at the community level, and is often practiced in the United States by those associated with the Agricultural Extension Service and by the United Nations and various international service agencies. Each of these activities has a rich and interesting history and each deserves elaboration.

RESOURCE DEVELOPMENT

Social work as a profession in the United States was largely the invention of the late nineteenth century charity organization movement. That movement established social work as a professional, "scientific" process, and liberated aid to the poor from its association with church morality or political ideology. The charity organization society (COS) was a manifestation of a public morality concerned with aiding the poor in a responsible, scientific way that would not interfere with the justice of the marketplace or the overall development of society. It was heavily influenced by nineteenth-century moralism and by social Darwinism, but it was basically secular, optimistic, and rationalistic, believing in the capacity of persons to change and the obligation of persons to move themselves, others, and the society toward perfection. One of the problems in implementing this vision was the proliferation of private, often religion-affiliated, organizations providing aid to the needy. As its name implies, the COS would organize charities so that only the needy would receive aid and only in the proper amount from a single source. The charity organization societies grew rapidly over the 1880s and early 90s in larger American cities and engaged in what must be regarded as the earliest professional community organization in social work. The COS concern with raising money, with creating widespread support among the better-off members of the community, and with planning the expenditure of money in a rational, efficient, and effective way (appealing to the dominant values of American society) began a process that we would all recognize as alive and well today in our own community's United Fund. Today's United Fund is a nearly direct descendant of the community welfare councils first organized in 1908, and those councils were the indirect descendants of the COS.

This sort of fund-raising, support-building, allocation, and planning activity was surely the dominant form of community organization practice in social work in the first decades of the twentieth century, and may be fairly regarded as dominant throughout the century. But it is inherently incrementalist and conservative, representing as it does the more established interests of community. It is a process little interested in social reform of any basic sort or in the development of insurgent leadership. This is often overtly acknowledged in social work literature. King, in 1939, wrote in regard to community welfare councils, "The Council . . . is not organized for social action in its own name. Problems which require professional skill are referred to agencies where that skill is located."[5] Community improvement from this perspective is understood to be the development of social services and mechanisms for the support and nurture of social services that would be able to respond to individuals who need aid, or in the words of the 1939 Lane Report to the National Conference of Social Work (and echoed by many since), to bring about a balance between the "social welfare needs and resources" of the community.

5. L. King, *Community Welfare Councils: Social Work Yearbook* (New York: Russell Sage, 1939), p. 100.

Prior to World War II, community organization was regarded as a professional activity supportive of social work but somewhat ancillary to it in the sense that it was not pure social work. Pure social work was based upon a medical model of diagnosis of an underlying pathology on the basis of symptomology, and the treatment of the pathology by direct professional means. Social casework and group work fit this model but community organization did not seem to. The Lane Report of 1939 considers the "social treatment" dimensions of community organization but holds the integrative, capacity-building, or community treatment purposes of community organization as plainly secondary to the more traditional construction of the purpose of community organization as program development. But by the middle 1950s the emphasis had clearly shifted to the treatmentlike purposes of community integration and capacity development. A number of writers contributed to this shift, but none is more representative or influential than Murray Ross. Ross published his *Community Organization: Theory and Principles* and a companion casebook in 1955. In his writing, community organization is clearly a social method in which professional agents of social change influence the associational patterns in a community to effect not merely some specific objective but the health of the community as a social organism. The professionally directed process "extends and develops cooperative and collaborative attitudes and practices in the community." What community organization is about, according to Ross, is not simply a "new nursery, water system, or housing project, but an increased capacity to undertake cooperative projects."[6]

This extraordinarily important work, so influential in the education of a whole generation of social workers, established community organization as a practice method in social work fully parallel, if not equal, to casework and group work. The community was now the client and the professional social worker the diagnostician of community problems and the agent of community treatment. This was overtly acknowledged in the 1958 report of the NASW Commission on Practice, which wrote a rather inclusive definition of practice that clearly could incorporate a "process"-oriented community organization.

The 1960s were not kind to the process orientation of community organization so carefully developed in the 1940s and 1950s. The civil

6. M. Ross, *Community Organization: Theory and Principles* (New York: Harper & Row, 1955), p. 50.

rights movement, urban rebellions of the middle 60s, the antiwar movement, and militance of public employee and community groups generally did little to support the view that community progress comes through cooperation and accommodation. Conflict and agitation were common elements in American community life. There were those who saw these conditions as normal, functional, or even therapeutic, and they advocated that social work should abandon its traditional associations with the well-to-do and its emphasis upon cooperation. Those who stood by the more traditional view were attacked directly. Saul Alinsky, the late high priest of the hard-nosed school of community organization, wrote:

> The means-and-ends moralists, consistently obsessed with the ethics of the means used by the Have-nots against the Haves, should search themselves as to their real political position. In fact, they are the passive—but real—allies of the Haves.[7]

But cooperation and accommodation continued, even if somehow they had lost the moral and intellectual high ground. The 1960s witnessed some dramatic changes in the actors and interests represented in community decision making. Some of these changes were accompanied by substantial conflict wrought through planned social action. The speed of social change and the apparent change in the boundaries of what was acceptable in social processes spurred many schools of social work to revamp their curricula in the direction of broadening the scope of concern to include social change generally and the processes of social planning beyond the pre-60s community organization view.[8] But the 1970s and early 1980s have witnessed a slow but sure lessening of interest in social work as a promoter of fundamental social change and a return to a predominant emphasis upon cooperative, rational, network-building processes in community organization. The emphasis in social work literature of the 1980s related to community work is framed in terms of organizational analysis, institutionalized social planning, program evaluation, and the management of social conflict. It is interesting to note, however, that little remains of the social psychological orientation of Ross and

7. S. Alinsky, *Reveille for Radicals* (Chicago: University of Chicago Press, 1946).
8. A. Gurin, *C.O. Curriculum in Graduate Social Work Education* (New York: CSWE, 1970).

the other writers of the 1950s. The value of participation was described in social work literature of the 1950s as promoting social solidarity, cooperation, and social integration. Participation in decision making escalated in the 1960s and early 1970s, in terms of both people and (perhaps more important) interests, but few social analysts would argue that social solidarity, cooperation, or social integration has increased. Indeed, the more common view is that expressed by Huntington:

> The essence of the democratic surge of the 60's was a general challenge to existing systems of authority, public and private. In one form or another, this challenge manifested itself in the family, the university, business, public and private associations, policies, the governmental bureaucracy, and the military services. People no longer felt the same obligation to obey those whom they had previously considered superior to themselves in age, rank, status, expertise, character, or talents.[9]

While social work and community organization may have returned to a somewhat more cooperative, and substantially more technical emphasis, the cultural effects of the 1960s are still very much with us and are an established part of the social context in which social workers must search for effectiveness.

SOCIAL ACTION

A recently published textbook in community organization rather surprisingly begins as follows:

> Community organizing spurs change. The history of community organizing's effect on our society is rich. Neighborhoods have organized to demand building and health code enforcement in housing. Disability rights groups have used organizing to win educational rights for all school age children . . . activists, students, union, churches and other citizens groups organized to pressure the government into ending its involvement in the Vietnam war. Ecology groups organized for the clean air and water acts. Homeowners' groups have organized to expose industrial dumping of toxic wastes in their communities. Civil rights advocates forced the integration of lunch counters, transit systems, schools, public accommodations. . . . Poor

9. S. Huntington, "Democratic Distemper," *Public Interest* 41 (Fall 1975), p. 15.

people have used organizing to fight forced relocation . . . welfare recipients have organized to demand and win increases in welfare benefits.[10]

Organized to "spur," "demand," "win," "pressure," "expose," "force," and "fight," society is a system by which resources are generated and distributed. Reallocations, historically and currently, have often come through conflict. The institutionalization of this conflict as a relatively routine aspect of our political system is one of the hallmarks of Western governments. Indeed, the escalation of identifiable interest groups and their claims on social resources (and the governments' power to reallocate them) has moved more than one social observer to despair. Worsthorne, a prominent British social critic, writes:

> Western society is being obsessed . . . to the point where the strong, the fit, the well-balanced, the rich, and the happy begin to be seen as eccentrics, got to say undesirables . . . as if God first created a universe of patients inhabiting a giant hospital and then, as an after thought, a few doctors and nurses to look after them.[11]

Whether one approves of it or not, it is rather apparent that our government in the United States, at every level, is greatly influenced by organized interests. We live in a time in which the old issue of government activism versus severely limited government has been resolved in the direction of activism. Lowi refers to the dominant aspect of our public life as "interest-group liberalism," arguing that every sort of interest group now looks to the government as a first-level source of resolution of its perceived problems.[12] The difference between conservative and liberal governmental administration is not so much whether government shall intervene in social and economic life, but what the character of that intervention shall be and in whose interests it shall be carried out. The American government has enormous resources at its command: fiscal, regulatory, and police power resources. These resources have been and are being used to benefit some and cost others. It only stands to reason that citizens of all types will observe and learn from this and will assert their interests in an organized way.

10. D. Biklen, *Community Organizing: Theory and Practice* (Englewood Cliffs, NJ: Prentice-Hall, 1983), p. 3.

11. P. Worsthorne, "A Universe of Hospital Patients," *Harper's* (June 1976), p. 35.

12. J. C. Farrell, *Beloved Lady* (Baltimore: Johns Hopkins University Press, 1967).

Social work's professional involvement with this process is a long but rather tentative one. It is rather commonly asserted in the social work literature that the settlement house movement of the Progressive era was overtly reformist and represents the first association between organized social work and social action. Some social settlements were quite active in their communities for reforms in local government, improved municipal services, housing codes, and the like. Jane Addams, Lillian Wald, the Abbott sisters, and other notables were reform minded and associated with the Progressive movement generally, and the Bull Moose ticket of 1912 specifically. The idea of an expanded and socially responsive government concerned with regulation of labor and trade practices and the creation of economic security through social insurance and other programs was a central element in their thinking.[13] Jane Addams, the most famous of the settlement workers, was involved in the world of politics in Chicago and Hull House was a place of political strategizing. But many settlement workers and Progressives were reluctant to support labor organizing or other direct mobilizations of the poor. The Progressive movement, like most reform movements in the United States, was primarily a movement of middle-class intellectuals driven by a desire, as Crunden calls it, to "preach without pulpits."[14] Patterson is probably accurate in his characterization of settlement houses as staffed by people "younger and more dedicated than the Lady Bountifuls of the Charity Organization Societies" who had supported preventive reforms but who had

> another goal—instilling middle class aspirations among the poor. . . . This is not to say all settlement workers were paternalistic: Thorsten Veblen was unfair in describing them as "young ladies with weak eyes and young gentlemen with weak chins fluttering confused among heterogeneous foreigners offering cocoa and sponge cake as a sort of dessert to the factory system." But they did hope to impress upon immigrants the value of education.[15]

Nevertheless, social work's historical association with social reform is largely a product of the settlement movement. That

13. J. Addams, The Social Thought of Jane Addams (ed. C. Lasch) (New York: Irvington, 1982).

14. R.M. Crunden, Ministers of Reform: The Progressives' Achievement in American Civilization, 1889-1920 (New York: Basic Books, 1982).

15. J.T. Patterson, America's Struggle Against Poverty, 1900-1980 (Cambridge, MA: Harvard University Press, 1981), p. 25.

movement played a role in the larger Progressive movement, which altered in a fundamental way American ideas about the scope and responsibility of government and set into motion, principally at the state level, programs of government regulation, social aid, and social services that would form the foundation upon which the New Deal era of the 1930s would expand. In essence, the Progressives ushered in at the beginning of the twentieth century the basic elements of a welfare system that has allowed social welfare and the professions that serve it to grow and, periodically, to prosper.

While many notable individual social workers participated in social reform efforts, particularly during the 30s, there was little general professional concern with social action. Especially during the 40s and 50s, the profession was busy educating its members to engage in increasingly "scientific" and psychologically based casework or the development and administration of agencies to deliver casework services. By the middle 1950s, however, rumblings from various sources suggested that change might be coming. The Chicago School of Sociology was emphasizing the social organization of communities, and chronicling their failures. This was particularly the case in regard to juvenile delinquency, which represented to many sociologists both the breakdown of community, in the inability to socialize all its members, and the quest of persons for small communitylike groups in which identity could be found and enjoyed.[16] Paul Goodman, the noted social critic, has argued that American society was closed to many and promoted a meaningless rat race for those unlucky enough to be within the enclosure.[17] He, too, was fascinated by delinquency. Nisbet, as already noted, had detailed the decline of community in America in 1931 in his *Search for Community.*

These writers of the 50s, however much they emphasized rather common themes, offered no program—especially none emphasizing professional services as an answer to American social problems. But such a program was not long in coming. Indeed, one advocate of planned, professionally directed social action had published his *Reveille for Radicals* in 1946. Saul Alinsky, a product of both Chicago sociology and the trade-union movement, had been organizing the Back of the Yards neighborhood action groups in Chicago for many

16. A. Cohen, *Delinquent Boys: The Culture of the Gang* (New York: Free Press, 1953).

17. P. Goodman, *Growing Up Absurd* (New York: Random House, 1960).

years. His perspective was the rough and tumble of Chicago politics, and he saw in it a model for change for all American communities. His basic orientation, as described by one sociologist, was that in the process of community change there is no give and take, only take. He advocated the organization of militant, disciplined units of community activists who would use any tactics, including disruptive ones, to accomplish their ends. Although he was often criticized for his militancy and that of his followers and his rhetoric was often rather harsh (including his penchant for quoting Lenin favorably), he had an enduring intellectual effect upon community organization, and upon social work more generally. He caused the profession to wonder if professional distance and neutrality were really desirable, and whether social change really comes through cooperation.

Among the many contributions to the discussion in the early 60s of professional, planned intervention as a catalyst in social change, none was more influential than Cloward and Ohlin's *Delinquency and Opportunity: A Theory of Delinquent Gangs.*[18] Here was a masterful reanalysis of juvenile delinquency that did not place this "deviant" behavior in the category of personal pathology; rather, delinquent behavior was seen as an inevitable and understandable product of a society that simultaneously creates expectations for money, status, and power and restricts opportunities to get them. Thus the gang was found not to be alien to American life, but to provide an alternative route to established social values—no bad boys, only bad social structures; and structures can be changed. Cloward and Ohlin's theories, in one of the more remarkable examples of social research with real consequences, led directly to the creation of Mobilization for Youth (MFY) in New York City in 1961. This program was funded initially by the National Institute of Mental Health and was a direct forerunner of the community action programs of the middle 60s. MFY had many features, but prominent among them was an emphasis upon neighborhood-based organization of the "unaffiliated" for social action purposes.

By the time of the passage of the 1964 Economic Opportunity Act, the idea that professionally planned social reform was desirable and possible was well in place.[19] And what sort of social reform? The

18. L. Ohlin and M. Cloward, *Delinquency and Opportunity: A Theory of Delinquent Gangs* (New York: Free Press, 1960).
19. T. Morris and M. Rein, *Dilemmas of Social Reform: Poverty and Community Action in the U.S.* (New York: Atherton, 1967).

dominant social analysis of the time, derived from sociological theories of alienation as well as community "power studies," emphasized exclusion of the poor and minority from American social life: Local governments were responsive to downtown merchants and real estate interests (that is why urban renewal had failed); public welfare agencies were accountable to middle-class county commissioners or city politicians; public schools didn't have local "neighborhood" boards; minorities in the cities weren't being courted by political organizations and in the South blacks were actively restricted from voting. Every wrong-headed social policy of the past and every nonexistent but needed social program was chalked up to the absence of power and influence of the poor at the community level. The solution to this problem was clear enough: Organize the poor and demand accountability of public services and political processes to the interests of the poor. The Office of Economic Opportunity (OEO) program, with funds available under its Community Action title for neighborhood service programs and with its seemingly innocuous requirement of "maximum feasible participation of the residents of the areas to be served," initiated a long and nearly all-encompassing effort to change participation in decision making in American communities. The very structure of the system for funding programs was radical. Rather than the federal government providing funds to lower levels of government to carry out social programs (as was the case with urban renewal and virtually every other similar prior effort), the legislation established a funding process borrowed from the foundations that had pioneered the community reform work. That process allowed private, nonprofit associations to form and apply for federal funds essentially independent of local governmental agencies. As one Chicago critic reportedly told President Johnson in 1966, "This is a matter of the federal government going to war not against poverty, but the local governments and the established interests they have built themselves upon." And so it seemed. In many communities the CAP agencies, as they were called, promoted organization of the poor in voting rights groups, in welfare rights groups, in tenant unions, in consumer rights groups, in neighborhood political action groups, and in school "community control" groups. City halls, welfare departments, public schools, and more were under siege by their long-time voiceless poor consumers. This was justified at the time by some on the grounds of practical hard-nosed politics, but most professionals in social work saw this as vaguely therapeutic. In the words of the original MFY proposal:

> The task is to direct the expression of alienation against the social structure which is its cause and to discourage its expression in delinquent acts. In this way, the discontented may help to alter the very inequalities which oppress them.[20]

In 1967 the Green Amendment to the Economic Opportunity Act of 1964 brought CAP programs somewhat closer to local governments by requiring greater participation of local governmental officials. This, along with the growing concern of many governors and national legislators, had a somewhat restraining effect upon community action efforts. But while the high-water mark of community activism of the poor may have passed, the general emphasis upon citizen participation was to continue and even expand in programs funded by the Office of Economic Opportunity and the Model Cities Act of 1966, and even in federal public education reforms. By the 1970s virtually no piece of federal legislation for social purposes did not contain elaborate requirements for citizen involvement.

Over the course of the 1970s and 1980s, social action initiated by or on behalf of the poor diminished. Neighborhood-based organization is now associated more with middle-class neighborhoods, where issues of crime control and environmental protection have made neighborhood groups in many communities a political force to be reckoned with. In addition, recent years have seen the development of many interest groups, often national in organization but with active local chapters. These interests groups are often referred to as "single-issue" groups because of their focus on a narrow set of policy choices. Independent of direct association with political parties, they are capable of exercising considerable influence in both general public opinion and political choice. Such groups cluster around issues generally associated with the political left (nuclear disarmament, pollution control, pro-choice, and prison reform groups, for example) or the political right (pro-school prayer, anti-abortion, anti-busing, and anti-gun control groups, for example).

The involvement of professional social work with the new issues-oriented organizations is not great. Indeed, there is a common

---

20. Mobilization for Youth, Inc., *A Proposal for the Prevention of Delinquency in Expanding Opportunities* (New York: Author, 1961), p. 69.

view that professionalism and organizing do not mix: "When organizers become professional organizers they stop organizing," says Biklen.[21] Professional social work has had a role to play in citizen participation, however, with myriad citizens' policy advisory groups and public hearing processes being built into virtually every major area of public social service. This is a direct legacy of both the participatory emphasis of the 1960s and the development of federal revenue sharing with state and local governments, which has required that states and local governments develop decision-making procedures for allocating these new revenues.

COMMUNITY TREATMENT

In addition to the streams of resource development and social action that constitute community organization in social work, there is a third, less clearly identifiable, stream of community treatment. Overlapping with both resource development and social action as well as with the social work method of group work, community treatment may be more properly regarded as an element of community organization thought as opposed to a clearly developed practice stream.

As noted earlier, community organization in social work has often been cast in terms of improving the social functioning of the community. Both Ross in the 1950s and Cloward and Ohlin somewhat later, while representing divergent views relative to cooperation in communities, justified community work on the basis of its contribution to community functioning—the increase of community integration and the reduction of alienation. Social action and reform or the development of social resources such as social services may have apparent social benefits, but the process by which these things have come to pass is argued to be an important element in the benefits individuals and the community overall derive. This orientation had an important manifestation in the previously mentioned proposal to establish Mobilization for Youth in New York City, and it is apparent in much of the social welfare literature of the early 1960s.[22] Many studies published between 1961 and 1964 argue for the social psychological benefits of planned community intervention.

21. Biklen, *Community Organizing.*
22. For example, see D. Cartwright, "Power: A Neglected Variable in Social

This orientation reached its greatest influence in the middle 1960s, with the emergence of the community mental health movement. That movement was concerned with the spread of availability of mental health services and contributed to the passage of the Community Mental Health Act of 1963, but an important element in community mental health thought was a view that community processes contributed to, and were perhaps the cause of, behavioral disorders.[23] The logical extension of this idea is to treat the environment directly as the "patient." This was advocated by many academics, but mental health practitioners, including social workers, had a great deal invested in direct service to individuals; and practical implications of "community psychiatry" were simply too radical to have staying power. Nevertheless, the elaborate social psychological basis for community work was to contribute to the view that the ends of community work are no more important than the means and to provide general support of the view of social problems as having an origin outside of individual pathology.

The community treatment orientation remains today, but it has been less encompassing in its purposes than it was in the 1960s. The emphasis upon general social reform as a primary means to improve social functioning and mental health is diminished, at least for a time. But the orientation is still quite evident in social group work, in the multitude of self-help groups, and in many delinquency prevention projects that emphasize the creation of "new, intermediate" social structures (often at the neighborhood level) to control deviant behavior.

COMMUNITY DEVELOPMENT

The terms "community organization" and "community development" have often been used interchangeably; the distinction between the two is not always easy to discern. This is especially the case in the literature of community development. For example, a recent text, *Community Development in America*, defines commu-

Psychology," in *The Planning of Change*, ed. W. G. Bennis et al. (New York: Holt, Rinehart & Winston, 1976).

23. D. Klein, *Community Dynamics and Mental Health* (New York: John Wiley, 1968).

nity development as a "(1) group of people (2) in a community (3) reaching a decision (4) to initiate a social action process (i.e., planned intervention) (5) to change (6) their economic, social, cultural, or environmental situation."[24] Certainly everything done in the name of community organization could be incorporated under such a definition. But a look at the sites of community development projects, the professional participants, the target participants, and the apparent purposes reveals some differences.

Perhaps the most evident difference is that community development in the United States is principally a rural or small community phenomena, while community organization has been primarily urban. The Cooperative Extension Service of the U.S. Department of Agriculture, and its state counterparts, is certainly the most significant employer of persons considering themselves community development specialists. State land grant universities, with their departments of rural sociology, provide the academic support for community development. The Community Development Society, the major organization of community development practitioners and academics, has derived its leadership primarily from these academic institutions.

Perhaps another difference is that community development projects often involve the creation of new economic resources for a community. The introduction of new agricultural technology, along with the social rearrangements necessary to accommodate new technology, is one of the more common elements of community development work, both in the United States and internationally. Community organization, by contrast, has been concerned more with the reallocation of existing economic resources than with the creation of new ones.

Internationally, community development has been promoted by the United Nations, especially UNESCO, and by governmental foreign aid programs such as the Agency for International Development (AID). It is also promoted within many countries to stimulate and guide change in underdeveloped regions. Everywhere the themes of participation and modernization seem to be present.

Professional social work participation in community development is less common than participation by those trained in education and

24. J. Christenson and J. Robinson, *Community Development in America* (Iowa City: Iowa State University Press, 1980), p. 12.

rural sociology, but social workers have been utilized in many international community development projects, particularly those associated with the United Nations. Within the United States, professional social work involvement is most likely with city government departments of communty development, which are concerned with (among other things) coordinating citizen participation in housing programs, city planning processes, and revenue-sharing decisions.

THE COMMON CONCEPTUAL BASE

All of these strands of community organization have, of course, a common element. They are all planned interventions into social life in order to produce some predictable increase in human welfare. Such interventions may occur in the name of the common good, but usually there are winners and losers in social interventions—some who gain in material welfare, status, power, or pride and some who lose. Most social interventions in the name of community organization or social work are designed to improve the social lot of those who are perceived to be the relative losers in social allocative processes that would continue if it were not for the intervention. Whether it is the organization of support for a new social service, creation of a neighborhood group to enhance police protection, organization of an insurgent group, or linking of agricultural production in an isolated community to a larger market, there is a goal that can be expressed as improved social welfare and some effort to rearrange associations between persons to effect the desired change. The social worker, community organizer, community developer, or whoever must have some plan of intervention, based upon some analysis of the social system in question, that is reasonably likely to produce the intended consequences.

Every social welfare problem can be cast as a distributional problem. Social welfare problems are usually constructed in terms of deficiencies of some tangible or less tangible social resource: Money, jobs, housing, health care, education, social services, power, and legal rights are some of the social resources that are typically regarded as deficient. Social intervention is designed to alter the existing distribution of these social resources. This alteration might occur through change of the personal aspects of some of the actors in the distributional system (for example, through education, training, or counseling), through creation of a new source of supply for the resource that is deficient (for example, public housing or nonmarket food distribution), or through a change in the pattern of relationships among the actors in the distributional system to effect a different outcome (for example, by organizing a union or a political group, or by changing a law or regulation so that it gives greater legal protection to those seeking jobs or housing).

Kunkel, applying a behavioral approach to social intervention, argues that successful social programs, whether designed for individuals, groups, or communities, have much in common: (1) specificity of the program goal (whose behavior must change to improve the situation and how); (2) knowledge of the situation (an analysis of how the existing problematic behavior of actors in the system is being maintained); (3) deprivation (a program intervention that creates a need for the resource that is used to reward the desired behavior when it occurs); (4) contingency management (a process of rewarding the problem-reducing behaviors and establishing these new behaviors as permanent); (5) monitoring behavior (an ongoing evaluation system that feeds back to the intervener, who makes adjustments accordingly); and (6) relation to the "real world" (program should lead directly into social roles and rewards that are part of the established social system).[25] Kunkel provides a number of examples of successful program planning or implementation, two of which—a community-based rehabilitation center for delinquents and the famous Vicos hacienda community development project in Peru—are directly related to social work. Levine, an economist with an interest in public policy, comes to a rather similar conclusion in his *Public Planning: Failure and Redirection,* in which he argues the failure of directed social planning because it has ignored the creation of incentives for people to behave in ways that promote the social goals of public policy.[26]

Such calls for the development of powerful, behavior-specific tools for use by social planners and social programs raise the issue of who has the right to plan and intervene for and to whom. While it is possible to identify a common set of conceptual issues that unite social planning, community organization, and social intervention generally, the practice is still more art than science. It is perhaps

25. J. Kunkel, *Behavior, Social Problems and Change* (Englewood Cliffs, NJ: Prentice-Hall, 1975).

26. R. Levine, *Public Planning: Failure and Redirection* (New York: Basic Books, 1972).

fortunate that the great diversity of community organization—in setting, concept, purpose, and method—in social work gives evidence that the situation is not likely to change in the near future.

SUMMARY AND CONCLUSION

Clearly, community organization is a method of social work practice. On the other hand, the method of community organization practice is difficult to describe through identification of specific community organization practice skills. As the discussion of community organization has shown, practice skills associated with this method of social work may differ widely, depending upon whether the social worker is involved with resource development, social action, community treatment, or community development.

The skills associated with resource development depend upon developing a dialogue, or a process among local social service providers, determining the kinds of services that should be emphasized, and finding sources of financial support to establish those services. The skills associated with social action depend upon organizing residents, assisting them to articulate their views about what would improve their community, and assisting these groups through a variety of tactics to achieve their self-determined objectives.

The skills associated with community treatment and community development are more difficult to specify. Community treatment requires some of the same skills as resource development and community action. These skills are directed toward strengthening the existing structure of the community so that it can respond more productively to whatever expectations are made of it by residents of that community. The same is true of community development, except that community development often requires skills in technology transfer. This means that a community organizer must be able to take technologies that worked in one place and make those technologies work somewhere else. Day care, for example, is a social technology that helps working mothers reduce their workloads. Transferring this technology from the middle-class suburb of Shaker Heights, Ohio, to the slums of Hough, in Cleveland, requires special process skills, in addition to citizen organization skills and skills in developing financial support.

Even this discussion of community organization method skills may leave many social workers still wondering exactly what kinds of things community organizers do. This is another way of examining community organization method skills, but, in this view, many of the activities of community organizers are not greatly different from those of caseworkers or group workers. Community organizers must engage people with problems. They must explore the range of the problem and plan with people how to address the problem. Certainly, community organizers intervene in existing circumstances and evaluate the products of their activities. More significant still, community organizers are most likely to carry out these activities and to practice their skills in and with groups. Therefore, community organizers must understand groups and must possess effective group helping skills.

The divergent and wide-ranging skills associated with the community organization method of social work raise questions as to whether any social worker has the kinds of skills to be a community organizer, and whether beginning social workers have enough skills to practice this method of social work. The answer to both questions is a qualified yes. Probably no social worker covers the whole spectrum of community organization practice. Specialization takes place very quickly. Moreover, the whole of a community organization activity seldom takes place within a single context; for example, developing a day-care center requires activities in a number of centers—social agencies, client groups, government regulatory structures, and centers of finance. One community organizer seldom spans the range of these centers.

Because community organization is practiced in such diffuse settings, and with such wide-ranging method skills, community organization has not held a consistent spot in the collection of social work methods. Sometimes, as discussed in the beginning of this chapter, community organization practice is at the center of social work practice; however, at other times it seems to be on the fringes. But regardless of where community organization practice may be located along the spectrum of social work practice at any point in time, it is a reliable and significant social work method that has enhanced the profession of social work.

SUGGESTED READING

Kramer, R., and H. Specht. *Readings in Community Organization*. 2nd. ed. Englewood Cliffs, NJ: Prentice-Hall.

Perlman, R., and S.A. Gurin. *Community Organization and Social Planning*. New York: John Wiley.

10

SOCIAL WORK
WITH FAMILIES

JANE H. PFOUTS

Professor, School of Social Work
University of North Carolina, Chapel Hill

The United States is currently experiencing a revolution in family life. Although a trend toward greater flexibility in marital and parental roles has been evident for half a century or more, it was during the turbulent 1960s that the family, along with other societal institutions, came under serious attack. Since that time, sweeping changes in male-female relations, sex norms, birthrates, and divorce rates have been occurring at an accelerating pace among all segments of the population, and the end is not in view. People today become sexually active earlier, marry later, have fewer children, and divorce more frequently than in the past. Nontraditional alternatives to marriage, such as living together, communal families, and one-parent families by choice, have emerged along with a confusing variety of other experimental arrangements. Within traditional marriage, couples are attempting to achieve maximum self-actualization through open marriages, shared roles, and new approaches to child rearing.

These important changes in family life reflect equally important changes in our culture. Since the mid-1960s, the society has been characterized by fierce power struggles between the sexes and generations and by rising expectations concerning standards of role performance in marriage and family life. For the first time in history, the majority of people have the means to separate sex from procreation through widespread access to effective birth control methods and legal abortion. "Women's work" has acquired a new meaning, as over half the women have left full-time homemaking to move into the labor force. All of these changes, taken together, have profoundly altered the nature of male-female and parent-child relationships in every major social institution, and especially within the family.

It is important to remember, however, that a successful social revolution cannot occur until the society is ready to accept it. The family revolution was not "caused" in any basic sense by such recent harbingers of the time as the new feminism, permissive child rearing, or the self-actualization movement. The true causes can be found in the vast social and economic changes brought about by industrialization, which has given us a new kind of society that demands a new kind of family. Child psychiatrist Bruno Bettelheim believes that

> the conditions which gave substance to the earlier family and made for its cohesion—or forced such cohesion on what, even then, may have been a reluctant or disappointed partnership in a common enterprise—are no longer present. In the past, companionship—under the most desirable circumstances, intimacy—was based on and the consequence of dire necessity. Now companionship is expected to hold the family as successfully together, when the necessity of living together as a group has been replaced by other social and economic conditions. Today it is quite feasible for males and females to succeed in life as well when they are single as when they are married, and often a single parent can readily afford to raise children. No longer does survival command that all family members stay and work together in order to avoid extreme emotional, social, and economic deprivation. Choice became available only when affluence no longer required the coordinated labor of all family members to guarantee their survival. . . .

With so many reasons for its existence removed, marriage necessarily becomes more problematic.[1]

Whether one views present trends with approval or alarm, it is obvious that we are living in a period in which traditional family norms have become blurred and in which new guidelines for courtship and marriage have not yet been clarified. Nor has a satisfactory substitute for the traditional nuclear family yet been found to take responsibility for the socialization of children. It is a time of ambivalence and flux in family life and in the practice of social work with families as well. Social work faces new and perplexing questions as it seeks to help troubled families cope with the dilemmas and realize the possibilities inherent in family life today.

FAMILY THERAPY: A NEW APPROACH TO PRACTICE WITH FAMILIES

During the second half of the twentieth century, a challenging new approach to practice with families has gained a secure foothold within social work. It is an approach that focuses on the total family system rather than on the individual as the unit of study and treatment. This approach is based on the belief that within the family unit can be found both the source and the solution for a wide range of problems of individual maladjustment. The target of intervention is the existing family system, and the clinician joins the system in order to facilitate change from within. The goal of intervention is not so much to help family members find reasons for current difficulties in past mistakes as it is to assist them in restructuring their present family life in new and better ways. Because this orientation focuses mainly on observable problems in the here and now, rather than on tracing the tangled threads of causation, it is applicable to types of clients and problems considered inappropriate for individual insight therapy. Family units need not be middle class, highly verbal, or introspective to be able to work together to solve their relationship problems with one another. They only need to want to be a family and to improve life within the group for all its members. Although casework and group work with families are still indicated in many cases, family therapy is the treatment of choice, either alone or in conjunction with casework, in those situations where it appears that

1. Bruno Bettleheim, "Untying the Family," *Center Magazine* (September-October 1978), pp. 5-9.

overall family patterns are detrimental to the functioning of one or more members.

The assumptions and methods of family therapy highlight dynamics of family life that are familiar to social work practitioners. Caseworkers have always been aware that in many instances, individual clients have failed to solidify gains made in treatment because the family system has sabotaged their efforts to change. It has been equally apparent that when a family system is functioning badly, all members suffer, although in differing degrees. Vulnerability to particular family problems varies among members, depending on such factors as age, sex, temperament, and role differences.

Although only a minority of social workers are engaged primarily in family therapy practice, the principles generated within the family therapy literature are highly relevant for social work practitioners in a wide variety of settings. This is not to say that the family therapy method, as practiced in a relatively small number of mental health clinics and family agencies where entire family groups are seen over a period of time, will ever be either appropriate or feasible in most social work settings. Nor is it true that all human problems originate within the family. In some cases, the principal locus of difficulty is within the individual; in others, the problem has its origin in the larger society. Nevertheless, family therapists have made us aware that family structure must be taken into account by all practitioners, because in most instances it plays a part, either central or peripheral, in the creation or solution of clients' problems.

Differences Between Family Therapy and Casework

Casework is oriented primarily toward change in an individual client, while family therapy focuses on changing the organization of the family. Family therapists believe that if any aspect of the family structure is changed, all members, including the client, will also change because alterations anywhere in the system affect the entire system. Thus, while caseworkers see the individual as the site of pathology, family therapists look for the roots of individual malfunctioning within the family system in which the individual functions.

In comparing the two methods, a leading family therapist, Salvador Minuchin, has likened the therapist who works with individuals to

a technician using a magnifying glass. The details of the field are clear, but the field is severely circumscribed. A therapist working within the framework of structural family therapy, however, can be compared to a technician with a zoom lens. He can zoom in for a closeup whenever he wishes to study the intrapsychic field, but he can also observe with a broader focus.[2]

For example, a young housewife with three preschool children comes to a mental health clinic with complaints of anxiety and depression. In working with this woman, a worker with an individual orientation would be likely to concentrate on the client's feelings about herself and her family, and would almost certainly hold individual interviews with the client's husband and perhaps other family members as well. In contrast, a family therapist would meet with husband, wife, children, and other significant household members *together* in order to discover, by direct observation, why the family has a member who is symptomatic. Perhaps the husband, who earlier appeared highly solicitous and reasonable in an individual interview with the worker, will reveal by manner, gesture, tone, or words in his interactions with his wife and children that in actual practice he is neither helpful nor supportive. Indeed, it may be clearly demonstrated that he is not even fully aware of the heavy domestic burden carried by his wife. The worker may also see that, because of low self-esteem, the wife actively encourages her husband and children to make ceaseless demands on her time and energy while she makes none on theirs. This is a group problem, with responsibility scattered among individual members, although only one member has sought help. For this reason, the family therapist would work wih the total group toward changing family structure in the direction of greater equity in domestic responsibilities and rewards. In the same situation, a caseworker would probably work primarily with the wife to help her shift her position in the family structure. It is likely, however, that the wife would find it very difficult to restructure the system if other family members were not also helped to work with her in effecting the desired change.

Differences Between Family Therapy and Group Work

Family therapy uses many of the concepts of group work (such as values, norms, roles, structure, process) because the family is a small

2. Salvador Minuchin, *Families and Family Therapy* (Cambridge, MA: Harvard University Press, 1974), p. 3.

group. However, small group theory cannot be applied to families without modification because the family is a unique small group. Social group workers generally deal with artificially constructed groups of unrelated children, adolescents, or adults who meet for a specified length of time to deal with an agreed-upon set of problems and to achieve specified goals.

In contrast, a family is a group of individuals who are united by bonds of blood in a relationship that, far more than any other, is central to the emotional development and life chances of all its members. Unlike other small groups, which tend to be homogeneous, the family is composed of members of different ages and sexes and is heavily weighted with dependents. Other small groups are time limited, but families have a past and a future. Membership in most small groups is a voluntary commitment, but this is not true of the family group. One does not choose one's family members (except for a mate), and kinship is a permanent condition, whether the individual wishes it or not and regardless of separations in time, space, or circumstances of life. Therefore, the group worker who does family therapy must change some techniques and modify others in order to deal with the qualitative differences between family groups and groups of unrelated individuals.

Old Concerns and a New Focus

What is new about family therapy? Certainly, social work's involvement with families is not new. Social work has always acknowledged the critical importance of the family in the development and functioning of the individual, and practice has traditionally emphasized problems of husband-wife and parent-child interactions. The family-centered focus of social work was made explicit as early as 1917 in Mary Richmond's classic text, *Social Diagnosis*.[3] In this book, which guided practice in its time, major attention was given to the importance of the family unit, to interpersonal relationships within the family, and to cultural, social, and economic forces impinging on the family. A decade later, however, the social work focus had shifted away from families as the unit of concern to the incorporation of Freudian theory into casework practice with individuals. Unfortunately, as psychological knowledge increased, social factors assumed less importance in social work theory. As a result, for almost forty

3. Mary E. Richmond, *Social Diagnosis* (New York: Russell Sage Foundation, 1917).

years, from the late 1920s through the early 1960s, the psychosocial balance that is the hallmark of social work remained tilted in favor of the inner life of the individual at the expense of the social reality of the environment. In 1958, Robert Gomberg, an outstanding family theorist in social work, pointed out that

> our conceptualization has been primarily in relation to individual personality, growth, pathology, adjustment, and so on. All of us are aware that in our practice we have worked with families, have planned with and for them, and were helpful to them. Yet there is no doubt that our diagnostic formulations have been framed in terms only of the individual and lack any crystalized conceptual system of family dynamics and family interaction which dealt with the family as a unitary organism.[4]

Family treatment, then, is not a new concern in social work. In fact, we should not forget that long before psychiatrists and psychologists were paying any attention to family systems at all, there were a minority of social workers in family agencies who were doing something very similar to what today would be called family therapy.[5] In addition, social workers in all settings traditionally have taken family histories, interviewed clients' family members, and given help to families in crisis. However, in most social work settings the focus has been almost exclusively on the individual client and his or her perception of the family, rather than on direct clinical observation and treatment of the total family system. Indeed, the reciprocal influence of the family system and the individual client on one another has often been completely overlooked because the significance of family interactional variables has not been recognized by either worker or client.

What is new in family therapy is that it gives primary emphasis to the family as a system of patterned activities that shapes the behavior of all family members in important and often unintended ways. By clarifying the psychosocial linkages between the individual personality system and the family social system, family therapists have made available to all social workers a useful set of concepts and techniques that, like psychoanalysis in the 1920s, adds a new dimension to prac-

4. M. Robert Gomberg, "Family Diagnosis: Trends in Theory and Practice," *Social Casework* 38 (February-March 1958), p. 74.

5. Morton D. Schumann, "The Social Work Relationship to Family Therapy in Perspective: Past and Future," *The Family* 2 (Spring-Summer 1975), pp. 4-10.

tice. According to family social work theorist Sanford Sherman, family therapy has raised its clinical eye one notch in the social organizational continuum, and in so doing has demonstrated the clinical advantage of moving back and forth between the atomized level of the individual and the nuclear level of the family.[6] As a result, social workers in all settings are becoming better able to explore the client's family world and to use this knowledge to help both client and family achieve higher levels of functioning.

FAMILY THERAPY: THEORY AND PATTERNS OF PRACTICE

The body of theory on which family therapy is based is drawn from psychiatry, psychology, and the social sciences. Among the theoretical contributions that have helped shape practice are the following: general systems theory; the ego psychology of such neo-Freudians as Hartmann and Erikson; the Parsonian theories of socialization and family interaction; role theory; small group theory; and the clinical research of the Bateson, Lidz, and Wynne groups with families of schizophrenic children.[7]

The practice of family therapy reflects a similar professional diversity, with representation among psychiatrists, psychologists, social workers, and a variety of other therapeutically oriented groups. With a high tolerance for professional differences within their ranks, practitioners from different disciplines frequently collaborate as co-therapists in treatment, carrying joint responsibility for conducting family sessions. Interdisciplinary co-therapy most frequently involves a social worker who is teamed with a psychiatrist or psychologist, but family therapists also engage in a range of less traditional collaborative arrangements. In general, co-therapists are selected on the basis of such considerations as the nature of the

6. Sanford N. Sherman, "Family Therapy," in *Social Work Treatment: Interlocking Theoretical Approaches*, ed. Francis J. Turner (New York: Macmillan, 1974), p. 459.

7. See Gregory Bateson et al., "Toward a Theory of Schizophrenia," *Behavioral Science* 1 (October 1956), pp. 251-264; Theodore Lidz, *The Family and Human Adaptation* (New York: International Universities Press, 1963); and Lyman Wynne, "The Study of Intrafamilial Alignments and Splits in Exploratory Family Therapy," in *Exploring the Base for Family Therapy*, ed. Nathan W. Ackerman et al. (New York: Family Service Association of America, 1961).

problem, the complementarity of the personalities and skills of the two therapists, and the ability of the therapists to work together. For example, a marriage counselor and a psychiatric nurse with skills in the area of parent-child relationships might be selected as the members of a clinic team best suited to work with a family characterized by marital strife and inadequate parenting.

One reason for the widespread use of co-therapists in family therapy is that the therapeutic complexity of working simultaneously with several family members can be shared. In addition, in some family situations it is considered clinically useful to have male and female therapists work together because in their interactions with one another and with family members they can serve as spousal or parental role models. For example, for a family that does not permit its members to disagree with one another, it can be instructive to see that the co-therapists can differ openly and even angrily, at times, and still maintain a good relationship.

Given the traditional interest of social workers in the family, it is not surprising that of all professions, social work is the one most highly involved in the practice of family therapy. According to a 1970 survey conducted by the Group for the Advancement of Psychiatry, 40 percent of family therapists were social workers.[8] The growing body of social work literature devoted to family therapy reflects this high professional involvement.

Because family therapy is still in its infancy and because diverse helping professions are actively engaged in formulating its principles, there are many differences of opinion concerning specific treatment issues. Nevertheless, consensus about certain basic principles has been established. It is these principles that the social work profession is beginning to incorporate in its own way to meet its own needs in such varied settings as social service departments, health agencies, correctional institutions, retirement homes, and day-care centers.

CHARACTERISTICS OF THE FAMILY SYSTEM

What is meant when the family is described as a social system? According to social group work theorist Grace Coyle, a social system is "a set of interacting relationships which has a life of its own, a

8. *The Field of Family Therapy* (New York: Group for the Advancement of Psychiatry, 1970).

relation to the larger social and physical environment, a differentiation among its interacting parts, and a constant interaction with individual personalities."[9] Because family systems are highly complex and intensely personal, they do not yield the nature of their transactions easily to outside observers—even when that observation is sought. It takes time, a trusting relationship, a clinical ability to move back and forth between the individual and group levels, and considerable diagnostic skill to unravel the complexities and understand the meaning of family system patterns.

Membership in the Family System

The first problem in working with a family system is the definition of family boundaries. Who are the members who constitute the primary family system, and who are the significant relatives outside the nuclear family who influence its functioning? The matter is more complicated than simply widening the circle to include extended family members who live with or in close proximity to the nuclear family.

Sometimes a close family friend serves as honorary kin, with great influence on the family system. In other instances, ghosts from the parents' families of origin haunt family interaction. In still other cases, a deceased parent, an absent son, or a former spouse continues to influence family functioning. It is essential for the therapist to take account of all members, present and absent, who are included by the family in its psychological world, even though the actual treatment group is necessarily much smaller.

Maintenance of the Family System's Boundaries

A family maintains its boundaries by erecting barriers between the family system and the environment. Boundary maintenance is necessary to preserve the integrity of the system. Outsiders must gain membership at the boundaries before they are admitted, and the culture of the nonfamily world must be evaluated before it is accepted. In a well-functioning family system, the screening process is neither so restrictive that the system becomes isolated nor so nondiscriminating that the system disintegrates.

9. Grace Coyle, "Concepts Relevant to Helping the Family as a Group," *Social Casework* 43 (July 1962), p. 350.

Social workers frequently deal with families whose boundaries are so diffuse that the family system has begun to dissolve. Such families often become our clients as a result of problems stemming from a weak relationship system, such as child neglect, truancy, marital conflict, or desertion. Social workers also work with families who guard their boundaries so vigilantly that members are virtually sealed in, with the rest of the world sealed out. Usually it is not the family itself, but someone from the community, such as a neighbor or teacher, who becomes alarmed at the inappropriate behavior of individual family members and refers them to a mental health clinic or social agency. Because closed family systems are deprived of both input and corrective feedback from the environment, they sometimes develop rigid, maladaptive social systems that are particularly vulnerable during times of stress that demand new behaviors. Such closed family systems, in extreme cases, are fertile breeding grounds for severe neurosis, psychosis, child abuse, spouse abuse, or incest.

Goals of the Family System

An important reason that family systems vary is that individual families differ in what they want to accomplish. Briar has pointed out that only by examining the goals of a particular family can the social worker determine the criteria by which it structures its members' interactions and evaluates its performance.[10] Although in a highly general sense all families share similar goals (the socialization of children and the meeting of adults' needs), there are wide differences among families in the relative importance they attach to a wide range of specific goals. One family may consider the occupational advancement of the father to be paramount, another may center its activities around the parenting function, a third may put the mother's career ahead of her homemaking role, and a fourth may favor expressive husband-wife activities at the expense of parent-child interactions. An understanding of the specific group goals that motivate the family gives the social worker a valuable diagnostic key to the puzzle of why family power, communications, tasks, and feelings are sometimes structured in ways that on the surface appear to be irrational. Such an understanding also enables the social worker to work directly with the total family system to find more effective ways of meeting group goals.

10. Scott Briar, "The Family as an Organization: An Approach to Family Diagnosis and Treatment," *Social Service Review* 38 (September 1964), p. 248.

It is also important to determine the extent to which consensus exists among family members concerning the ranking of group goals. Lack of consensus may pass virtually unnoticed so long as the family system has the resources to meet the preferred objectives of all members. In times of crisis, however, when some goals must be abandoned or modified if others are to be accomplished, families are often torn by conflict or indecision in assigning priorities among competing goals. For example, a young father may want to go back to school in order to get the academic qualifications he needs for a desired promotion. Such a move would require the family to live on a drastically reduced budget for a period of months or years, and would also involve the temporary absence of the father from the home except on weekends. If the husband considers his career advancement the most important priority for the family but the wife puts family "togetherness" first, conflict over goals is likely to ensue.

Structure of the Family System

One of the best ways to gain understanding of a particular family system is to analyze its structure. Family "structure" refers to patterned interactions among family members. All families, no matter how disorganized they may appear to the outside observer, operate under some set of stated or unstated norms. Because the family is a unity of interacting personalities, the interdependence of its members must be coordinated by a set of rules, however primitive or ill defined, that specify members' relationships and roles and the allocation of resources. According to Briar, structure tends to develop in each of the major areas of family life.[11]

(1) Division of Labor. To what extent are adult male and female roles segregated or shared? Is the division of labor equitable? Is too much or too little responsibility given to children? Is there agreement among members concerning allocation of tasks? Are tasks performed poorly or well? Are some tasks overemphasized at the expense of others? Is family life orderly and predictable or chaotic on a day-to-day basis?

(2) Distribution of Power and Authority. Can this family be characterized as patriarchal, matriarchal, democratic, or anarchic? Is the use of power and authority reasonable, consistent, and nonpunitive? Do

11. Briar, "The Family as an Organization," pp. 251-254.

all family members accept the distribution and use of power and authority as legitimate?

(3) Assignment of Roles. What are the roles the family has implicitly or explicitly assigned to individual members (for example, the good child, the bad child, the drudge, the scholar, the scapegoat)? What behaviors do these roles involve? What family needs are met by specific role assignments? What is the effect on members of their role assignments?

(4) Patterns of Communication. Who speaks to whom, who is left out, and who speaks for whom? What types of communication are not permitted? Is the communication network open and direct, or blocked by distortion and ambiguity? Do members communicate their feelings of sadness, anger, tenderness, or delight appropriately, or is the manner of speaking at variance with the words spoken? How are differences of opinion handled?

(5) Relationships Outside the Nuclear Family. How close and extensive are family ties to kin? Is the family estranged from one or more close relatives? Do relatives help the family when it is under stress? To what extent are family members involved in community affairs? What are the family's patterns of entertaining and visiting?

(6) Handling of Feelings. Do family norms encourage or discourage spontaneity and the open expression of both positive and negative feelings among members? Under what conditions will nurturance and praise be given, and by whom? Is the family characterized by excessive displays of anger, hatred, or physical abuse? What is the role of the family's pet in the emotional life of the family?

(7) Family Rituals. How does the family celebrate birthdays, anniversaries, and national holidays? What are family meals like? What leisure time activities does the family share? Does the family have its own private terminology, jokes, rituals, and symbols? Are all members included in family rituals?

Variations Among Family Systems

Just as there is variation among total family structures in their effectiveness in meeting members' needs, so do different areas within the family show variation. Some families are very well organized in certain areas and poorly organized in others. For example, the affectional substructure may be strong, but the performance of housekeeping tasks weak. The distribution of power and authority may be unclear, but the communication among family members direct and unambiguous. Or the division of labor may result in a very smoothly run household that does not include warm and loving interactions among family members.

It is also important to remember that family structures vary in the degree to which the needs of all members are met. For example, the division of labor may be completely satisfactory from the point of view of the husband who is exempt from chores, but much less satisfying for his overburdened wife. Or the family may be structured around the needs and wishes of children at the expense of their parents' marital relationship.

Caseworkers and group workers, as well as family therapists, must look closely at family structure when it appears to be operating in such a way as to distort or inhibit the client's growth. In order to do this, it is often necessary to arrange one or more home or office appointments with the entire family. Only by direct observation can the social worker hope to get a clear diagnostic picture of the strengths and weaknesses of a particular family structure. Because a family that is not in family therapy is unlikely to view itself as a "client," there are limits to what the worker can do to effect extensive structural change, and it is unlikely that in the few interviews that can be arranged the family will shift its label of "problem" from the client to itself. However, at the very least, the worker has the opportunity to assess the strengths and weaknesses of the family structure and to enlist the help of the family in making specific structural changes that appear essential to the client's welfare.

In addition, seeing the interaction of the client with other family members provides diagnostic and treatment clues that can be obtained in no other way. Family sessions bring out aspects of the client's behavior that are less evident in individual treatment sessions. For example, it is in the interaction of family members that the worker can observe, perhaps for the first time, the manipulative techniques of the family martyr, the provocative behavior of the family scapegoat, or the emotional coldness of the dutiful parent, all of whom may be unaware of their part in creating family problems.

Variations in the Complexity
of Family Systems

Individual families differ markedly in the extent to which the behavior of members is structured. At one extreme are overorganized families that inhibit spontaneity and restrict the development of personal autonomy. In these families, members adhere to a tight schedule of duties, allowing scant opportunity for self-directed leisure. At the opposite extreme are under-organized, chaotic families that fail to provide the secure and nurturing environment that is essential for socialization and emotional well-being. All members in such an unpredictable environment—adults as well as children—suffer losses that can be attributed directly to the underdevelopment of the family system.

Variations in Members' Participation in Shaping the Family System

Families also vary in the degree to which individual members have a role in shaping the system within which they live. In some cases, it is the patriarchal father or the matriarchal mother who sets all the rules; in others, parents divide or share this responsibility; in still others, the children also have a voice, sometimes a very powerful one, in effecting modifications of the system. None of these ways of distributing family power has been shown to be markedly superior to the others in terms of family happiness or the performance of the members; however, professional bias tends to favor equalitarian norms, which may prejudice the worker against a client's family system if it does not conform to this model. It is easy to forget that, contrary to liberal mythology, there are countless well-adjusted, happy families in which husband and wife do not share interests, roles, or power to any appreciable extent, and in which little weight is given to opinions voiced by children in shaping family policy. What is important is not whether the client's family system fits some preconceived model in the worker's head, but whether it appears to suit the needs of its members and the social norms of the group to which they belong.

Variations in Members' Consensus Concerning the Family System

It is important to determine the extent to which the family system's rules represent consensus among family members. In every family, no matter how well integrated, almost all aspects of the structure inevitably elicit a certain amount of discontent and rebellion among members. Unfortunately, the "perfect" family does not exist, except in children's books, television dramas, and advertisements aimed at the family market, and as an idealized belief about how other families behave in the minds of millions of members of imperfect real-life families. Conflict is as integral a part of family life as consensus. However, in families whose consensus about basic family values, norms, and routines is very weak or nonexistent, the survival of the family unit is in jeopardy.

Variations in the Efficiency of Family Systems

Family systems differ in the extent to which they display overall efficiency and rationality. Regardless of income, some families make better use of their resources and are more effective in meeting their goals than are others. Many highly inefficient families manage to rock along quite well until a crisis occurs in which efficiency is essential because resources are sharply diminished or members' needs are greatly increased. At this point, unless new coping abilities are learned, the family system begins to break down and a once marginally functional unit becomes dysfunctional. Poor families of this type are particularly vulnerable in times of crisis, because they live close to the edge of economic disaster at all times and have no financial margin to allow for meeting the crisis in customary ways. Affluent families, too, are sometimes characterizd by family systems that lack the efficiency and rationality to cope with serious problems. Help for such floundering families, on all economic levels, might well include short-term material and emotional support to deal with the crisis; but a family therapy focus would suggest that the long-range goal would be to work with the family as a unit to increase competence in family system management.

Subsystems

Within the general family system there are three distinct subsystems: husband-wife, parent-child, and sibling. Each subsystem has a life of its own in the sense that it meets needs of members that are not satisfied elsewhere in the system. Husband and wife meet one another's adult needs in the sexual, affectional, social, economic, and homemaking spheres. Parents satisfy their children's needs for nurturance, protection, and guidance. Children, in return, satisfy powerful parental needs. Siblings serve as near-in-age companions, rivals, models, and teachers, and in their relationship with one another first learn the costs and rewards of interacting with peers.

Ideally, all subsystems in the family operate equally well and are coordinated into a smoothly functioning whole. In the real world, however, this is usually not the case. Few families are either problem free or problem ridden in all three systems. A highly satisfactory husband-wife relationship does not ensure good performance in parent-child interactions. A very satisfactory son or daughter is sometimes an unloving sibling. An exemplary parent may be a deficient spouse. One might assume—in view of the strengths exhibited by family members who need help because of uneven role performance—that the modification or elimination of dysfunctional relationship patterns would be a relatively straightforward therapeutic task. But practitioners have learned from bitter experience that too often this is not the case. Now, family therapy is helping social workers to see more clearly why families, even when they bring many assets to treatment and appear to welcome therapeutic intervention, may sabotage help. By carefully observing family systems in action, family therapists have been able to monitor the chain reaction experienced throughout the entire family system when any part of the system alters its interactional patterns. Family therapists have documented how therapeutic gains in one subsystem may cause painful losses in another, and how family systems are able to mobilize powerful resources to defeat the efforts of outside change agents to disturb their pathological equilibrium. On the basis of these observations, family therapists are convinced that the only therapeutic strategy that can successfully effect permanent change in a client's family relationships is one that involves the total family system in the change process.

Both the literature and the direct experience of family therapists provide numerous examples of specific ways in which pathology originating in any of the three subsystems can spread throughout the entire family system. Family therapists believe that the most important and far-reaching effects of family systems are those originating in the husband-wife subsystem. It is in this adult relationship that the family has its beginnings, and it is here that the greatest power to shape parent-child and sibling interactions resides. For example, it is not uncommon for parents who are unhappy in their marriage either to overidentify with their children, in an effort to gain the love and approval not available in the adult relationship, or to blame the children for causing problems that, in fact, stem from the adult relationship. Sometimes, parents actively or covertly involve the children in their marital struggle as scapegoats, pawns, or allies. When this occurs, the siblings are drawn into an adult conflict that they neither understand nor want to be a part of, and as a result may become divided from one another in their loyalties. If the marital conflict persists over an extended period of time, a new equilibrium will be established. No longer will the family system be composed of three interdependent subsystems working together in the service of the family's well-being; it will have been replaced by a system characterized by polarized hostile coalitions and isolates, functioning in the service of family pathology.

It is also common for transactions within the parent-child subsystem to enhance or diminish both the spousal and the sibling relationships. For example, marital difficulties can result from the husband's resentment toward both spouse and children when he feels that his wife is over-involved in the role of mother and underinvolved in the role of wife. A wife, too, may feel deprived by her husband's greater interest in the children; but, in our culture, it is more likely that her rival for her husband's attention will be his job or hobbies rather than his absorption in the parental role. The parent-child subsystem can also adversely affect the sibling subsystem in cases where parental favoritism and differential treatment greatly exacerbate sibling rivalry and jealousy.

Finally, transactions within the sibling subsystem can contaminate the entire family system if they are marked by extreme hostility. On the other hand, if they are marked by sibling solidarity under all circumstances, the flow of essential information from children to parents is blocked.

In summary, family therapists believe that disequilibrium in any of the subsystems leads to disequilibrium throughout the entire family system. Families, however, do not make this assumption, and they seldom seek help for system-level problems. Indeed, they strongly resist the suggestion, however tactfully put, that the family system may be part of the client's problem. The family seeks treatment not for itself, but for a deviant member who needs to be straightened out so they can all get back to normal. Therefore, when a family comes for social work help with a subsystem problem that, in the worker's view, is causing or is caused by problems elsewhere in the family system, the worker must help the family see that within the total family system can be found both the cause and the cure of subsystem dysfunction.

Effects of the Helping Process on Family Systems

Social workers sometimes underestimate the impact of the helping process itself on the family system. Systems theory reminds us that unless the effect of the helping process is taken into account, the family system may suffer. In some instances, social work intervention may solve one problem only to create another. For example, an unemployed father may feel that his authority has been seriously undermined when publicly funded training and job opportunities are available for his wife and teenaged children but not for him. A family may be broken by desertion because needed welfare assistance is less apt to be forthcoming if there is a marginally employed father in the home. Outpatient care for a mentally ill mother may enable her to remain with her family, but a high price may be paid in the disruption of family routines.

The social worker whose clinical eye is focused on the total family system rather than on the individual client is more likely to recognize that help, even when it is essential, may be a mixed blessing for the family unit. As a result, the family-focused worker is more apt to arrange sessions with the entire family to help them deal with the dysfunctional aspects of change so that the functional aspects will not be undermined or canceled out.

The Family Life Cycle

The nuclear family, like the individual, moves through a progression of developmental stages. The family's life cycle begins with a marriage, expands as new members are added, contracts as members leave the group, and disappears as a unit when its founders die.

Each stage of family development involves both losses and gains for the individual members and contains the potential for family crisis. For example, the newly married couple must be able to break infantile ties to parents and establish an adult heterosexual relationship as husband and wife. When the family adds a new member, the dyadic marital relationship must be drastically altered, and a new balance must be achieved between spousal and parental roles. As the years pass, parents must be flexible enough to give infants and growing children the nurturance they need while at the same time encouraging age-appropriate independence; and children must be willing to accept the responsibilities of increasing maturity. Inevitably, if the life cycle progresses normally, parents are faced with the task of letting their grown children go, and children must find the courage to reject dependency and accept autonomy. As the family cycle of the parental marriage enters its final stages and the new family cycles of the children and their spouses begin, both parents and children have the task of accepting a new kind of closeness and a new kind of difference, unencumbered by feelings toward one another of anger, guilt, or dependency.

Families often seek help from social workers when members are experiencing problems in moving from one stage of development to another. Sometimes the very strengths that made an earlier stage successful become liabilities when new behaviors are required. For instance, a highly nurturing mother may cope very well with the needs of babies and small children, but may find herself unable to accept the emerging sexuality and independence of the early adolescent period. A man may be a loving and supportive spouse but an impatient or disinterested new father.

Transitional stress, if not successfully resolved, can result in permanent family dysfunction, since the tasks of each stage of family development must be mastered successfully in order for the family to move on to the next phase. Sometimes, for this to occur, the social worker must work with all family members to help them resolve their ambivalence about change and accept new tasks and new roles.

The Process of
Multigenerational Transmission

Although parents die and siblings scatter, adult children continue to carry their families of origin within themselves as long as they live. Thus there is a strong thread of continuity from generation to generation as children who were socialized in one family become spouses and parents in another, bringing to their family of procreation patterns of behavior they learned in their family of origin. Most clients are unable initially to see the clinical relevance of the extended family to their here-and-now problems, but family therapists are convinced that difficulties within the current family are often best understood as reflections or extensions of unfinished relationship struggles in the family of origin. Murray Bowen, an eminent family therapy theorist, believes that the family projection process continues to operate through many generations. In this process, the weakest members of each generation are the most vulnerable to pathological patterns of family behavior, while stronger members are less affected. In extreme cases, a downward spiral can occur in which the most impaired members of the family transmit ever more virulent family pathology from generation to generation.

Bowen believes that a downward spiral lasting for eight to ten generations can produce a schizophrenic child.[12]

The strength of the multigenerational transmission process lies in its obscurity. Clients do not know that they are crippled in their present family relationships by a burden of unfinished emotional business with parents, siblings, and other relatives. Many family therapists help troubled nuclear families to reestablish contact with kin in order to reevaluate the past with adult eyes and to establish a new basis for mutual support and understanding within the extended family. Indeed, family therapists believe that, for all of us, therapists and clients alike, maladaptive relationships with our families of origin can exert a continuing negative influence on our relationships with our spouses and children unless we recognize and deal with our heritage of unfinished family business.

Family Interactions

Patterns of family interactions reflect a basic dilemma of human existence—the desire for both closeness and distance in relationships with others. The never-ending struggle between the "I" and the "we" can be seen in the shifting balance of family alliances. Members vacillate along an emotional continuum, between the ever-present dangers of total fusion at one extreme and total detachment at the other, in the one-to-one relationships of husband-wife, parent-child, and brother-sister. Most families are able to avoid the extremes, but a minority of troubled families can be characterized as either enmeshed or detached. Murray Bowen describes the highly enmeshed family as "an undifferentiated ego mass" in which the boundaries between individual members are blurred and the unique characteristics of members are submerged in order to eliminate the possibility of difference or conflict. In contrast, a detached family is characterized by the extreme individualism of members and the emotional distance that separates one from another.[13] In either case, the focus of a social worker using a family systems approach would be primarily on reframing dysfunctional relationships between family members and only secondarily on treating individual pathology.

---

12. Murray Bowen, "Theory in the Practice of Psychotherapy," in *Family Therapy: Theory and Practice*, ed. Philip J. Guerin (New York: John Wiley, 1976), p. 86.

13. Bowen, "Theory in the Practice of Psychotherapy," pp. 65-75.

Triangles

Inevitably, when any dyadic relationship becomes too threatening, too demanding, or too intense, one of the members moves to create distance between the two by bringing a third person, object, or issue into the system. Converting an unstable twosome into a triangle eliminates the need to deal directly with the other person. All people regulate their dyadic relationships through the use of triangles, and in most cases triangles serve the very useful purpose of defusing the inevitable tensions of daily interactions. In some situations, however, triangles are harmful because they are used to evade serious interpersonal problems that demand solutions. For example, a husband and wife may avoid marital strife by making their child a scapegoat for their frustrations with one another. Or the wife may bring a sympathetic friend into the relationship to listen to confidences about marital problems that cannot be confronted openly. Or the unwary social worker may become part of a triangle when a husband-wife dispute somehow becomes the fault of the worker. The third component of the triangle may be the couple's political differences, a mutual enemy, or the high involvement of one spouse with television, golf, or gardening. In fact, anything or anybody that allows the couple to avoid the real issues between them can serve as the stabilizing factor in the relationship. Unfortunately, as long as the triangle persists it prevents any straightfoward resolution of dyadic problems.

The aim of a social worker who finds dysfunctional triangles operating within a family should be to help the individuals involved move back into dyadic interactions in order to work out their relationship problems directly. A family functions best when each member is able to relate to all other members openly and responsibly, even though conflict may increase in the short run as the triangles are being dissolved.

THE FAMILY TREATMENT PROCESS

According to David Freeman, family treatment consists of three stages: definition, working through, and termination.[14] In the first

14. David Freeman, "Phases of Family Treatment," *Family Coordinator* 25 (July 1976), pp. 265-270.

stage, the social worker has the difficult task of reassigning the role of client from an individual member to the total family unit. This is a new and frightening approach, and most family members initially resist changing their definition of the problem.

If the family-focused view of the social worker prevails, treatment moves into the middle stage, in which the examination by the family of its own interaction processes constitutes the most crucial part of the treatment. In this stage the family no longer concentrates on the shortcomings of the original client, but works on problems and issues affecting the entire group. During this often painful process of self-examination, the family itself does most of the therapeutic work, and it comes to know that it is its own best treatment resource. The worker helps the family members define the issues, encourages them to deal directly with one another, insists that members take responsibility for their own actions and their own statements, and works with them in extending their family boundaries to include kin and community resources in their support system.

The ending stage is reached when the family sees that it has acquired the necessary internal and external resources to deal with its problems alone. Because the relationship between the worker and the family is usually much less intense than that between worker and client in individual treatment, transference and dependency problems are less likely to hinder termination. Indeed, it has been demonstrated that many families can successfully complete treatment within the relatively short span of eight to twelve sessions.

In all stages of the treatment process, the family therapist tends to be more active, more spontaneous, and more present oriented than is the therapist who is working with an individual client. In the dual role of participant and observer, the family therapist faces the ever-present danger of being caught up in the family's pathology because of unresolved conflicts from his or her own past. For this reason, it is essential that workers come to terms with their personal family histories so that their own unresolved feelings about family life will not handicap them in their efforts to help other families.

FAMILY TREATMENT IN THE 1980s

Specific treatment modalities go in and out of fashion in the practice community. Traditionally, casework has been the most universally used method, and it will almost certainly continue in that role in the future because one-to-one interactions are as fundamental in social work practice as they are in human affairs. However, even casework has had its ups and downs, and other practice methods have enjoyed brief periods of extremely high popularity, such as community organization in the 1960s and group work in the 1970s. In this sense, the 1980s belong to family therapy.

Social workers, like the population generally, tend to be somewhat excessive in their temporary allegiances to specific problems and specific methods of solution. Today, the institution of the family is a national preoccupation and is also being discussed endlessly by social workers at professional meetings and in the literature. Students currently are fascinated by family therapy, and many practitioners consider it to be the treatment of choice in dealing with a wide range of family problems. What began in the United States in the 1950s as an unorthodox approach, espoused by a handful of iconoclasts, has now spread throughout the practice world. In the 1980s, family therapy has become thoroughly respectable in the United States and England; it is taught, researched, and practiced in most Western European countries and in such far-flung places as South Africa, Israel, Australia, and Argentina.

At some point, probably within this decade, it is inevitable that the current popularity of family therapy will diminish as the novelty wears off and as new areas of interest and new practice modalities appear. Still, it is clear that social work with families will never be quite the same. Family system variables will continue to be taken into account, whatever the fate of family therapy as a treatment method, just as intrapsychic variables remain central to all social work practice even though the psychoanalytic method itself has declined in influence in recent years.

Because the family therapy method is still in a relatively early stage of development, many questions about its use remain unanswered at the present time. Therefore, workers must rely, to some extent, on their own judgment in choosing among a variety of theoretical emphases and practice principles. Is a particular family best served by a family approach alone, a combined family and individual approach, or individual treatment only? Are there instances in which open communication among family members is more harmful than helpful? To what extent should the sexual or financial concerns of parents be discussed in the presence of children? Should young children be included in the treatment group at all? Should family treatment be denied to families if one member refuses to participate? Should past family relationships with parents and other kin be emphasized, or should the focus be on current family functioning? Is it fair to aging parents, who are not in therapy, to be forced by their grown children, who are, to reopen old wounds and reexamine long-ago parenting failures, real or imagined? As yet, there are no definitive answers to questions such as these. Social work practitioners and researchers must continue to learn more about specific ways in which a family systems orientation can be used to enhance our services and to strengthen family life.

SUGGESTED READING

Bowen, Murray. *Family Therapy in Clinical Practice.* New York: Jason Aronson, 1978.

Goldenberg, Irene, and Herbert Goldenberg. *Family Therapy: an Overview.* Monterey, CA: Brooks/Cole, 1985.

Hoffman, Lynn. *Foundations of Family Therapy.* New York: Basic Books, 1981.

Kaslow, F. W. "History of Family Therapy in the United States: A Kaleidoscopic Overview." *Marriage and Family Review* 3 (1980-B):71-111.

Lasch, Christopher. *Haven in a Heartless World.* New York: Basic Books, 1977.

Minuchin, Salvador. *Families and Family Therapy.* Cambridge, MA: Harvard University Press, 1974.

Nadames, Cloé. *Strategic Family Therapy.* San Francisco: Jossey-Bass, 1981.

Okun, Barbara F., and Louis J. Rappaport. *Working with Families.* Belmont, CA: Wadsworth, 1981.

Rueveni, Uri. *Networking Families in Crisis.* New York: Human Sciences Press, 1979.

Satir, Virginia. *Conjoint Family Therapy,* rev. ed. Palo Alto, CA: Science and Behavior Books, 1967.

Watzlawick, P. *The Language of Change: Elements of Therapeutic Communication.* New York: Basic Books, 1978.

11

CASE MANAGEMENT

PETER J. JOHNSON
Assistant Professor, School of Social Work
University of North Carolina, Chapel Hill

Every community has a substratum of people who cannot function without massive, long-term support. Some are protected and cared for by relatives all of their lives; family members carry primary responsibility for their welfare, often at great emotional and financial cost and with few community resources to help. Too often, however, family support is unavailable or insufficient, and the society must act as parent to its rejected members. Dependent and damaged persons who have no personal resources must make do with whatever help the society is willing to provide.

Social workers articulate the needs of these people, provide services to them, and advocate on their behalf. This chapter discusses a current approach used by social workers to meet the multiple service needs of chronically dependent people within the community. The approach involves selective use of all of social work's methods—casework, group work, family therapy, and community organization. Based on the assumption that social work methods must be blended in a new way to meet the needs of some groups of clients, the approach is called "case management."

DEINSTITUTIONALIZATION:
THE IMPETUS FOR CASE MANAGEMENT

As we have seen in earlier chapters, the movement to remove certain classes of people from institutions has gained momentum slowly over the past century. During the nineteenth century, there was a strong belief that for society's outcasts, custodial group care was humane and in the best interests of all concerned. And, indeed, in many instances, group care was an advance over local community care, which was idiosyncratic at best and nonexistent at worst.

It is, however, the fate of reforms to need reform themselves, and for solutions eventually to become new problems. Thus, beginning in the mid-nineteenth century, voices were raised to document and deplore the shameful conditions of institutional life. In every generation thereafter, social reformers have spoken out against the evils of custodial institutions. By the turn of the century, a social revolution against institutionalization had begun, as one dependent or deviant group after another was given options other than institutional care. Today, the orphan asylum has almost disappeared, to be replaced by foster care and adoption; the Social Security Act has removed the specter of the poorhouse; probation and parole have eliminated or decreased penal incarceration. The most recent groups to return to the community in large numbers have been juvenile status offenders, who formerly were sent to training schools; severely handicapped children, who now leave their homes and residential schools to be "mainstreamed" in public schools; and mentally ill persons, who are offered community-based services as an alternative or follow-up to hospitalization.

The deinstitutionalization of patients from state mental hospitals has been the rallying cry of civil libertarians, many mental health professionals, and others since the mid-1950s. As one enthusiastic advocate put it, "There is only one way to deal with state hospitals, or for that matter, prisons: empty them, close them, and blow them up."[1] In the 1980s, however, such professional euphoria has been replaced by sober second thoughts and, once again, the solution has been found to generate problems of its own. It is becoming increasingly more evident that community-based care must be made less a slogan and more a reality if it is to provide a better quality of life for people who can be "freed" from institutions.

Where Do All the Ex-Patients Go?

John is a 42-year-old male who was discharged eighteen months ago from a New York state hospital after fifteen years of intermittent stays there. Last night, he was picked up at the New York City bus terminal once again (sleeping on benches is considered loitering, which is illegal). This was John's eighth such arrest in six weeks.

He has no family. His relatives "disowned" him several years ago after his second hospital admission for acute schizophrenia. He has no job, no place to live, and no friends. His possessions (an extra pair of sneakers, a transistor radio, a few clothes, a copy of Milton's *Paradise Lost,* and about a hundred thorazine and artane pills) are carried in a shopping bag.

John sometimes receives food from the Salvation Army; sometimes he finds his meals in garbage bins behind restaurants; sometimes he doesn't eat at all. He often weeps for no apparent reason; he says he is being tortured by "evil thoughts that won't go away."

John is a victim of the shortcomings in the current movement to deinstitutionalize state mental hospital patients. While well-meaning legislators and mental health planners continue to applaud and promote the movement because of its theoretically positive benefits, there are thousands of people like John whose sad circumstances raise important questions about the massive discharge rates of mental institutions. Any of us, having had John's experience, might well prefer to return to the safety of the state hospital.

In 1955, there were more than 565,000 patients in state mental hospitals; today, there are fewer than 180,000. Thus deinstitutionalization is an empirical fact. But it is also a process and a philosophy. As a process, deinstitutionalization decreases the use of institutions while

---

1. G.R. Redding, "Letter," *Psychoanalytic News,* 1 May 1974.

expanding community-based care of mentally disabled people.[2] As a philosophy, deinstitutionalization is promoted because community-based care is considered preferable to institutional care.

Periodically, throughout the first half of the twentieth century, widely acclaimed exposés of mental hospitals were written, such as the famous account by Clifford Beers of his experiences as a patient and Mary Jane Ward's best seller, *The Snake Pit*.[3] It was not until 1948, however, that the time was ripe for a book, *The Shame of the States*, by Albert Deutsch,[4] to arouse more than temporary public indignation. In the 1950s and 1960s, the advent of anti-psychotic medication and an emphasis on patients' legal rights further contributed to reform efforts, as did the increased availability of nursing homes and psychiatric wards of general hospitals, and an increase in insurance coverage for such care. Finally, the creation of a national network of community mental health centers, initiated in 1963 by Congress through the Community Mental Health Centers Act (P.L. 88-164), served to justify and propel the fact, the philosophy, and the process of deinstitutionalization.

Unfortunately, some important factors were ignored by the movement. State mental hospitals were labeled unacceptable because they had failed to demonstrate success as treatment centers. But critics overlooked the hospital's crucial functions of protection and custody—of providing a safe refuge for persons who cannot survive independently because of their emotional state or bizarre behaviors. Moreover, there did not exist—and there still do not exist—an adequate supply of community places of asylum for the chronically mentally disabled. (This latter problem, incidentally, was discussed in Chapter 8 as being a major impetus for establishment of state mental hospitals in the first place.)

Today's widespread belief that community resources exist to meet all the needs of deinstitutionalized people is, however, only one of many mistaken assumptions that have proved to be pitfalls in the process of deinstitutionalization. Other fallacies are that community

2. Leona L. Bachrach, "A Conceptual Approach to Deinstitutionalization," *Hospital and Community Psychiatry* 29 (September 1978), pp. 573-578.

3. Clifford Beers, *A Mind that Found Itself* (New York: Longmans, Green, 1908); Mary Jane Ward, *The Snake Pit* (New York: Random House, 1946).

4. Albert Deutsch, *The Shame of the States* (New York: Harcourt and Brace, 1948); see also Albert Deutsch, *The Mentally Ill in America*, rev. ed. (New York: Columbia University Press, 1949).

residents are willing to accept mentally disturbed people in their midst, that community mental health workers have both the interest and the repertoire of skills to sustain severely mentally disabled persons, and that there exists an integrated network of community services to respond flexibly to the overwhelming and critical needs of the mentally ill.[5] Indeed, it is the very lack of an integrated network of services for chronically mentally ill persons—as well as for the mentally retarded, the physically handicapped, and multiproblem families—that has caused case management to emerge as an interventive strategy.

The Needs of Deinstitutionalized Persons

Chronically mentally ill people, such as John,

suffer severe and persisting mental and emotional disorders that interfere with their functional capacities in relation to such primary aspects of daily life as self-care, interpersonal relationships, and work or schooling, and that often necessitate prolonged hospital care.[6]

They display "lifelong patterns of non-productivity, dependency, isolation, and psychiatric symptomatology."[7] Effective implementation of the process of deinstitutionalization offers them their only hope to escape from spending most of their lives in state mental hospitals.

Given the severity and chronicity of the problems of this segment of the population, what are their needs, if they are to be expected to survive in the community? John Talbott, a professor of psychiatry at Cornell Medical Center, has suggested that they need access to 24-hour, 7-day-a-week crisis services; they need programs to instruct them in the fundamental skills of everyday living; they need vigilant

5. See, for example, Uri Aviram and Steven Segal, "Exclusion of the Mentally Ill: Reflection of an Old Problem in a New Context," *Archives of General Psychiatry* 29 (July 1973), pp. 126-131; Peter Johnson and Joseph Beditz, "Community Support Systems: Scaling Community Acceptance," *Community Mental Health Journal* 17 (Summer 1981), pp. 53-60; and Gerald Klerman, "Better but Not Well: Social and Ethical Issues in the Deinstitutionalization of the Mentally Ill," *Schizophrenia Bulletin* 3 (1977), pp. 617-630.

6. Howard H. Goldman, Antoinette A. Gattozzi, and Carol A. Taube, "Defining and Counting the Chronically Mentally Ill," *Hospital and Community Psychiatry* 32 (January 1981), p. 22.

7. W.S. Deitchman, S.D. French, and T.C. Weerts, "Defining Chronic Psychiatric Disability: Preliminary Results," *Community Support Service Journal* 6 (Winter 1981), p. 6.

medical attention; they need a broad spectrum of both supervised and unsupervised housing; they need financial support and employment opportunities; they need vocational rehabilitation and welfare services; they need meaningful daytime and evening activities and social contacts; and they need the continuity of ongoing counseling and support.[8] Indeed, the needs of the chronically mentally disabled are so massive and so diverse that a program description of the Community Support Branch of the National Institute of Mental Health (NIMH) called for the

> active involvement of a wide range of interest groups: consumers, parents, citizens, employers, landlords, neighbors, hospital and community mental health workers, and administrators and policy-makers at all levels. What seems to be needed is a broad-based coalition of concerned agencies and individuals working toward mutually determined goals.[9]

Unfortunately, such a broad-based coalition of groups (who, in any event, often work at cross-purposes) has been imperfectly realized in many communities and not at all in even more. As a result, we read newspaper stories about patients going from the "back wards" of state mental hospitals to the "back alleys" of communities, and "falling through the cracks" of the service delivery system. The *New York Times* editorialized that deinstitutionalization tended to result in

> sick and fearful people . . . needing to . . . shift for themselves in an often hostile world . . . to drag out a hungry and derelict existence in a broken hotel if they are lucky; victimized if they are not . . . by greedy operators of so-called halfway houses that are sad travesties.[10]

The Importance of Social Networks

We all need social networks to meet our emotional, social, and physical needs—whether natural networks based on commonalities such as religion, kinship, hobbies, or ethnicity, or formal networks,

8. John A. Talbott, "Toward a Public Policy on the Chronically Mentally Ill," *American Journal of Orthopsychiatry* 50 (January 1980), pp. 43-53.

9. National Institute of Mental Health, Community Support Branch, *The NIMH Community Support Program* (Rockville, MD: National Institute of Mental Health, 1977), pp. 3, 4.

10. Editorial, *New York Times*, 8 April 1975.

such as social welfare agencies, that compensate for breakdowns in the informal networks. Some natural networks, such as juvenile gangs or organized crime syndicates, have negative effects; on the other hand, informal and spontaneous helping networks occur more often than we sometimes realize. Examples of such informal networks include the supportive listening of beauticians, bartenders, and clergy; the baby-sitting services offered by friends; the rebuilding by neighbors of a farmer's barn destroyed by fire. "Were it not for the informal services of natural helping networks," according to Collins and Pancoast, "social agencies would be swamped."[11] The mentally disabled among us are no exception to this universal need. Two examples will serve to illustrate how helping networks can operate with respect to mental illness.

The first example is that of an informal, naturally occurring network. In a survey of attitudes toward the community-based care of mental illness, one of the 574 randomly selected interviewees said, "I've got a few friends who 'aren't playing with a full deck.' If it weren't for some of us helping them through rough times, they'd be in an institution today."[12] The speaker may not have been professionally qualified to diagnose and assess the severity of mental illness, but the fact remains that there are people whose crippling disabilities are made bearable because they have family or friends to offer support and encouragement.

The second example is a vignette. Although the client's identity is disguised, it is a factual report of a formally devised support network taken from my experience as a social worker at a mental health center.

> Fred, a middle-aged man, was discharged from the state hospital after a five-year admission. He had had a psychotic depression, with frequent suicide attempts. The worker linked Fred with Phillip—an ex-client of the mental health center—who agreed to share his apartment with Fred. The worker also linked Fred with a group of men who played checkers at the town's recreation center. The mental health center also had a weekly activities and social program that Fred was invited to attend. Phillip's landlord had received training as a mental health volunteer and offered his services. Arrangements were made with a

11. Alice Collins and Diane Pancoast, *Natural Helping Networks* (Washington, DC: National Association of Social Workers, 1976).

12. Peter Johnson, "Community Support Systems for the Mentally Ill: A Study of the General Public, Mental Health Workers and Board Members in Leon County Florida" (Ph.D. dissertation, University of Michigan, 1980).

physician to supervise Fred's medication. Fred received enough money from social security to pay his room and board; he also received a small income from the town in return for janitorial work. Eventually, he became a full-time municipal employee.

The worker met regularly with Fred for the first few months; then their meetings tapered off. However, when Fred either stopped taking his medication or withdrew from his regular activities, his community support network (Phillip, the landlord, the physician, Fred's employer, the activities program staff—even some of the men with whom Fred played checkers) alerted the worker, who would again become more directly involved. This plan had Fred's prior approval.

On one occasion, Fred became so depressed that he had to return to the state hospital for his own protection (he had threatened to kill himself). This stay was for only seven days, however, and when he returned to the community, Fred said "It is good to have a home to come back to."

Among the many reasons for the vastly differing circumstances of John, who was arrested for sleeping in the bus terminal, and Fred, not the least is the fact that case management was viewed by Fred's mental health center as an important approach. Case management is defined as *the development, coordination, and monitoring of a supportive network of services and resources–both from the informal (neighborly) and formal (social agency) caregiving systems–that is tailored to the unique needs and interests of a particular client.*

In the remainder of this chapter, I will review aspects of the case management approach by focusing on its utility in working with chronically disabled clients who have been discharged from state mental hospitals. Some of the settings where it is practiced, its major functions, the knowledge skills and values of case managers, and the place of case management within the social work profession will be discussed.

CASE MANAGEMENT SETTINGS

Case management is performed in many types of settings under varied auspices. In fact, its very diversity impedes development of one clear, standard definition that would be acceptable to all who use the approach. At the federal level, case management was incorporated in two recent laws: the Developmental Disabilities Training and

Bill of Rights Act (P.L. 95-602) of 1978, and the Mental Health Systems Act (P.L. 96-398) of 1980. Both of these laws require programs receiving federal funds to have staff members who can coordinate services as well as provide support and advocacy for disabled clients. The former law remains intact; the latter, however, is subject to state interpretation. Several states (for example, New York, Minnesota, Georgia) already have created case management systems; in Florida, case managers are pivotal staff members in a Human Services Department that combines eleven previously separate functions such as youth services, welfare, and public health.

Case managers are employed in many (but not all) community mental health centers and in the "psychosocial rehabilitation centers" that were launched in the late 1970s by NIMH. Many of these community support programs were modeled after Fountain House in New York City and actually predate the NIMH initiative.

The Fountain House Model

Fountain House resulted from the efforts of ex-mental hospital patients who formed WANA (We Are Not Alone) in the mid-1940s. A social worker, John Beard, assisted WANA members in developing their own helping social network. The organization grew rapidly, and by 1965 it had built a six-story clubhouse in Manhattan. Today, as many as 500 discharged patients visit Fountain House each day and participate in programs that offer prevocational experiences (learning basic job skills), temporary job placement (four hours per day, leading to full-time employment), living arrangements (including apartments owned by Fountain House), and social activities.

There are now 108 programs in the United States that were developed on the Fountain House model. These programs bear a strong resemblance to the late-nineteenth-century settlement houses of Britain and the United States, which attempted to develop a sense of community and potency among disadvantaged people. The settlement workers' orientation of reform, spirit of egalitarianism, and belief in working through existing social structures were remarkably similar to the staff patterns of contemporary community support programs.

What makes programs such as Fountain House successful in helping people who once were doomed to live out their lives in state hospitals adjust to community life? A case example may help to answer this question.

The Case of Jimmy

It is 7:15 on a Monday morning. Most of the drivers who are stopped at the traffic light are yawning or gearing themselves up to face the grim realities of another week. But a 30-year-old man who is sitting behind the wheel of an ancient car is smiling.

Jimmy is looking forward to a full week of work. This $5/hour job was a recent promotion, and it helped him buy the used car—the first he has ever owned. Jimmy is living independently; in addition to owning a car, he holds a job and pays his portion of the rent on the apartment he shares with a friend. This self-sufficiency may not seem startling until it is put in the context of Jimmy's having been told, only eighteen months earlier, that he would probably spend his entire life in a mental hospital. No wonder Jimmy is smiling!

Jimmy's dramatically changed life is the result of several factors: his own fierce determination, caring people who support his efforts, a flexible employer who is willing to hire mentally disabled people, and the staff and members of Friendship House, a community-based, self-help rehabilitation program. Jimmy had lived in institutions for the last twenty years, and a gloomy prediction had been reasonable in light of his history. He had frustrated the efforts of the best "teaching centers" in his part of the country; he had been the subject of scores of important case conferences; he had been diagnosed at various times as autistic, a childhood schizophrenic, and a chronic undifferentiated schizophrenic; he had made numerous suicide attempts, usually by overdosing or slitting his wrists. Looking back, Jimmy commented that hospital staff "seemed to expect the worst from me, and I didn't disappoint them." Years of taking antipsychotic drugs had left Jimmy with tardive dyskinesia, which causes some facial muscle distortion and slurred speech. Otherwise, it would be impossible to guess that this pleasant-looking man ever had been mentally ill.

Jimmy's sister, Polly, had stayed in touch with him throughout his long institutionalization. Their parents had necessarily become involved with their own deteriorating health, and their father had died four years earlier. Their mother lives in a small town, supported by her income from sewing and her husband's life insurance. Polly had heard about Friendship House through a friend whose uncle had a successful experience there after having been in a state mental hospital for five years. Polly had long wanted her brother to have another chance to live in the community, but other "chances" seemed doomed to failure. There was no outreach to deinstitutionalized patients, no job training programs; only rat-infested tenements and lots of medication. In contrast, Friendship House offered a comprehensive approach toward self-sufficiency, including decent housing, ongoing socialization, and temporary job placement. Its goals were accomplished through active coordination, continual support, occasional advocacy, and ongoing assessment.

Before Jimmy was discharged from the state hospital, a social worker from Friendship House met with Jimmy and hospital personnel to determine Jimmy's needs and strengths. The case did not appear promising, but Jimmy's motivation and Polly's support could not be denied. The social worker learned of Jimmy's difficulties in handling stress—his tendency to bang his head against a wall when he became frustrated; his withdrawal when people attempted to become close to him; and his many compulsive routines, such as constantly filing his nails, taking showers, and smoking cigarettes. The social worker also learned that Jimmy's IQ was reported as 128 on the Wechsler Intelligence Scale for Children, which had been administered when Jimmy was 6 years old. The worker noted that Jimmy seemed to count things constantly and that he knew the batting average of every major league baseball player.

A more comprehensive assessment of Jimmy's interests, strengths, and needs was undertaken after he was discharged and became a member of Friendship House. That assessment, and other activities on Jimmy's behalf, are described in the next section.

THE FUNCTIONS OF CASE MANAGEMENT

The aftercare needs of chronically mentally ill persons are extensive, often spanning many formal and informal support networks. Five major components of case management have been identified by the Joint Commission on Accreditation for Hospitals (JCAH), although the emphasis may differ according to the setting. These functions, which are also endorsed by the NIMH Community Support Program and by various states in their job descriptions for case management personnel, are assessment, developing an individualized service plan, linking and coordinating, monitoring, and advocacy.

Assessment

The process of assessment involves gathering information from the client, from interested family members and friends, and from social and health agencies. The information can be classified within six areas: (1) interests and capabilities, (2) material resources, (3) social supports, (4) interpersonal skills, (5) ego strength, and (6) motivation and interest in maintaining a life outside the institution.

Interests and Capabilities

Questions that were asked to obtain information about Jimmy's interests and capabilities include the following:

- Does he really want to leave the hospital?
- What was aversive and what was pleasant, for him, about the hospital?
- What does he say he wants at this time? Where does he want to live, with whom, and what would he like to do?
- What hobbies does he have?
- What is his work history?
- Does he have any special skills and/or training?
- Does he have any particular capabilities or limitations?
- Does he need special supervision (that is, is he continent, can he feed himself, does he have medical problems or physical handicaps)?
- What medications does he take? Is there a complicated medication regimen, or one requiring nursing care?

Jimmy was interested in obtaining a job, maintaining his own apartment, owning a car, and seeing the Braves play the Dodgers. These were very ambitious goals for Jimmy, given the extent of his impairment.

In terms of capabilities, Jimmy's skills at computation was real. At Christmas, the Mental Health Association had given him a calculator, which he taught himself to use; since then, the calculator had been an extension of his right hand. Jimmy's other capabilities included punctuality, responsiveness (usually) when asked a question, dependability, and physical strength.

On the other hand, there were significant deficits. He had little knowledge of nutrition; left to his own devices, he would eat nothing but candy bars. He was not at all assertive; he clung to female authority/parental figures to the extent that he would refuse to make decisions in their presence. Occasionally (once or twice a year), he would react to not getting his own way by regressing to a fetallike posture and refusing to move. He had no experience of ever having had any major responsibilities such as holding a job or paying for his room or board.

Material Resources

It was necessary to evaluate the extent of material resources available to Jimmy when he returned to the community. This information was gathered by asking questions such as these:

- What sources of income does Jimmy have (for example, social security, welfare assistance, food stamps; personal insurance, savings, or pensions; family support)?
- Is shelter available through Jimmy's, or his family's or friends', resources?
- Is appropriate housing (supervised, semisupervised, unsupervised) available in the community?

Jimmy had inherited $2500 in life insurance after his father's death, and he would be likely to be eligible for SSI benefits. Otherwise, his resources were limited. Polly could provide emergency shelter, but her assistance was limited by her marriage, young child, and employment.

Social Supports

The worker assessed the extent of Jimmy's social support system by investigating these topics:

- Are there willing and responsible family and/or friends who can take care of Jimmy? Who are they? Where do they live?
- Have there been occasions when members of the support system lost patience with Jimmy? Which of his behaviors were difficult for his support system to accept?
- Do particular circumstances seem to induce Jimmy to withdraw or exhibit bizarre behavior?
- Does Jimmy display behaviors that could mitigate developing new relationships for emotional support?
- Are there some types of people who are threatening to Jimmy? Are there some types of people with whom he feels more comfortable?

Polly's own circumstances prevented her being of help to Jimmy except for limited periods of time. Jimmy's mother wanted to help, but she wanted to continue living in her small-town home. Since the town had stigmatized Jimmy, living with his mother would not facilitate his integration into community life. Moreover, Jimmy quite understandably did not like his hometown. Thus, at the time of his discharge, Jimmy really did not have an adequate system of social supports.

Interpersonal Skills

This category is similar to that of social supports, but includes more specific information about the client:

- How does Jimmy present himself to others? How does he introduce himself? How much eye contact can he tolerate? How closely does his conversational style approximate social norms?

- Does he have specific psychiatric disorders (such as pronounced projection, paranoia) that would interfere with his ability to develop interpersonal relationships?

Jimmy presented himself to new acquaintances in a pleasant but somewhat rigid and guarded way. He smiled appropriately, but his manner tended to be robotlike. He would look only briefly at a person to whom he was introduced; then his glance would dart alternately between the person and a corner of the room.

Jimmy was overly sensitive to others' comments and placed undue emphasis on schedules and sequences. If a hospital nurse was fifteen minutes late in dispensing medication, or if the volleyball game was played on Tuesday instead of Wednesday, Jimmy would make a series of critical comments that others found irritating.

Jimmy also had some strengths. He was considered very loyal by people with whom he was friendly. He had an uncanny memory for every detail ever mentioned in his presence by his friends, including ward attendants and nurses.

Ego Strength

Evaluating Jimmy's ego strengths involved asking questions such as the following:

- Does he have the ability to tolerate frustration at not having his needs met, having to wait, and the like?

- Are his perceptions of other people or situations accurate?
- Is his judgment sound?
- Is his control of impulses weak or strong?
- Is his self-image strong and appropriate?
- Can he develop and maintain interpersonal relationships with appropriate boundaries to allow for separateness?
- Which of the defense mechanisms does he use? Does he blame himself or others excessively?
- Can he concentrate on tasks that require mental or physical work?

Jimmy's major defense mechanism was compulsivity. In fact, whenever his counting behavior and memory for details decreased, he would regress or decompensate. He never blamed anyone but himself for his problems; to a fault, he experienced a full range of difficult feelings without ever attempting to deny them or project them onto others. For several years, Jimmy's major difficulty had been his inability to repress his painful and scary feelings, but this had recently abated, most likely as a result of medication and group therapy.

The supportive milieu of the state hospital, with its comforting familiarity and expressions of caring from staff members, had seemed to help Jimmy slowly build his self-esteem and confidence. He was gaining a realistic self-image. He knew he was different from other young men of his age, that he was sick, and that his life circumstances were not as favorable as those of other people. But this awareness seemed only to strengthen his desire to be more like "normal people," as Jimmy put it.

Another problem for Jimmy was his difficulty in coping with the erratic schedules of some professionals, with the terse and demanding behavior of some attendants, and with visits from his mother, who treated him as though he were a preschool child. When things didn't go according to schedule, Jimmy was apt to pout or bang his head against a wall. Jimmy was also uncomfortable with, or did not understand, more abstract emotional concepts such as ambivalence or the need for two people to maintain some distance while still feeling a sense of belonging. Jimmy much preferred to deal with concrete issues.

Motivation and Interest in
Maintaining a Life in the Community

This category is similar to interests and capabilities, but its aim is more toward evaluating the client's ability to deal with the demands of community life. The importance of this information derives from Bachrach's poignant discussion of how the community—usually thought to be the "least restrictive environment"—may, in fact, be more restrictive in individual cases than is the institution. Bachrach writes, "It is quite conceivable that for some patients the least restrictive environment is an institution, if the only available community settings fail to provide conditions that enhance their well-being."[13] Thus, for Jimmy, the fundamental questions were these:

- What are Jimmy's particular needs and interests at this time, with respect to living in the community?
- What community facilities and programs are available that mesh with his needs, clinical history, and interests?

Jimmy's motivation to develop a life like that of others his age was very strong. In fact, it was such a driving obsession that there was reason for the social worker to be apprehensive. In the past, when things hadn't gone his way, Jimmy withdrew, banged his head, or attempted suicide. Thus his wish for self-sufficiency, although understandable, would have to be tempered; unreasonable expectations would only ensure failure. It would be essential to instill in Jimmy some idea of what a realistic pace would be for him in developing a "normal" life. Jimmy would also have to acquire a clear understanding of the ways in which he would never be completely free. This would require his acknowledgment and acceptance of the fact of his vulnerabilities.

Summary

Assessment, as a function of case management, spans many topics and requires much skill. The client's strengths and limitations are not the only focus; the potential support of family, social, and agency networks also must be addressed. Little attention is given to

13. Leona L. Bachrach, "Is the Least Restrictive Environment Always the Best? Sociological and Semantic Implications," *Hospital and Community Psychiatry* 31 (February 1980), p. 99.

attempting to ferret out the "causes" of problems suffered by emotionally disturbed clients; given our present state of knowledge, all that can be said for certain is that many genetic and environmental factors probably play a role in the etiology of mental illness. Rather than pinpointing causes, the case manager attempts to identify those present circumstances that either facilitate or hinder the client's adjustment.

In addition, the rights of others in the environment must be taken into account. Case management cannot remove from the client a personal responsibility for behavior that harms or offends others; nor can it ignore the reality that a family's patience and resources may be exhausted after years of trying unsuccessfully to cope with a disabled member. The damaging effects a mentally ill person can have on the family are underscored in the story of Sylvia Frumkin (a pseudonym), a 32-year-old woman who had been hospitalized scores of times, in several institutions, since the age of 15. For two days, after returning from one of her hospitalizations,

> Sylvia fought with her mother. One afternoon, she tossed some of her clothes and books into a small suitcase and ran out of the house. Several hours later, one of the neighbors happened to see Sylvia walking on the grass adjacent to a busy expressway opening and closing her suitcase as she walked. He brought her home. Sylvia's mother opened the suitcase. Sylvia's clothes and books were gone. In their place were aluminum cans, cigarette butts, and pieces of old tires. Sylvia said she was "helping to clean up the ecology."[14]

On another occasion, Sylvia

> got drunk and returned to a hotel where she danced around the fourteenth floor in a nightgown ornamented with jujubes. She then grabbed an armful of records, danced around Greeley Square, giving records to the crowd which had gathered. [Mrs. Frumkin was summoned.] . . . "Look at that crazy girl," a woman standing next to Mrs. Frumkin said, pointing to a young woman who was dressed only in a bra and a half-slip as she danced and distributed records. "You should be thankful it's not your daughter," Mrs. Frumkin said to the woman.[15]

14. Susan Sheehan, "The Patient," New Yorker, 25 May 1981; 8 June 1981; 15 June 1981; 22 June 1981.
15. Sheehan, "The Patient," New Yorker, 15 June 1981, p. 48.

Those of us whose family members' deviance is of the more usual variety find it difficult to imagine the strain of living all one's life in the company of the Sylvia Frumkins of the world.

Assessing the suitability of an emotionally disturbed patient for deinstitutionalization and the case management approach requires an intensive gathering of fragmented information. It calls for a realistic evaluation of the client's motivation, strengths, interests, and limitations. It demands a sensitivity to the family's threshold for coping with the client's difficult behaviors. It requires a thorough appraisal of the resources and limitations of the community environment to which the client returns.

Developing an Individualized Service Plan

An individualized plan to provide services to a client is developed on the basis of the information gathered during the assessment. The plan is not tailored to the treatment preferences of staff members, or even to currently available facilities. The client's level of functioning, service needs, and role performance are the major determinants of whether a plan will restrict or extend freedom and independence and whether it will promote or mitigate comfort and safety.

Two other general principles also guide development of the treatment plan. First, the client is included in the process, as are collateral persons who will be involved in implementation, such as family members, friends, and the caregiving personnel of formal support systems. Second, short-term objectives are established, against a backdrop of the client's long-term goals (for example, "to be on my own," "to be like everybody else," "to own my own business"). The time period of the short-term goals may vary, but three months can be considered typical. Short-term objectives should be set for all areas of social functioning; they should be written in concrete and specific terms; and they should become progressively more advanced in accord with the client's interests, motivation, and history of performance.

When Jimmy's assessment was completed at Friendship House, a service plan for the next three months was developed. Setting some short-term goals was presented to Jimmy as a necessary first step toward his eventual self-sufficiency. Jimmy's plan highlighted his needs for room and board, daytime activities, supporting relationships, and medication. His long-range plan included temporary job placement, with the idea that success at progressively more responsible jobs might lead eventually to a position in which he could use his quantitative skills.

Linking and Coordinating

The process of linking coexists with the development of a treatment plan, and it continues as long as the case continues. Linking, according to the Joint Commission on Accreditation for Hospitals, is the process of referring or transferring individuals to all required services in the mental health agency, the overall formal caregiving system, and the naturally occurring "folk-support" system.[16] In addition to being aware of the services that are available, the case manager must be adept at manipulating agency bureaucracies and must act as an entrepreneur in finding or creating natural helping networks.

The process of coordinating involves not only identifying service providers and linking the providers to clients, but also linking providers to one another. There may be differences in treatment philosophies among the caregivers of various agencies that require expertise in the emotional/expressive as well as pragmatic/instrumental problems of implementing the service plan.

Both linking and coordinating require that case managers have certain knowledge and skills, including the following:

- being aware of services available in social, health, legal, and vocational agencies
- identifying potentially supporting people or groups outside the formal caregiving system (for example, self-help groups)
- mobilizing the resources of the formal caregiving system
- encouraging or persuading natural helpers to become involved
- assembling groups and guiding discussions and decision-making sessions of relevant professionals, the client, the client's family, and significant others, to formulate goals and design an integrated intervention plan.
- acting as liaison between client and family, and between client and relevant professionals, programs, and informal resources, to help the client verbalize preferences and secure services

16. Joint Commission on Accreditation for Hospitals, *Principles of Accreditation for Community Mental Health Centers* (Chicago: Joint Commission on Accreditation for Hospitals, 1973).

- acting as liaison among programs, to ensure a smooth flow of information and to minimize conflict among subsystems

- establishing and maintaining credibility and effective public relations with formal and informal systems, to mobilize community resources for current and future clients

Jimmy's case manager at Friendship House linked Jimmy with other program members who lived at the same boarding home and could "look out" for him. Jimmy was also helped to establish a positive relationship with the boarding home's operator. Staff members linked Jimmy with Bill, who could be a companion to Jimmy on Saturdays when Friendship House was closed, and they arranged for Polly to take Jimmy to visit with her family on Sundays. Other linking activities would be required when Jimmy was ready to move out of the boarding home into an apartment of his own. In arranging for Jimmy's temporary employment, considerable skill was required to convince an employer that Jimmy could be an asset to the business. Additional linking was done with community volunteers and social agencies such as the Mental Health Center, the Social Security office, Vocational Rehabilitation, and the Department of Social Services.

Monitoring

Monitoring is the continuous evaluation of the client's progress, leading to reassessment of goals and development of new service plans and linkages. It also includes "following up" service provision and "following along" the client's progress. More specifically, monitoring includes the following:

- ensuring that promised services are delivered
- observing the client's use of services
- being available for troubleshooting
- providing support or consultation to natural helpers and families
- providing support to the client through encouragement, accessibility, and sensitivity to the client's vulnerabilities

Monitoring was essential to the success of the complex support system built to meet Jimmy's needs. It meant watching for breakdowns in the system, supporting the informal helpers and volunteers, and being available to offer Jimmy encouragement and, when necessary, to set limits.

Advocacy

Advocacy is the process of interceding on behalf of clients to assure that entitlements are received and rights are protected. Advocacy may require case managers to negotiate their way through agency bureaucracies to gain benefits for clients who cannot assert or articulate their needs. Or it may require arranging for legal services for clients whose civil rights have been denied.

In Jimmy's case, two situations required staff advocacy. When Jimmy moved to town, he applied for the SSI benefits to which he was entitled as a mentally disabled person. He needed the money to pay his room and board and other living expenses, but benefits initially were denied on a technicality. When a Friendship House staff member intervened on Jimmy's behalf, the decision was reversed in Jimmy's favor. On another occasion, staff advocated for the interests of several clients who lived in a group home when neighbors attempted to have the home "zoned" out of their neighborhood. By mobilizing influential citizens and agency board members, and by presenting testimony at the zoning hearing, Friendship House helped the group home obtain a favorable ruling.

DIFFERENCES BETWEEN
CASE MANAGEMENT AND CASEWORK

Case management differs in some fundamental ways from the more traditional casework offered in mental health centers. Caseworkers usually meet with their clients for regularly scheduled office appointments. They are also likely to place less emphasis on the impact of social forces in sustaining or undermining their clients' disabilities. The needs of the chronically mentally ill require that case managers possess the same skills of psychiatric diagnosis and clinical interviewing used by their casework counterparts. Arguing against the use of case managers solely as service coordinators, Richard Lamb states:

> The case manager should not be simply a broker of services, but should have the primary relationship with the patient . . . the patient's primary

therapist. . . . To help the long-term patient establish a satisfying life in the community requires a person who provides support and encouragement, has a thorough understanding of that patient, and has earned the patient's trust.[17]

Lamb does not recommend, however, that case managers engage in in-depth psychotherapy. He asserts that "the most meaningful psychotherapy with long-term patients is dealing with the realities and day-to-day issues of life and survival in the community."[18] In light of the many barriers facing ex-patients, it is certain that they cannot make the adjustment alone, nor can they survive if they are aided only by occasional refills of prescriptions and verbal therapies in a clinic office.

Thus a distinctive feature of case management is the need to intervene in neighborhood settings, bus terminals, police stations, and private homes. Traditionally trained caseworkers who become case managers often need retraining to free them from their attachment to the office. The Southwest Denver Community Mental Health Center, nationally recognized for its excellence in developing alternatives to hospital care, faced the problem of shifting the locus of intervention from the office into the natural environment:

> Initial evaluation procedures usually take place at home, at work, or in other real-life settings. [Although this] concept is attractive, actual implementation has involved substantial problems. Staff members need to learn how to operate in much less controlled and predictable environments. . . . This often threatens [their] authority, competence, and potency. . . . Members of the helping professions have a particular affinity to territoriality in the use of office space. Each treatment session is likely to be preceded by non-verbal signalling reaffirming the dominant position of the therapist. Patient-staff contact is decreased and stereotyped and the clinician is highly unlikely to be exposed to the real-life territorial space of the patient. Like the male stickleback, the courage of the mental health professional decreases in direct proportion to the distance from the nest. . . . [Our solution] was quite simple: we eliminated all staff offices."[19]

17. Richard Lamb, "Therapists-Case Managers: More than Brokers of Services," *Hospital and Community Psychiatry* 31 (November 1980), pp. 762-764.

18. Lamb, "Therapists-Case Managers," p. 764.

19. Paul R. Polak, "A Comprehensive System of Alternatives to Psychiatric Hospitalization," in *Alternatives to Mental Hospital Treatment*, ed. Leonard I. Stein and Mary Ann Test (New York: Plenum, 1978).

CASE MANAGERS' SKILLS, KNOWLEDGE, AND VALUES

To carry out the major functions of case management, competence in several roles is required. The worker must be able to meet the unique demands of working with chronically mentally ill persons, creating broad-scale supportive networks and often working outside an office in the "real world."

Case management is both a direct and an indirect service. There is considerable face-to-face contact with individual clients and others who are significant to them, but there is also much behind-the-scenes work with community groups. Examples of these indirect services include such activities as problem solving with a mental health association to develop appropriate housing, establishing an interorganizational council of agency staff members to promote delivery of services, conducting public forums to discuss the needs of mentally ill persons and debunk the myths about them, and inviting a state legislator to meet with concerned relatives about passing a bill to increase funding of community programs.

None of the services of case management, either direct or indirect, is unique to the process; yet the total configuration distinguishes it quite sharply from other forms of human services. On a typical day, for example, a case manager might provide therapy to a client in the morning, lead a support group of clients' families after lunch, and present evidence before a zoning board in the evening. This switching of roles is at once the most exhilarating and most difficult part of the job for most case managers.

The case management approach, which utilizes all of social work's methods, requires the worker to develop a broad knowledge base. In the area of mental health, for example, the case manager must be well versed in the subjects of legal rights, psychopathology, psychopharmacology, interagency policies and protocol, group theory and practice, principles of crisis intervention, social systems theory, and advocacy.

Certain aspects of the case manager's value system are unique. Perhaps the most fundamental value is that each client has dignity and is worthy of support in his or her attempt to create a satisfactory existence. This value is particularly crucial for case managers because their clients tend to be society's scapegoats and outcasts. Indeed, the case examples of Jimmy, John, Fred, and Sylvia would be disparaged by many community mental health workers as a "bunch of chronics."

Clinicians who use such terms admit they find aftercare clients unattractive, and their indifferences can lead to the creation of mass-production medication groups as an "efficient" way to "process" people who do not respond to their offers of verbal therapy. Case managers, on the other hand, work on behalf of any and all clients, personally attractive or not, because they emphasize the value of individual dignity and worth. Such a value, in turn, increases workers' satisfaction when even modest changes occur.

Case managers also have a unique ideology—a theory that incorporates their knowledge, skills, and value system. The ideology that guides case managers and motivates them to sustain their efforts, even in difficult or frustrating circumstances, includes the following beliefs:

- All people have an equal right to comfort, safety, and opportunity for social advancement.

- The chronically mentally ill (as well as all who suffer discrimination) may not have attained these basic rights, and their deprivation warrants extraordinary effort and compassion.

- Case managers become allies of clients and their families because some opportunities continue to be closed.

- The community can become more accepting—even part of the care-giving system—if its members are properly sought out, consulted, and nurtured in their efforts.

- The relationships between case managers and clients and between case managers and the community are egalitarian.

- The real-life environment of the client is often a more effective location for intervention than is the clinic office.

Franco Basaglia, an Italian psychiatrist, eloquently summarizes the ideology of working with the mentally disabled in the community:

For the mental health worker, this means an entirely new role: instead of acting as a go-between in the relationship between the patient and the hospital, he has to enter into conflicts in the real world—the family, the workplace, or the welfare agencies. These become the new arenas of "treatment," as the patient's private problems are turned back into public ones. Moreover, mental health workers are no longer impartial: they have to face the inequalities of power which engendered these crises, and put themselves wholeheartedly on the side of the weak. Acting outside the asylum (institution, clinic) situation, they of course lack any established expertise or authority: thus they have to function without any predetermined responses, on the basis of nothing more or less than their total commitment to the patient.[20]

SOCIAL WORKERS AS CASE MANAGERS

Just who are these renaissance people who perform the functions and possess the ideology of case management? Actually, the requirements described in this chapter are deliberately comprehensive, encompassing a range of services in a variety of programs. Nonetheless, there is a common denominator of functions that distinguishes case management from other methods of intervention. It is the blending of psychotherapeutic and sociotherapeutic orientations, and the conviction that the problems of the chronically mentally ill are caused and maintained by an interplay of psychological and social forces, that a complete "cure" may never occur, and that an assortment of direct and indirect services are needed for successful community adjustment.

If any profession can claim leadership in this arena, it is social work. The claim can be made on empirical grounds, because social workers are employed as case managers more frequently than are members of other professions, and because job descriptions often require social work education and/or officially classify positions as those of social work. However, there are also strong theoretical and historical reasons case management falls within the domain of social work.

From the theoretical perspective, a definition of the function of social work shows how it meshes with the function of case management:

Social work is the science and art of aiding people whose personal and/or family resources are insufficient. . . . Social work is . . . concerned with . . . :
1. Personal care and support
2. Advice and/or counseling in regard to personal and behavioral problems
3. Advice in establishing, improving and/or utilizing opportunities and resources such as housing, income, employment, health, legal counsel, social services, education, and case and class advocacy.[21]

20. Franco Basaglia, "Breaking the Circuit of Control," in *Critical Psychiatry: The Politics of Mental Health*, ed. David Ingleby (New York: Pantheon, 1980), p. 190.
21. John B. Turner, "Excellence in Social Work Education," paper presented at Rutgers, the State University of New Jersey, 25 May 1981, pp. 8-9.

This definition is compatible—almost identical—with the function and ideology of case management. Indeed, the raison d'être of case management—active, ongoing development and coordination of services for persons who are unable to care for themselves—is remarkably similar to social work's function of "aiding people whose personal and/or family resources are insufficient."

Historically, the fundamental tenet of social work has been the worth and dignity of the individual, and this is a guiding principle of case management. Many social work ideals harmonize with case management, for example: Morris's assertion of the appropriateness of caring for disabled persons; Pincus and Minahan's notion of expanding the "action system"; Levy's call for advocacy for disadvantaged groups; Collins and Pancoast's principle of linking; Reid's concept of task-centered practice; and Lubove's "mezzo-system" of intervention.[22] Thus there is strong precedent in social work for the case management ideology.

The social worker as case manager combines casework with group work, family work, and community organization. This constellation of roles differentiates social work from more narrowly bounded professions and places social workers at the cutting edge of expanding opportunities in the human services. Although the unavoidable ambiguity of combining functions and balancing social and psychological orientations leads to occasional and tiresome debates over the question "What is social work, anyway?" it is precisely this fluidity of function and mental agility in balancing perspectives that makes social work the keystone profession in developing community support systems.

CASE MANAGEMENT IN THE 1980s

Case management is still emerging as a formal method of social work practice, and there are many issues to be resolved before it attains the recognition enjoyed by more traditional forms of practice. Moreover, although there are convincing logical grounds for social

22. Robert Morris, "Caring for Versus Caring About People," *Social Work* 22 (September 1977), pp. 353-359; Allen Pincus and Anne Minahan, *Social Work Practice: Models and Methods* (Itasca, IL: Peacock, 1973); Charles S. Levy, "Advocacy and the Injustice of Justice," *Social Service Review* 48 (March 1974), pp. 39-50; Collins and Pancoast, *Natural Helping Networks;* William J. Reid and Laura Epstein, *Task-Centered Casework* (New York: Columbia University Press, 1972); and Roy Lubove, *The Professional Altruist* (New York: Athenum, 1972).

work to lead in the development of the method, many social workers do not, in fact, want to be case managers.[23]

A fundamental issue is disagreement about a definition. The Case Management Research Project found that emphases in case management activities varied. Mental health settings used a "mixed model," with primary emphasis on "extensive client contact with therapeutic counseling as the focus, and on extensive evaluation of the client's psychological status." Case managers in community mental health centers were least clear, of all settings examined, about expected tasks and activities, and were least committed to the case management approach. The researchers concluded that this emphasis on psychotherapy represented "a critical barrier to the development of case management systems."[24]

Several other factors have probably contributed to the limited development of case management in mental health settings. Fiscal realities, for example, may be inhibitory, because community mental health centers rely heavily on "reimbursable services" such as psychotherapy for their survival. Public funds are declining in the 1980s, and indirect services are not covered by Medicaid or private insurance plans. Public support of case management may increase in the future, however. The continued interest of most states in the process of deinstitutionalization, if only for financial reasons, is certain. Some programs of community-based care have been demonstrated to be cost-effective,[25] and it is likely that many states will fund similar programs in the coming years.

At this early stage of its development, it is impossible to assert that case management is superior to the more traditional methods of service. We do know that some model programs have produced favorable results, and that the severe needs of the chronically mentally disabled have not been well served by other efforts. We also know that community support for the mentally ill must be nurtured

23 Allen Rubin and Peter J. Johnson, "Practitioner Orientations Toward the Chronically Disabled: Prospects for Policy Implementation," Administration in Mental Health 10 (Fall 1982), pp. 3-12.

24. David M. Austin and Penelope Caragonne (co-principal investigators), A Comparative Analysis of Twenty-Two Settings Using Case Management Components (Austin: Case Management Research Project, University of Texas at Austin School of Social Work, 1981).

25. Les Greene and Arnold de la Cruz, "Psychiatric Day Treatment as Alternative to and Transition from Full-Time Hospitalization," Community Mental Health Journal 17 (Fall 1981), pp. 191-202.

slowly, because fear and prejudice still exist; and we know that not all human service professionals have the enthusiasm and requisite skills for case management. We have not found a reliable way to instill a sense of dedication to this population in community mental health workers, and we have not strengthened organizational reward systems for case managers. However, the need for case management will not abate in the coming decades; political and economic uncertainties notwithstanding, there will probably be a slow but sure increase in the number of community support programs, with a corresponding increase in employment opportunities for case managers.

So far, social work's claim to leadership in developing community support programs has been quiet and uncertain; but there is every reason for it to be loud and clear. Social workers who take pride in their profession's diverse repertoire of skills and its history of championing society's rejects can find professional satisfaction in working as case managers. The combination of enabling individuals to become more competent and enlisting the compassionate strength of communities on their behalf is at the heart of both traditional social work and case management.

SUGGESTED READING

Bachrach, Leona L. *Deinstitutionalization: An Analytical Review and Sociological Perspective*. Rockville, MD: National Institute of Mental Health, 1976.

Collins, Alice H., and Diane L. Pancoast, *Natural Helping Networks*. Washington DC: National Association of Social Workers, 1976.

Morris, Robert. "Caring for Versus Caring About People." *Social Work* 22 (September 1977):353-359.

President's Commission on Mental Health. "Community Support Systems" and "Deinstitutionalization," in *Task Panel Reports*, Vol. 2. Washington, DC: Superintendent of Documents, 1978.

Reid, William. *The Task-Centered System*. New York: Columbia University Press, 1978.

Segal, Steven, and Jim Baumohl, "Social Work Practice in Community Mental Health." *Social Work* 26 (January 1981):16-24.

Stein, Leonard I., and Mary Ann Test, eds. *Alternatives to Mental Hospital Treatment*. New York: Plenum, 1978.

Talbott, John A., ed. *The Chronic Mental Patient*. Washington, DC: American Psychiatric Association, 1978.

PART IV

SOCIAL WORK PRACTICE IN VARIED SETTINGS

Now that you understand the scope of social work practice, the range of policies and programs available to social workers to help people, and the contemporary methods by which this helping takes place, it is important to see how these three elements of social work come together in a helping process. To illustrate this coming together, Part IV of this textbook provides seven examples drawn from real-life social work practice. These examples were prepared by the social workers who were responsible for the various activities reflected in the case studies. But although the examples are real-life situations, and although the people who have written about these situations are real-life social workers, the names of the people worked with (and sometimes the names of the organizations that provided the services) have been changed. These changes are necessary to protect the clients from any sense of exploitation that might result from the presentation of these teaching-learning case studies.

Because these examples of social work practice are included in this text as a means of illustrating the materials presented in the first three parts of the book, it might be more useful to draw on this illustrative material throughout the use of this textbook rather than waiting until the end. At any rate, the materials in Part IV show clearly the overlapping elements of social work. For example, methods, philosophy, and services are interwoven in all these examples. Furthermore, the examples illustrate the overlap and complementarity of the social work methods themselves. Finally, the examples show that professional social workers do some things that are not explained by the materials in this textbook. This is due to several factors: There is still much about social work practice that is not known; social workers have many individual talents that they use in helping situations; and the structure of agencies that provide services often requires unique practice activities.

Because these are real-life examples, students may question whether the services are offered in the right way, or even if the workers always did the right thing. The real world of social work practice differs from the world of theory as presented in earlier parts of this book. These are frustrations that social workers face when, despite everything they do, situations do not improve, and there are always limitations placed on workers as to what they are allowed to do. Thus these examples also illustrate patience and personal dedication, which are professional attributes that are difficult to teach. The case of protective services for Tom Raymond (Case 1) and the story of Nickie (Case 2) demonstrate that social workers also need to have a fundamental concern for the welfare of others in order to express the devotion and patience such cases require.

Case 3 is an unusual story of the development of better social resources for ethnic and minority populations. Little has been said in this textbook about the plight of this disadvantaged group, whose members often are not disadvantaged through any fault of their own but because some Americans do not like the color of their skins. Such prejudices are so deeply ingrained in American society that often social work goes about its professional business without special attention to such forms of discrimination. Case 3 should be a strong reminder of social work's commitment to racial and ethnic minorities while serving as an illustration of how social work help can serve to bridge the social distance between idealism and reality in American life.

Case 4 is another excellent example of how social work methods become mixed depending upon the field of social work. In this case the field of medical social work requires a different mixture of methods than does the field of child welfare. Case 5 illustrates the application of social group work. It is interesting to contrast the social work outcomes of Case 5 with those in Case 6. Despite the fact that different methods are employed by the social workers, many of the results are the same. Thus a comparison of these two examples illustrates how different agency structures and different social resources may require different methods in order to reach the same basic goals. Finally, Case 7 illustrates the diversity of social work practice and its common helping themes; consultation in industrial settings shows the need to blend several social work methods that emerge in what seems to be a unique way of practicing social work. It is through an expanded process of such blending of methods that old methods of social work practice are changed and new methods are institutionalized.

This textbook closes with an important summary section by John Turner. With considerable candor, Turner discusses several of the most important debates in social work that often confuse beginning social workers. Often the introduction to the field of social work is so ensnarled with long-standing debates over its mission in society that beginning workers lose sight of the fundamental unity that binds social workers and social work practice together. From the broader view that Turner provides, many of the dilemmas that served to divide social workers—such as methodological debates or debates over who is to be served—become not so much obstacles as benchmarks in the development of a profession and guidance for its future development.

One major fact stands out above all others in Turner's discussion, and in the discussion of many of the other contributors: The future development of social work is closely related to the American commitment to set aside resources for its disadvantaged people. America has always been the land of hope and opportunity, and these lofty ideals have been realized through the generosity and social commitment of Americans. No textbook, no profession, no college or university degree can ensure such commitment among Americans. As with other American ideals, commitment to others must be borne by all of us.

CASE 1

PROFILES OF ABUSE AND NEGLECT
Protective Services for Children in a Department of Social Services

LANE COOKE

Social Worker, Department of Social Services
Orange County, North Carolina

ROBERTA KYLE

Social Worker, The Treehouse
Chapel Hill, North Carolina

LINDA REIFSNYDER

Social Worker, Department of Mental Health
Orange County, North Carolina

The status of children as individuals with certain basic rights has been acknowledged by all of the states and the District of Columbia since 1964, when the last state passed laws related to child abuse, neglect, and dependency. In 1974, the federal government made protective services for children mandatory for states receiving federal funds for social services (Title XX of the Social Security Act).

The words *abuse, neglect,* and *dependency* may have different connotations for different people, but each state defines them legally in order to limit the situations in which society may intervene to protect children, with or without permission of their caretakers. *Abuse* is usually defined as intentional physical or mental injury inflicted on a child by the parent or caretaker. *Neglect* refers to a lack of proper supervision or attention to a child's medical, educational, or physical care. The term *dependency* describes the status of a child who has special needs that cannot be, or are not being, met by the parent or caretaker. Taken together, these legal terms describe a group of children who are in need of community intervention on their behalf.

The Child Protective Services (CPS) unit of the Department of Social Services accepts referrals from anyone in the community who is seriously concerned about a child's welfare. Occasionally, self-referrals are made by children or parents. The identified problems can vary greatly; they include excessive conflict and violence within the family, extreme poverty and deprivation, running away from home, and emotional disturbance or retardation that cannot be dealt with by the parents. After the referral is received, the CPS worker gathers facts and assesses the situation. Assessment is accomplished by visiting the family at home and by talking with others who have knowledge of the child's status. CPS agencies usually provide 24-hour coverage for emergency referrals and are legally required to respond to all referrals within a stated period of time.

When all of the pertinent information has been gathered, the CPS worker decides to what degree, if any, the child is at risk of serious harm and whether the environment is dangerous enough to warrant removing the child. Removing a child from home can be traumatic, and such a decision is made only after careful assessment of the family's ability or willingness to protect the child.

Although other community workers (for instance, school social workers, psychologists, mental health center staff workers) also assess family problems, it is usually the CPS worker's responsibility to take whatever legal action is required to remove the responsibility for the child temporarily from the parent or caretaker. Whether the child remains at home or is placed in a safer environment, the CPS worker is also responsible for devising a treatment plan to resolve the family's identified problems. The CPS case is not closed until the child is receiving all necessary care or attention and the agency no longer needs to oversee the child's welfare.

The following cases illustrate two common types of family responses to CPS intervention. The first is a case of abuse and the second is one of neglect.[1]

A CASE OF ABUSE

Rebecca Jones, a CPS caseworker at the Department of Social Services, was on emergency call Friday night, when the police social worker called to report a complaint she had received from Tom Raymond, a 10-year-old boy. Tom said he decided to call after seeing the police worker's number listed under "child abuse" in the telephone book. He stated that his stepfather had beaten him with a belt, leaving bruises across his legs and buttocks, and that he was tired of being threatened and hit.

Initial Home Visit (May 1980)

On Saturday morning, Ms. Jones went to Tom's home, a large and imposing house in an upper-middle-class neighborhood. As she approached the immaculately tended house and grounds, her anxiety increased. Although Ms. Jones had been working in CPS only a few months, she knew the Raymonds were a well-educated professional couple who were highly respected in the community. As the provider of an "involuntary" social service, Ms. Jones was bringing the Raymonds a message from the community that there was a concern about how they were caring for the safety of their child. It would be natural for the Raymonds' defenses to be raised, and she expected that this first contact would have some elements of an adversary relationship. In order to get the parents' side of the story, she would need to convince the Raymonds that she was open to their explanation and to focus the discussion on sorting out the family's problems.

Ms. Jones was met at the front door by Mr. and Mrs. Raymond. They were shocked to learn that the reason for her visit was that a report had been received about their son's having some physical injuries.

1. The names, personal characteristics, and circumstances of clients have been changed to protect their anonymity.

Ms. Jones explained her legal responsibility to check on Tom's safety after the report had been filed. She also explained that, by law, the CPS worker must keep confidential the identity of the person who made the referral, although in this case it seemed easy for the Raymonds to guess that Tom himself had told someone about the spanking. As they went into the living room, Mr. Raymond told Tom to go upstairs to his bedroom and watch television.

Mrs. Raymond told the caseworker that Tom had been spanked the day before because of his behavior at school. As John Raymond told the story of the whipping, he became uncomfortable and finally said he wanted his attorney to be present before they went any further. As the couple's surprise diminished, their anger at Ms. Jones's visit increased, and Ms. Jones responded by saying that she would return in an hour.

During the intervening hour, Ms. Jones enlisted the help of another CPS worker so that one of them could interview Tom while the other talked with his parents. The second worker was a more experienced CPS staff member, and Ms. Jones welcomed her support. When the two returned to the Raymonds' home, they found the couple's attorney waiting for them with the Raymonds. Apparently he had advised the parents to cooperate with the agency because they appeared to be more receptive. The more experienced worker met with the parents while Ms. Jones interviewed Tom upstairs, with his parents' permission.

Mr. Raymond said he had whipped Tom with a belt because Tom had told his teacher to "go jump in a lake." This was just one of many similar incidents, and the parents were frustrated by their inability to control Tom's behavior. They also remarked that it was a serious blow to their egos to have someone come to their home to question their ability as parents. The CPS worker did not personalize the Raymonds' anger and hostility. She knew they needed this opportunity to express their feelings. Abusive or neglectful parents usually can come to respond positively if the worker shows sincere concern and interest in their problems.

Meanwhile, Ms. Jones encouraged Tom to talk with his mother and stepfather about his feelings of fear and shame. Later, with Ms. Jones's support, Tom was able to tell his parents that he was afraid much of the time and didn't like being threatened and spanked constantly. The workers advised the Raymonds that a medical evaluation would be necessary to determine whether Tom had any injuries (he had not allowed Ms. Jones to inspect his bruises). They encouraged Mrs.

Raymond to take Tom to his pediatrician. She agreed to do so, and the workers praised her for her cooperation. The subsequent physical examination showed five areas of bruised and broken skin on the backs of Tom's legs and buttocks, most of which were about 4 × 4 inches in size. The bruises were dark colored and approximately three days old. Other than the bruises and cuts, the thorough examination showed no other physical problems.

Investigation

As part of the family assessment, Ms. Jones talked with Tom's teacher and explored his family background through medical histories and school records. Tom's teacher reported that Tom had transferred from another elementary school during the year because of a "personality conflict" between Tom and his former teacher. The new teacher found Tom to be a bright student, but one who was in constant trouble because of hitting people, stealing, and talking back to the teacher.

In a telephone conversation with the guidance counselor at Tom's former school, Ms. Jones discovered that the Raymonds had removed Tom from the school following a disagreement with the counselor and the school principal, who had recommended that the family seek counseling or therapy. A picture of Tom and his family began to emerge from these discussions.

Family History

The family history that Ms. Jones pieced together revealed that in 1977, Tom's mother and father had been divorced, and Tom subsequently spent some time with his father, whom he began to idolize. The next year, following a two-month illness, Tom's father died. Next, Tom turned to his paternal grandfather, upon whom he began to depend as the male adult in his life, but the grandfather also died suddenly during that year. At about the same time, Tom's mother began to date John Raymond, and Tom could not allow Mr. Raymond to take the place of his biological father or grandfather. Tom began to feel rage toward Mr. Raymond, especially when his mother married Mr. Raymond in 1979. His acting-out behavior at school, which had begun during the time of his parents' divorce, increased steadily. Tom's new stepfather began to use physical discipline in an attempt to gain control over the boy's behavior, and on this latest occasion had apparently lost his temper while whipping Tom. The situation had deteriorated to the point where Tom was being threatened and spanked almost daily.

Consultation

The Raymonds continued to resist CPS agency intervention, maintaining that they were able to handle the situation. Feeling a need for consultation, Ms. Jones asked for a meeting of the community's multidisciplinary child protection team (composed of a pediatrician, mental health center staff member, child psychologist, public health nurse, and attorney). The team's function was to make recommendations for family treatment plans when CPS staff needed assistance. Mr. and Mrs. Raymond were informed about the meeting and invited to attend, but they chose not to be present.

After reviewing the information presented by Ms. Jones, the team concluded that Tom had not resolved his feelings about recent major changes in his life. They wrote a letter to the Raymonds, strongly recommending that Tom and his parents seek counseling with a social worker, psychologist, or psychiatrist. The team reassured Ms. Jones that since Tom had notified the proper authorities on the last occasion of excessive discipline, they believed he would do so if there were future episodes.

Ms. Jones met with Tom at school to talk about her concern for his safety, and Tom said he would contact the agency if any further serious problems arose. Next, she talked with the Raymonds, who said they had made plans for Tom to attend a summer camp. Ms. Jones found their plans to be appropriate and adequate.

Closing the Case (October 1980)

At the end of the summer, Ms. Jones received a letter from a local clinical psychologist who was seeing all three Raymonds in family therapy. The psychologist reported that both Tom and his stepfather were making efforts to relate to one another, and that he had observed in Tom some beginning affection for Mr. Raymond. He planned to continue meeting with the family as a group and with Tom individually.

Ms. Jones was satisfied that the family was receiving the help it needed, and that the danger of physical abuse of Tom was past. Therefore, the CPS file on the Raymond family was closed.

A CASE OF NEGLECT

The Jacksons lived in a two-bedroom public housing unit. The family included Mr. and Mrs. Jackson, their daughter Susan, and Susan's three children. Mr. and Mrs. Jackson also had three older children who no longer resided in the state.

At the time of the family's contact with the CPS unit of the Department of Social Services (DSS), Mr. Jackson was 48 years old, had been disabled in an accident, and was receiving social security benefits. Mrs. Jackson (age 46) worked seven days a week as a kitchen helper in a local restaurant. Susan, who was 20, had dropped out of school at the age of 14 when she became pregnant (the same age at which she was put on probation for assaulting a teacher). Susan's three children were Tina (age 5), Danny (age 4), and Willy (age 8 months).

Initial Family Request for Service (October 1978)

Mrs. Jackson telephoned the DSS to request that her grandchildren, Tina and Danny, be placed in foster care because their mother, Susan, was rarely at home to care for them. When a worker visited the home the next day, however, both Susan and her parents denied any problems and refused services. No further action was taken by the DSS.

Second Family Request for Service (December 1978)

Susan telephoned the DDS to request that Tina and Danny be placed in foster care "so that I can get out on my own." Again, when a caseworker visited the home, the family denied any problems and no further action was taken.

First Community Referral (April 1979)

The DSS received a referral from a local hospital concerning Susan's failure to bring her newborn son, Willy, for his scheduled checkup. Because this referral was a community report of possible neglect, the CPS worker assigned to the case was legally required to investigate and to keep the case open until appropriate action was taken.

The worker visited the Jackson home that afternoon, where she talked with Mrs. Jackson about the importance of Willy's pediatric checkups. Mrs. Jackson was furious and said, "Why are you bothering me? I'm not Willy's mother and he's not my responsibility. Talk with Susan if you have a problem." Then she stormed out of the room.

The worker learned from a neighbor that Susan had left the home several days earlier without warning and had not yet returned. The worker remained nonjudgmental about this information, because she knew that in some communities and cultures it is not only acceptable, but often necessary, for extended family networks to care for children, sometimes without identification of a primary caretaker. Still, she was puzzled by Mrs. Jackson's apparent lack of concern for Willy's welfare.

The next day, the CPS worker telephoned Mrs. Jackson to ask if they might talk about Susan, since her absences seemed to be causing a problem for the family. Mrs. Jackson, sensing that the worker was sympathetic to her stress, hesitantly agreed. During their meeting, the worker again explained that Willy's pediatrician was concerned about the child's medical condition. The worker knew that neglect often stems from family stress, and she suggested that Mrs. Jackson probably had many reasons for feeling angry at the worker's implication that Willy was not being well cared for, as well as for being angry with Susan for leaving her with the responsibility of three young children. Mrs. Jackson broke into sobs as she recalled her own experience of having been bounced from caretaker to caretaker following her mother's death when Mrs. Jackson was 2 years old. She also told the worker that she had dropped out of school at the age of 12 to go to work, and described not being able to meet her family's financial needs. She had to work at night in order to care for her disabled husband during the day. Finally, Mrs. Johnson said, "It's more than I can handle." This early "owning" of problems surprised and pleased the CPS worker. The ultimate goal of CPS is to turn an involuntary intervention into a therapeutic relationship, a goal that can be accomplished only if the family can recognize and "own" their problems. Usually, because of the adversary relationship involved, it takes some time for families to accept their problems as their own.

Having acknowledged Mrs. Jackson's pain and struggle, the worker again emphasized Willy's need for medical care, and asked how she and the family could work together to accomplish that goal. Mrs. Jackson suggested that if the worker arranged the appointments, she could take Willy to the clinic, provided she could find someone to watch Tina and Danny. The worker agreed to make the appointments and further offered to arrange day care for the three children. Perhaps most important, however, was the fact that Mrs. Jackson agreed to meet weekly with Susan and the worker to discuss the routines and responsibilities of child care and to monitor the progress they were making in their plans for day care and medical work. Despite all efforts, Susan never met with Mrs. Jackson and the worker. Tina and Danny's father agreed to provide some clothing and to visit the children twice a month, but Willy's father could not be located.

Second Community Referral (May 1979)

On a Monday morning, the CPS worker received a call from Willy's day-care teacher. Willy was severely dehydrated and had a temperature of 104° and a serious diaper rash. The teacher had rushed him to the hospital, but parental consent was needed to admit him for observation. After four hours of searching, the worker was still unable to locate any family member, and the physician believed the child could no longer wait for treatment. Having consulted with her supervisor, the worker contacted the juvenile court judge and explained the emergency. Next, she filed a petition that cited the fact that the child required immediate medical treatment and parental consent could not be obtained. The judge signed an order granting temporary custody of Willy to the CPS agency, an action that is taken only when a child's health or welfare is at risk. The more usual procedure is first to hear the parent's side of the story.

That afternoon, while having Willy admitted to the hospital, the worker had an opportunity to talk with hospital and day-care personnel. She learned that Willy had had an ear infection on Friday. The day-care nurse had taken him home and explained to Susan how to administer the necessary medication. Willy's hygienic condition on Monday was such that the physician was sure Willy had not been bathed or had his diapers changed during the entire weekend. In fact, the physician wondered if the child could have survived one more day in his crib at home. The severity of the ear infection indicated that Willy had not been given any of the medication.

When she left the hospital, the CPS worker stopped at the Jackson home to explain that Willy was in the hospital. Susan was not at home, and the worker was shocked by Mrs. Jackson's nonchalance about the hospitalization and custody proceedings. Mrs. Jackson's concluding statement was, "You'll never take Tina and Danny away from me, but I never want to see that worthless child again. His father once murdered a man and nobody ever wanted that child." Now the worker had a clue as to why Willy had received less care and attention than his older siblings.

During the next three days, the worker met with day-care and hospital staff in preparation for the required juvenile court hearing. These professionals gave detailed accounts of their involvement with Willy and his mother and compared Willy's hygienic and physical condition on Friday and Monday. The physician stated that Willy had been critically ill upon admission to the hospital.

Susan appeared at the court hearing on Friday and requested that an attorney be appointed by the court to represent her because she was unable to pay for legal services. The hearing was scheduled to be held in two weeks, and in the meantime the judge granted the CPS agency an extension of temporary custody so that Willy could be placed in a temporary foster home when he was released from the hospital the next day.

Two weeks later, the CPS agency presented evidence at the hearing that Willy's family was unwilling or unable to cooperate in assuring that Willy would not continue to be a neglected child. This legal procedure through the juvenile court is the only avenue through which a parent's decision-making rights can be removed. On the basis of the evidence, the judge found Susan to be a neglectful parent and awarded custody of Willy to the agency. Willy's foster-care placement was to be continued, and the case was to be judicially reviewed in six months.

Susan refused to talk with the CPS worker after the hearing. She did not appear to be upset over the judge's decision, but the worker could not tell whether her reaction reflected apathy or a feeling of helplessness, both of which are commonly found among neglectful parents. Susan left town the next day and was not heard from again by the agency or by the Jackson family.

During her continued weekly visits with Mrs. Jackson, the worker was unable to detect any grief reaction on the grandmother's part to the fact that Willy had been removed from the home. In fact, Mrs. Jackson appeared to be relieved that she no longer had responsibility for Willy, and she refused to visit him, stating, "Like I said, I never want to see him again." In contrast, Mrs. Jackson's care of Tina and Danny improved significantly. She and the worker negotiated a six-month contract in which the worker agreed to help the Jacksons obtain legal custody of the two children, to arrange for physical and dental examinations, to help Mrs. Jackson apply for financial aid and food stamps, and to help register Tina for kindergarten in the fall. Mrs. Jackson, in turn, agreed to continue meeting with the CPS worker weekly to discuss the children's progress, to cooperate with all legal, financial, and medical requirements, and to attend all appointments. She also agreed to visit the day-care center monthly to meet with Tina's and Danny's teachers. The worker had carefully designed the contract so that it was based on Mrs. Jackson's needs and strengths and actively involved the client in working toward realistic short- and long-term goals. The language was behavior-specific and clear, and the activities were set within definite time limits.

Progress Report (September 1979 to February 1980)

A Legal Aid attorney helped the Jacksons obtain custody of Danny and Tina, and the family's financial distress was relieved by AFDC checks, which began to arrive in September. Both children had physical examinations and were found to be healthy and normal; their immunization records were brought up to date. Meanwhile, Tina started kindergarten. The teachers reported that Tina and Danny were "different children" than they had been in April—much calmer and happier, and less dependent and demanding of constant attention. Mrs. Jackson glowed when she received these reports as well as the worker's repeated praise for her increasing attention to the children.

Willy continued to grow stronger and healthier in his foster home. He no longer resembled the scrawny, dirty, emotionless child of three months earlier. The agency permanency planning team met in November to discuss placement goals for Willy. The purpose of permanency planning is to avoid the necessity of having children remain in foster care for indefinite periods. When children remain in impermanent situations for long periods of time, they cannot develop clear feelings of belonging and security. The goal, therefore, is to return foster children to their natural families as quickly as possible or to find permanent adoptive families. In Willy's case, since no family member was willing to care for him, the decision was that Willy's best interests required adoption as soon as possible. In January 1980, Willy's biological parents' rights were terminated by the juvenile court. Neither parent appeared at the hearing. Permanent adoption plans were formalized to allow Willy's foster parents to adopt him, and the adoption was completed in February.

Closing the Case (November 1980)

When their six-month contract expired, Mrs. Jackson and the CPS worker met to review their progress toward mutual goals. Mrs. Jackson had been kept informed of the adoption plans for Willy and had begun to express the feeling that "it is the best thing the family can do for him, just as we are doing for Tina and Danny." While Mrs. Jackson and the worker agreed that it was time for the Jackson family to proceed without further assistance, Mrs. Jackson assured the worker that she would feel comfortable in contacting the agency in the future if further problems arose. The two bid a warm farewell, each with a feeling of accomplishment.

CASE 2

NICKIE'S STORY
Specialized Adoption Services in a Department of Social Services

ANN SULLIVAN
Lecturer, School of Social Work
University of North Carolina, Chapel Hill

THE SETTING

Traditionally, adoption services in the United States have consisted mainly of the placement of the newborn infants of unmarried mothers with white middle- or upper-class couples who were unable to produce children biologically. Recently, however, social changes have profoundly affected this traditional pattern of service. Widespread use of effective birth control measures, changing mores that allow unmarried mothers to keep their children with less social stigma, and legalized abortions have all contributed to a significant decrease in the number of infants available for adoption. Concurrently, societal developments have contributed to an increased awareness of and concern for children who are growing up without nurturing families or stability. These developments include more extensive knowledge of the effects of growing up in poverty, increased public awareness of the incidence of child abuse and neglect, and the civil rights movement, which sanctions the concept of children's rights as well as parents' rights.

Ideally, child welfare services represent a continuum of supportive services to families and children, including preventive and protective services, temporary foster care, group home and institutional care, and adoption. For several decades, however, little was done to develop effective preventive services to help families stay together. Rather, temporary foster care was frequently offered as the service of choice. Although foster care is a valuable part of the complete range of services, too often the temporary plan has become the permanent solution, and countless children have grown up in foster care inappropriately, sometimes living out their childhood years in a series of foster homes.

Over the last fifteen years, changes in society have led to a rethinking of the role of families and the needs of children. Faced with a shortage of infants and with large numbers of childless couples who want to adopt a child, some adoption agencies have begun to experiment with placing children who formerly were considered "unadoptable." This new facet of adoption, which has evolved since the late 1960s, is usually referred to as *specialized adoption*. Specialized adoption responds to a recognition of the fact that the needs of older, minority, and handicapped children can be better met through adoption than through foster care. The concept is based on the conviction that adoptive families can be found for children who once were considered unadoptable, if agencies aggressively recruit families and prepare them for this radically different form of adoption. Nickie, whose story follows, is one child who was served through a specialized adoption program in a county department of social services.

NICKIE'S HISTORY[1]

Nickie was almost 8 years old when he came to the attention of the Department of Social Services' adoption unit. Nickie's foster-care worker had requested a conference to determine whether an adoptive home could be found for him, even though his chances seemed remote. At the conference, Nickie was described by the foster-care worker as a small, fragile-looking youngster with light blond hair, very pale complexion, and dark brown eyes. He was underweight, wore thick glasses, and was on medication for hyperactivity. He had periodic episodes of internal bleeding, the cause of which was unknown. Nickie participated in a day-care program for seriously disturbed children at the state hospital. Each evening, he returned to his foster family. However, his worker was expecting the family to request Nickie's removal in the near future, and she had been able to find no other family with whom he might live. Having heard that the agency was placing older and handicapped children for adoption, the foster-care worker wanted to investigate the possibility of finding someone to adopt Nickie, although both she and her supervisor saw little hope for this solution.

During the conference, the foster-care supervisor stated that Nickie had lived in sixteen homes since entering foster care at the age of 2. This was an unusually high number of foster-care placements at such an early age. Only incomplete information was available, but it appeared that Nickie had been moved often because of his destructive behavior, including attacks on other children in the foster homes, stubbornness and moodiness, and soiling. Before considering Nickie's prospects for adoption, the adoption unit requested further information about Nickie's current functioning, his developmental history, and his placement history, including the reason for initial placement.

During the second conference, the foster unit worker provided the following information. At the hospital program, Nickie was described as hyperactive, a condition for which Ritalin was being administered. His behavior was confusing; some days he was cooperative,

---

1. Nickie's name and those of his temporary caretakers and adoptive family have been changed to preserve their anonymity.

perceptive, and sensitive to those around him, was quite verbal, and displayed a good sense of humor. On other occasions he was destructive, stubborn, and nearly nonverbal. There seemed no obvious reason for his wide mood swings. He loved all kinds of music and enjoyed contact with the other children in the program. At times, however, he became so destructive that he had to be removed and physically restrained. Nickie had many fears—the dark, the devil, ghosts, fire, getting hurt, and bathrooms. His fear of bathrooms was intense, including resistance to entering a bathroom, resistance to using the toilet, a dread of flushing the toilet because he feared going down the drain with the water, and a fear of being left alone in a bathroom. Nickie frequently used bad language, and seemed to enjoy shocking adults with his extensive and colorful vocabulary. He was also described as having a voracious appetite; he ate any food available, even to the point of making himself ill. Dental problems, gastrointestinal difficulties, diarrhea, soiling, and periodic episodes of blood in his stools were chronic and unresolved problems. Despite this multitude of problems, however, the hospital staff remained optimistic about Nickie, indicating that he had made "tremendous progress" since entering the day-care program. They were opposed to any suggestion of institutionalizing Nickie and, perhaps surprisingly, described him as an appealing child "in his own way."

Nickie had come into foster care on an emergency basis at the age of 2, after he had witnessed the murder of his mother by his father. When he entered care, he was thought to be retarded. He was described as extremely nervous, and was given tranquilizers for stomach and digestive problems. He had frequent problems with diarrhea, earaches, and colds, and was found to be anemic. Tests indicated a possibility of minimal brain injury. Ritalin was prescribed to control his hyperactivity when Nickie was 4 years old.

Several months after Nickie entered foster care, both sets of grandparents were located and consulted about an appropriate plan. The families were still grieving over the tragedy and thought it would be better if Nickie did not live with either family because he would be a constant reminder of the murder. The grandparents provided minimal information about Nickie's early development, including an indication that Nickie's mother had had a normal pregnancy and delivery. They described Nickie as a fat, healthy baby who walked at 10 months and talked at 18 months. His only health problems during the first 18 months had been several episodes of diarrhea, and pneumonia at about age 1 year. Because, at that time, the agency was placing only infants for adopion, and because the grandparents did not want the child, long-term foster care was the plan selected for Nickie.

Thus Nickie came to experience an extremely unfortunate series of sixteen moves from one foster home to another between the ages of 2 and 7. Some of these moves were due solely to problems within the foster families, such as illness, a serious fire, or moving out of the state. Many of the moves, however, were a direct result of Nickie's increasingly destructive behavior, moodiness, stubbornness, and continued problems with diarrhea and soiling. Several of the placements were for brief stays in emergency shelters or receiving homes, an action made necessary when one plan broke down and another had not yet been developed.

At the conclusion of the second conference, alternative methods for helping Nickie were outlined. These included continued placement with foster families, placement in a group home, institutionalization, or adoption. Before settling for any of the other alternatives, the workers decided to try to locate an adoptive family for Nickie.

INTERVENTION

Because Nickie's current placement was tenuous, the first task was to determine whether either an adoptive family or another foster family could be found. Nickie's background information was given to all of the staff members of the adoption unit. They were asked to screen families currently under study and those already approved for adoption to determine if any families already known to the agency might be possible resources for Nickie. Three families were identified, but the available information indicated that none was a suitable resource. Next, the search for a home for Nickie was expanded to include contacts with foster-care supervisors in the Departments of Social Services in surrounding counties. One of these supervisors indicated that a recent applicant, Ms. Dwyer, might be helpful. Although their study of Ms. Dwyer was not complete, the supervisor recalled that this applicant was a psychiatric social worker who had expressed interest in providing foster care to boys. She had extensive professional experience in working with children and adolescents, in both residential and outpatient settings as well as in summer camps for disturbed children.

Nickie's adoption worker contacted Ms. Dwyer about the possibility of providing temporary care if it became necessary to move Nickie while searching for an adoptive family. The staff of the adoption unit thought Ms. Dwyer's professional training would enable her to provide invaluable help in gaining a better understanding of Nickie's problems and his potential for overcoming them. After careful consideration and an opportunity to observe Nickie at the hospital day-care program, Ms. Dwyer agreed to become Nickie's temporary foster mother and was licensed to so do.

Within three weeks of the initial referral conference, a media recruitment plan focusing specifically on Nickie's need for a family had been developed and implemented in another part of the state. Five families responded to this recruitment effort, and studies of the five families were initiated. Two families decided they were not interested in adopting such a severely traumatized child and withdrew from consideration. After completing studies of the other three families, the workers agreed that none seemed exactly right for Nickie. At this point, the adoption supervisor decided that a group meeting of the families, plus the three previously identified families in her own county, might be useful. The purpose of the meeting was to review with all of the families the agency's assessment of Nickie's needs and strengths.

During this time of study and recruitment, the staff had been learning more about Nickie from Ms. Dwyer. Nickie's foster family had asked to be relieved of his care shortly after Ms. Dwyer was licensed, and Nickie was moved to her home. The first several days were difficult, with Nickie lashing out physically at Ms Dwyer; but, having worked with similar problems in the past, Ms. Dwyer was able to control his destructiveness. Then Nickie became terribly ill one night, with high fever, diarrhea, internal bleeding. Ms. Dwyer rushed him to the hospital and stayed with him constantly for the next three days, taking leave from her job, while neurological, allergy, and other tests were completed to search for the causes of Nickie's problems. Food allergies were considered possibly related to both his health and behavioral difficulties. Nickie's medication schedule was drastically reduced while he was in the hospital.

Following hospitalization, Nickie became very dependent on Ms. Dwyer. He clung to her constantly, and would become upset if she left the room even momentarily. Ms. Dwyer would put him to bed in his own room at night, only to find him asleep at the foot of her bed in the morning. She was finding the experience exhausting, but she remained committed to helping Nickie. She found that he responded positively to an extremely regular schedule of meals, medication, bedtime, and school. Any variation in the schedule precipitated a period of disorganization. This included friends dropping by unexpectedly to visit, or even changes to the schedule that Nickie himself requested.

Yet, in spite of the problems, it was obvious that the two liked each other and enjoyed much of their time together. Ms. Dwyer reported that Nickie could be quite talkative and curious about the world. He loved being read to and enjoyed all kinds of music. A radio by his bed solved the problem of keeping him in his own room at night. After overcoming his fear of the water, he liked going to the swimming pool. Most of all, he enjoyed riding the bike Ms. Dwyer bought for him. He would ride it for hours in front of their apartment, and learned to obey the rules about staying near the building. He also loved wearing the new clothes she bought him and began to take pride in his appearance. Several of Ms. Dwyer's friends became Nickie's friends as well, and provided some much-needed relief for her and new experiences for Nickie. Eventually Nickie was able to tolerate being left with one of these friends for an hour or two while Ms. Dwyer was out.

Ms. Dwyer was an effective reminder to the agency of its commitment to seeking a permanent family for Nickie. She was informed of the progress being made with home studies and the plan for the group meeting of the six prospective families. Staff consensus following the group meeting was that only one of the six families might be able to meet the challenges presented by Nickie. Three families seemed to be good resources for other children waiting for adoption, and the other two decided to wait for a younger child.

The family under consideration, the Hamiltons, had a son who was 14 years old and two daughters, ages 9 and 11. They wanted another boy to balance their family, and they were receptive to the idea of taking a school-aged child. The Hamiltons' outstanding characteristic was their commitment. At several times during the group meeting, they indicated that whatever child came into their family would remain a part of the family, regardless of the problems encountered. They clearly understood the nature of the commitment necessary in adopting a child like Nickie. The staff were also impressed with the Hamiltons' relaxed attitudes about parenting and their knowledge of the kinds of problems Nickie might present. They seemed open to seeking professional help, and presumed such help would be necessary for Nickie. They also had the advantage of living in a community where there were excellent school resources for emotionally disturbed children.

Dr. Hamilton was a mathematician and Mrs. Hamilton was a trained rehabilitation counselor. They were active in their community and church. In many respects, however, they were an unconventional couple. Mrs. Hamilton wore no makeup, did nothing to her hair except shampoo it, was somewhat overweight, and seemed totally unconcerned about her clothing and appearance. All of this gave her a rather eccentric quality. Dr. Hamilton wore a handlebar mustache and a hairstyle that gave him an old-fashioned appearance. The Hamilton children seemed to be independent and self-directed. They appeared to be highly motivated toward having Nickie as a brother, and were fairly realistic about the problems that were likely to arise.

Arrangements were made for the Hamiltons to meet with Ms. Dwyer and Nickie's worker. During the meeting, Ms. Dwyer described Nickie's problems and his appealing qualities in detail, and outlined his daily schedule. The Hamiltons seemed enthusiastic about continuing the process by getting acquainted with Nickie, so a series of visits was arranged.

The first several visits took place at Ms. Dwyer's home, since that was the most comfortable environment for Nickie. More than the usual number of visits were scheduled so that Nickie could become thoroughly acquainted with this new family. Several one-day visits were followed by Nickie's spending three weekends with the Hamiltons. Then the Hamiltons and their children spent a week at the beach with Nickie and Ms. Dwyer. Throughout the process, Ms. Dwyer consistently provided Nickie with permission and encouragement to move away from her into the Hamilton family. All of the children became well enough acquainted during the visits to begin bickering and arguing, but they continued to favor the placement. Following the week at the beach, the Hamiltons signed the adoptive placement agreement and took Nickie home to live with them.

During the early months of the adoptive placement. Ms. Dwyer stayed in touch with the family by telephone and letters. These contacts were intended to provide some continuity for Nickie and support for the Hamiltons. They occurred less frequently as the need appeared to decrease. After about six months, the Hamiltons needed emergency care for Nickie when they had to leave town for a week because there had been a death in their family. They asked Ms. Dwyer if she would care for Nickie while they were gone, and she agreed to do so. After that, the Hamiltons asked Ms. Dwyer to care for Nickie for several weekends each year.

NICKIE'S PROGRESS

Nickie has made remarkable progress since his adoption. A close relationship has developed between Nickie and the younger of the Hamilton daughters, 9-year-old Tammie. This bubbly, delightful little girl has done much to draw Nickie into the family, and both children seem to have benefited from the relationship.

During the first two years of his adoptive placement, Nickie attended special classes for emotionally disturbed children. At the end of the second school year, however, he was recommended for placement in a regular classroom, where he has remained. He is reading at grade level, although sometimes he doesn't know what all the words mean. He loves spelling, but he is still behind in math skills, a subject with which he will probably always have trouble.

Six months after the adoptive placement, Nickie was off all medication. The internal bleeding had been found to be associated with an allergy to milk and eggs, and diet has largely corrected the problem. His appetite is still good, but he eats more appropriate amounts. Since his diet was adjusted, his color has been better and he is no longer so underweight.

Most of the time, Nickie is a verbal child who is curious about his environment. Although he still has moody spells, he reaches out to people, starts conversations, and continues to love music. He is still challenging and sometimes frustrating to his new parents, but he has come a long way.

Nickie's growing self-confidence and sense of security are a reflection of his family's remarkable commitment and perseverance. He is 12 years old, now, so his story is still incomplete. But those who have shared his experiences for the past five years are cautiously optimistic about his future.

CASE 3

FAMILY CRISIS
Medical Social Work
in a Teaching Hospital

JANICE JACOBSON RYAN
Social Worker, Student Mental Health Center
University of North Carolina, Chapel Hill

THE SETTING

The North Carolina Memorial Hospital is a state-supported, 700-bed teaching hospital affiliated with the School of Medicine of the University of North Carolina. The hospital's medical and psychiatric facilities include a social work department of approximately 45 social workers with the MSW degree. Each social worker is assigned to a specific medical service (for instance, surgery, obstetrics, or oncology). Within that service, the worker often functions as a member of an interdisciplinary team, which always includes physicians and nurses and usually includes members of allied disciplines (such as physical or occupational therapy, psychology, or vocational rehabilitation). On most services, the interdisciplinary teams hold regular meetings to discuss individual patients and general service needs.

Working through an interdisciplinary team can be both rewarding and frustrating. Professional growth can be enhanced by exposure to new knowledge and different points of view; satisfaction can be taken in the knowledge that one has assisted other professionals in increasing their understanding of nonmedical factors in illness; and personal reward can be found in knowing that one's participation in group decisions has improved the quality of health care. It can be frustrating, however, to deal with the role conflicts that can occur if, for example, the physician does not understand what the social worker can contribute or is unaccustomed to dealing with aspects of care that are not directly related to medical diagnosis and treatment. In addition, problems of role overlap can arise in the form of territorial disputes, and such problems must be resolved quickly and straightforwardly to prevent interference with the achievement of goals and optimal patient care. But when interdisciplinary teams work well—and they do, more often than not—service to patients is enhanced and collegial relationships are strengthened. For most social workers, collaborative service delivery is one of the most satisfying aspects of medical social work.

The duties of the social worker in a teaching hospital are multifaceted, often involving direct service to clients, consultation, program planning, teaching, and research. For most workers, the bulk of time is devoted to direct service. The primary service goal is to help individual patients take advantage of medical care in such a way as to regain optimal physical, social, and psychological health.[1] The goal is accomplished by assisting the patient and family to prepare for hospitalization, helping them come to terms with the illness, linking the patient to community support systems and resources, and facilitating plans for the future in light of the medical diagnosis, prognosis, and treatment.

Medical social workers must develop specific skills and knowledge beyond those that are general to the profession. For example, they

1. Margaret Brock, *Social Work in the Hospital Organization* (Toronto: University of Toronto Press, 1969).

must understand the workings of the highly complex modern hospital, in order to bring available resources to bear on individual cases. They must learn to speak the medical language, in order to communicate effectively with medical staff and to translate medical recommendations into an idiom that is comprehensible to patients. They must learn to be flexible, appropriately assertive, and well organized. They must be able to respond quickly and effectively to a wide variety of demands while recognizing the realistic limits of personal time and emotional involvement.

the following case is presented to show how all of these factors interact in the practice of medical social work.

THE CASE OF LAURA AND MS. F

The Referral

A child on the inpatient pediatric unit had just been diagnosed as having cystic fibrosis, a genetically determined disorder that is present at birth and terminal in nature. The disease causes an abnormal production of mucous which, in turn, leads to lung damage and digestive disorders. Affected children often appear malnourished. Because the disease is difficult to detect, it may be improperly diagnosed for months or even years.

At the North Carolina Memorial Hospital, a pediatric social worker assigned to the Chest Clinic is routinely involved with all families of children with cystic fibrosis because of the devastating impact of the disease. In the case presented here, the referral was made early by the attending physician in order to alert the social worker at once to the additional emotional and financial stresses that were likely to be present in this single-parent family. Nursing staff had also found the young mother to be hostile toward their instructions about caring for the child.

At the time of diagnosis and referral, 10-month-old Laura[2] was living with her 18-year-old mother (Ms. F), an aunt who was 17 years old, and a 1-year-old cousin. The family lived in a low-income housing project in a town located about ninety miles from the hospital. Ms. F was unmarried, unemployed, and receiving AFDC for Laura's care from the county Department of Social Services.

2. The names of Laura and Ms. F have been changed to disguise their identities.

Initial Interview

After reviewing the medical chart to determine Laura's current medical status, the social worker formulated goals for the initial interview with Ms. F. It would be necessary to obtain additional social history, to establish an alliance with Ms. F, and to begin to formulate a diagnostic impression that would be helpful to the interdisciplinary pediatric team.

During the initial interview, Ms. F appeared to be anxious and uncomfortable with the worker and had difficulty establishing eye contact with her. She was cooperative, however, and responded with detailed information about her background when questioned directly. An only child, Ms. F had been abandoned in infancy by her own mother, and her father had arranged for an aunt and uncle to provide primary care. From that time on, Ms. F's father seldom came to see her. She could not recall ever having had a close and trusting relationship with him. She continued to live with the aunt and uncle throughout childhood and early adolescence, but their relationship was conflictual and Ms. F left home several times to stay briefly with friends or other relatives. During those troubled years, Ms. F was frequently absent from school. She finally left school at the age of 16, having completed the eighth grade. She felt very much alone and adrift, with weak ties to family and peers.

At the age of 17, Ms. F decided to become pregnant "to have someone to love," as she put it. She was involved at the time in a relationship with a man whom she had no intention of marrying. Laura, who was conceived as a solution to her mother's emotional deprivation, was born shortly after Ms. F's eighteenth birthday. Motherhood, from which so much had been expected, proved to be very difficult from the beginning. Laura had been sick from birth, with frequent hospitalization because of a failure to thrive. Since she did not understand the cause of Laura's difficulties, Ms. F felt responsible for the child's illness and viewed herself as an inadequate mother.

Laura was referred to the North Carolina Memorial Hospital at age 10 months by a local physician who had been unable to discover the cause of her illness. The diagnosis of cystic fibrosis was made shortly after Laura was admitted to the hospital. Although she was relieved to learn that her daughter's illness was not her fault, Ms. F was understandably fearful of the implications of this serious illness and did not fully comprehend either the disease or the treatment plan.

Initial Impression

After the initial interview, the social worker concluded that this young mother had experienced a life almost entirely devoid of emotional support or parental modeling. She had become self-sufficient at too early an age and was painfully aware of her inadequacies as an individual and as a mother. She was investing a great deal of time and energy in her child, but was unsure of her parenting techniques. Yet her inability to trust other people resulted in her becoming defensive when hospital staff offered suggestions about the care of the child.

The social worker also observed that Ms. F had some strengths. The young mother had relaxed a bit during the interview and had begun to relate to the social worker more comfortably, even smiling and joking occasionally. The social worker interpreted this behavior as a positive indication that medical staff would be able, in time, to develop a supportive and educational relationship with Ms. F. It was also apparent to the social worker that Ms. F cared very deeply for her child.

Direct Services

During the next few weeks, the social worker met with Ms. F regularly and began slowly to develop a positive and trusting relationship. Ms. F herself began to initiate contacts with the social worker to voice concerns and questions about her child's illness. Her concerns included feeling incompetent to manage a chronically ill child, frustrations with child management problems, difficulty in learning to trust the hospital staff, and fears about Laura's eventual death.

Consultative Services

At the same time that Ms. F was developing a trusting relationship with the social worker, the nursing staff was continuing to express, both individually and in team meetings, concerns about Ms. F's inappropriate interactions with her child and hostility toward staff. Laura was hospitalized on a unit with a "primary nursing" concept, which meant that she was assigned to one nurse who took care of her on every shift that the nurse worked. In the case of Ms. F, the primary nursing concept proved to be especially helpful because of her difficulty in establishing relationships and her tendency to be overwhelmed in interactions with a number of different nurses.

The social worker met regularly with Laura's primary nurse and helped her understand Ms. F's behavior in terms of the psychosocial history. The social worker also provided the nurse with a number of strategies that might help her interact more effectively with Ms. F. As a result, Ms. F came to develop a strong identification with the primary nurse and began to accept her gentle suggestions and to model her physical management methods and parenting techniques.

Referral Services

The social worker's next step in managing this case was to make referrals to community resources. Laura was to be discharged from the hospital soon, to return periodically for outpatient visits, and the interdisciplinary team believed it would be crucial for Ms. F to receive continued support in her home community. With Ms. F's consent, the social worker referred her to the local Health Department, which would provide visiting nursing services and nutritional supplements; to her county Department of Social Services, for additional financial support and advocacy services; and to an Early Childhood Intervention program, which could work with Laura and Ms. F at their home, to improve parenting skills and provide appropriate stimulation for the child. During the latter period of Laura's stay in the hospital, Ms. F was also referred to a hospital support group for parents of chronically ill children. This group had been organized by the pediatric social workers, who recognized the value to clients of self-help peer counseling.

Progress Report

After Laura was discharged from the hospital, the social worker continued her contacts with Laura and Ms. F during their regular visits to the outpatient clinic. A subsequent development in the family challenged the social worker's ability to remain objective and refrain from allowing her personal beliefs to interfere with the client's right to make independent decisions.

After months of struggling alone, Ms. F reported that she was considering marrying a 17-year-old boy whose chief attraction was that he shared responsibility for Laura's care and had a steady income. Ms. F's family was encouraging her to marry the young man, and plans for the wedding were already being made. But Ms. F had some reservations; she felt a strong need for adult support apart from that of her extended family, but she was unsure about her feelings toward her fiance.

During one clinic visit, Ms. F asked the social worker for her opinion about the impending marriage. The worker believed that the marriage would be a mistake, but she struggled to refrain from voicing her opinion because she also believed in the principle of self-determination. Therefore, instead of pointing out what seemed compelling evidence that Ms. F was choosing to marry for the wrong reasons, the worker maintained a supportive and nonjudgmental attitude while providing the client with an opportunity to discuss her positive and negative feelings about her decision. By the end of the interview, Ms. F had acknowledged her ambivalence, but a few weeks later she decided to marry the young man for what she considered to be good, pragmatic reasons. The marriage lasted three months. This unhappy episode, although it confirmed the social worker's apprehensions, helped Ms. F to learn that marriage in itself would not magically solve her financial and emotional problems, nor would it relieve her of the burden of her chronically ill child.

In the year following the diagnosis, Laura's health was good enough that she required only one hospitalization. Although Ms. F continued to have difficulty developing long-term relationships, her parenting skills improved considerably, as did her understanding and management of Laura's illness. She is now learning to use family and community support systems, is doing a remarkably good job of caring for Laura, and is beginning to take control of her own life.

DISCUSSION

The case of Ms. F illustrates some of the many economic, social, and psychological needs of parents who are struggling to cope with the chronic illness of a child. With inherited disorders such as cystic fibrosis, there are likely to be strong guilt feelings about having produced a "defective" child. In some instances, this sense of guilt may last a lifetime and may be channeled into overidentification with the child. Siblings may be neglected as the parents focus on the needs of the sick child, and marital relationships may suffer.[3]

3. Ruth K. Young, "Chronic Sorrow: Parents' Response to the Birth of a Child with a Defect," *American Journal of Maternal Child Nursing* (January-February 1977), pp. 38-42.

If the illness is a fatal one, family members must live with terrible feelings of anxiety, and they often are inadequately prepared to meet the formidable demands imposed by the illness. In addition, they may be caught in a dilemma of deeply resenting the demands while being unable to acknowledge personal negative feelings. These feelings of inadequacy, unexpressed anger, sadness, and anxiety may be compounded by frequent separations caused by hospitalization; and parents may find it difficult to form a satisfying relationship with the sick child, especially if hospitalization occurs during the first months of life, when bonding takes place. Parents sometimes find some temporary relief from all of this discomfort by blaming the medical staff for inadequate treatment or delayed diagnosis, or by putting responsibility on God or on people in the environment. But if the parents can be helped to become more comfortable in caring for their child and learn that their feelings are normal, the need to project their feelings onto others should diminish.[4]

The demands of chronic illness can be overwhelming for any family, whether the patient is a child or an adult. In almost all cases, there is a need for financial support, emotional support, or both. Linkages with community resources and education about the illness are essential. In the case of terminal illness, grief counseling can be crucial. Most families eventually adjust reasonably well to the presence of a chronically ill member. They may need social work intervention only in times of crises such as diagnosis, first hospitalization, or the terminal stage of the illness. Sometimes, however, personal and marital problems interfere with the family's ability to cope, and continued social work intervention is called for.

Because of the wide variety of illnesses and coping styles, the medical social worker must learn to assess family functioning quickly, form relationships easily, and identify potential crisis periods in the lives of patients and their families. Although the demands are great, practice in the hospital setting is rewarding for the social worker who observes change and growth in families such as that of Laura and her mother.

4. Rudolph H. Moos, "The Crisis of Illness: Stillbirth and Birth Defects," in *Coping with Physical Illness,* ed. Rudolph H. Moos (New York: Plenum Medical, 1977).

CASE 4

WOMEN WITH WEIGHT PROBLEMS
Group Treatment in
Social Work Practice

SIBYL M. WAGNER
Private Practitioner
Chapel Hill, North Carolina

TREATING OBESE CLIENTS

Weight problems are notoriously difficult to solve. Bruch has stated that a major goal of therapy with either obese or anorexic persons should be to help them become aware of their needs and how to respond to them.[1] Interpersonal relationships should be

---

1. Hilde Bruch, *Eating Disorders: Obesity, Anorexia Nervosa, and the Person Within* (New York: Basic Books, 1973), p. 336.

examined in depth so that eating cannot serve as a way to avoid conflict. Although Bruch usually treats clients individually, she tries to create change in family members as well.

Minuchin et al. and Palazzoli have found Bruch's conceptualization of the personal and family structures related to eating problems useful in their work with eating disorders.[2] Palazzoli cited a personal sense of independence and worth as significant in helping clients overcome eating problems. Weight problems appear also to be maintained by family patterns. Minuchin et al. defined four family characteristics that emerged in their studies of psychosomatic disorders: enmeshment, overprotectiveness, rigidity, and lack of conflict resolution. Both Minuchin et al. and Palazzoli stress the need to change the family structure in order to help the symptomatic member.

Thus the focus in the treatment of eating problems is the person in context; that is, working with clients in the settings where they have had difficulty directly experiencing, expressing, and satisfying their needs. With a child, it is possible to work with the family. However, with adults who are struggling to establish a personal identity or for whom family members are unavailable, group treatment offers several advantages. There is opportunity to rework issues with siblings and parents through group interactions.[3] Clients can gain some relief simply in talking with others who share their problems. In seeing that other group members are bright, talented, and likable, they can begin to believe that they might share some of these qualities.[4] Orbach points out that women use their obesity to convey messages about their needs and desires without having to express them explicitly.[5] In the group, each woman's obesity is unique, and each client is forced to express herself more directly[6] and to develop new coping mechanisms. Finally, in observing others who are losing weight, clients can see that success is indeed possible.

2. Salvador Minuchin, Bernice L. Rosman, and Lester Baker, *Psychosomatic Families, Anorexia Nervosa in Context* (Cambridge: Harvard University Press, 1978), p. 30; Mara Selvini Palazzoli, *Self-Starvation* (New York: Jason Aronson, 1978), p. 155.

3. Irvin D. Yalom, *The Theory and Practice of Group Psychotherapy* (New York: Basic Books, 1975), p. 15.

4. Susie Orbach, *Fat Is a Feminist Issue* (New York: Berkley Publishing, 1978), p. 131.

5. Orbach, *Fat Is a Feminist Issue*, p. 133.

6. Orbach, *Fat Is a Feminist Issue*, pp. 134-135.

THE SETTING

My office was located in an attractive area of the city, in a neighborhood of older homes. Most of the residents were Chicano. There were a few other small offices and business in the neighborhood. My building was converted from an old home, and it retained a sense of homelike comfort. The office itself was furnished with a sturdy couch and chairs that were large enough to hold quite obese clients.

When I decided to form a group for obese women, my first job was to determine the structure of the group. I set the meetings for Saturdays to accommodate the working hours of potential members, and decided that each sesson would run for one and one-half hours. I placed a notice, announcing formation of the group, in a local newspaper. Then, as applicants began to call, I arranged to interview each woman who seemed, during the telephone call, to be a likely candidate for the group.

PREGROUP INTERVIEWS

Some of the women I interviewed were in need of other kinds of assistance. For example, one woman with symptoms of anorexia, including severe underweight, amenorrhea, and facial hair, needed medical supervision and more intensive care than I could provide. She was referred to a physician who specialized in eating disorders.

I also referred a woman with a low educational level, transportation difficulties, and a terminal illness. I had had some experience in dealing with terminally ill clients, and I would have liked to provide a warm, supportive structure for this woman, but this particular group was not an appropriate one to help her cope with approaching death. I had a professional responsibility to provide a group structure in which members could concentrate on the topic of weight loss.

Another woman wanted to deal with her eating problem on a behavioral level. She did not want to explore the underlying conflicts behind her eating patterns. I referred her to a psychologist who used behavior modification techniques in treating eating disorders.

At the end of one interview, I asked a young woman, "Is there anything else you want to ask me, or tell me about, in our last ten minutes today?" There was a brief silence. Then she blurted, "My mother killed my father and sisters. I'm afraid that a killing instinct runs in my family, in our genes, and that I might kill my boyfriend and his kids." Significant material often is withheld until the end of a session! I told the woman that this worry must be difficult to handle; since it was so painful, perhaps it wouldn't be fair to start her out in group therapy where she would be required to set aside her own needs and listen to those of others. I suggested that individual counseling might be a more appropriate way for her to begin, with the option of joining the group later. She seemed relieved, and readily agreed to this plan.

The pregroup interviews can serve functions other than screening. The worker can stress the importance of regular and punctual attendance at group meetings. Individual and group goals and expectations can be discussed, to ensure their compatibility. There are, in fact, indications that the greater the number of pregroup sessions, the lower the dropout rate once group sessions begin.[7] The pregroup interview can also be useful in giving the worker a comparison between the client's behavior in a one-to-one interaction and her functioning in the group.

It is important to discuss the matter of fees and attendance during the pregroup interview. I told each candidate that those who joined the group would be charged a monthly fee, with no refund for illness or absence. I explained I had made this somewhat arbitrary decision because I wanted to assure both excellent attendance and total commitment. Also, I did not want group time to be spent on deciding whether someone had a good enough excuse not to have to pay for a missed session. I preferred to deal with the meaning of absences on other than financial grounds. Each woman was also told that if she could not attend a meeting she was to call in advance and let me know.

The pregroup sessions were used to help prepare clients for some of the stresses of joining a group. I warned the women, for example, that people often have an initial weight gain when they join a group; increased eating reflects a concern that food will soon be taken away. I asked the women to use this period before the first session to gather more information about their eating patterns and to see it as a responsive behavior. I also used the pregroup sessions to help the women identify ways they could sabotage the group as well as

7. Yalom, *The Theory and Practice of Group Psychotherapy*, p. 287.

enhance success. And throughout the pregroup sessions, I made an effort to help each client learn to trust me so I would be able to help her weather some of the inevitable group crises.

FORMING THE GROUP

Eight women met the qualifications for group membership and decided to join the group. A brief description of each is presented here.[8]

Maria. An attractive Mexican woman in her late 20s, Maria was from a large family and had moved to the United States at the age of 18. Since that time, she had earned a high school diploma and had worked steadily as an aide at a senior citizens' recreation center. For two years she had been dating a serviceman who was gone frequently for extended periods. Maria had a long history of being about 30 pounds overweight.

Pam. A stylish woman in her mid-20s, Pam was 35 pounds overweight, living with a boyfriend who was critical of her weight. Pam's weight gain was directly related to two events. As a young, inexperienced actress, she was overwhelmed by the sexual pressures of the movie industry. While she was trying to cope with that pressure, her sister died suddenly of cancer. Pam was convinced that her mother, a widow, resented the fact that the "good" daughter was the one who had died. When the group began, Pam had given up her theatrical ambitions and was working in a small business. She had tried college several times, but had always been unable to complete the courses.

Jean. A blond, divorced woman in her mid-30s, Jean had already lost 30 pounds, but had 40 more to go. She worked full time as an evening bookkeeper for an airline. Jean complained at length about her salary, but she liked the travel benefits. To save money, she shared a small apartment with another woman. When Jean was a child, she and her mother had been left by her wealthy father, who was a compulsive gambler. Her mother, with whom she still lived, was distant and critical. Sixteen months earlier, Jean had had a severe depressive episode during which she was unable to stop crying. She stayed home for three months, except for attending sessions with a psychiatrist, whom she was still seeing weekly.

8. Group members' names have been changed to ensure their anonymity.

Nancy. A quiet, 28-year-old single woman who looked ten years younger, Nancy had become overweight while on her present live-in job as attendant for a handicapped woman. Nancy was 20 pounds overweight; she had lost 50 pounds before joining the group and wanted companionship and encouragement in continuing her weight loss. Nancy had a college degree in art. Her father was no longer involved with the family; her mother lived in New York. Nancy had to travel 20 miles by bus to attend the group sessions.

Margaret. Margaret was the one member who was not self-referred. Her mother had seen the notice about the group and called for information. Margaret was discouraged, having already tried Weight Watchers, Overeaters Anonymous, and medication. At 32 years of age, she was 100 pounds overweight; she had always been obese. Margaret had just moved into an apartment with two friends, but she maintained daily contact with her family. She held a low-paying job, but one that offered attractive travel possibilities after the first year. Her relationships with men were restricted to business contacts. Margaret spent much of her free time writing a novel.

Ann. A single woman in her mid-30s, Ann was in the second year of medical school. She had a long history of weight fluctuation. That fall, she had gained 60 pounds while recovering from a back injury. She was now 20 pounds overweight and was terrified of becoming more obese. Ann was involved in a turbulent relationship with an attorney whom she had been dating for a year. The man had told her he did not find her physically attractive. Ann was also having trouble getting along with the women with whom she shared an apartment. Despite her academic success, Ann's family was critical of her and doubted that she would succeed professionally.

Debbie. A 26-year-old woman who was 45 pounds overweight, Debbie had recently quit her latest job as a bookstore clerk and had been looking unsuccessfully for a new job for three months. Her financial problems were exacerbated by the fact that she lived alone in an expensive apartment. Debbie's depression was expressed in her feelings of hopelessness and her poor personal grooming. She denied any suicidal ideation and refused to consider the psychiatric evaluation I suggested. Her family lived in the northern part of the state, but was in frequent contact with her.

Heather. A single, 30-year-old graduate student in psychology, Heather had a history of obesity since the onset of puberty. She was skeptical about her ability to lose weight; she was from a large family in which all of the women were overweight. As a clinical intern, she had extremely high self-expectations and easily became discouraged. During her early 20s, Heather had lived with a man for four years, but she had avoided close relationships with men after he left her for a mutual friend.

BEGINNING PHASE

At the beginning of the group's first meeting, I reviewed my goals for the group. I said that I hoped each woman would develop a greater understanding of the function her weight problem served in her life, and that the group would help her develop alternative coping skills to make overeating a matter of choice. I described the group as a place where members could try out new interpersonal behaviors in a supportive environment, and emphasized each woman's responsibility for making the group worthwhile by helping to keep the group focused and letting the group know if her needs were not being met.

Margaret asked how the group would differ from something like Overeaters Anonymous (OA). I said my understanding was that OA believed members could not handle their eating problems, that eating was out of their control. I explained that I believed eating was something that the individual does control. I added, however, that some people receive strength from OA and group members should feel free to attend OA meetings if they wished. One similarity between OA and our group was that all members of the group—myself included—had eating problems, and we all had ideas on how to approach the problem and how to support each other. Direct information and clarification of this kind is vital in the early stage of group formation. Anxiety is high, and the leader needs to reduce uncertainty.[9]

Another early aspect of group definition involved explaining that the group would begin and end on time. This structure is especially

9. Maxine Loomis, *Group Process for Nurses* (St. Louis, MO: C. V. Mosby, 1979), p. 84.

important for a group with eating and dependency needs, whose members may feel that their needs are endless. By establishing limits, the worker helps group members use their time actively, thus reducing the sense of insatiability.[10]

When we had completed the process of structuring the group, I asked each woman to tell a little about herself and her eating problem. To help her gain experience in acknowledging her strengths, I asked each woman to mention five things she liked about herself. Quickly, the level of excitement and anxiety rose. There was envy when Pam talked of her work as an actress and the public recognition she had achieved. Ann's status as a medical student and an especially attractive member of the group set her apart initially. Jean quickly earned respect because of her feminist activities, and possibly because of her obvious anger toward men. The members were drawn to Maria, who described warmly and positively her struggles to become an independent woman in a new homeland. Nancy was quiet and attracted little attention. Margaret seemed uneasy, but she formed an early alliance with Jean because both had jobs in which a major goal was to travel. Heather's graduate study of psychology raised anxiety among the other group members, who seemed unclear about whether to treat her as another client or as a therapist. Heather, too, seemed ambivalent, and carefully avoided revealing personal material.

At the end of the first session, I asked the members to keep journals, recording their eating patterns, activities, and feelings. For the next session, they were to bring photographs from various points in their lives to share with the group.

The second session started with a discussion of Debbie's and Heather's decision to leave the group. There was much anxiety that the group might fall apart. Memories of earlier disappointments, in therapy and in other relationships, surfaced. The women talked about how hard it is to trust other people when the others may leave. Several members began to talk of how much they needed this group. They used the early loss of two members to consider how they could help the group stay together. Jean asked if they could exchange phone numbers so that if someone were tempted to binge, the others could offer emergency support. The group decided this would be helpful,

10. Orbach, *Fat Is a Feminist Issue*, p. 137.

although Ann said her schedule made it difficult to have other commitments and suggested the group not depend on her too much for help.

Next, the group members shared their weight histories. They used their photographs to show the times when their weight had been satisfactory as well as the times when weight had been a problem. This was an emotional experience for the group, during which they discovered some of the deep sorrows in each others' lives.

Ann revealed her history of serious binge eating. The group was struck by the contrast in her photos, which showed a period of six months when she had gone from being thin and sexually appealing to being sixty pounds overweight, pimply, and withdrawn. Ann shared her recent embarrassment over having eaten a whole box of chocolates that her roommate had been given by a date. She was tormented by the contrast of her role as a bright, helpful medical student with her feeling of being a crazy woman who was destroying her relationships. She voiced her concern that no one in the group would like her, and no one would understand how much she needed help.

Nancy said it really helped her to hear Ann's problems. She had been afraid that Ann wouldn't be interested in her because she wasn't pretty or well educated. Other members admitted they had been both shy and resentful of Ann's beauty. Jean verbalized the group's general feeling that if you are thin, you don't have problems. In this regard, Jean suggested that in some ways, Ann's weight was a way of saying that she had suffered. Jean also admitted that she had felt distant from both Ann and Pam because they looked so stylish and self-assured. This confession precipitated a tearful discussion during which Pam said she wanted to feel that she deserved to belong to the group and that, in fact, she did belong.

I supported these attempts by the group members to get to know one another in order to establish a strong and caring group. I reflected aloud that it would be exciting for them to watch each member find support within the group so that there would be no need to resort to binges or other crises in order to "deserve" attention.

Having established their group structure and membership, the six women were able to settle down in the remaining sessions of the beginning phase to discussing their weight histories and what they were learning from their journals. A strong common bond was established. Members began to identify patterns in their eating behavior and their moods.

THE MIDDLE PHASE

The middle phase of group development has been described as the period of greatest conflict as well as a time of working on group goals, and this group was no exception. After the group had been meeting for a month, Jean came to one session at which she sat quietly but appeared to be angry. With some prodding, she complained that she had gained ten pounds since joining the group, that obviously group membership was hurting rather than helping her. Ann asked Jean to describe what she thought was the cause of her weight gain. Jean explained that her job entailed working until eleven o'clock at night; after work, she usually went out with her coworkers and would have several mixed drinks as well as hors d'oeuvres. Then she would go home and eat a full dinner. Pam asked Jean how she wanted the group to help her with this pattern. Jean said she had hoped the group would help her feel less stress so she could lose weight. She expressed concern that I might not be good enough, saying that perhaps she needed an older therapist.

The group helped Jean divide this issue into two parts. On a practical level, they suggested she limit herself to one glass of wine after work. Then she was to go home and take a long, leisurely bath rather than eating another meal. Jean agreed to try this plan for a week and to report on how it had worked. The other part of the issue was what Jean wanted from the group, and especially from me. As they discussed this topic, Jean began to view her passive stance in a new light. She realized she had hoped to be "cured" by joining the group, waiting for others to help her without changing her own habits. Other group members shared with Jean their own feelings of sadness at the realization that losing weight meant changing personal habits, that it could not be accomplished without great personal effort. Along with the realization came the knowledge that I would not provide the total support and control that they had wanted from their parents. This issue emerged with decreasing frequency during the middle phase as members looked to me when discussing a problem only to hear me say, "There's a lot of experience here; what do you all think?"

Another major area of work in the middle phase involved changing the members' patterns of behavior within the group. In the early sessions, for example, Pam had been active in supporting others and drawing out the quiet members. The role of "helper" enhanced her popularity in the group, which was something Pam said was important to her. In this role, Pam appeared very kind and self-possessed. During the sixth session, however, Pam arrived late, looking disheveled and tired. I commented on her tardiness and asked if there was some reason that made it hard for her to face the others.

After some hesitation, Pam asked the group if they had time to listen to her. She was afraid she would monopolize the group and what she had to say could wait. The group encouraged Pam to tell them what was going on. Pam reported that she had stayed home from work one day that week because she was sick, and she had asked a friend to substitute for her at the shop. During Pam's absence, a man entered the shop and raped Pam's friend. Pam knew she was the one who would have been raped if she had not been sick, and her old guilt surfaced about living while the favored sister had died. Pam apologized for discussing this personal problem during group time, because she thought it wouldn't help the group members to deal with their weight problems.

Jean and Nancy sat with Pam and held her while she cried. Margaret gently pointed out that Pam was in the group to help herself as well as the others, and it made her feel needed to hear what had happened to Pam and to be able to offer support. Margaret added that she thought this issue was, indeed, tied into the problem of weight. Pam might be using eating as a substitute for the help she was afraid to ask for directly. Margaret also wondered how eating might be related to Pam's method of coping with her sense of guilt by taking care of others instead of looking out for her own needs. Maria added that she, too, had always thought the only way to get people to like her was to be a helper. She said she felt even closer to Pam, now, as she observed Pam asking for help. Maria thought that perhaps she too might be able to let people know more about her needs, now, without worrying that her needs would frighten other people away.

This session proved to be a major turning point for the group. Toward the end of the meeting, Maria and Nancy began to talk about how many important issues they had discussed, and they wondered if the group could be extended beyond the two months initially set. We decided to take time at the next session to discuss that possibility.

The group did decide to extend its existence for another two months. During that time, they dealt with many conflicts revolving around self-worth, self-image, and trusting others. Maria and Jean both had lengthy and turbulent visits from their mothers; they used the group to talk over some of their sadness and anger, and explored alternative ways of coping during these stressful visits other than by eating. As various members of the group began to lose weight, those who did not lose weight learned to deal with their admiration and envy. When they felt jealous, they began to ask themselves what the other person had that they wanted and what they could do to get it. During this period, Nancy started to plan how she could leave her lonely job and move closer to her family, who lived in New York.

ENDING PHASE

Issues of termination did not occur with this group in the usual fashion because two special events occurred. First, I invited the group to attend my wedding, which was to take place on the weekend preceding the group's last meeting. All of the group except Ann and Maria attended the wedding. During the eighty-mile trip to the wedding, the four decided they would continue to meet after the group had terminated. They planned to invite the other two members to join them. Thus there would be no immediate termination.

In addition to giving the group an opportunity to plan for future meetings, the wedding served as a focus for their hopes and their own futures. They had identified with me as we had discussed my own struggle with weight and with a previous divorce. We had discussed their jealousy over my marriage and my satisfactory professional life. We had all emerged from this ambivalence with a feeling of closeness and greater confidence. Attending the wedding was a positive experience for the group; without my guidance, it provided a less structured relationship in a social context.

During the final group session at my office, Ann appeared only briefly, explaining that she needed the meeting time to study.

(Skipping the last session, or attending only briefly, is a behavior often used to avoid intimacy and the pain of dealing with endings.) Ann had decided not to continue in the self-help group; she chose instead to concentrate on her studies and on her relationships outside the group.

Nancy had postponed her move to the East Coast so she could attend the final meeting of the group. Although she would be unable to join the self-help group, she promised to keep in touch with the members by mail.

The other four—Maria, Pam, Jean, and Margaret—agreed to continue their relationships. I later learned that they frequently got together for a supportive meeting, eating at a restaurant that served dietetic foods. When Nancy returned to live in the area a year later, she eagerly joined the self-help group. Maria had visited her in the East, and Nancy had kept up a correspondence with the group in the meantime.

Most of my postgroup contacts with these women have been through letters and phone calls. Jean briefly joined another of my groups when she was laid off from work and needed help in coping with the anxiety of having a limited income. She also worked on achieving more satisfying relationships with men, now that she had reached her desired weight and was dating.

The strength of the self-help group became dramatically apparent when Margaret's mother died in an automobile accident six months after the self-help group was formed. The members are still providing the strong support that Margaret needs to help her weather this crisis. They turn to me only for affirmation that they are doing a good job.

EVALUATING THE GROUP'S EFFECTIVENESS

It is difficult to evaluate the effectiveness of a short-term group in which the members' goals are to lose weight. Obviously, the short-term group is not the place to achieve the loss of 100 pounds, for example. Such a rapid weight loss would be unhealthful, if not impossible. Thus the group must be evaluated in terms of changes in eating patterns that result from exploration of the underlying causes of the weight gain. In this section I will focus on change in three areas —amount of weight lost, improvement in autonomous functioning, and the possibility of future progress. For the six members who attended this group to its conclusion, there was a range of improvement that is to be expected in any group.

Maria. Maria achieved her weight goal. Her depression has lessened, and although she continues to be shy, she is beginning to see friends outside of work. She is attending college on a scholarship, majoring in recreation. Family contacts are now less overwhelming for her, and she has started to date a man who is interested in marrying her.

Pam. Pam achieved about two-thirds of her desired weight loss. Pam's obesity is reactive (related to specific events) and she will need continued support to reach her goal. She has been active in the self-help group, and this may be all the support she will need. Pam is enrolled at a community college and is working hard to maintain average grades. She and her boyfriend have entered couples therapy at a family counseling center.

Jean. Jean achieved her weight goal. In any evaluation of group effects, it is impossible to determine whether it was the group or other factors that had the greater influence on outcomes. In Jean's case, she was in individual psychotherapy throughout the time of the group, and we cannot tell what improvement might have occurred without the support of the group. We do know that Jean's history of serious depression and her strong dependency needs not only did not interfere, but seemed to serve as a positive force in her active use of the group.

Nancy. Nancy achieved her desired weight and showed real improvement in both appearance and self-esteem. Although she believes the group helped her to modify her withdrawn behavior, there have since been some signs that Nancy may have gone to an opposite extreme. I can only hope that her positive experiences in the formal and self-help groups will lead her to seek further support if her new image causes her future discomfort.

Margaret. Margaret showed considerable weight fluctuation while in the group, and was slightly heavier when the group ended than she had been at the beginning. Here, again, external forces were at work. Margaret had been extremely dependent on her mother and was undergoing a major transition in finally leaving home at the age of 32. She had more weight to lose than did any of the other group members, and she had not joined the group on her own initiative. She is an active member of the self-help group, whose members helped her to work through her feelings about her mother's death, and we can only hope that the self-help group will sustain her until she is able to proceed on her own motivation to achieve her weight loss.

Ann. Ann showed the least progress of any of the six members who attended all of the group sessions. Her weight varied increasingly as termination approached. She tended to arrive late for sessions, wanted to be the center of attention, and had trouble listening to the other members. The heavy demands of medical school made it difficult for Ann to maintain a strong commitment to the group and to develop satisfactory relationships with other members. Ann probably would have responded more positively to an individual treatment approach.

Debbie and Heather. These two women, who attended only the first session of the group, require special evaluation. Why did they leave the group so early, and what pregroup information might have uncovered the fact that the group experience would not have suited them? It is only speculation, of course, but Debbie joined the group at a time when she was financially troubled. Perhaps she might have profited from individual treatment, where a problem-solving approach could have been used to develop a plan of action and reduce her anxiety. Heather might have benefited from more adequate preparation in the pregroup session. She had extremely demanding self-expectations and became discouraged easily; I should have anticipated that she would have higher expectations than the others for my work as therapist, because she herself was a graduate student in a helping profession.

My overall evaluation of the group is positive. Yalom has said that the optimal size for a group is six to ten members, and that it is usually a good idea to begin with extra members because one or two will drop out, even with careful selection.[11] This group began with eight members, and two dropped out after the first session. The six who remained developed a group cohesiveness that resulted in their forming a self-help group at the conclusion of our meetings.

Every group develops its own personality, and it is interesting to compare the rather tranquil ending of this group with others I have

11. Yalom, *The Theory and Practice of Group Psychotherapy,* p. 284.

led that met for longer periods. Most of my weight groups have displayed considerably more acting out, with eating binges, suicidal ideation, and anger expressed by various members. Perhaps because this was a relatively short-lived group, its members were less dependent on me. Another possibility, of course, is that this group's members did not develop sufficient comfort to express their anger; or perhaps these women approached problem solving in a way that did not require dealing with anger. Certainly their decision to become a self-help group made ending the formal group less traumatic for all of us.

Would a similar group offered by a social work agency have been equally as satisfactory for these women? Yes, provided such a group was offered and was structured to meet the requirements of these particular women for privacy and for holding sessions in other than regular working hours. But the kind of group these women wanted, structured in the way they wanted, was available only in the private sector. For them, private practice offered the best opportunity to meet their needs.

CASE 5

HELPING A COMMUNITY GROW
Community Organization with a Minority Population

FEDERICO SOUFLÉE
Lecturer, School of Social Work
University of Texas, Arlington

The sociopolitical climate of the late 1960s and early 1970s fostered the development of human service programs specifically designed to address the needs of racial and ethnic minorities. Fueled by the civil rights movement and legitimized by Great Society social legislation, the rhetoric of equality and justice found concrete expression in a variety of programs dealing with oppressed and disadvantaged populations.

Concomitantly, the helping professions began to recognize the existence of diverse cultures within our society and to appreciate the role that culture plays in the determination of behavior.[1] The prevailing view of culture as a monolithic phenomenon defined by national boundaries and nationalistic axioms started to yield to the concept of cultural pluralism, with culture viewed as a dependent as well as an independent variable: dependent in the sense that an ethnic or racial group's culture is shaped by the group's unique psychohistorical, religious, sociopolitical, and socioeconomic experiences; independent because of the culture's impact on the group's collective behavior and on that of its individual members. Thus the helping professions began to appreciate culture for what it is: a highly complex, difficult to analyze, yet critically important factor in the definition of a group's human condition.[2]

These general developments were paralleled in the social work profession by two important policy commitments. One was a requirement by the Council on Social Work Education that graduate schools of social work, in order to remain or become accredited, "provide racial and cultural diversity" as reflected through their student bodies, faculty, and staff.[3] The other was the adoption by the National Association of Social Workers of a goal to eradicate poverty and racism, thereby focusing the profession's attention on the insidious effects of these oppressive forces.

At the federal level of government, despite attempted cutbacks in appropriations by the Nixon administration, initiatives dealing with minority needs were being translated into requests for proposals for demonstration projects. Within the Department of Health, Education and Welfare, the National Institute of Mental Health (NIMH) in particular began to explore ways, through its Manpower and Training Division, of supporting efforts on the part of the mental health professions to upgrade knowledge and skills in the provision of services to Native Americans, Blacks, Puerto Ricans, Asian Americans, and Chicanos. The Division's Social Work Education Branch, at the time a major source of support for graduate social work

1. Dorothea C. Leighton, "Cultural Determinants of Behavior: A Neglected Area," *American Journal of Psychiatry* 128 (February 1972), pp. 183-186; Bernard Bandler, "Interprofessional Collaboration in Training in Mental Health," *American Journal of Orthopsychiatry* 43 (January 1973), pp. 101-110.

2. E. Fuller Torrey, *The Mind Game: Psychiatrists and Witchdoctors* (New York: Bantam, 1972); Clifford Geertz, *The Interpretation of Cultures* (New York: Basic Books, 1973); Edward T. Hall, *Beyond Culture* (Garden City, NY: Doubleday, 1976).

3. Council on Social Work Education, *Manual of Accrediting Standards* (New York: Council on Social Work Education, 1971), p. 6.

education, was considering a number of alternatives for the training of social workers in the provision of professional services to members of these minority groups. One option under review was the establishment of national independent training centers.

It was out of the convergence and interaction of these events and processes that the Chicano Training Center was created. What follows is an abbreviated account of how this minority human service organization was born and how it developed and survived over a period of ten years.

ORGANIZATIONAL BIRTH AND DEVELOPMENT

Human service programs are born out of recognized need. The extent to which need is recognized can vary, as can the means of recognizing it.[4] In this instance, the need for a national Chicano mental health training center was felt and expressed by a now defunct, loosely organized assemblage of Chicano social work educators and practitioners known as Trabajadores de la Raza (TR), who took it upon themselves to convey this need to NIMH. Armed with anecdotes and impressions of institutional racism practiced on Chicano consumers of social services, TR initiated an arduous and at times acrimonious relationship with NIMH aimed at the funding of an organization that would if not eliminate at least reduce the inability of mental health professionals to meet the needs of bilingual and bicultural recipients of services effectively.

From TR's perspective, the community mental health development was a modern-day extension of Anglo America's persistent colonization of its Chicano minions. Mental health professionals were seen as control agents conveying a technology insensitive to and incompatible with Chicano cultural realities. A partial solution to this problem was to sensitize mental health professionals to Chicano cultural realities and to provide them with culturally compatible models of practice. What was needed was a massive training effort, endorsed, supported, and advocated by the federal government as a matter of national policy and practice. TR not only requested this of NIMH, they demanded it.

4. Rino J. Patti, *Social Welfare Administration: Managing Social Programs in a Developmental Context* (Englewood Cliffs, NJ: Prentice-Hall, 1983).

NIMH, on the other hand, saw this as an understandable, albeit unreasonable, demand. To retrain thousands of mental health professionals on the scale demanded by TR would require resources beyond NIMH's command. Not only was TR being unreasonable, it was being ungentlemanly in its courtship of a lady less bountiful than it presumed. Meetings between the two dissolved into shouting matches. There were confrontations, walkouts, shutouts, and other similar exchanges of political greetings. Finally, cooler heads prevailed, accord was reached, and a truce declared. NIMH would entertain a written proposal from TR that, if approved, would be funded at an affordable level. Refunding would depend on initial performance, the merits of the renewal application, and the availability of funds.

A proposal was written and submitted. In April of 1971, NIMH announced the award of a $100,000 grant for the establishment of the Chicano Training Center (CTC). Since TR was not a duly incorporated entity and therefore ineligible to receive federal funds, it was to identify a bona fide fiscal agent to act as receptacle and manager of project funds. The committee that had been appointed to develop the proposal was to act as CTC's policy and governing body until such time as CTC became a nonprofit corporation with a duly constituted board of directors. In addition, the committee was charged with making two decisions immediately: the hiring of an executive director and the selection of a site for the organization. NIMH had to approve the fiscal agent selected and was to be involved in the determination of CTC's director and geographic location.

Given the political climate, organizational pitfalls, and technological obstacles facing CTC from the start, it is remarkable that the organization survived its birth and early development. What follows is a discussion of the organization's genetic defects and how they were corrected or compensated for during the first two years of program operations.

Developmental Disabilities

Organizational Environment

From the beginning, CTC's organizational environment was characterized by varying degrees of political strife and stress. Whereas the discord between NIMH and TR was contained once the former agreed to fund the training program, it did altogether dissipate once the grant award was announced. Conflict again surfaced during the deliberations for the selection of the site. The newly appointed policy committee, assuming that it had final authority to decide CTC's location, selected San Antonio, only to be immediately informed by NIMH that its decision was unacceptable. The reason given was that San Antonio was too politically fractious, especially within its Chicano community. NIMH's overruling of the committee's decision not only resulted in the resignation of two members, but served as well to rekindle feelings of suspicion and mistrust toward NIMH. Moreover, the ultimate selection of Houston as the site for CTC was forever to be regarded by certain San Antonio TR members as a conspiracy between NIMH and Houston TR members to curtail San Antonio's political clout within TR nationally. Others felt that this was NIMH's way of getting even with San Antonio's more contentious TR members. Whatever the motive, NIMH's behavior in the site selection process only served to exacerbate the political conflict attendant upon CTC's birth.

Organizational Goals

A memorandum circulating in NIMH at the time described the stages that minority groups go through as they seek funding. The first stage is that of confrontation, characterized by accusations of racism and demands for retribution. This is followed by a state of shock induced by the funding source's willingness to fund a grant proposal. This triggers delusions of grandeur, as reflected in the group's initial proposal, with its global goals and matching budget request. Once the proposal is funded, but at a radically reduced level, the group begins to come down to earth and to accept and deal with its reality. Finally, the group gets down to the serious business of developing and operating a limited program with limited funds.

This describes what happened to CTC. Fortunately, NIMH gave the nascent organization time for reality to sink in and for it to align its goals with its budget allocation. Had a program evaluation been conducted during the initial funding period based on the attainment of original program goals, NIMH would have had technical grounds for defunding the organization.

Organizational Boundaries

That CTC was funded before it actually came into existence resulted in all kinds of organizational confusion and diffusion. The official grant applicant and grantee was the Southwest Council of La Raza (SCLR), a Phoenix, Arizona, nonprofit corporation involved in housing and job development, with no official ties to TR and no prior experience with NIMH or in mental health training programs. However, it was the only Chicano organization around at the time with a track record with federal funding agencies, and it was willing to serve as CTC's fiscal agent and to let the policy committee govern all other program operations.

This arrangement created an interorganizational monster. First there was NIMH, a somewhat skeptical and reluctant participant. Then there was TR, a nonbureaucratic coterie or idealists whose representatives on the policy committee discerned no pitfalls in the arrangement. Next, there was SCLR, an innocent but obliging bystander carrying full legal responsibility and liability for the program. Finally, there was CTC itself, a legal nonentity governed by a legally nonaccountable committee and administered by a director whose orders came from the committee but whose salary was paid by SCLR, and who suffered from recurring nightmares that the monster would eventually rear its ugly head. Miraculously, through a strategy of shuttle diplomacy, interorganizational crises were averted. But it was difficult to answer the very basic question: "Who's in charge?"

Organizational Technology

Another problem confronting CTC at the beginning was its technological unpreparedness. The mission and function of the organization, as initially stated, involved the development and mounting of a national interdisciplinary training program for mental health practitioners and educators, including social workers, psychiatrists, psychologists, and psychiatric nurses. Yet, the staff the program attracted and hired were social work practitioners with no experience or formal educational preparation in curriculum development or training. This technological dilemma was an inescapable consequence of two factors: budgetary restraints and a policy that required all staff to be bilingual and bicultural (that is, Chicanos or close approximations thereof). At the time, however, the number of Chicanos who possessed the technology required to plan and carry out such a project was extremely limited. Those who had these technologies were securely employed and unwilling to join a highly uncertain and relatively low-paying soft-money venture, no matter how committed to the cause they might have been.

Not only did the CTC trainers lack the basic technology of training and curriculum development, they were faced with the additional problem that the state of the technology of cross-cultural training in mental health was virtually nonexistent. No one had ever developed or implemented a program to train non-Chicanos to work with Chicanos. Moreover, professional literature contained almost no content on Chicanos. What content did exist was to be found in anthropological and sociological studies—studies for which the methodologies and findings were under attack by the scientific community. Out of all of this, one fact emerged: The organization's technology had to be developed from scratch.

Corrective and Compensatory Strategies

Faced with these initial developmental problems, CTC had to undertake a number of activities to ensure its survival. All of these activities were tasks familiar to community organization practice, but seldom did one community organization assignment encompass such diverse activities.

Organizational Environment

One of the first tasks facing CTC was the reduction of political conflict and uncertainty in its environment. The first order of business was to establish a close professional relationship with the principal component of its environment, NIMH. The second was to deal with the San Antonio Community to resolve whatever conflict remained from the site selection controversy. The first task was accomplished with little fanfare. The CTC executive director had not been part of the negotiations between TR and NIMH. He also had been employed by the Department of Health, Education and Welfare prior to his CTC appointment. From the start, the CTC executive director and the NIMH project officer found a common ground for professional communication, and they formed a relationship based on mutual trust and respect. The second political dilemma was resolved through a strategy of "cooptation." The newly emerging leader of the San Antonio TR group was appointed to the CTC policy committee. Thus one TR group was given some share of authority in charting the course of CTC.

Contributing as well to the environmental survival of the organization was the receptiveness and support that CTC experienced from the Chicano community generally and the Houston community specifically. Locally both the Chicano and the social welfare communities were pleased to be associated with or to support the aims of the enterprise. The Houston United Way provided CTC with a $10,000 no-strings-attached grant to help it get started. The chairman of CTC's policy committee was a widely popular and respected political figure in Houston, and CTC's executive director had been the administrator of one of Houston's largest social agencies prior to joining HEW. Finally, since CTC was the only organization of its kind in the country, it did not have to contend with competitive elements in its broader environment.

Organizational Boundaries

By the end of its initial budget period, CTC had become a chartered nonprofit corporation legally empowered to deal directly with NIMH on all matters, including the receipt and management of program funds. No longer requiring a fiscal agent, CTC parted company with SCLR. The policy committee was reorganized as a legally responsible and accountable board of directors, rather than representative of TR. The act of incorporation greatly reduced the interorganizational complexities that marked CTC's beginnings. Organizational boundaries, and therefore a better organizational identity, emerged. There was no longer any doubt as to who was in charge, and CTC became clearly identified with Chicano concerns.

Organizational Goals

At a meeting held early during the second year of the program, the board of directors made a series of decisions that were to have a long-lasting impact on the mission and functions of the organization. First of all, the board agreed that the goal of providing training to all of the professions involved in the mental health field was an unrealistic one in the light of budgetary constraints. Therefore, for purposes of the NIMH grant, the trainee population was restricted to social work educators, principally those in graduate schools. The board further set a limit on the number of educators to be trained, and that decision was tied in to the amount of funds awarded for that purpose. This decision still left CTC with a modest role in the mental health training field, but with a readily available and identifiable market (social work educators) for its services (training) and products (curriculum materials).

Next, the board decided that training provided to groups other than social work educators would not be supported by the NIMH grant, but by fees charged to those groups. Finally, the board broadened CTC's mission to include the provision of well-designed but modest social services to Chicano groups and the engagement in

Chicano-related research activities, thereby opening the door for market, service, and product diversification. These decisions set the stage for CTC's development from a sole-purpose project, dependent on a single funding source, to a multipurpose organization in search of varied sources of financial support.

Organizational Technology

During the first two years, the CTC staff spent a considerable amount of time in the development of knowledge, skills, curriculum development, and training. Consultants were brought in to train staff, and staff attended numerous related workshops and conferences throughout the country, including those sponsored by the Council on Social Work Education's Chicano Faculty Development Project. During the same time, the organization amassed a sizable library of Chicano material and professional publications, which staff methodically reviewed and selectively incorporated into its evolving curriculum. It started to publish some of its own curriculum materials[5] by the third year of program operations, by which time CTC was actively involved in the actual provision of training. The initial technological unpreparedness had to a large extent been overcome.

ORGANIZATIONAL DIVERSIFICATION

CTC's diversification strategy was based on the realization that the NIMH grant would run out eventually, and that to be totally dependent on one source of funds for organizational survival is to court organizational suicide. Yet CTC's basic identity was tied to its NIMH training function. In order to maintain that identity and its new commitments, CTC had to maintain and find support for new functions. At the same time, the organization would go after funds to establish badly needed bilingual and bicultural professional counseling services at the local level. This would serve two purposes: An unmet need would be addressed, and the practice experience would serve as a source of content for the training curriculum. As funds became available, a research component would be created to

5. Federico Souflée and Graciela Schmitt, "Educating for Practice in the Chicano Community," *Journal of Education for Social Work* 10 (Fall 1974), pp. 75-84; Federico Souflée, "Chicano Curriculum Design and Social Work Education," in *Chicano Content and Social Work Education,* ed. M. Sotomayor and A. Ortego y Gasca (New York: Council on Social Work Education, 1975).

generate knowledge that would enhance both the training and the social service components. CTC would become a synergistic and heuristic system of interrelated and interdependent parts.

Armed with this new mission and vision, CTC began to implement its diversification strategy. Summarized below are the major projects launched by the organization during a ten-year period dating from April 1971 to September 1981.

Training and Curriculum Development

Mental Health Training Project

This was the program that gave birth to the agency. It ran its full seven-year course as a demonstration project—from 1971 through 1978. During that time, training was provided to hundreds of faculty and students in graduate and undergraduate social work schools and programs from throughout the country. A significant number of curriculum materials were published and distributed, and several staff members attained national prominence in the Council on Social Work Education and the National Association of Social Work.

Bilingual-Bicultural
Social Work Education Project

This project was also funded by NIMH for a seven-year period. It called for the training of social work students in the provision of bilingual and bicultural social services to Chicano clients. Graduate students primarily from Texas schools of social work were provided a stipend to do their second-year field placement with CTC, in its social services division. In addition to regular field instruction, students received intensive instruction in written and conversational Spanish, as well as in Chicano culture. Approximately forty Anglo and Chicano students participated in this program.

Model Course Syllabi Project

Also funded by NIMH, this two-year project had as its objective the development of model course syllabi incorporating social work and Chicano content in three major areas of social work study: policy, planning, and administration; human behavior and the social environment; and direct social work practice. This project was a response to the "apparent need in social work education for specific and readily applicable content materials reflecting Chicano cultural, social, and psychological perspectives, and for the integration of these perspectives into the social work curricula."[6] With the involvement and assistance of graduate and undergraduate social work educators from Texas, a compendium of model course syllabi was produced. Once published, it was distributed to all graduate and undergraduate social work education programs in the country.

Training Contracts

A considerable amount of unrestricted funds were generated over the years through contractual training agreements with a number of human service organizations, including United Way agencies, community mental health centers, departments of human resources, and Chicano grass-roots agencies in various parts of the nation. Even the U.S. Military Academy at West Point and the Colima, Mexico, campus of the University of Oklahoma availed themselves of CTC's training services. Funds from these contracts served two purposes: They were used to pay for expenditures not covered by project grants, and they allowed CTC to continue operating during the impoundment of funds during the Nixon administration.

Conferences

Support from various private foundations and federal and state agencies permitted CTC to organize and sponsor a number of special-interest conferences and symposia between 1974 and 1978, including an international conference on immigration held in Houston during the early Carter administration. This conference involved notables from the United States and Mexico, including respective presidential assistants, secretaries of labor, undersecretaries of state, and scholars. It was shortly thereafter that CTC's board president was appointed as commissioner of the U.S. Immigration and Naturalization Service.

Social Services

By providing social services for Chicanos, CTC kissed a benevolent local environment good-bye. Simply by seeking funds for counseling services for Chicanos, the organization disturbed the placid relationships it had enjoyed with the United Way and a number of its member agencies. CTC became an agitator for local response to

6. Norma Benavides and Federico Souflée, eds., *A Model Course Syllabi Compendium: Social Work and Chicano Content* (Houston: Chicano Training Center, 1978).

Chicano community needs and a competitor with other agencies once funding sources started paying attention. It was history repeating itself; now the struggles were between CTC and the Houston United Way rather than with TR and NIMH. Ironically, CTC had few political problems with funding its social service programs other than the United Way. This was because local political leaders had been sensitized to the human needs in Chicano communities, but, despite its initial support, the Houston United Way had not. This challenge was addressed directly by the CTC staff, and through extensive relationship-building efforts CTC and United Way eventually became friendly partners in service to the Houston Chicano community. By 1981, the following social service projects were in place:

(1) *Clinica de Consulta Familiar.* Begun with a grant from the Texas Commission on Alcoholism and later funded by United Way, this Chicano family counseling agency was CTC's initial social service component. It became the training ground for students on the NIMH Bilingual-Bicultural Training Program. Located in the midst of one of Houston's largest barrios, it became a potent declaration of CTC's intent to address the counseling needs of Houston Chicanos.

(2) *Mexican American Child Abuse and Neglect (MACAN) Project.* Funded by the National Center on Child Abuse and Neglect and the Harris (Houston) County Child Welfare Unit, this program dealt with prevention of child abuse and neglect in Chicano families referred to the local protective services agency.

(3) *Mexican American Youth Assistance (MAYA) Project.* This program was concerned with the prevention of juvenile delinquency and school truancy and dropout. Initially funded by the City of Houston, it was later, in modified form, supported by the United Way.

(4) *Reuniones Familiares.* Funded by the Texas Department of Community Affairs, the DAPP was designed to serve Chicano youth susceptible to drug use and abuse.

Research

Unlike training and social services, the research component never got off the ground in the ten-year period covered by this report. CTC's only attempt to develop a bicultural treatment framework based on statistically quantifiable scientific inquiry was discontinued once CTC realized that its paid research consultant was unprepared to conduct this type of study. The lesson learned by CTC from this experience was that if it wanted to conduct research, it had to develop its internal expertise in this area. The experience taught that diversification often requires the incorporation and control of those environmental elements that are essential for organizational achievement.

ORGANIZATIONAL SURVIVAL

In June of 1978, CTC's original training grant from NIMH expired. During the last year of the project, a new grant application had been prepared and submitted to NIMH. The project called for the training of personnel in community mental health centers and facilities in the state of Texas, a somewhat downscaled version of the 1971 grant application. Although endorsed by all of the major community mental health centers in the state and every single Texas congressional delegate, the application was denied, thereby putting an end to CTC's major training function.

Fortunately, the agency's social service component had by that time grown to the extent that organizational survival was assured. However, its training mission had come to an end and, with it, CTC's original identity changed. Once the identity changed, CTC's function changed as well. Thereafter, CTC remained an exclusively local social service agency. In keeping with its redefined identity, the organization changed its name accordingly and to this day continues to thrive and serve Chicanos in the Houston area.

CONCLUSION

CTC's experience illustrates how one minority human service enterprise was created, how it developed, and how it managed to survive in spite of numerous technological, political, and environmental obstacles. In a decade, it grew from a sole-purpose project to a multipurpose organization. Its structure changed as its functions grew and as its environment became more turbulent.

Not all obstacles were overcome, not all political battles won. However, the organization developed enough technological proficiency, political sophistication, and environmental support to keep itself afloat under the stormiest of conditions. Infused with values from its supporters and its geographic environment, CTC almost fulfilled its original promise of becoming an institutionalized national training resources. Whether or not CTC could have achieved this objective is a subject of community organization debate. There are many questions about whether community organizations are a method of practicing social work or whether they constitute a group of activities undertaken to achieve well-defined social objectives. As an example of a method of social work practice, the social service activities undertaken by CTC were examples of effective community organization. Once resistant to allocation of resources to Chicanos, the Houston community eventually embraced and funded a broad-based set of programs for Chicanos through CTC. CTC and its activities on behalf of Chicanos have become part of the fabric of the Houston community.

Whether the community organization activities, as a method of social work, were successful in institutionalizing broader social change such as might be realized through an institutionalized national training resource is less clear. CTC was highly instrumental in interjecting a Chicano presence in social work education and practice. CTC also provided a visible base from which Chicanos could move into national decision-making positions. Both consequences of CTC will continue to produce noticeable changes. But some question must be raised as to whether community organizations, as a method of social work, possess sufficient breadth to institutionalize broad social change of the type envisioned by CTC's founders. More likely, such broad-scale social changes are a product of many forces and professional activities, of which social work practice is a necessary but not sufficient component of such levels of success.

CASE 6

THE SEARCH FOR SELF-UNDERSTANDING
Long-Term Treatment in a Family Service Agency

ALLAN A. BLOOM
Private Practitioner
Raleigh, North Carolina

THE SETTING

Family Service Agencies were providing counseling to clients throughout the United States more than fifty years before the first community mental health center opened its doors. Unique among settings in which social workers offer clinical services, the organization is staffed entirely by social workers. Psychiatrists or psychologists sometimes are used as consultants, but social workers in this setting work independently rather than within the traditional hierarchy or as members of a treatment team. There is a wide range of social services offered to individuals and families of all social, religious, and economic categories. Marriage counseling, individual/family/group treatment, adoption, foster care, refugee resettlement, and homemaker services are examples. Behind all of these diverse activities lies the purpose of the Family Service Agency—the enrichment of family life.

The case that follows illustrates the long-term treatment of a Family Service Agency client. It is not an atypical case except for its length; most cases are of shorter duration (six interviews or less). The case was chosen to demonstrate how an experienced clinical social worker who has had appropriate supervision and training can provide treatment to a client who is suffering from both environmental and intrapsychic problems. All identifying material has been changed to protect the client's anonymity.

INITIAL INTERVIEW

Mr. Brown was referred to the Family Service Agency by the local community mental health center after he had requested help in working out problems with his wife, who had recently left him for another man. According to the information on his application form, he had a college degree but was employed in a blue-collar technical job unrelated to his education. This tall, heavy-set, 25-year-old man arrived for his interview dressed neatly and appropriately, if somewhat casually, in a sport shirt and jeans.

He talked readily, answered questions easily, and volunteered a good deal of information. His speech was direct and to the point, neither rambling nor circumstantial. He became tearful on several occasions as he described his wife's desertion and his own lonely and angry feelings. In discussing the situation, he showed no evidence of any thought disorder. His mood was what one would expect of anyone who had recently suffered a serious loss—flat, sad, low-key; in a word, depressed. He was having some difficulty sleeping, his appetite had been poor, and he reported that for the past two weeks, since his wife had left, he had been "doing a lot of drinking and crying." He did not request medicine for his depression, however, and said he had been able to continue working and getting together with friends. He did not admit to having any suicidal thoughts.

Consequently, I did not suggest a psychiatric evaluation, as I would have done had he appeared psychotic, suicidal, or homicidal.

According to Mr. Brown, his wife left him after four years of marriage, announcing "out of the blue" that she did not want to stay married anymore. The client was not at all in favor of the separation, however, and reported that he had been "entirely happy for four years. My wife provided everything I needed." His initial request had been for "help in putting my marriage back together again," and he concluded our first meeting by saying, "I definitely need help." When I asked if he could describe more clearly what it was he thought he needed help with, he replied that he wanted to try to sort out some things in addition to the marriage that were making him unhappy. "The insecurities . . . I have a great need to have friends, to talk to people, but I have the hardest time initiating things." I offered him the opportunity to come back to sort out his confused feelings and he accepted, but I was more than a little doubtful that he would return.

Since he was so upset over his separation, we discussed his family of origin only briefly in the first interview. He mentioned that he had two brothers and a sister; the client was the oldest sibling. His father, an alcoholic and "generally a good person," worked as a carpenter but had always disliked his work. Mr. Brown was quick to point out his own similarity to his father in hating his occupation, commenting, "I've never really been able to find anything I like." He said his father, "used to scream and yell a lot, but I always knew that he cared." He described his mother as "quiet and strong," but did not elaborate.

Evaluating the Initial Interview

In casework, as elsewhere, one must always be cautious of making judgments based on limited information. First impressions can serve merely as tentative guideposts; abundant data are needed to make a useful assessment. With this caveat in mind, I considered what Mr. Brown had revealed about himself in the first hour.

He seemed motivated. He arrived on time, was friendly and cooperative, answered questions, volunteered information, and accepted an offer to return. One of the most favorable indications of his motivations was the fact that he sought treatment voluntarily. He knew he was troubled and upset, and was consciously asking for help. Coming to treatment of one's own volition makes a big difference, both in the kind of help the caseworker can give and the prognosis for improvement. However, this conscious motivation is only the tip of the iceberg. Even the best motivated of clients keep within the self a core of resistance to change, to being honest, to "getting well." It is crucial that the caseworker understand and accept this basic fact of life: There is within each of us a potent fear of change, even for the better.

Mr. Brown showed no evidence of psychosis. His affect (the manner in which he displayed his inner feelings) fit his situation. One would expect him to feel and act sad, and he did. This, too, was a good sign. It showed that he was not too removed from his own feelings and that his defenses were neither too rigid nor too loose and fluid. That he did not request drugs to obliterate his suffering might speak well of his tolerance for frustration and his realistic understanding that caseworkers are not wizards who magically cure pain and sadness with pills. On the other hand, frequently clients really do need psychotropic medicine but refuse it, either feeling too threatened to accept help or fearing that medication will place them too firmly under the worker's control.

Another strength Mr. Brown displayed in the first interview was his capacity for introspection and self-observation. For instance, he made the connection himself between his plight of being stuck in a hated job and his father's similar unhappy fate. True, he offered no explanation for this similarity, but that was no cause for concern. Treatment is not so much a matter of finding answers as it is learning to ask the right questions.

There was evidence of other strengths in the fact that the client had graduated from college, thus indicating intelligence, ambition, a reasonably inquiring mind, and the capacity to defer gratification. These last two qualities would be important in assessing his suitability for long-term treatment, which is a tough and sometimes painful journey with little promise of quick or easy rewards.

In addition, Mr. Brown was aware that he had problems apart from the immediate crisis of his wife's leaving. He wanted to sort out the other things that were making him feel unhappy: "The insecurities . . . I have the hardest time initiating things." Few clients show such insight in the first interview, and many never do so. There is a crucial difference between seeing the problem as being "out there" and seeing it as being "inside"; that is, coming from within the client. Most people believe, in effect, "It's they (or he, or she) who are making me miserable. If only they (or he, or she) would change, I would be all right." There was, of course, no question that the reality of his wife's desertion was what precipitated Mr. Brown's depression.

But we would need to ask (though not in the first interview, and probably not for many weeks) what part Mr. Brown himself played in the separation. Was it really "out of the blue," as he believed, or had he been refusing to face the truth about his marriage for a long time? And even if he were not in any sense an unwitting accomplice (suppose, for example, that his wife had been killed by a truck), the manner in which he handled the loss, the time it took to recover, the intensity of his suffering would all be, to some extent and on some level, under his control. Freud put it nicely when he was asked just what psychotherapy could accomplish: "Psychotherapy can replace neurotic suffering with ordinary unhappiness."[1]

As important as it was for me to assess Mr. Brown's strengths carefully, it was equally important to estimate his deficits and weaknesses. Even in the first hour, Mr. Brown hinted at some personality problems. For example, he had a college degree but worked at a technical job having nothing to do with his education. He hated his work and knew he was not making full use of his abilities. A healthy person can work and love, Freud said. Was Mr. Brown a failure at both?

What did he mean when he said he wanted help with "insecurities . . . I have a great need to have friends and to talk to people but I have trouble initiating things"? Was he warning me that passivity was a problem for him? If so, manifestations of this problem would almost certainly occur in treatment. Indeed, no problems are displayed in treatment that do not also occur "outside." Conversely, given enough time and a suitably neutral atmosphere, almost all central problems of the outside world will eventually show up in the client's relationship with the caseworker.

Did Mr. Brown view his "great need to have friends" as shameful, as a threat, or (more probable) a weakness? Such sentiments would affect his willingness and ability to accept and use help. Waiting to ask for help until his situation appeared desperate and possibly hopeless suggested a reluctance to admit that he couldn't take care of his problems himself. This reluctance would need to be addressed quickly and repeatedly if treatment were to be successful.

To illustrate what I mean about the difficulty of accepting psychological help, compare going to a social worker with going to a dentist. Most people do not like going to a dentist, but that dislike

---

1. Sigmund Freud, *The Standard Edition of Complete Psychological Works of Sigmund Freud,* vol. 2, trans. James Strachey (London: Hogarth, 1955), p. 205.

pales in comparison to their distaste for seeing a caseworker. People are not ashamed of cavities, but they are ashamed of psychological and interpersonal problems. No one attempts to drill his or her own teeth, but most people feel weak, inadequate, and morally reprehensible if they cannot resolve emotional problems without help.

Planning Treatment

Mr. Brown was verbal, intelligent, and unhappy. Moreover, he showed the capacity to defer gratification, control his impulses, and look at himself introspectively. For these reasons, I decided he might be an appropriate candidate for primarily *uncovering* rather than *supportive* treatment. Let me explain the difference between the two modes. In supportive treatment, the caseworker does not challenge the client's defenses; rather, there is an attempt to bolster and augment them. The worker offers the client encouragement, reassurance, suggestions, and understanding. In uncovering, or insight-oriented treatment, the primary tools are understanding and interpretation; the goal is insight and ego-autonomy. Ego-autonomy is the ability to understand oneself and function as a self-directed, volitional person. Many people who come to social workers for help do not feel they are their own persons; they feel driven and manipulated by other people and outside forces. "I just couldn't say no"; "I didn't mean to say it"; "It feels like something just makes me do it"; we hear these phrases over and over from our clients. Ego-autonomy, then, is the ability to say and do what one means to say and do, to feel that one is in control of one's own life.

I do not mean to imply that uncovering and supportive treatment are dichotomous—that one method is used with a client to the exclusion of the other. The caseworker who has formed an adequate relationship with a client, using supportive treatment, eventually can interpret to some degree in some areas. On the other hand, even the most insightful client usually has a few areas that remain impenetrable, and they are likely to be extremely important. But the clinical social worker must understand the use of the two modes and when to apply them, considering the client's strengths, weaknesses, and needs.

Let me illustrate with an example. A 12-year-old girl is brought to treatment by her adoptive mother because the girl is chronically moody, irritable, tense, and belligerent. She has no friends; she picks fights with her schoolmates and family for no apparent reason. Her parents, who adopted her when she was 6, are kind, loving, and patient people who are at a loss to know how to help their daughter. Her history shows that the girl was given up for adoption at 2, and spent two years in each of two foster homes, where she was abused and neglected. Then, at 6, she was adopted into her present home. She continues to see the world as a hostile, unfriendly, dangerous place, full of people who will get her if she doesn't get them first. The fact is that although her world was once a dangerous place, it no longer is. Yet she persists in behaving as if nothing had changed. Her defenses, once appropriate, are now obsolete.

In supportive treatment, the caseworker would tacitly accept the girl's view of the world and help her find ways to make her stay in it as pleasant as possible. "You need to think before you speak," the caseworker might suggest, thereby helping her stay out of trouble with parents and other authorities. Eventually, the girl might learn to control her temper and tame her aggressiveness, and the change in outward behavior might elicit friendlier reactions from others. But friendliness may be what she fears and mistrusts, and a paradoxical, more aggressive response would not be surprising. On the other hand, she might not react with further rancor; she might eventually become accustomed to the idea that most people are not as mean and dangerous as those she had known earlier. She might, in time, settle down to live a relatively symptom-free life. However, this type of adjustment might give rise to another problem when, as an adult, she is again faced with the possibility of forming an intimate relationship. A revival of her unresolved conflicts and fears might be anticipated. A good marriage and the rewards of fidelity, care, and love might be difficult or even unattainable. Unfortunately, a solution of papering over and shoring up, similar to the one just described, is the best some people can ever realistically achieve.

Using the techniques of insight-oriented treatment, the caseworker would not accept the girl's view of the world as dangerous and hostile. Rather, the attempt would be to help her give up this illusion. She would be helped to relinquish the defenses to which she has clung tenaciously in her mistaken belief that she still needs to guard vigilantly against the dangers of personal involvement. The success of this approach would presuppose the existence of a stable ego (a firm foundation on which to build)—autonomy, initiative, identity, and intimacy, in Erikson's terminology.[2]

In comparing these two strategies, we are talking about the difference between symptom relief and a more radical reorganization of the personality. Many of the clients whom clinical social workers treat are incapable of such restructuring. They lack the necessary foundation of basic trust. In any case, it is not unusual for caseworkers to employ a prolonged trial of supportive work to bolster the ego before engaging in the more intensive, insight-oriented treatment. We will see how this worked with Mr. Brown, as we return to our discussion of his treatment.

BEGINNING TREATMENT

Mr. Brown did, indeed, return for his next appointment. The beginning phase of treatment (the first few months of weekly sessions) consisted mainly of his ventilating his feelings of sadness and anger. He talked repeatedly of how hurt, bitter, and outraged he felt. He complained about the injustice of his situation, how unfair it was that he should have been dumped in such a brutal matter. His wife, Joyce, had been the only woman he had ever loved. Their relationship had been altogether happy. Sex was good, they got drunk and stoned together, she cooked and cleaned for them. Then, "for some reason," Joyce decided to go back to college to study music. She met new people who took her time and energy away from him. She stayed late to practice and study, and struck up a friendship with Larry, another student. Larry and Joyce began seeing each other frequently. Joyce assured her husband that her new relationship was strictly platonic, and Mr. Brown believed her. Then suddenly, one day, Joyce dropped the bomb. She was tired of being married and wanted out. She needed to "find herself." Her husband's pleas, tears, and tantrums were useless, and she left. Mr. Brown later discovered that she had been sleeping with Larry all along, and that the two had practically set up house together. Mr. Brown became virtually obsessed with a jealous rage that all but consumed him, but he did nothing to deal with the situation.

2. Erik H. Eriksen, *Childhood and Society,* 2nd ed. (New York: W.W. Norton, 1963), p. 263.

The Caseworker's Role:
Supportive Treatment

My comments during this beginning stage of treatment were, for the most part, reflective and empathic: "It's understandable that you would feel so hurt." "You must have felt angry." "There must be times when you just don't want to go on anymore." Mostly, I listened. I tried to help Mr. Brown feel that someone cared and understood. This man's self-esteem, pride, his very manhood, had been brutally shattered. He felt empty and alone and worthless. Most important, he was ashamed and humiliated.

My first task was to create an emotional connection, or to establish a relationship, as social workers usually call it. Without an emotional connection, there could be no "cure." While the relationship itself can have a healing effect, its primary importance is that it keeps the client involved in treatment. Mr. Brown would have to work hard, and eventually the going would be rough. An emotional connection to me would nourish and sustain the process. So I began to build the relationship by slowly and patiently reiterating my understanding and concern in a nonjudgmental way. I did not take sides, reassure, or offer sympathy. I did not even ask many questions. At this point, my job was to put Mr. Brown's feelings into words for him, to help him verbalize, and thus make comprehensible and tolerable whatever it was that he thought he needed to fear. I did not ask such questions as "How did you feel about that?" or "Why do you think you felt that way?" These gratuitous requests for emotional clarification are only confusing to a client who is trying to recover from the jolt of painful rejection.

The History Begins to Emerge

As Mr. Brown became more comfortable with talking about his feelings, he began to volunteer details about his family and childhood. He grew up in a small rural town. His father was a chronic and abusive alcoholic who despised his job as a carpenter. Mr. Brown recalled many times in his childhood when his mother sent him to fetch his father from the neighborhood bar. Upon arriving home, the father would cause a violent scene, hitting his wife, smashing household objects, and screaming at the children who cowered in terror. Mr. Brown's mother was a quiet, passive woman who bore in martyrlike fashion the abuse inflicted by her husband. The client described her as "cold and distant," a woman who was restricted and cut off from her feelings. "She was just there," he said with bitterness. Whatever nurturance and security Mr. Brown had received was provided by his maternal grandmother, who lived close by. She died when he was 9, and he grieved for her terribly. She had been his "haven in a heartless world."

Mr. Brown had been an average student, performing well below his potential while in public school. In education, as in other spheres of his life, he was conflicted and inhibited. He kept mostly to himself in high school. What few friends he had were loners and drinkers— "weirdos, like me." His high school record was undistinguished, as was his work at the state university he attended. He joined the army to escape the draft, but was dishonorably discharged on drug charges. He habitually butted heads with authority in the army, a pattern than had solidified by this time. After being discharged, Mr. Brown returned to his hometown, where he met Joyce. They were married after a brief courtship and then moved to a larger city. He took the hated job, but only for the pay. "I was never interested in it," he confided. He continued to smoke marijuana daily, a habit that persisted for many years.

The Caseworker's Role: Insight-Oriented Treatment

Mr. Brown did not reveal all of this information at one time, nor was it all offered spontaneously. Pieces emerged gradually, and I had to probe actively for many details. The essential facts emerged without much difficulty, but as he related his story Mr. Brown habitually left out the feelings associated with events, omissions I repeatedly called to his attention. "Do you notice how, once again, you didn't say anything about how you felt when your father came home drunk that night and slapped you?" There was a reason for my phrasing the question in that particular way. It is important for the client to understand and acknowledge his feelings. But simply to ask Mr. Brown what feelings he had would not address the more far-reaching issue of his chronic avoidance of emotions. When I asked, "Did you notice that you neglected to mention your feelings?" I was not directing Mr. Brown to tell me what his feelings were. Rather, I was enlisting his active cooperation in our mutual venture of exploring how he lived his inner life. "Look here," I was saying in effect, "let's examine what you are staying away from, and why. If we can figure that out, it might tell us something very useful about you."[3]

In addition, I continually endeavored to help Mr. Brown link his past to his present. For many months, he resisted the notion that his past and his family background had anything to do with what he was like today. However, through repeated confrontations and interpretations, this point gradually was brought home. The wedge that was driven into the client's awareness was the inescapable fact of his father's chronic drunkenness and mistreatment of the family. Mr. Brown began to speak of his angry and disappointed feelings toward his father, and initially he sided with his mother, who he viewed as innocent victim while his father was cast as villain. As we talked about his family, Mr. Brown repeatedly discussed how much his father hated his work. It was his cognizance of the similarity between his father and himself that made him aware of the effect the past can have on the present.

Following the initial phase of building a relationship, my chief concern was to teach Mr. Brown how treatment works and to help him become an active participant. Another aim, however, was for the two of us to construct as complete a history as possible. Of course, the history can never be completely reconstructed, and usually it is tactless, not to mention futile, to obtain a history through a barrage of direct questions. One can easily become mired down in facts that serve as intellectualized armor against feelings. There are situations that require that the worker take a formal, structured social history, but allowing the client to set the pace yields a far greater emotional payoff. The worker can nudge the client to discuss personal history by saying something such as, "Please tell me about your family," which allows the client freedom of movement. Then clarifying questions such as "How do you mean that?" can be asked to aid the data-gathering process.

As I listened to Mr. Brown's history, I began to piece some things together. He had remarked in our first meeting, "My wife provided everything I needed." This statement had an infantile ring to it, and I wondered if he was not reexperiencing the trauma he had suffered when his grandmother died. Depression is a pathological reaction to loss, and once again Mr. Brown had been abaondoned. He had been entirely dependent on Joyce, as he had earlier been on his grandmother, for emotional nurturance. It was likely that an old

3. See J. H. Paul, *Letters to Simon* (New York: International Universities Press, 1973).

wound, which had never properly healed, had been reopened with this new crisis of abandonment.

Mr. Brown had described an early childhood largely devoid of emotional security, and I wondered if his chronic failure to reach goals in school work and relationships represented a wish to remain attached to a miserable, yet familiar and hence comfortable, pattern set in childhood. In refusing to succeed in life he was, after all, imitating or identifying with his parents, especially his father. He confided that he stayed intoxicated with beer and marijuana almost constantly, rationalizing that "all my friends stay stoned." But eventually he admitted that he used drugs and alcohol to try to escape the pain of loneliness and the rage and disappointment in his life.

THE MIDDLE PHASE OF TREATMENT

About eight months after Mr. Brown began treatment, Joyce and her lover died in a fire. We worked together to overcome this new crisis, as Mr. Brown wrestled with the sadness, regret, rage, and guilt he felt over the permanent loss of his wife and his failure to prevent her death. He believed he had not been "man enough" at the time of the separation, and he berated himself for not having beaten or killed Joyce's lover. Later, we talked about his feelings of hatred and the death wishes he had directed toward Joyce following her desertion. He conceded that his guilt revolved in part around these destructive feelings, which we brought to the surface and discussed. "There's nothing we can't talk about," I told him repeatedly. Gradually he came to see the truth and importance of this statement concerning the nature of the therapeutic relationship.

As the months passed, we spent more and more time talking about how his early family life had affected him. He was able to tolerate increased self-honesty due to the level of positive attachment (transference) that had developed. He confessed how furious he was at his parents, and how much he had felt the burden, as oldest child, of looking after his mother in his father's place. Mr. Brown understood, now, that his parents had forced him, from early childhood, to deny his own need for nurturance. We discussed how little emotional support he had received from his mother; indeed, how little she was able to give emotionally to anyone. Mr. Brown was beginning to view his parents more realistically. Mother no longer was the unblemished angel; father was not entirely the wicked villain.

We did not dwell only on the past, however. As treatment progressed, Mr. Brown's character patterns emerged more clearly. He became a volunteer at a local drop-in crisis center, and eventually he quit his hated job to work as an aide at a Goodwill Industries workshop. Although his altruism appeared to be a step forward, his motivations were unclear to either of us. Together we examined, in a number of ways, these efforts to help others. First, we speculated that he was acting out a long-standing character pattern of taking care of others, as he had felt driven to do with his mother. Second, we discussed the possibly defensive quality of these altruistic endeavors. Specifically, we looked at how Mr. Brown might, through defense mechanisms, be covering up his deep-seated anger and aggression. "Look what a wonderful, loving person I am. I don't have an angry bone in my body," he might be trying to say. Moreover, because he habitually denied his dependency needs, we also speculated that he was doing for others what he wished would be done for him; he wanted to be taken care of but simultaneously feared closeness and dependence. Third, we looked at these behaviors from the point of view of what they might be saying about his self-esteem; he might be gaining a sense of superiority by associating with other people who were even more emotionally distraught than he.

The Caseworker's Role: Dealing with Transference

From the beginning of treatment, Mr. Brown's style of relating to me had been superficially cooperative, with an underlying tone of hostility and challenge. Time and again, he would mention friends who were successfully involved in group therapy such as EST, Life Spring, and Re-evaluation Counseling. He talked repeatedly of how expensive and elitist individual treatment was, although he himself was a low-fee client who payed only a few dollars a session. Beneath the hostility in these comments, however, I detected a strong defensive quality. I believed that in behaving this way, Mr. Brown was trying to protect himself from passive and affectionate feelings. The fear of becoming dependent on the caseworker was an issue Mr. Brown himself frequently mentioned. "I could really get to like coming here," he said. It was obvious that prospect bothered him.

Initially, Mr. Brown belittled or ignored my suggestions that it would be useful for us to examine his feelings about me in more detail, especially the thinly disguised angry ones. "What difference does that make?" he would say with a shrug, adding, "You take all this too personally." But I repeatedly interpreted and confronted him with the veiled manifestations of his hostile feelings toward me—being late for or missing appointments, using a sneering tone of voice. As treatment progressed, we spent more and more time on the theme of his fear of dependence and his profound difficulty in accepting my help.

There were elements of positive transference, as well. For example, I saw Mr. Brown's helping others as an identification with me. I was becoming, for him, the good parent; and he was shifting his identification from his depressed, hostile, and unfeeling parents to what he saw as the kind, understanding, benevolent caseworker. However, I did not voice this interpretation to him. As a rule, caseworkers interpret transference only when it impedes treatment. That is to say, we need to discuss with clients promptly and frankly their angry, fearful, and disappointed feelings about us in order to help clients understand how they are inappropriately transferring negative attitudes from past relationships to the present situation. Without this intervention, treatment might collapse under the weight of too much hostility and unpleasantness. On the other hand, unless the client's loving, friendly, erotic feelings toward the caseworker reach such an intensity that they too become an impetus to flee ("I am so involved with you that I must get away from here"), we simply tacitly accept these positive emotions. They become, as in Mr. Brown's case, the vehicle that carries the client forward toward health and growth.

The Client Learns from
the Treatment Relationship

When one sees a client only once or twice a week, one must pick and choose what to emphasize and what to ignore. These are not easy decisions, and there are no hard-and-fast rules. In working with Mr. Brown, I decided that his anger and fear of closeness deserved priority. I tried not to miss any opportunity to explore this issue, especially in his interactions with me. The reason for "dwelling" (his word) on us, I explained, was that in so doing we could both get a close-up, undiluted look at how we felt and behaved in other relationships. I agreed that discussing his relationship with his girl friend, mother, or boss was important, but I pointed out how much more powerful it can be to deal with a relationship in the here and now. For instance, Mr. Brown's habitual pattern of arriving early for appointments came to be seen as another example of his way of guarding against a desire to stand me up. By the same token, it was an example of his wish to be a good client—the dutiful son he had tried to be as a boy. As we explored both sides of this ambivalence, the client's hostility toward me began to abate. This movement was accompanied by a rise in the frequency and intensity of his expressions of negative feelings about his parents. He began to discuss his childhood in greater detail. He gradually shifted from viewing his father as the family villain toward seeing him as an unhappy, depressed, and pitiful man who tried hard but received little emotional support from his wife. Mr. Brown's mother, on the other hand, lost her status as blameless victim and became a cold, somewhat hostile, very disappointed woman. As the view of his mother became less idealistic, Mr. Brown was able to look more realistically at his relationships with other women. He acknowledged his tendency to become involved in frustrating relationships with women who were needy, unemotional, and sexually frigid. The positive results of these explorations were apparent. Mr. Brown became more careful in his choice of dates and remained with unsuitable partners only briefly. However, he continued to deny for a long time that a lasting, close heterosexual relationship was possible, since the two most important women in his life—his mother and his wife—had turned away from him.

THE LATER STAGE OF TREATMENT

In the third year of treatment, there occurred a major shift for the better. Mr. Brown's social functioning had improved greatly. He developed goals to return to school, became a graduate student at the university, and did well. In Erikson's terminology, Mr. Brown was mastering the tasks of industry and identity, which Erikson defined as necessary achievements of latency and adolescence, respectively. Thus he climbed the developmental ladder, and was stuck at the next step, "intimacy versus isolation," the characteristic conflict of the young adult.

Mr. Brown attended his treatment sessions regularly and worked hard in them, producing appropriate material. He was doing a good deal of casual dating, but had not yet become seriously involved with any one woman. However, he now admitted, both to himself and to me, that he wanted and felt capable of achieving a close, caring relationship.

As trust between us strengthened, Mr. Brown disclosed his worries over his tendency to get drunk and stoned on marijuana every night. He continued to deny that getting high was a problem, but I confronted him repeatedly with the truth: He was running away from his feelings, especially aggressive ones, by means of drinking, smoking pot, and indulging in the grandiose fantasies that accompanied these bouts. He understood my comments and admitted that, when alone, he liked nothing better than to play on his stereo what he called "angry music" (punk rock), yelling and dancing around all by himself. In these cathartic escapades, he was a frenzied, violent little boy throwing a tantrum. As I had anticipated, Mr. Brown did not appreciate my suggestion that he had a drug problem. He became angry with me for this confrontation and was deeply offended by the merest suggestion that he couldn't control himself. I wanted to deprive him of beer and pot, he complained, and he was not going to put up with it. However, it was he, not I, who pointed out how once again he was copying his alcoholic father's behavior. Then, too, the strength of the positive transference was sufficient to hold him in therapy during this difficult period. We struggled together to understand his motivation to become stoned. He responded well to my interpretation that the deeper motives that brought him to use drugs were not so different from the motives that brought him to seek treatment—he was looking for something to give him comfort and peace.[4]

TERMINATION

After three and a half years, termination is in sight. There is still unfinished business, as there is in every termination, such as drug and alcohol abuse and unresolved relationship problems; but Mr. Brown has made real strides toward achieving autonomy. I have assured him that he is ready to terminate so that he can feel free to continue the movement away from me that is already under way, but at the same time he can feel free to retain some contact without fear of overdependency. I have reminded him that the issue is not whether

4. Siegfried Berthelsdorf, "Analysis of a Heroin Addict," in *Psychoanalytic Study of the Child*, vol. 31 (New Haven, CT: Yale University Press, 1976), p. 171.

treatment should be continued, but rather where it will be con-tinued—with me, or on his own.

Termination is always difficult for both caseworker and client, particularly when a long-term relationship has been established that is important to both. In the case of Mr. Brown, however, termination also involves a sense of accomplishment. Although Mr. Brown undoubtedly will have problems in the future, he is no longer bound by forces from the past to the same crippling extent as he was when he first came for help with his failed marriage.

CASE 7

INDUSTRIAL SOCIAL WORK
Direct and Indirect Services and Consultation

PHILIP W. COOKE

**Professor, School of Social Work
University of North Carolina, Chapel Hill**

Industrial social work is an expanding area of practice involving activities performed by social workers in the work place. Although these activities are basically similar to those performed by social workers in the public and private welfare systems, practice in the industrial arena involves differences as well. Industrial social work takes place in an environment where goods or services are produced and distributed for financial profit, and social workers are employed by management for the purpose of helping to achieve the goal of profit. Ideally—and usually in actuality—this organizational goal coincides with social work's goal of improving the working conditions and personal lives of workers. It is this meshing of organizational and social work goals that makes a fruitful collaboration possible.[1]

The principal activities of an industrial social worker involve direct services to troubled employees. In making such help available, the organization is interested primarily in minimizing the negative impact of an employee's personal problems on work performance. The organization generally wants to do what it can to enable a troubled employee to remain productive, particularly when the employee has served the organization well in the past. The social worker's direct services may include counseling, organizing and leading self-help groups, consulting with supervisors, and making referrals to community agencies and resources.

To a lesser extent, social workers perform what are called "indirect" services. Within this framework, social workers provide consultation with managers regarding personnel policies and group training of employees or managers in such areas as communication skills, conflict management, and work-group dynamics. The social worker may help to diagnose and solve organizational problems through consultation with both workers and managers, or may help managers implement difficult or unpopular decisions. These kinds of activities are sometimes called "organizational development."

Since World War II, there has been considerable growth and expansion of employee benefit programs within industry. This expansion has occurred for a variety of reasons, including a strong labor movement, a better educated work force, new laws governing the work environment, extension of the mandatory retirement age to 70, a changing work force with the addition of more women and minorities, and a growing recognition by mangement that employee benefit programs contribute to productivity. Social workers are particularly well suited to this area of practice; until recent years, however, there has been little interest on the part of educators or practitioners in this type of employment in the private sector.

One type of employee benefit program that has expanded greatly since World War II involves in-kind benefits. These services are provided either internally (by the organization) or externally (by purchase from a service provider). In-kind benefits usually are identified as "employee assistance programs" and include such services as counseling programs for alcoholism or marital problems,

---

1. Paul A. Kurzman and Sheila H. Akabas, "Industrial Social Work as an Arena for Practice," *Social Work* 26 (January 1981), pp. 52-60.

day care for the children of working parents, health clinics, legal assistance, and financial and career planning services. One of the purposes of an employee assistance program is the early identification of employees who are experiencing personal or medical problems that adversely affect job performance. It is the responsibility of the employee assistance program first to discover existing problems through screening and diagnosis, then either to provide short-term counseling or to refer the case elsewhere for services. Referrals are generated in several ways. Some employees are referred to the employee assistance program by supervisors who have noted a decline in job performance. Others are self-referred. Family members usually are also entitled to service, and may enter the program as self-referrals. Members of the managerial staff also may seek help. Some large corporations, for example, employ social workers to counsel executives and their families regarding the emotional difficulties associated with frequent company transfers to new communities.[2]

Colleagues from other disciplines are also engaged in these activities. Along with nurses, clergy, psychologists, and guidance counselors, social workers may be employed either full time by an industry or through a contractual agreement to perform employee assistance services. At the time of the activities described in the two cases that follow, the social workers were employed full time by large industrial organizations.

DIRECT SERVICES
TO A TROUBLED EMPLOYEE:
THE CASE OF HENRY JOHNSON

April 16

When I returned from lunch, my secretary informed me that Allan Simpson, a supervisor in the assembly section, had called to discuss an employee's situation. I knew Mr. Simpson slightly as a member of a group of line supervisors I had organized recently to discuss employee morale and ways of identifying employees who were having difficulty with such problems as drinking, burnout, or stress overload.

---

2. Martha Ozawa, "Development of Social Services in Industry: Why and How?" *Social Work* 25 (November 1980), pp. 464-470.

When I reached him by telephone, Mr. Simpson suggested that we meet during his coffee break. I arrived at the appointed time, and we drank two cups of coffee without getting to the point of our meeting. It was apparent that this supervisor was struggling with his strong disinclination to talk about an employee's personal problems, so I suggested that we go for a walk on the company grounds. We spent the next ten minutes exhausting the subject of the beauty of the landscaping and its importance to the company in creating a good public image. Finally, I brought the conversation to the reason he had called me.

Mr. Simpson began by talking about his years as a line supervisor, the trust he felt from his crew, and his reluctance about being a "fink." I remarked that I was aware of his good reputation as a supervisor and could understand that he did not want to feel as if he were betraying one of his men. I also recognized, however, that there are times when a supervisor must "meddle" in a worker's private life because of job performance and concern for the worker. Given this reassurance, Mr. Simpson began to talk about Henry Johnson, a senior welder on his work crew. Apparently Mr. Johnson had come to work several times during the last month with the smell of alcohol on his breath; he had been late for work on a number of occasions and had taken two days of sick leave during the past two weeks. Although Mr. Simpson had not noticed any decrease in Mr. Johnson's productivity, he was concerned because Johnson's work involved occasional contact with dangerous materials. Mr. Simpson went on to explain that Henry Johnson had been a steady, dependable worker for many years, and until recent weeks had shown no signs of a problem with alcohol.

I reassured Mr. Simpson that his concern seemed justified and asked him how he thought the situation should be handled. After thinking for a moment, he somewhat reluctantly suggested that he guessed it was up to him as supervisor to initiate action. I agreed, and we spent some time discussing how he might approach Mr. Johnson and route him to the employee assistance office. After we had decided on a plan, I promised to keep Mr. Simpson informed of any actions taken, should Mr. Johnson decide to avail himself of my services.

Because industrial social work is a relatively new profession, social workers spend much of their time educating employees about the nature and availability of services. This educational process can occur on a one-to-one basis or through formal group training programs. In either case, the social worker must establish a relationship of trust and comfort with the "gatekeepers"—those persons who are apt to come in direct contact with troubled workers. In industry, the key gatekeeper is the line supervisor, and social workers devote much of their time to coaching line supervisors on how to respond to workers and their needs. The line supervisor's function is to oversee production and deal with whatever issues impede production. The social worker's task is to assist in that function as a human relations consultant. To be effective, the social worker must respond to the line supervisors in terms of "where they are" and must work with them in ways that make the supervisors feel most comfortable. The role of the social worker as consultant or coach is achieved through an evolutionary process, as the worker gains trust and respect by demonstrating the usefulness of social work services.

April 18

Henry Johnson came to my office to make an appointment with me. He stonily explained that he had been "sent" by Mr. Simpson to discuss his "problems." Mr. Johnson was a large man, in his mid-40s, with slightly stooped shoulders. His callused hands and rugged appearance suggested years of physical work. His manner was shy and reserved. His hesitance in speaking indicated that he was a person who had difficulty articulating his feelings. His mood was one of sadness.

I matter-of-factly and candidly explained that Mr. Simpson and I had discussed Mr. Johnson's frequent illnesses, tardiness, and arrival at work smelling of alcohol. Mr. Johnson responded by denying that he had a drinking problem. Rather than arguing the point, I invited him to tell me about himself and his family.

One of the more common problems dealt with by social workers in industry is alcohol abuse. In fact, many of the direct service programs in industry began because of concern over the effect of alcoholism on productivity. Companies and unions have found that in-house programs to reduce alcohol and drug abuse are both cost-effective and beneficial for employees.

Mr. Johnson slowly volunteered information about his 18 years with the company and his 22 years of marriage. The eldest of his three children had completed college and moved away, the middle boy was living at home and working, and the youngest child, a girl, was still in high school. As we discussed his family, it became obvious that Mr. Johnson was feeling increasingly depressed. I observed that he seemed down and wondered what was bothering him. He denied that anything was troubling him. I disagreed, and commented that perhaps he was bringing his troubles to work. After some hesitation, he spoke of a recent incident concerning his teenage daughter's experimentation with drugs. The incident had resulted in a "family fight" involving himself, his wife, and their daughter, during which all of them said a lot of "terrible things" to each other. We explored this incident, along with others that had occurred on previous occasions. It became evident that the Johnson family had been having trouble for some time and that the focus of the trouble was the teenage daughter. Mr. and Mrs. Johnson had tried to handle the situation without outside help, hoping that their efforts and time would provide a solution.

After discussing how most families attempt to handle their problems privately at first, I recommended to Mr. Johnson that he, his wife, and their daughter seek family counseling. I pointed out that they could use the services of the local family service agency or see a counselor in private practice. I said I would be glad to arrange an appointment, and told him that his company insurance plan would cover the cost. At first, Mr. Johnson was reluctant to commit himself, saying he was not sure that his wife and daughter would agree to the idea of counseling. I offered to talk with them, but Mr. Johnson decided that he should be the one to discuss my recommendation with them. He promised to let me know the results of that discussion on the following day.

April 19–Morning

Mr. Johnson stopped by my office briefly and explained that to his surprise, his wife and daughter had actually welcomed the idea of going to see a family counselor. They had decided that they would prefer seeing someone in private practice. It was apparent that Mr. Johnson was feeling a great deal of relief as a result of this family decision. His manner and mood were more relaxed and hopeful. I promised to make some inquiries and let him know when I had some more information for him.

April 19–Afternoon

I went to the area where Mr. Johnson worked and gave him the name of an excellent family counselor in private practice whom I had called in the meantime. Mr. and Mrs. Johnson and their daughter had been given an appointment the following Friday. With Mr. Johnson's permission, I told Mr. Simpson of the plan. Mr. Simpson was pleased, and he and I agreed that together we would monitor Mr. Johnson's progress on the job.

Termination of Service

The case of Mr. Johnson illustrates the most common type of social work activity in industry. The worker initially appeared to have a drinking problem that could intefere with his productivity, and the social worker was asked to intervene. As is so often the case, the drinking behavior was found to be symptomatic of family problems, and the client and his family were helped to secure appropriate community services.

Mr. Johnson's case also illustrates the general pattern of brevity in providing industrial social work practice. The time spent in meeting with Mr. Johnson was the smallest amount of time spent on the case. The focus was on a responsive helping intervention with the goal of improving job functioning. In this instance, the social worker employed a variety of skills, including group training and coaching of gatekeepers, confrontation, counseling, referral, and follow-up consultation with the supervisor in order to help Mr. Johnson deal with a family problem that was affecting his job performance.

CONSULTATIVE SERVICES TO MANAGEMENT

This case illustrates the role of an industrial social worker as a consultant to management. As a training specialist in the human resources development unit of the company's personnel department, the social worker cooperates with other trainers representing such disciplines as business administration, adult education, and psychology. Services provided to improve organizational interactions include employee skill training, supervisory training, consultation to management and labor on specific issues such as work-group acceptance of new technology or procedures, data collection and feedback, team or work-group development, and analysis of problems of work-group morale. In the case presented here, the social worker performed a variety of these activities while assisting a group of supervisors to form a more effective work team.

January 3

For the past several months, I had been conducting a series of training seminars for division managers on the topic of the issues and technology involved in evaluating employees' performance. Joe Baker, division manager for product development, had asked me during one of the training sessions to drop by his office when I had the chance. Now that I had some free time, I called Joe and made plans to have lunch with him. Over lunch, Joe explained that there were six work units in his division, each headed by a supervisor who was very capable in his particular technical area. Individually, each work unit was performing well, but increasingly there were situations in which the units and their supervisors had to work together. Joe's approach in the past had been as a "one-to-one" manager with each of his supervisors, but now circumstances required that all of them work together as a management team. He asked me to help him and his six supervisors become an effective working group.

Before responding to his request, I explored with Joe a number of concerns regarding other agendas he might have for wanting the supervisors to become a group, his personal approach to management decision making, the degree of time and energy he wanted to put into the effort, and other components that would help me develop a feel for how I should proceed. Our discussion made it quite evident that Joe and his supervisors were all competent managers, and that my interventive strategy should be one of building on their strengths rather than correcting their deficiencies. Joe had already discussed his interest in a team development effort with his supervisors, and I agreed to meet with them to plan together how we would proceed.

January 6

In my exploratory session with Joe and his supervisors, we agreed that we would meet every other week for a period of four months. Meetings would be devoted to group task activities and interpersonal exercises. During the initial sessions, I would provide the agenda and direction; in later stages, the group would design and implement its own agendas. The first step would be to undertake a series of management self-inventories to help group members become aware of their individual differences in perceptions, values, preferences, and ways of dealing with managerial tasks.

February 11-28

I met individually with Joe and each of his supervisors in order to understand the perspective of each and give all of them an opportunity to evaluate me as a potential group facilitator—and, perhaps, to begin to develop trust in my goodwill and competence.

March

The work group and I met for three sessions in March. During this time, Joe and the supervisors participated in a management approach inventory, a learning style inventory, and a decision-making assessment exercise. My role with the group was to help the members feel comfortable in sharing personal information with the group and to help them recognize and value each other's strengths. We also used our interactions during these sessions as a basis for discussing how groups make decisions and handle conflict.

April

During the early part of the month I helped the group members clarify their expectations of each other on the job and participate in exercises designed to increase feelings of mutual trust. The final meeting of the month was focused on an obvious conflict that had developed between Joe and two of his supervisors. Two extra sessions were held to permit the group to discuss and negotiate this conflict.

May

I met with the group twice during the month of May. The sessions now took on a task orientation, with each supervisor presenting and discussing his unit's six-month work plan. The group also made plans to hold a "take stock" session during the first week in June.

June 4

Joe, the supervisors, and I spent this concluding session reviewing the meetings of the last four months. Everyone felt that good progress had been made in the group's ability to function as a team. All of us shared impressions of the dynamics that had contributed to or detracted from the growth of the group as a working unit. I contracted with the group to continue to participate in monthly meetings for the next six months.

July

I received requests from two other divisional managers to assist them in forming their supervisors into a work team.

EPILOGUE

REFLECTIONS ON THE FUTURE OF THE FIELD OF SOCIAL WORK

JOHN B. TURNER

Dean, School of Social Work
University of North Carolina, Chapel Hill

In this book's opening chapter, the social work profession was described as "unity in diversity." Throughout the book, social work educators and practitioners have demonstrated in a variety of ways that social work is, indeed, a cohesive profession in which practitioners in varied settings remain united by a common bond of characteristics, values, and competencies. The authors have also spoken to the challenges and satisfactions of practice, as well as to its frustrations, ambiguities, and mixed outcomes. Their discussions and case examples have given the student a beginning sense of what day-to-day practice involves for the thousands of social workers who are helping real people in the real world with personal and social problems that threaten their well-being and that of their families. Although we have not touched upon every problem, described every arena of practice, or mentioned every helping technology, and while authors have indicated that there are gaps in knowledge and areas in need of exploration and development, the reader is left with the impression that social work is a vibrant profession that is relevant to the human needs of society.

Looking ahead, some basic questions come to mind rather quickly. Will social work continue to be needed by society, or will it be replaced by other helping professions? Will it enjoy more or less status than it has today among other professions and within society? Will it continue to struggle with the internal issues of the past, or will new issues emerge to replace the old? What advances are likely to take place in its technologies for helping people with problems?

Several of the authors have consulted their crystal balls and made predictions in their areas of expertise for the remainder of this decade. The conclusions they have drawn are resoundingly positive but not utopian. Students can rest assured that there is, indeed, a future for social work. The nature of that future depends on what happens within the profession itself, as well as upon events that occur in the larger political, economic, and social systems. In this concluding section, I will discuss three major dilemmas that social work must solve in the years that lie ahead. How we deal with these issues will affect our professional future in fundamental ways.

DILEMMAS OF RANGE AND DOMAIN

The debate between the generalists and specialists in social work will be with us for a long time. Those who urge greater specialization and clearer definition of professional boundaries point out the obvious disadvantages of attempting to be all things to all people. The generalists argue, equally compellingly, that a holistic view of clients and a generalist approach to practice distinguish social work as the only helping profession that cuts across specializations in our increasingly segmented world.

The generalist approach demands that in the process of dealing with the specific problems presented by clients, social workers must consider other factors on the individual, family, and community levels that interact with or result in the specific problem at hand. Realistically, help must be circumscribed to some degree; having gained an understanding of the client's functioning within his or her social system, the worker must decide what assistance should be rendered, who can provide it, how long the process will take, and by what means help will be delivered. Thus the holistic approach calls upon the social worker to master four separate but related techniques: (1) how to help resolve the presenting problem, (2) how to get others to help with related aspects of the problem, (3) how to get the client to accept and use help with issues other than the one for which help was sought, and (4) how to allocate responsibility for success and failure among those who cooperate in the helping process.

This holistic view of people and problems has led social work to carry out its practice in a variety of settings and with many kinds of human problems. Social work provides help to infants, children, adolescents, young adults, and the elderly. It seeks to help with the problems of the poor, the ill, the disadvantaged, and the severely distressed, regardless of the source of the stressors, by working with individuals, families, and organizations. This broad dispersal of effort among a multitude of settings, problems, and clients causes uncertainties of professional identity, definition of service, and interorganizational relationships, both within and outside the profession.

The view of social work as holistic pays high dividends in practice, because it accurately reflects the way most people in trouble see themselves. Yet, in this age of specialization, survival becomes increasingly precarious for a generalist profession such as ours. It is almost inevitable that hard choices will have to be made to define more clearly the specific client groups and clinical competencies that constitute social work's domain, as other specialized professions lay claim to segments of practice that once were the sole province of social work. Sooner or later, the profession must create some kind of workable compromise between the breadth that has been its hallmark and the depth that characterizes specialization.

DILEMMAS OF
WHO IS TO BE SERVED

A profession, in order to survive and flourish, must seek the esteem and secure and maintain the support of the broadest possible range of individuals and groups within the society. The more the services of a profession are universally recognized as being of value to the entire population, the more likely it is that the profession will be accorded public esteem and support. Conversely, if those in need of the profession's services are a stigmatized, powerless minority, and if ambivalence exists within the society about the desirability of helping these "outsiders," significant dilemmas are posed. Two serious consequences result from society's distancing itself from the stigmatized and their helpers: Public support tends to be given on the least favorable terms, and there tends to be a withdrawal of public esteem.

These dilemmas can be viewed in terms of certain dualities. Shall social work be concerned primarily with those who are the most or least vulnerable, the most or least able to use help, the most or least able to pay for service? Shall social work practice and education be concerned primarily with those having the greatest needs, the fewest resources for meeting their needs, and the greatest degree of stigma? Or shall the profession seek to increase its public esteem and support by catering to those who need its services less because they have a variety of other resources available to them, can pay for services, and are among the least stigmatized members of the society?

The reader may protest that stating the problem in terms of polarities omits many facts, and that great variations in need exist between these two positions of service to the most vulnerable and service to the least vulnerable. This is true, of course, for we are dealing with very complex phenomena. But does such criticism blur the accuracy, relevance, or significance of the polar distinctions? Nor is this issue debated only on the very broad policy level. Dilemmas of choice of clients are posed in all areas of practice: social and fiscal policy, administration, human resources development and allocation, research, and service delivery policy and procedures. Each social worker, every day of practice, must struggle with the dynamics of choice. What clients and which problems should receive priority, and on what bases should priorities be assigned?

These delimmas are also apparent in questions about what levels of intervention are appropriate. To what extent should practice focus on personal change, societal change, or both? Some within the profession regard social work's duality as competitive rather than complementary. Thus the traditional dichotomy of casework and community organization, which was articulated clearly in the 1960s, is played out in some form in every generation, mirroring the insoluble dispute between the individual and the social as both cause and cure of social ills. A part of social work's ambivalence on this issue derives from recognition that it is difficult to achieve success in helping individuals when one is dealing with problems that stem from the behavior of the social order. There is, in addition, the fact that traditional social agencies seem unsure of their sanction to engage in efforts to improve environmental factors, including making broad changes in policy.

This particular tension is an old one. It is unlikely to be resolved merely by limiting professional concerns to particular kinds of problems, clients, or interventions. Indeed, it is likely to continue to be an issue as long as social work practice focuses on the interaction of the individual and the environment. It is very difficult for the profession to maintain an appropriate balance between a commitment to the personal problems of individuals, families, and small groups and a focus on social action; yet good practice demands this duality. Social service that benefits all classes and social action on behalf of stigmatized and deprived groups are two sides of the same coin. To minimize either in favor of the other is to reduce professional effectiveness.

DILEMMAS OF
SUPPORT AND ALLIANCES

Effective social work practice requires cooperation and support from a wide range of publics, institutions, and disciplines. If our client's problems are to be dealt with adequately, and if stigmatized client groups are to receive the services they need, social work must struggle constantly to maintain the financial and political support required to get the job done. In short, the profession needs to maintain alliances with the organizations and sectors of society that can effectively support its goals and policy objectives. The ultimate logic of this analysis is difficult to refute.

During the early years of social work, alliances were forged with labor, corporate interests, special interests groups, and a variety of religious, fraternal, and community organizations. More recently, however, disturbing changes have occurred in those alliances. The conclusion to be drawn is that the alliances now seem less numerous and less strong. Many factors undoubtedly have helped to weaken the relationships, including the predominance of government in social welfare funding, the changing goals of the labor movement, the growing gap between corporate and local leadership, and social work's concern with securing its professional identity. One important consequence of these factors has been an increase in the social distance between organized social welfare and the citizenry. There is less involvement of volunteers in professionally directed social services and, as a result, there is among the general public a lack of familiarity with, and personal investment in, the agencies that work with social problems and disadvantaged people.

The continual need to mobilize public support for programs and policies, from budget period to budget period, presents a major, ongoing challenge to social work. In the 1980s, there are some new dimensions involved in orchestrating that support. There is greater competition for goodwill and financial support from citizens among the many local and national interests. There is greater residential stratification among socioeconomic classes, which reduces investment in and familiarity with the problems of the poor. There is uncertainty among both the general public and our traditional allies about whether our programs work. Finally, there is more highly organized opposition to causes that are perceived as "liberal."

What can social work do to establish closer alliances with citizens in order to acquire its needed bases of understanding and support? How are such alliances to be maintained and strengthened, and who has the responsibility for bringing them about? These questions must be addressed at every level of social welfare organization, in both the public and private sectors. As part of the process, it is essential that practicing social workers, who have daily, face-to-face contact with clients, find ways of sharing their experiences with volunteers and policymakers. As important as it is to communicate such knowledge anecdotally, however, it is even more important that a data base be compiled for use as a tool in policy formation. The availability of data to support a case is no guarantee of success, but many a valid cause has been lost for the lack of it.

We have taken a brief look at three basic social work issues: the scope of service, the types of clients, and the need for alliances. There are two reasons for singling out these issues for comment in speculating about the future of social work. First, discussion and actions about these issues tend to take enormous amounts of professional time and energy that could be used to better advantage;

they should be settled and put aside. Second, whatever the final solutions may be, resolution of these three dilemmas will profoundly influence the field of social work. In the years ahead, social workers on all levels—direct service workers, supervisors, administrators, researchers, educators, and policy consultants—will have the opportunity to contribute toward solving these problems. In doing so, they will be shaping the social work profession of the future.

Index

Abbot, Grace (1878-1939), 63, 232
Abbot, Edith (1876-1957), 63, 232
Abortion, legal, 245
Abels, Paul, 188-221
Abels, Sonia, 188-221
Addams, Jane (1860-1935), 62-63, 222-223, 232
Adoption: as an alternative, 270; a case study, 315-321; specialized, 313-314
Agency for International Development (AID), 239
Aging, 123-124
Agriculture, Department of: Cooperative Extension Service of, the, 239; Food Stamps, 132, 137
Aid to Families with Dependent Children, 71; Department of Economic Assistance and, 154; guaranteed minimum income and, 155; inadequacies of, 146-149; poor families and, 78-79, 113; poverty and, 116; "right" or "wrong," 103
Agency system, 74
Alcoholism, 378, 381
Alcoholics Anonymous, 178, 189, 220
Alinsky, Saul, 229, 233
American Association of Retired Persons (1958), 94
American Geriatrics Society (1942), 94
Antipsychotic medicine, 272
Area Agencies on Aging (AAA), 125
Asian Americans, services for, 347

Battered women, 27
Basaglia, Franco, 293
Beard, John, 277

Beers, Clifford W., 87-88, 272
Bettelheim, Bruno, 245
Better Jobs and Income Program (BJIP) (1977), 147
Biklen, 237
Birth control, 245
Blacks, provision of services to, 347
Block grants, 138-139
Bloom, Allan A., 360-376
Bowen, Murray, 264
Booth, Charles (1840-1916), 62
Brace, Charles Loring, 77
Brown v. Board of Education (1954), 108, 115
Break-point, 36-38
Breckenridge, Sophinisba, 63
Bruch, Hilde, 330

Cabot, Richard C., 82
Cannon, Ida, 82
Carnegie, Andrew, 114
Carter, Jimmy, 131, 147
Carter administration: national health insurance and, 149-150; welfare reform and, 139, 147-148
Case managers: as advocates, 289; in community mental health centers, 277, 291; ideology of, 293; knowledge base of, 292; in psychosocial rehabilitation centers, 277; skills of, 292; value system of, 292
Case management, 160; assessment process in, 280-286; a case study, 278-289; casework and, 289-291, definition of, 276; individualized service plan, 286-287; linking and coordinat-

ing, 287-288; in the 1980s, 295-296; settings, 276-277
Case Management Research Project, 291
Casework, 158, 159. See also Social casework
Caseworkers, 158
Charity Organization Society (COS), 61, 151, 226
Chicago Juvenile Psychopathic Institute, 87
Chicanos, provision of services to, 347
Chicano Training Center, 348-359
Child abuse: a case study, 303-305; protective services and, 301-302; as a social cause, 27
Child-care facilities, licensing of, 114
Child-care programs, 114
Child guidance clinics, 86-87
Child neglect, 254; a case study, 307-312; protective services and, 301-303
Child Protective Services (CPS), 302-312
Child welfare services, 87
Cloward, M., 234, 237
Children: delinquent, 90; emotional disturbance in, 302; family violence and, 302; legal rights of, 90; neglected, 90; poverty and, 302; retardation in, 302; running away from home, 302
Children, dependent, 90; defined, 302; institutional care, 76-79; services for, 74; warehousing of, 77. See also Adoption; Foster care
Children's Aid Society, 76
Civil rights movement, 27, 346
Collins, Alice, 275, 295
Commission on Practice, of the NASW, 228
Committee for the Advancement of Social Work with Groups, 219
Committee on Economic Security, 101
Commonwealth Fund, 81, 86-87
Community Action Programs, 235-236
Community, as client, 21, 228
Community Mental Health Act (1963), 238, 272
Community mental health centers, 272; and case managers, 277, 291
Community mental health services, 87-89

Community mental health movement, 238
Community mental health workers, 273
Community Development in America, 238
Community Development Society, 239
Community organization, 159-160; a case study, 348-359; community development and, 226, 238-240, 242; community treatment and, 228, 237-238, 242; interest groups and, 226, 231; with a minority population, 346-359; planned intervention and, 237, 240, 241; program development and, 228; resource development and, 226-230, 242; social action in, 229, 230-237, 242; social planning in, 241; as social work practice, 242
Community organizers, 242-243
Community Organization: Theory and Principles, 228
Community Services, Department of, 154
Community Social Services Act (1979), 154
Community Support Branch of NIMH, 274
Comprehensive Education and Training Act (CETA) (1977), 147
Comprehensive health care, 84
Congressional Budget Office (CBO), 103
Consumer rights groups, 235
Cooke, Lane, 301-312
Cooke, Philip W., 377-385
Cooperative Extension Service. See Agriculture, Department of
Correctional institutions, 91-92
Correctional programs, 93
Correctional services, 89-93
Council on Social Work Education, 24, 193, 347
Counseling, as a correctional program, 93
Coyle, Grace Longwell, 65, 192, 219, 252
Crunden, R. M., 232
Culture, a component of client's problem, 36

Darwin, Charles (1809-1882), 57
Day care, 152, 379

Deinstitutionalization: case management and, 270; community-based care and, 272; in the correctional field, 93; juvenile status offenders and, 270; state mental hospitals and, 270-273

Delinquency and Opportunity: A Theory of Delinquent Gangs, 234

Delinquent youth, a welfare concern, 76

Dembo, Tamara, 67

Dependent people, chronically, the case-management approach to, 269

Depersonalized society, 35

Depression, the Great, 99, 100, 139

Deutsch, Albert, 84, 272

Distributional problem, 240

Dix, Dorothea Lynde (1802-1887), 61

Dobelstein, Andrew W., 9-13, 98-127

Domestic assistance, 152

Drug abuse, 27

Dynamic theory. See Social work practice, theory of

Eating disorders, 331, 332

Economic Assistance, Department of, 154

Economic Opportunity Act (1964), 234, 236

Education, Department of, 132

Elderly citizens: housing for, 122; programs for, 123-126; services for, 154

Elderly Nutrition Program (ENP) (1972), 110, 125

Entitlement programs, 74, 137

Environment, 21

Epstein, Laura, 295

Equity, horizontal and vertical, 115

Ethics, social work code of, 16, 23, 167

Family Assistance Plan (FAP), 147

Family: as client, 21; interactions of, 264; social work with, 160

Family life: ambivalence in, 246; cycle of, 262; in flux, 246

Family Service Agencies, 360-376

Family system: boundaries of, 253; characteristics of, 252; goals of, 254-255; helping process, effects of, 261-262; intervention in, 246-247; membership in, 253; multigenerational transmission in, 263; structure of, 255-256; subsystems in, 259-261; treatment of, 250; variations of, 256-259

Family therapy: co-therapy and, 251-252; as a new focus, 249; practice of, 251; theory of, 251

Family treatment: a case study, 360-376; definition of, 265; in the 1980s, 266-268; termination of, 265-266, working through, 265-266

Farmer's Home Loan, 122-123

Financial assistance programs, 143-144

Fink, Arthur E., 9-13, 73-97

Flexner, Abram, 51

Food Stamps: debates over, 112; the Department of Agriculture and, 132; new federalism and, 138; the working poor and, 137

Ford, Gerald, 110

Foster care: as an alternative, 76-78; a public program, 78; as a social cause, 27; as a social service, 361

Fountain House, 277

Free market, intervention in the, 113

Freud, Sigmund (1856-1939), 84

Freudian concepts, 88

Freudian theory of personality, 57

Friendly Visiting Among the Poor (1899), 157

Friendship House, 278-279

Funding patterns, 31

Gault v. Arizona (1967), 90

Gay rights, 27

General Assistance, 154

Gerontological Society (1945), 94

Goodman, Paul, 233

Gomberg, Robert M., 250

Green Amendment to the EOA (1967), 236

Greenwood, Ernest, 52

Group, as client, 21

Group dynamics, 54

Group treatment, a case study, 330-345

Group Work with American Youth, 65

Guaranteed minimum income, 135, 155

Handicapped children, mainstreaming of, 270

Head Start, 115

Health and Human Services, U.S. Department of (DHHS), 131

Health, Education and Welfare, Department of (DHEW), 347
Health Care Financing Administration, 135-136, 150
Healy, William, 87
Helper, personal qualities of, 48-49; relationship with client, 42-47
Helping: co-planning in, 35; giving and taking, 38-41; skills, 15, 16; the therapeutic, 34
Henry Phipps Psychiatric Clinic of Johns Hopkins Hospital, 87
Heredity, as a cause of social problems, 57
Hewitt, Abram, 223
Hobbes, Thomas (1588-1679), 114
Home-care programs for the elderly, 95
Homemaker services, 95, 361
Hoshino, George, 128-156
Hospital. See Medical social work; Mental health services
Host agency, the school as, 79, 80
Housing Act (1933), 119
Housing Assistance, 121-122; and HUD, 132
Housing and Community Development Act (1974), 120
Housing and Urban Development, Department of (HUD), 132
Housing for the Elderly and Handicapped, 122
Housing programs, 71, 119-123
Howard, Johns (1826-1890), 60-61
Hull House, 62-63, 232
Human behavior, laws of, 56
Hopkins, Harry (1890-1946), 63

Immunization programs, 114
Individual: dignity of, 28, 29; and environment, 390; and society, 21
Industrial social work: a case study, 379-383; consultant to management, 378, 383-385; counseling in, 378; employee assistance programs, 378; referrals, 378; self-help groups in, 378
Institutionalization: an alternative, 270; of the chronically ill, 95; of dependent children, 74, 78, 79; of the mentally ill, 84, 85
Interests groups. See Single-issue groups.

Interior, Department of the (Bureau of Indian Affairs), 132
Intervention, planned, 234, 237, 241
Introduction to Social Work Practice, 170

Jarrett, Mary C., 85, 86
Johnson, Peter, J., 269-296
Joint Commission on Accreditation for Hospitals (JCAH), 279
Juvenile court, 89-91
Juvenile correctional facilities, 90, 91
Juvenile delinquency, 234

Kadushin, Alfred, 55
Kahn, Albert, 152
Keith-Lucas, Alan, 33-49
Kent v. District of Columbia (1966), 90
Kiester, Dorothy J., 19-32
King, L., 227
King, Martin Luther, Jr., 101
Kunkel, J., 241
Kyle, Roberta, 301-312

Labor, Department of, Work Incentive Program, 132
Lane Report (1939), 227, 228
Lanham Act, 115
Lamb, Richard, 289
Lebeaux, Charles, 115
Lehman, Herbert (1878-1963), 63
Levine, R., 241
Levy, Charles S., 295
Lewin, Kurt, 54, 67, 204
Lowell, Josephine Shaw, 222
Low-Income Energy Assistance, 137

Manpower and Training Division, of NIMH, 347
Marriage: alternatives to, 244-246; counselor, 252; counseling, 361
Marx, Karl, 51
Meals on wheels, 152
Medicaid, 136; amendment to Social Security Act, 96; and the Department of Economic Assistance, 154; health insurance for the aged, 149; social workers and, 154-155
Medical social work, 82-84; a case study, 324-329; with chronic illness, 328-329; consultative services, 326-327; direct services to client, 326; with

fatal illness, 328-329; and interdisciplinary teams, 323; referral services, 327

Medical social workers, skills and knowledge of, 323-324

Medicare, 135; amendment to Social Security act, 96; health insurance for the aged, 149

Mental health centers. See Community mental health centers

Mental health services: development of, 84-86; and Department of Community Services, 154

Mental health workers, 88

Mental Health Systems Act (1980), 277

Mental illness, as a social cause, 27, 87-88

Mentally ill persons: aftercare needs of, 279; deinstitutionalization of, 270-274; needs of, 273-274; quality of care, 85

Mental retardation, as a social cause, 27

Meyer, Adolph, 87

Minahan, Anne, 295

Mind that Found Itself, A, 87

Minuchin, Salvador, 247

Minorities: and community action, 235; needs of, 347; and the school system, 81; and social work, 23-24

Mobilization of Youth in New York City, 234, 237

Model Cities Act (1966), 236

Morris, Robert, 295

Mothers Against Drunk Drivers (MADD), 189

National Association of Social Workers (NASW): a policy commitment, 347; and social work's purpose, a statement, 20, 167

National Committee for Mental Hygiene, 87

National Conference of Social Work, 227

National Council on Aging (1960), 94

National Council of Senior Citizens (1962), 94

National health insurance, 149-151, 155

National Institute of Mental Health (NIMH), 277, 347

National Retired Teachers Association (1947), 94

Native Americans, services to, 347

Neighborhood political action groups, 235

New federalism, 138-139, 149

NIMH Community Support Program, 279

Nisbet, Robert, 224, 225, 233

Nixon administration: and cutbacks in appropriations, 347; Family Assistance Plan, 147; and national health insurance, 149; and welfare reform, 139

Nuclear family, 246

Nursing homes, 95

Office of Economic Opportunity (OEC), 235-236

Ohlin, L., 234, 237

Old Age Survivors and Disability Insurance (OASDI), 132-134

Older adults. See Elderly citizens

Older Americans Act (1965), 96, 110, 124

Older citizens, services to, 94-96

Organization, as client, 21

Organizational analysis, 229

Overeaters Anonymous, 336

Pancoast, Diane, 275, 295

Parents Anonymous, 189

Parents Without Partners, 178, 189

Parole, 92-93; as an alternative, 270

Patients' legal rights, 272

Patterson, J. T. 232

Pennsylvania, University of, psychological clinic at the, 87

Perkins, Frances, Secretary of Labor (1935), 101

Personality, as a component of a problem, 36

Pfouts, Jane H., 9-13, 19-32, 73-97, 244-268

Polansky, Norman, A., 50-67

Pincus, Allen, 295

Poverty: eradication of, 347; a social problem, 116

Principles of practice: codifying and transmitting, 64-66; practice theory, 64-66

Pressures, as a component of a problem, 36

Prison, 92

Probation, 91, 92; as an alternative, 270

Professionalization of social work, 51-53, 64, 167
Program evaluation, 229
Progressive movement, 232, 233
Psychiatric social work and workers, 85-87
Psychiatrists, 85
Psychopathic hospitals, 85
Psychosocial aspects of illness, 83
Psychosocial rehabilitation centers, 277
Public health inspections, 114
Public Housing, 120-121; and HUD, 132
Public Planning: Failure and Redirection, 241
Public welfare: defined, 129-131, federal, 131-132; local, 141-142; reform of, 146-149; as scapegoat, 27; state, 139-141
Public welfare policy, 98-127; defined, 100; philosophical bases of, 111, 117; as a political process, 101; as a reflection of the times, 100; "right" or "wrong," 102, 104
Public welfare programs, 109, 129-154; voluntary, 116
Puerto Ricans, services to, 347
Putnam, James J., 85

Racism, eradication of, 347
Rank, Otto, 168
Rape victims, 27
Reagan, Ronald: and block grants, 118; and welfare costs, 148
Reagan administration: and national health insurance, 150; and new federalism, 138-139, 148, 150
Reform: desire for, 24; and social work, 26-28
Reformatory, 92
Refugee settlement, 361
Residential care, 152
Reid, P. Nelson, 222-243
Reid, William J., 295
Resource development, 226-230, 237
Resources: available to clients, 30; and older people, 69; redistribution of, 111-113
Reveille for Radicals, 233
Richmond, Mary E., 65, 157, 158, 167, 249

Ross, Murray, 228, 229, 237
Roosevelt, Franklin D., 99, 100
Rothman, Daniel, 84
Ryan, Janice Jacobson, 322-329
Ryland, Gladys, 65

School "community control" groups, 235
School meals, 132
School Social Services. See Social services in schools
Schwartz, William, 193, 215
Search for Community, The, 224, 233
Self-determination for clients, 24-25, 28, 30
Self-help groups, 189, 220-221
Siporin, Max, 170
Service delivery systems, 31
Settlement movement, 62-63, 232
Shame of the States, The, 272
Sherman, Sanford N., 251
Shulman, Laurence, 215
"Single-issue groups," 236
Smith College, 85-86
Snake Pit, The, 272
Social action, 230-237, 242
Social agencies: and appropriations, 27; and history, 73
Social casework: and crisis intervention, 168; existential and systems theory, 168; individualized assistance, 163-165; multiple interviewing, 168; objectives of, 165; problem solving in, 168; psychosocial diagnosis in, 168
Social caseworker: cognitive skills of, 50; and disengagement, 185; and engagement, 170-175; and evaluation of client's progress, 184-185; and exploration of client's problem, 175-177; and the helping process, 170; preparation for practice, 166; and intervention, 169, 175, 180-183; and relationship with client, 166, 168-172; and resources, finding needed, 177-180
Social causes, in and out of fashion, 27
Social conflict, management of, 229
Social Diagnosis (1916), 65, 158, 249
Social Group Practice (1949), 65
Social group work, 158, 159; action in a group, 213-216; child guidance work

and, 192; commitment of a group, 216; engagement of a group, 216; interactional model of a group, 191; in medical and psychiatric settings, 192; and personality treatment, 192; point of concentration, 189; organizing a group, 194-196; social goals of a group, 192-193; termination of a group, 216-218; treatment orientation of, 191-192
Social intervention. See Community organization; Intervention, planned
Social justice, 27, 115
Social networks: formal networks, 274, 275; importance of, 274-276; natural networks, 274, 275. See also Fountain House
Social planning, institutionalized, 24
Social programs, 70; development of, 73-97
Social reform, 232-233
Social Security Act of 1935, 71, 95, 99-103; and children in foster care, 78; income maintenance programs within, 119; and older citizens, assistance for, 94; and social welfare policy, 100, 102; Title II (Old Age Retirement), 115; Title XX of, 110, 118, 119, 302
Social Security Administration, 109, 132-135, 152
Social services, personal, 151-154
Social Services Block Grant Act (1981), 154
Social Services, Department of, 302
Social treatment, 55
Social welfare programs, 70, 106
Social work: as an art, 16; in the community, 222-225; definition of, 16, 20-22; education in, 31; future of, 386-392; generalist (holistic) approach, 387-388; helping skills in, 15; knowledge base of, 15, 16, 50-67; methods of practice, 157-161; as a profession, 15; research, 66-67; specialist approach, 387-388; theory, 16, 51; values, 15, 16
Social Work, journal of NASW, 20
Social Work with Groups, 219
Social Work Encyclopedia, 66

Social work practice, 69; definition of, 50; and evaluative research, 58; theory of, 55-58
Social Worker's Creed, A, 29
Social Worker in the Group, The, 193
Social workers: Certification of, 22; credentials of, 22, 31; education of, 22; and idealism, 16, 24, 25; licensing of, 22; practice competencies of, 30-31; and the public, 26; and reform, 26; and self-awareness, 24, 26, 28; and self-discipline, 47; as social welfare leaders, 70
Souflée, Federico, 346-359
Southard, Ernest E., 85
Special interest groups, 27
State mental hospitals, 61. See also Deinstitutionalization
Sullivan, Ann, 313-321
Supplemental Security Income (SSI), 134-135, 155
Support groups, 204
Supreme Court of the United States, 90
Swift, Linton A, 29

Taber, Lois R., 163-186
Taber, Richard H., 163-186
Talbott, John, 273
Tardive dyskinesia, 278
Tenant unions, 235
Townsend, Frances, march on Washington, 101
Training school, 92
Turner, John B., 386-392

UNESCO, 239
United Fund, 227
United Nations, 239
United Way of America, 118

Veterans, and psychiatric disabilities, 88
Veterans Administration, 88
Voting rights groups, 235

WANA (We Are Not Alone), 277
Wagner, Sibyl M., 330-345
Wald, Lillian, 232
War on Poverty, 26
Ward, Mary Jane, 272
Webb, Beatrice (1858-1943), 61-62

Webb, Sydney, 62
Welfare departments, local, 155
Welfare rights, 35, 235
Weeping in the Playtime of Others, 90
White House Conferences on Aging, 94, 124
Wilensky, Harold, 115

Wilson, Gertrude, 65
Witmer, Lightner, 87
Women's movement, 27
Wooden, Kenneth, 90
Work release programs, 93
Working poor, the, 144-149; and Food Stamps, 137